ANCIENT EGYPT

UNDER

THE PHARAOHS.

By JOHN KENRICK, M.A.

> Ἀριπρεπέων γένος ἀνδρῶν
> Οἱ πρῶτοι βιότοιο διειτήσαντο κελεύθους,
> Πρῶτοι δ' ἱμερόεντος ἐπειρήσαντο ἀρότρου,
> Πρῶτοι δὲ γραμμῇσι πόλον διεμετρήσαντο,
> Θυμῷ φρασσάμενοι λοξὸν δρόμον ἠελίοιο.
> Dionysii Periegesis, 232.

IN TWO VOLUMES.

VOL. II.

ISBN: 978-1-63923-674-9

All Rights reserved. No part of this book maybe reproduced without written permission from the publishers, except by a reviewer who may quote brief passages in a review to be printed in a newspaper or magazine.

Printed: February 2023

Published and Distributed By:
Lushena Books
607 Country Club Drive, Unit E
Bensenville, IL 60106
www.lushenabks.com

ISBN: 978-1-63923-674-9

CONTENTS.

VOL. II.

ANCIENT EGYPT (continued).

CHAPTER XXIII.
Animal Worship.

Pag

Local worship of animals in Egypt.—Their maintenance and treatment.—Fanaticism of the people.—Embalmment of the sacred animals.—Explanations of the origin of animal worship.—Analogies in the sentiments and practice of other nations.—Causes of its intensity in Egypt.—Reasons alleged for the appropriation of certain animals to particular gods. —Honours paid to Apis.—Effect of animal worship on the national character.................................. 1–27

CHAPTER XXIV.
Constitution and Laws of Egypt.

Tenure of land.—Rent paid to the king.—Monopoly of political power by the king, the priests, and the warriors.— Hereditary succession the law of the monarchy.—Female reigns.—Mode of election when the throne was vacant.— Early kings also priests.—Control exercised over the king by the priests.—Regulation of his daily business and habits. —His power limited by law.—Posthumous judgement of his character.—Wisdom and mildness of the Egyptian government.—Splendour of the court.—Wealth and influence of the priests.—Their exclusive possession of scientific knowledge.—Whether they were the sole physicians.—Their judicial functions.—The military class.—Their duties and prerogatives.—The other classes of the population.—The law of caste—to what extent it prevailed.—Division of Egypt into Nomes.—Their number.—Administration of justice.—The Supreme Court.—Character of the legislation.—Criminal law.—The *Lex Talionis*.—Labour in the mines.—Law respecting thieves.—Law of sacrilege.—Condition of women.—Polygamy forbidden to the priests.—Civil laws. . 28–59

HISTORY OF EGYPT.

INTRODUCTION.

Authorities for Egyptian History.

SECT. I.—*Greek Writers.*

Uncertainty of the commencement of Greek intercourse with Egypt.—Notices in the Homeric poems.—Opening of Egypt to the Greeks in the reign of Psammitichus.—The Persian dominion.—Commencement of Greek prose history.—Cadmus, Hecatæus, Hellanicus, HERODOTUS.—Analysis of his History of Egypt.—Philistus.—Establishment of the power of the Ptolemies.—DIODORUS.—Analysis of his account of Egypt.—Discrepancies of Herodotus and Diodorus 63–87

SECT. II.—*Egyptian Authorities.*

MANETHO—his History and dynasties.—Genuine and spurious works.—The Christian chronologers, Africanus, Eusebius, Panodorus and Anianus.—Syncellus.—Reign of the Gods, Heroes and Manes in Manetho.—His chronology—whether artificially adapted to the Sothiac period.—No Æra used in Egypt.—The Old Chronicle.—The Laterculus.—The Sothis.—Whether Manetho's dynasties were all successive. ERATOSTHENES.— His discrepancies from Manetho.—

CONTENTS. v

Bunsen's theory for their reconciliation.—Probable origin of the List of Eratosthenes.

Antiquity of records among the Egyptians.—List of 330 kings read to Herodotus.—Early use of the art of writing.—The papyrus of Sallier and other ancient fragments.—Sacred literature enumerated by Clemens Alexandrinus.—Hieratical Canon of Turin.—Existence of popular historical poetry among the Egyptians. — The Tablet of Abydos. — The Tablet of Karnak.—Successions of kings at Benihassan and Qoorneh, Thebes and Tel-Amarna.—Invasion of Judæa by Sheshonk (Shishak) the earliest synchronism in Egyptian history.—Division of the entire History into the OLD, MIDDLE, and NEW MONARCHY.—Its duration according to Manetho 87–110

BOOK I.

The Old Monarchy.

The First Dynasty.

Menes.—Athothis.—Ouenephes 111–123

The Second Dynasty.

Boethos.—Kaiechos.—Binothris.—Nephercheres.—Sesochris. 124–129

The Third Dynasty.

Necherophes.—Tosorthrus 129–130

The Fourth Dynasty.

Suphis.—Souphis.—Mencheres.

Discrepancies in the accounts of the building of the Pyramids.—Internal structure of the Great Pyramid.—Chufu or Cheops.—Noum-Chufu or Chembes.—Shafre, Chephren, or Chabryis.—Menkera, Mencheres or Mycerinus. — The Shepherd Philition.—Extent of the dominion of Egypt under this dynasty.—The state of science, art, and civilization. 131–143

The Fifth Dynasty 143–145

The Sixth Dynasty.

Othoes.—Phiops.—Menthesuphis.—Nitocris.—The kings Pepi and Remai.—Distinction of the titular and phonetic shields of kings.—Royal standard.—Share of Nitocris in building the Third Pyramid.—Story of Rhodopis.............. 145-152

The Seventh to the Eleventh Dynasty 152-157

The Twelfth Dynasty.

Opinions of Champollion, Felix, Wilkinson and Hincks respecting this dynasty.—Lepsius' arrangement of the succession—Ammenemes I.—Sesortasen I.—Ammenemes II.—Sesortasen II.—Sesortasen III.—Ammenemes III.—Ammenemes IV.—Omission of the Hyksos period on the Tablet of Abydos.—Confusion respecting the name Sesostris.—Dominion of the kings of the twelfth dynasty.—Tomb of Nevopth. — Grottoes of Benihassan. — Ammenemes III. founder of the Labyrinth. — Statements of the ancients respecting it.—Duration of the Old Monarchy 157-177

BOOK II.

The Middle Monarchy.

The Thirteenth to the Seventeenth Dynasty.

Manetho's account of the invasion of the Hyksos.—Probability that some of these dynasties are contemporaneous.—Hyksos not the Jews.—Silence of the Greek historians respecting their invasion.—Connexion of Phœnicia with Egypt referred to this event.—Exaggerations in the history, and uncertainty of the chronology 178-197

BOOK III.

The New Monarchy.

The Eighteenth Dynasty.

Differences between the lists and the monuments.—Probable

CONTENTS. vi

order of succession.—Amosis, 204.—Amenophis I., 206.—Thothmes I., 209.—Thothmes II., 213.—Thothmes III., 215.—Amenophis II., 232.—Thothmes IV., 233.—Amenophis III., 234.—Horus, 247.—Rameses I., 249.—Setei-Menephthah, 253.—Rameses II., 268.—Rameses III. (Sesostris), 271.—Menephthah II., 293.—Setei-Menephthah II., 296.—Chronology of the eighteenth dynasty, 297 198-298

The Nineteenth Dynasty.

Suspicions of its identity with the latter part of the eighteenth.—The Pheron and Polybus of the Greeks.—Reflections on the history of Egypt under the eighteenth dynasty.—Extension of dominion to Asia.—Importance of Palestine and Syria to Egypt.—Historical character of the Egyptian monuments.—Connexion between Egypt and Greece.—The Exodus of the Israelites.—Date of their going down into Egypt.—Manetho's account of their expulsion 298-325

The Twentieth Dynasty.

Rameses IV., 326.—Rameses V.-XIV., 337.—Relations of Egypt and Assyria.—Decline of art.................... 325-340

The Twenty-first Dynasty.

Antiquity of Tanis.—Deficiency of monuments.—Relations of Judæa and Egypt 340-344

The Twenty-second Dynasty.

Bubastis—its description by Herodotus.—Sheshonk, Sesonchis, the Shishak of Scripture, 347.—Osorthon (Zerach), 353.—Takellothis 345-357

The Twenty-third Dynasty 357-359

The Twenty-fourth Dynasty.

Sais.—Settlement of the Greeks in Egypt.—Reign of Bocchoris 359-363

The Twenty-fifth Dynasty.

The Ethiopians of the 8th century B.C.—Sabaco, 367.—Sevechus, 369.—Tirhakah, 370.—Invasion of Sennacherib 363–377

The Twenty-sixth Dynasty.

The Dodecarchia.—Psammitichus, 385.—Neco, 399.—Psammitichus II. (Psammis), 410.—Uaphris (Apries, Hophra), 413.—Amasis, 427.—Psammenitus 378–445

The Twenty-seventh Dynasty.

Cambyses, 445.—Darius, 473.—Xerxes the Great, 482.—Artabanus, 484.—Artaxerxes Longimanus, 484.—Xerxes II.—Sogdianus.—Darius Nothus, 491 445–492

The Twenty-eighth Dynasty.

Amyrtæus 492

The Twenty-ninth Dynasty.

Nepherites, 496.—Achoris, 497.—Psammuthis, 499.—Nepherites, 500 494–500

The Thirtieth Dynasty.

Nectanebes (Nectanebus I.), 500.—Teos (Tachos), 504.—Nectanebus II., 509.—His flight into Ethiopia 500–514

Reconquest of Egypt by Darius Ochus, 514.—Final conquest by Alexander the Great, 515.—Division of Alexander's empire and establishment of the dynasty of the Ptolemies.. 514–518

Index 519–528

ANCIENT EGYPT.

CHAPTER XXIII.

ANIMAL WORSHIP.

AMONG the marks of an excessive superstition which characterized the ancient Egyptians, nothing struck the traveller of another nation more than the honours paid to brute animals, and their employment as representatives of their deities. The representation of the gods under such forms had ceased among the Greeks; the legends of Io and the Minotaur prove that their practice had once been partially influenced by that of the Egyptians and Phœnicians; but the mythic explanations which had been framed of these symbols at Argos and in Crete, show how remote must have been the æra of their introduction, and how repugnant the worship to which they belong to the refined taste of the later Greeks. A slight mixture of the animal with the human form, and that in the person of an inferior deity—a Faun, a Centaur, or Medusa—was the utmost that it could tolerate. In poetry, art and divination certain animals were appropriated to the different gods,—the eagle to Jupiter, the raven to Apollo, the goat to Pan, the bull in later times to Bacchus; but they were not kept within their temples or approached with divine rites, as their visible representatives; much less was the whole race consecrated to them, and the life of every individual protected by law or popular superstition. Herds of cattle, exempt from the yoke and from all profane uses, fed in the groves and pastures included within the sacred precincts of the temples; but though consecrated to the divinity, they were not considered as his emblems, and their inviolability was their only sanctity. The serpent of the temple of Epidaurus, who was sacred to Æsculapius, and seems in some measure to have been considered as the god himself[1], is the nearest approach that we find in Greece to the veneration paid to the sacred animals of Egypt[2].

As some of the gods of Egypt were held in equal honour throughout the whole country, while others enjoyed supreme rank in some one nome, and held only a subordinate place elsewhere, so some animals were partially, others universally worshiped. The ox, the dog and the cat, the ibis and the hawk, the fishes *lepidotus* and *oxyrrynchus* were held in reve-

---

[1] The serpent was taken to Rome A.U.C. 462, after a pestilence. "Quum civitas pestilentia laboraret, missi legati, ut Æsculapii signum Romam ab Epidauro transferrent, anguem, qui se in navem eorum contulerat, *in quo ipsum numen esse constabat, deportavere.*"—Liv. Epit. lib. 11.

[2] Plutarch, Isid. et Osir. p. 379 D, points out the difference between the Greek *consecration* of animals to the gods and the Egyptian *worship* of them.

rence throughout the land; the sheep only in the Theban and Saitic nomes, the wolf at Lycopolis, the cynocephalus at Hermopolis, the *Cepus* (an animal of the ape tribe) at Babylon near Memphis, the eagle at Thebes, the lion at Leontopolis, the goat at Mendes, the shrewmouse at Athribis, and others elsewhere[1]. According to Herodotus[2], all the animals which the country produced, whether wild or domestic, were sacred, and with a few unimportant exceptions this appears to be true. To every one of them curators male and female were appointed, probably of the sacerdotal order, whose office descended by inheritance. A portion of land was assigned for their maintenance, and the superstition of the multitude provided other means of supply. Parents made vows to the gods, to whom they were respectively sacred, for the health of their children, especially if they were sick, and the vow was discharged by expending on food for the sacred animals a weight of silver equal to that of the children's hair[3]. Their ordinary residence was within the precincts of the temple, and in its most sacred recess. "Among the Egyptians," says Clemens Alexandrinus[4], "the temples are surrounded with groves and consecrated pastures; they are furnished with propylæa, and their courts are encircled with an infinite number of columns; their walls glitter with foreign marbles and paintings of the highest art; the *naos* is resplendent with gold and silver and electrum, and variegated stones from India and Ethiopia; the adytum is veiled by a cur-

[1] Strabo, 17, 812, 813.
[2] 2, 65.
[3] Her. 2, 65. Diod. 1, 83.
[4] Pædag. 3, 2, p. 253, Potter.

tain wrought with gold. But if you pass beyond into the remotest part of the enclosure, hastening to behold something yet more excellent, and seek for the image which dwells in the temple, a *pastophorus* or some one else of those who minister in sacred things, with a pompous air singing a Pæan in the Egyptian tongue, draws aside a small portion of the curtain, as if about to show us the god; and makes us burst into a loud laugh. For no god is found within, but a cat, or a crocodile, or a serpent sprung from the soil, or some such brute animal; the Egyptian deity appears a beast rolling himself on a purple coverlet." "The temples of Egypt are most beautiful," says Diodorus; "but if you seek within, you find an ape, or ibis, a goat, or a cat." The choicest food was placed before them, cakes of fine flour, steeped in milk or smeared with honey; the flesh of geese, roasted or boiled, and that of birds and fish uncooked for the carnivorous class. They were placed in warm baths and anointed with costly perfumes; and everything was supplied to them which could gratify their appetites[1]. This charge was thought so honourable, that their curators, when they went abroad, wore certain insignia by which their office might be discriminated even at a distance, and were received with genuflexions and other marks of honour. When any of the sacred animals died, it was embalmed, swathed, and buried in a consecrated depository near the temple of its god; if a cat died even in a private house, the inmates clipped off the hair from their brows in

---

[1] Ὁμοφύλους θηλείας ἑκάστῳ τῶν ζώων τὰς εὐειδεστάτας συντρέφου-σιν, ἃς παλλακίδας προσαγορεύουσι. Diod l. 84.

sign of mourning; if a dog, from the head and body. Voluntarily to kill any one of the consecrated animals was a capital offence; involuntarily it entailed a penalty fixed at the discretion of the priests: but voluntarily or involuntarily to kill an ibis or a hawk, the sacred birds of Thoth and Horus, was capital; and the enraged multitude did not wait for the slow process of law, but put the offender to death with their own hands. On the part of native Egyptians it was an almost unheard-of crime; and so great was the dread of being suspected of it, that those who accidentally saw one of the sacred animals lying dead, stood aloof, protesting with lamentations that they had found it dead. Diodorus himself was witness to such a movement of popular fanaticism: a Roman had unintentionally killed a cat; the king Ptolemy Auletes had not yet been received into the friendship of the Romans, and it was an object of great importance, both to him and to the Egyptian nation, to give them no umbrage; yet neither the terror of the Roman people nor the efforts of the king, who sent one of his chief officers to intercede, could save the unfortunate man from death. Even in times of famine, when they were driven to consume human flesh[1], the Egyptians were never known to use the sacred animals for food. Antiquarian researches have confirmed the statements of ancient authors respecting the veneration paid to them; the embalmed bodies of bulls, cows and sheep, dogs and cats, hawks and ibises, serpents and beetles, and in short, nearly the whole zoology of Egypt, except the

[1] See vol. i. p. 85.

horse and the ass, have been found in excavations[1]. The numerous figures of these animals also, of all sizes and materials, from the colossal ram or lion of basalt or granite, to the portable image of bronze, wood or porcelain[2], were probably devoted to religious purposes, the larger having been placed in temples or *dromoi*, the smaller used in private devotion, as amulets and sacred ornaments, or deposited for good omen along with human mummies.

The origin of this characteristic superstition was the subject of various explanations by the Egyptians themselves, and by the Greeks and Romans. Manetho attributed the establishment of the worship of Apis and Mnevis and the Mendesian goat to the reign of Caiechos, the second king of his second dynasty. But specific dates of national religious usages are never much to be depended upon, and we seek some more general cause than the enactment of a legislator for a practice which had taken such deep roots among a whole people. In the age of Diodorus[3] the Egyptian priests alleged, that Isis had commanded them to consecrate some animal from among those which the country produced, to Osiris; to pay to it the same honour as to the god, during its life, and bestow the same care upon it after its death. This explanation has evidently been produced in an age when the worship of Osiris had become predominant over all others, and the rest of the gods were regarded as only different manifestations of him. The bulls Apis and

---

[1] Wilkinson, 5, 100, 103. Pettigrew on Mummies, 183–226.
[2] Birch, Gall. of Antiq. p. 49–60.
[3] Diod. 1, 21.

Mnevis, however, were said to be specially consecrated to him, and honoured by all the Egyptians without exception, in consequence of the service of the ox in agriculture, which Osiris taught mankind. Such was the sacerdotal account: the popular explanations were threefold[1]; according to the first, which Diodorus pronounces to be altogether fabulous, and savouring of antique simplicity, the original gods, being few in number, and no match for the iniquities and violence of men, took the shape of animals to escape from them, and afterwards, when they became masters of the whole world, consecrated and appropriated these animals to themselves, in gratitude. According to the second, the images of animals fixed on spears having been used as ensigns to distinguish the corps of the army and prevent confusion, victory followed, and the animals became objects of worship[2]. This explanation evidently inverts the order of cause and effect; the animals were used as ensigns, because they had previously been associated with the gods. The third reason is the only one which has any plausibility, or even partially attains the truth—that animals were consecrated on account of the benefit which mankind derived from them[3]; the bull and cow from their services in agriculture and in supplying man with nourishment; the sheep from its rapid multiplication and the utility of its fleece, its milk and its cheese; the dog, for its use in hunting; the cat, because it destroys asps and other

---

[1] Οἱ πολλοὶ τῶν Αἰγυπτίων τρεῖς αἰτίας ταύτας ἀποδιδόασι (Diod. 1, 86).
[2] Diod. 1,85. See vol. i. p. 228.
Rosellini, M. Civ. pl. cxxi. vol. 3, p. 229.
[3] Cic. N. D. 1, 29; Tusc. Quæst. 5, 27.

venomous reptiles; the ichneumon, because it sucks the eggs of the crocodile, and even destroys the animal itself, by creeping into its mouth and gnawing its intestines; the ibis and the hawk, because they destroy snakes and vermin. Till metaphysical reasons were devised, this seems to have been the explanation most generally received by the ancients; but it does not solve the whole problem. If the ichneumon or the hawk were worshiped because they destroyed serpents and crocodiles, why the serpent and the crocodile? Or if the ibis was worshiped because it devours snakes and vermin, why was it specially consecrated to Thoth, the god of letters?

Diodorus has elsewhere given a still more improbable explanation than any that we have mentioned[1]. He says that one of the kings of Egypt, more sagacious than the rest, seeing that the people frequently conspired against their rulers, established a separate worship in every nome, in order that, being alienated from each other by their religious usages and fanatical zeal, they might never be able to unite for the overthrow of the government. This explanation marks an age in which men not only theorized on the institutions of past times, but transferred to them the maxims of a vicious policy with which they were themselves familiar.

The hypothesis which Lucian proposes in his Astrologia[2], that the objects of adoration among the Egyptians were the asterisms of the zodiac, the Bull, the Ram, the Goat, the Fish, is sufficiently

---

[1] 1, 89. Plut. Is. et Os. 380.
[2] Lucian, Op. ed. Bip. 5, p. 215, foll.

refuted by the circumstance that many of their sacred animals are not found in the heavens, as the ibis, the cat, the crocodile. It is known too that all monuments of Egypt on which figures of animals appear in the zodiac, are of the Greek and Roman times. Porphyry[1], in his Treatise on Abstaining from Animal Food, says that "the Egyptians had learnt by practice and familiarity with the divinity, that the godhead pervades not man alone, nor does a soul make its only dwelling-place on the earth in him, but goes through all animals, with little difference of nature; and that hence, in making representations of their gods, they joined indiscriminately portions of the bodies of men and of brute animals, indicating that, according to the purpose of the gods, there is a certain community even between these. And for the same reason the Lion was worshiped at Leontopolis, and other animals at other places; for they worshiped the power that is over all, which each of the gods exhibited, by means of the animals which shared the same nomes with them[2]." That in the age of Porphyry animal worship was explained and justified by the Egyptians on this ground is not doubtful[3]; but it by no means follows that it originated in a conception which Porphyry himself says they had attained by means of practice and familiarity with the divinity[4]. Plutarch having enumerated various

---

[1] Euseb. Præp. Ev. 3, 4.

[2] Διὰ τῶν συννόμων ζώων. This is an unusual sense of σύννομος, but seems to be required by the connexion.

[3] He elsewhere says that the Egyptians worshiped animals because they believed them to be endowed with a rational principle and the knowledge of futurity.

[4] Ἀπὸ ταύτης ὁρμώμενοι τῆς ἀσκήσεως καὶ τῆς πρὸς τὸ θεῖον οἰκειώσεως.

opinions respecting the motive of the Egyptian worship of animals, concludes by saying that he approves most of those who honoured not the animals themselves, but the divinity through them. It is undoubtedly a natural impulse to assimilate our own intellectual principle to that of the Deity, and to attribute the imperfect reason of the brute animals to the possession of the same principle. "Wherever there appeared singular excellence among beasts or birds, there was to the Indian the presence of a divinity[1]." It is not, however, any Egyptian writer, but Heraclitus[2], whom Plutarch quotes as maintaining "that a nature which lives and sees, and has a principle of motion in itself, and knowledge of what is congenial or alien to it, has snatched an efflux and particle from that which devises the government of the universe." This therefore is probably also a refinement of philosophy. The doctrine of the Metempsychosis has been supposed to have had an influence in producing animal worship; but Sir Gardner Wilkinson has justly observed, that human souls, undergoing transmigration, were in prison and in purgatory[3], and therefore they were not likely to have procured divine honours for the animals in which they dwelt.

Since, then, it is evident that all which the ancients have left us in explanation of this subject, is only hypothesis more or less probable, we are at liberty to seek a solution for ourselves, either in analogies derived from other nations, or in the general principles of human nature. Such analogies

[1] Bancroft, Hist. of United States, 3, p. 285.
[2] Is. et Os. p. 382.
[3] Mann. and Cust. 5, 112.

are indeed chiefly valuable, as proving that the practice has a foundation in human nature. India is the land which in this respect most closely resembles Egypt; the cow is there an object of adoration, and no devotee of Isis or Athor could have regarded its slaughter for food with greater horror than a Hindoo. Annual worship is paid to her on the day on which she was created along with the Bramins; and those who are more than commonly religious worship her daily, feeding her with fresh grass, and walking thrice or seven times round her, making obeisance. The ape, under the name of Hanumân, has his images in temples and private houses, to which daily homage is offered. A statue of the jackal is seen in many temples, where it is regularly worshiped; when a Hindoo meets the animal on his way, he bows reverentially to it; and food, regarded as an offering to the god, is daily placed in a part of the house to which he resorts to consume it. Other animals, which are considered as the emblems, or, as the Hindoos express it, the *vehicles* of their gods, are worshiped on the days appropriated to these gods[1]. The *nelumbo* and the *ficus religiosa*[2] are as sacred to the native of India, as the *lotus* and the *persea* to the ancient Egyptian. Yet even if we had historical ground for concluding that these religious ideas and usages had been transplanted by colonization from India to Egypt, we should only have removed one step further back the difficulty which we seek to solve. In the same way, if we look to Africa rather than

---

[1] Ward's Hindoos, 1, 250.
[2] The *Pippul* or aspen-leaved fig-tree. See Ritter, Geogr. Asien, 6, 681.

India as the source of the Egyptian population, and find that among the Negro races or the Kafirs of the South[1], traces of animal worship similar to that of Egypt prevail, we may have obtained an ethnological argument for the African origin of the people, but no explanation of the motive of their superstition. The more wide indeed the diffusion of the same or similar customs, the less reason have we to seek special explanations. The cause is still to be sought, to whatever country the practice may be traced.

The sanctity of plants (it is said even of stones) among the Egyptians is the best proof that this cause is to be found in some simple, obvious, and general feeling, not in those metaphysical refinements respecting God and the soul to which it has been attributed. For it cannot be supposed that a custom so universal could have sprung from a conception so far removed from the popular apprehension, as that even a plant or a stone is informed by a portion of the universal spirit. The rites and forms of worship originate in the disposition of man to assimilate the Deity to himself, and appropriate to his god what gratifies his own sense of beauty, or excites his imagination. The lotus which so constantly appears in offerings to the Egyptian gods, the oak, the ivy, the olive, the laurel, consecrated respectively to Jupiter and Bacchus, Minerva and Apollo, are among the most beautiful of the vegetable productions of Egypt and Greece. It is not utility, in the vulgar sense of the word,

---

[1] Prichard, Researches, 2, 289, ed. 3. "Invenio scarabæum taurum supra dictum, in magno honore esse apud ultimos in Africa barbaros et velut bonum genium coli. Vide Kolben." (Zoega, Or. et Us. Obelisc. p. 450.)

which influences the selection; they would otherwise have preferred grain or pulse. Many plants, it is true, appear to have been selected as objects of superstitious reverence, both in the countries which we have specified, and in others where the same custom has prevailed, in which no special beauty appears. The peculiarity of their form may have established an association with some religious rite or doctrine, as the passion-flower has seemed to the eye of Christian piety an emblem of the cross, or the persea-fruit to the Egyptian to resemble a heart[1]; or their unusual growth, like that of the parasitic misletoe, may have afforded a slight impulse to the fancy, which in connexion with religion especially, suffices for the production of mystical feeling. Their real or exaggerated virtues in medicine may have led to their being regarded as the choice gift of a beneficent deity; their susceptibility to atmospheric influence may have invested them with a prophetic virtue in regard to changes of weather, and fruitful or sickly seasons, which imagination has exalted into a divinatorial power. The extraordinary longevity of trees may have caused them to be regarded as emblems of divine power and duration, and to be invested with something of that mysterions awe which attaches to everything that has witnessed ages and generations long passed away. We do not pretend to analyse the ingredients of an imaginative superstition as if it were a conelusion of the understanding, or to assign to every association of religious feeling with the vegetable world even a fanciful cause. It is suffi-

---

[1] Wilkinson, 4, 392.

cient to point out that everywhere certain of its productions do acquire a peculiar connexion with religious feelings and ideas. It may be checked by philosophy and die away before the progress of scientific observation; but it exists everywhere in human nature; and if instead of being discountenanced as in Christian countries, it were fostered by religion, it might easily attain the rank luxuriance of Egyptian superstition. It was said of this people in the times of the greatest corruption of their religion, that "gods grew in their gardens[1]." This however is a mere satirical exaggeration; it does not appear that anything which could be fairly called worship was ever paid by the Egyptians to plants. Juvenal infers that onions were gods to them, because it was a crime to eat them. Had this been the case, it would seem to have been only a restriction of diet imposed on the priests, or those who approached the gods as worshipers[2]. They were not only commouly eaten as food, but were actually offered to the gods[3]. As such they might be regarded sacred, and like any other "gift on the altar," be the subject of an oath[4], which, according to Pliny[5], was the case in Egypt. Lucian says the onion was a god at Pelusium[6]. To swear by plants was a

---

[1] Porrum et cæpe nefas violare et frangere morsu.
O sanctas gentes, quibus hæc nascuntur in hortis Numina!—Juv. Sat. 15, 9. Comp. Diod. 1, 89.

[2] Sitim excitant et comestæ ingratum spirant odorem. G. J. Voss. Idol. 5, 12. It was a local custom to abstain from particular vegetables, as from particular animals. Diod. 1, 89.

[3] Wilkinson, M. C. 4, 234. 2, 373.

[4] Matt. xxiii. 19.

[5] N. H. 19, 32 (6). Gellius, N.A. 20, 8, who gives as a reason that it grew as the moon waxed and shrunk as it waned.

[6] Jov. Trag. 6, 275, ed. Bip.

custom by no means confined to the Egyptians[1]. Christianity does not allow of a division of the godhead, nor consequently of such appropriation of trees and flowers to special divinities as prevailed among the heathen nations; yet our trivial names show a connexion in the popular mind with sacred or legendary history. It is not the religious feelings only which seek an expression for themselves in symbols and associations derived from the vegetable world; their beauty, variety and universal presence make them ready, pleasing and intelligible emblems of emotions which are striving for a sensible expression. Love and joy, sorrow and despair, memory and hope, all create to themselves a sympathetic relation with the form and colour, the structure and functions of plants and flowers; and the mind with difficulty guards itself against superstitious auguries of its own impending destiny from their health or decay.

This disposition in man to connect himself and his feelings with the objects of the world about him shows itself much more strongly in regard to animals. With them he has really a community of nature; they can not only render him services, but can reciprocate his kindness by marks of personal attachment. The absurd tales which Ælian relates concerning animals, show what licence man has given to his imagination in attributing to them the passions, thoughts, and even vices of humanity. Without having devised a formal theory that the same divine intelligence pervades the highest and

---

[1] Multi per brassicam jurarunt ut Hipponax in Iambis, ac Ionicum id fuisse juramentum Ananius, Teleclides et Eupolis prodiderunt. G. J. Voss. *ubi supra*. Zeno the Stoic swore *per capparim*.

the lowest of animated beings, he regards their instinct with a mysterious feeling. In the certainty with which it foresees the future, it surpasses his own reason; and his imagination, always prone to exaggerate, attributes to them a superhuman foreknowledge. The Romans kept sacred chickens, from whose feeding they derived omens of the issue of a battle. In all countries we find certain animals singled out which are specially objects of interest and attachment to man, whose familiarity is invited, whose lives are spared and protected, who are maintained, not for the services which they render so much as for the feelings of affection with which they are regarded, and whose death, if accidental, is mourned, if intentional, is resented, with passionate vehemence. Referring his own feelings to his divinities, it was natural that man should appropriate some animal as a special favourite to each god, and putting himself in his place, should cherish and honour it with the same elaborate study, as his own animal favourites receive from him. From pampering a brute animal with the choicest food, providing it with a luxurious bed, addressing it in the language of human affection, and mourning for its decease as if some human life had been extinguished, to burning incense and reciting a litany before it, is not so wide a step as it may seem[1]. Though the Greeks and Romans did not worship animals as the Egyptians did, they consecrated them, as we have before observed, to particular divinities, and believed them to regard their

---

[1] Compare Her. 2, 69. The crocodile of Thebes and the lake Mœris was treated like a favourite cat or lap-dog, and ornamented with earrings and bracelets.

whole species with a discriminating favour[1]. Even the fanatical fury with which the Egyptians punished the death of an ibis or a cat, is not without a parallel at Athens, where the people condemned a man to death for killing a sparrow sacred to Æsculapius, and another for plucking a branch from an ilex that grew in a grove sacred to a bero[2]. The feelings with which the stork is regarded in Holland, or the wren, the swallow and the lady-bird among ourselves, are such, that if religion lent its sanction to popular superstition, they might easily become as sacred as the ibis, the hawk and the beetle to the Egyptians. The Lemnians venerated the crested lark on account of its usefulness in destroying the eggs of the locust; and to kill a stork among the Thessalians was punished with banishment or death, so highly was it valued for its services in destroying serpents[3].

We need not, therefore, seek elsewhere than in the feelings and tendencies of human nature for the origin of a superstitious attachment and reverence for animals in Egypt, or their appropriation to the gods of the country. Nor shall we have much difficulty in assigning causes why this disposition in Egypt attained an intensity which rendered it a national characteristic. The power of the sacerdotal order was greater there than in any country of the ancient world, not excepting India, whose very extent produced a variety which is a species of liberty. Hence every influence of religion was carried in Egypt to the utmost possible degree; and

---

[1] Comp. Æl. N. H. 12, 40, where several instances are given.
[2] Æl. Var. H. 5, 17.
[3] Plut. Is. et Os. p. 380 F. Plin. N. H. 10, 31.

everything connected with its doctrines and rites so arranged as to make them most impressive to the public mind. The length of time during which it remained without counteraction from philosophy or contradiction from any rival faith, made every religious conception an inveterate prejudice. The multitude of temples, in each of which a special animal worship was established, concentrated the affections of the people on an object constantly within their view and within reach of their homage. The rivalry of neighbouring nomes, each jealous of the honour of its respective deity, would increase the fanatical attachment to the animal who was his type and visible representative[1]. It has been thought that the use of hieroglyphical writing among the Egyptians tended to produce animal worship. This could hardly be its origin, since the hieroglyphic signs of animals by no means correspond with the names of the gods, and some of their representations fill a humble phonetic office in the system of writing. But it is not improbable that the same habit of mind, that of expressing qualities symbolically by means of visible objects, which has given its peculiar character to the Egyptian mode of writing, had a share in producing the practice of denoting the specific offices and attributes of the divinities by means of living animals, kept in their temples and worshiped as their symbols.

What those analogies were which the Egyptians found or fancied between these attributes and the

---

[1] The Romans were compelled to employ an armed force to quell a civil war between Cynopolis and Oxyrrynchus, occasioned by the one party killing a dog, and the other eating the fish Oxyrrynchus (Plut. Is. et Os. p. 380).

specific qualities of the animals consecrated to them, we can in general only guess. The lordly bull, as a type at once of power and of production, seems a natural symbol of the mighty god Osiris, who whether he represented originally the Earth, the Sun, or the Nile, was certainly revered as the great source of life. The god of Mendes for a similar reason was fitly represented by a goat. The bright and piercing eye of the hawk made it an appropriate emblem of Horus, who was also the Sun; the crocodile might naturally be adopted as a symbol of the Nile which it inhabits, or from its voracious habits and hostility to man, might on the other hand symbolize Typhon, the principle of evil. We may fancy that the Cynocephalus was chosen to represent Thoth, the god of letters and science, from the near approach which this animal makes to human reason. The Oxyrrynchus[1] from his projecting snout may have suggested to the imagination of a votary the peculiar emblem of the Osiris whom Typhon destroyed, as the Hindu sees everywhere the sacred emblem of creative power. But why was the ibis appropriated to the same deity, or the cat to Pasht, or the ram to Kneph, or the vulture to Isis; or what made the scarabæus one of the most sacred of all the animal types of Egypt?

To these questions we can obtain only very unsatisfactory answers. Herodotus gives no explanation of the reasons why particular animals were worshiped, except that he attributes the worship of

---

[1] The sacredness of the Oxyrynchus was local; at least, the paintings represent it as being caught along with other fish (Wilkinson, M. and C. 5, 250).

the ibis to its utility in destroying serpents, an office which modern naturalists say that it is incapable of performing. He gives a romantic account of the battle which took place between the ibis and certain winged serpents which endeavoured to invade Egypt from Arabia in the spring[1]. The later writers, Plutarch, Porphyry, Horapollo, account for everything, but it is evident that their explanations are arbitrary and of no historical authority. Thus Plutarch tells us that the ibis was consecrated to Thoth (or the Moon), because the mixture of its black and white feathers bore a resemblance to the gibbous moon; besides which it forms an equilateral triangle from the tip of its beak to the extremities of its feet when extended in walking. Further it was consecrated to the god of Medicine, because it had been observed to drink only of the purest and most salubrious waters, and had given the first hint of a useful practice in medicine[2]. A Platonist devised a still more fanciful reason for the reverence in which it was held; it has the shape of a heart, and its feathers are black at the extremities, but white elsewhere, indicating that truth is dark outwardly, but clear within[3]. The crocodile, having no tongue, is a fit emblem of deity, since the divine reason needs no utterance, but governs all in silence. Its eye when in the water is covered with a membrane through which it sees, but cannot be seen[4],

---

[1] Her. 2, 75. Cuvier, Oss. Foss. Disc. sur les Révolutions du Globe, 1826. p. 175. Herodotus does not profess to have witnessed the combat; he only saw the spines of the serpents.

[2] Plin. N. H. 8, 41. Volucris in Ægypto quæ vocatur ibis, rostri aduncitate per eam partem se perluit qua reddi ciborum onera maxime salubre est.

[3] Hermias ap. Wyttenb. Plut. Is. et Os. p. 381.

[4] Plut. ibid.

as the deity beholds all things, being itself invisible. The scarabæus was an emblem of the Sun, because no females being found in the species, the male enclosed the new germ in a round ball, and then pushed it backwards, just as the sun seems to push the sphere of heaven backwards, while he really advances from west to east. The asp was likened to the Sun, because it does not grow old, and moves rapidly and smoothly without the aid of limbs. For the consecration of the cat to the Moon two reasons were assigned; the first, that this animal brings forth first one, then two, and so on to seven, in the whole twenty-eight, the number of the days of a lunation. This Plutarch himself thought to border on the fabulous; of the second he seems to have judged more favourably—that the pupils of the cat's eyes are round at the full moon, but grow contracted and dull as she wanes.

These instances are given, out of a multitude of equally fanciful explanations, to show that those from whom we derive our principal knowledge of Egyptian antiquities knew no more than we do of the real origin of the things which they undertook to explain. The ignorance[1] of the history and habits of the animals in question which they betray is not itself a proof that they are ill-founded; for popular superstitions respecting animals are frequently caused by ignorance, or at best partial knowledge; but it is clear that they are all conjectures; and were we to venture on other explanations, derived from a more ac-

---

[1] The amount of this ignorance is astonishing, as it relates to animals whose habits are obvious. It was said, for example, that the cat διὰ τῶν ὤτων συλλαμβάνει· τεκνοποιεῖ δὲ τῷ στόματι. Plut. Is. et Os. p. 381 with Wyttenbach's note.

curate zoology, we should not approach any nearer to historical truth. No doubt the cause of the appropriation was in many cases quite fanciful, but this makes the attempt more hopeless to ascertain what it was. It may also have been historical, and in this case, the history not having been preserved, no conjecture can recover it.

Of the animals which are described generally as sacred, some were held in a higher degree of reverence than others. It does not appear that all were kept in temples, or received divine honours, and we know that some which were deemed divinities in one nome were treated as nuisances and destroyed in others. The worship of Apis and Mnevis, the bulls consecrated to Osiris, exhibits perhaps the very highest point to which this characteristic superstition of Egypt reached. Apis was believed to be born from a ray which darted from heaven (Plutarch says from the moon) on his mother, who after his birth never brought forth again[1]. His colour was black, but he had a square spot of white upon his forehead; on his shoulders the resemblance of an eagle[2], the mark of a scarabæus on his tongue, and the hairs were double in his tail. It may be easily supposed that either some contrivance was used to produce such an unusual combination of marks, or, as is more probable, that credulity was satisfied with very general resemblances. It appears from Herodotus that a considerable interval sometimes elapsed between the appearance (*epiphaneia*) of one Apis and the death of the other. In Plutarch's time, on his

---

[1] Herod. 3, 28.
[2] Sir G. Wilkinson observes that the figures of Apis found in Egypt show that it was a vulture, not an eagle, which was marked on the back of Apis. (M. and C. 4, 349.)

death the priests immediately began the search for another. Under the charge of the hierogrammats, who repaired to the spot on the intelligence of his discovery, the sacred calf was fed for four months on milk, in a house facing the East[1]. At the end of this time he was transferred at the new moon, in a covered boat with a gilded house, to Memphis, amidst the rejoicings of the people. Psammitichus had built a hall, adjoining the temple of Ptah, the chief deity of Memphis, in which Apis was kept. There were two apartments, from one of which to the other he passed, and in the front a magnificent peristyle court, supported instead of the usual columns by caryatides twelve cubits in height. His food was selected with the greatest care, and lest in his state of confinement he should grow too fat, they abstained from giving him the water of the Nile to drink. In Strabo's time he was brought forth into his court to exhibit himself to curious strangers; in earlier times it is not probable that he was exposed to view except on solemn festivals, when he was led through the city in procession. Various modes of divination were practised by means of Apis; it was a good omen if he took food readily from those who offered it to him; but evil threatened them if he refused it. Public prosperity or calamity was portended by his entering one or the other of his two apartments. There were other methods which they employed to obtain a more specific knowledge of the future by his means. The children who walked before him in the public pro-

---

[1] Diodorus says that for forty days women only were allowed to see him, who stood before him, ἀνασυράμεναι. (1, 85.)

cession were supposed to acquire from his breath a gift of prophecy. Those who consulted him closed their ears after they had propounded their question till they had quitted the precincts of his temple, and the first words which they heard when they opened them again were the answer of the god to their inquiry. He was not allowed to live beyond a certain age, twenty-five years according to Plutarch, when he was secretly drowned[1]. Whether he died by the course of nature or by violence, his death was a season of general mourning; and his interment was accompanied with most costly ceremonies. The funerals of all the sacred animals were performed in later times, when superstition had reached its height, with a magnificence which sometimes proved ruinous to the fortunes of the curators; but that of Apis surpassed them all. In the reign of the first Ptolemy, Diodorus relates, Apis having died of old age, they not only expended on his funeral the large sum appropriated to this purpose, but also borrowed fifty talents from Ptolemy; and in his own time a hundred talents was no uncommon sum to be expended by the curators of the sacred animals on the ceremony of their interment. The body of Apis was afterwards embalmed, and mummies of bulls have been found in several of the catacombs; near Abousir eight chambers appear to have been filled with them[2]. The catacombs contain mummies also of most of the other animals which are known to have been held sacred among the Egyptians[3]. There are some

[1] See vol. 1, p. 336.
[2] Pettigrew on Mummies, p. 201.
[3] See the enumeration of them in Pettigrew, p. 178.

indeed which are not specifically mentioned as having been held sacred; and therefore it has been thought that sanitary, rather than religious considerations, led to their embalmment; but Herodotus says[1] that *all* the animals of the country were holy—of course not all everywhere, but in some part or other. In regard to Apis, we are distinctly told that the Egyptians honoured him as an image of the soul of Osiris[2], and that this soul was supposed to migrate from one Apis to another in succession[3]. He was therefore to the Egyptians the living and visible representative of their greatest and most universally honoured deity. Even in this case, it appears that they did not consider him as the god, but only as the living shrine in which the divine nature had become incarnate. It is doubtful whether in the age of Herodotus their belief had reached to this point of exaltation.

What was the precise amount of veneration paid to the other animals which are ordinarily said to have been worshiped in Egypt, it is impossible to define, from the loss of all record of the sentiments of the people by means of literature. No standard could be correct for all ages of the monarchy, or all minds. That it did not amount to a belief in the divinity of the animal is evident from the case of Apis; and between the honours which he received, and homage paid in outward forms as to the established symbol of divinity, there is room for a long gradation, according to the more or less enthusiastic

---

[1] Τὰ ἐόντα σφι ἅπαντα ἱρὰ νενόμισται (2, 65).
[2] Plut. Is. et Osir. p. 359 B.
[3] Diod. 1, 85.

character of the worshiper. For centuries the two great divisions of the Christian Church have been unable to agree in regard to the true nature of the use of images in religion, which one pronounces to be a direct worship, while the other declares it to be merely an act of reverence, worship being addressed exclusively to the supreme God. We see therefore how impossible it is to describe, in words of universal application, the sentiments with which an Egyptian regarded his sacred animals.

In itself, animal worship has nothing more irrational than the worship which the Scythians paid to a scimitar, or the Romans to a spear[1]; but there is more danger that gross minds should confound a living than a lifeless symbol with the god whom it represented; it affords more scope to an anxious superstition, in watching the indications of the future, afforded by the actions and state of the consecrated animal. Multiplied as the objects of this worship were in Egypt, it met the devotee perpetually, and its power was strengthened by the constant repetition of its rites. It is of a nature peculiarly calculated to lay hold of the feelings in early life, and thus preoccupy the mind with superstition, before reason has acquired any counteractive power. The variety and opposition of the rites of different nomes and cities produced a fierce and fanatical hostility between the Egyptians themselves, of which we have no example, among the other nations of the Gentile world. Many causes contributed to degrade their character to the state to

[1] Herod. 4, 62. Varro, Fragm. 1, p. 375, ed. Bipont.

which it had been reduced in the last age in which their native superstition remained, and which Christianity has done less to raise than for any other civilized people which has embraced it; but we cannot hesitate to place animal worship among the most efficacious causes of the narrowness and imbecility into which the Egyptian mind degenerated.

CHAPTER XXIV.

CONSTITUTION AND LAWS OF EGYPT.

In describing the constitution and laws of Egypt we labour under this difficulty;—that as the Egyptians have left us no history of their own, and no code of their laws has been discovered among the written remains which have come to light, we know not, except by a few doubtful traditions, what changes they may have undergone. The fullest account is that given by Diodorus[1], which he professes to have derived from the records of the priests, and which may be considered as representing the state of things during that period of the native monarchy which succeeded the expulsion of the Hyksos.

The whole of the land of Egypt was possessed by the king, the priests, and the military order[2]. Such a possession, however, like that of a feudal sovereign and aristocracy, cannot be exercised by the persons who claim it. The husbandmen occupied the land capable of cultivation, on payment of a small rent or proportion of the produce. It appears from the Book of Genesis, that before the time of Joseph, the mass of the people had been independent possessors of land, but parted with their rights to the crown, under the pressure of continued

---

[1] Diod. 1, 70 foll.
[2] Diod. 1, 74. Οἱ γεωργοὶ μικροῦ τινος τὴν καρποφόρον χώραν τὴν παρὰ τοῦ βασιλέως καὶ τῶν ἱερέων καὶ τῶν μαχίμων μισθούμενοι διατελοῦσι τὸν ἅπαντα χρόνον περὶ τὴν ἐργασίαν ὄντες τῆς χώρας.

famine[1]. They submitted in future to pay a fifth part of the produce to the king, and were thus placed in nearly the same condition as the people of India[2], where all the land belonged to the king, but was farmed on condition of paying him a fourth part of the produce. The priests are expressly mentioned as retaining their property[3]; of the military order nothing is said, but from analogy we should conclude that they also retained their rights, or speedily recovered them, as the account of Diodorus before quoted implies. After the change of tenure, the proportion of the produce did not exceed what had been taken by an act of power in the seven years of plenty[4]. Even after this annihilation of the rights of landed property, the condition of the peasantry in Egypt was better than in India, and not very different from that of the agricultural tenant among ourselves; for it appears from the evidence given before the Committees on the Corn Laws in 1814 and 1821, that rent is usually about a fourth part of the produce[5].

It is probable that the priests occupied a portion of their own land, and cultivated it by their hired labourers, as we know the military class did. Diodorus, speaking of the different classes and occupations of Athens, says, " The second class was that of the *geomoroi*, whose duty it was to possess arms

[1] Gen. xlvii. 26.
[2] Strabo, B. 15, p. 704.
[3] Gen. xlvii. 26. " Joseph made it a law over the land of Egypt unto this day, that Pharaoh should have the fifth part; except the land of the priests only, which became not Pharaoh's."
[4] Gen. xli. 34. " Let Pharaoh do this, let him appoint officers over the land, and take up the fifth part of the land of Egypt in the seven plenteous years."
[5] Rickards on India, vol. 1, p. 288 note.

and serve in war on behalf of the city, like those who are called husbandmen in Egypt, and who furnish the fighting men[1]." Now as the continued and personal cultivation of the soil would be inconsistent with military duty, we must suppose that at least that portion of the warrior caste which was in actual service, tilled their lands by hired labourers. Herodotus appears also to have included the possessors of land among the priests and the warrior caste, as he makes no mention of husbandmen among his seven classes.

The king, the priest, and the warrior were the privileged orders of Egypt; the rest[2], including the herdsmen of swine and cattle, the artificers, the retail traders, the boatmen and pilots, and in later times the interpreters, were excluded from all share of political power. Yet there prevailed in Egypt no notion of an aristocracy of descent; the priest and the warrior were honoured on account of the higher functions which their birth assigned them, but not for a patrician genealogy. In the funeral encomium no mention was made of descent, all Egyptians being considered as equally well-born[3].

Hereditary succession appears to have been the rule of the Egyptian monarchy. Diodorus says (1, 43), that in ancient times, according to the accounts which he received, kings were chosen for public services, but this occurs in a part of the history in which he is tracing the progress of society evidently according to a theory. In many instances a sove-

---

[1] Diod. 1, 28.
[2] Strabo, B. 17, p. 787. Plato, Tim. iii. 24. Isocrates, Busiris, p. 161, ed. Battie, arrange them variously.
Herodotus, 2, 164, reckons priests, warriors, herdsmen, swineherds, tradesmen, interpreters, steersmen.
[3] Diod. 1, 92. Vol. 1, p. 500.

reign is expressly said to have been succeeded by his son; on the monuments a king sometimes declares himself to be the son of his predecessor, and is found in the sculptures of his reign in the character of a prince of the blood, serving in the army or attending at a solemnity[1]. Females were not excluded from the throne; a queen Nitocris occurs in the sixth dynasty, Scemiophris in the twelfth, and other examples are found in the sculptures[2]. If it were necessary to have recourse to election, the king must be chosen from the priests or the soldiers; Amasis was a plebeian, and was on that account despised, but the monarchy was then approaching its termination. According to a late authority (Synesius[3]), the form of election represented all the elements of the community. The priests stood immediately around the candidates, then the warriors, and outside of all the people. But the priests possessed great prerogatives in voting; the suffrage of a *prophetes* counted for a hundred, that of a *comastes*[4] (one who carried the sacred images in processions) for twenty, that of a *neocoros*[5] for ten, while that of a warrior counted but for one. The common people probably enjoyed the same right as in the middle ages—that of approving by their acclamations the choice of the clergy and the military chiefs. If the election fell upon a soldier, he was admitted into the sacerdotal order, and made acquainted with

---

[1] Rosellini, Mon. Stor. iii. 2, 283; Champollion, Lettres d'Egypte, p. 351.
[2] Rosellini, M. St. iii. 1, 129. Comp. Luean, Phars. 10, 92.
[3] Quoted by Heeren, Ideen, 2, p. 335, Germ.
[4] Clem. Alex. 5, p. 671, Pott.
[5] Vol. 1, p. 451.

their hidden wisdom[1]. This initiation is perhaps represented in monuments, where the *tau*, the emblem of life and key of mysteries, is placed on the lips of the king[2]. To the shields of some of the early kings the word " priest " is prefixed[3].

The monarch was so entirely under the influence and control of the priests, that the hierarchy may be considered as in fact the governing body in ordinary times. Unlike the sovereigns of the East, he was not irresponsible master of his own actions. The forms of public business and even his daily habits of life were subject to strict regulation. "It was his duty," says Diodorus, "when he rose in the early morning, first of all to read the letters sent from all parts, that he might transact all business with accurate knowledge of what was being done everywhere in his kingdom. Having bathed and arrayed himself in splendid robes and the insignia of sovereignty, he sacrificed to the god[4]. The victims being placed beside the altar, the high-priest standing near the king prayed with a loud voice, the people standing round, that the gods would give health and all other blessings to the king, he observing justice towards his subjects. It was the priest's office also to declare his several

---

[1] Plut. Is. et Osir. p. 354 B; Plat. Polit. ii. 290. Steph. Ἐὰν τύχῃ πρότερον ἐξ ἄλλου γένους βιασάμενος, ὕστερον ἀναγκαῖον ἐς τοῦτο εἰστελεῖσθαι. Plut. Is. et Osir. c. 6. Οἱ βασιλεῖς καὶ μετρητὸν ἔπινον ἐκ τῶν ἱερῶν γραμμάτων, ὡς Ἑκαταῖος ἱστορήκεν, ἱερεῖς ὄντες.

[2] Hieroglyphics of Egyptian Soc. pl. 94.

[3] Wilkinson, M. and C. 3, 281. The shield of a king whose name is lost, in the papyrus of Turin, but who belonged apparently to the Sebekotphs, has a group of characters annexed to it, which have been read "chosen by the soldiers" (Lesueur, Chronologie, pp. 236, 321).

[4] We find accordingly in the monuments the king leading processions, pouring libations, dedicating temples, presenting offerings, and with his own hand sacrificing victims.

virtues, saying that he showed piety towards the gods and clemency towards men; that he was temperate and magnanimous, truthful and liberal, and master of all his passions; that he inflicted on offenders punishments lighter than their misdeeds deserved, and repaid benefits with more than a proportionate return. After many similar prayers the priest pronounced an imprecation respecting things done in ignorance, exempting the king from all accusation, and fixing the injury and the penalty on those who had been his ministers and had wrongfully instructed him." His pleasures and his exercise, the quality of his food, the quantity of his wine, were all prescribed by a minute ceremonial, contained in one of the Books of Hermes[1]. He was not allowed to be attended by slaves; sons of the priests, carefully educated till the age of twenty, surrounded his person night and day. The hierogrammat or sacred scribe then read from the sacred books precepts and histories of eminent men calculated to inspire the monarch with the love of virtue. His power over the lives and properties of his subjects was strictly limited by law, and nothing left to caprice and passion[2]. The right to enact new laws, however, resided with the sovereign: Menes and Sasyches, Sesostris, Bocchoris and Amasis are all celebrated as legislators[3]. The king was also a judge in certain cases which are not defined; but the ordinary administration of justice was left to the tribunals. A singular kind of posthumous judgement was exercised on his government and cha-

[1] Clem. Alex. Strom. 6, 4, p. 757, ed. Potter.
[2] Diod. 1, 70, 71.
[3] Diod. 1, 94.

racter. Before the embalmed body was placed in the sepulchre, any one who had an accusation to prefer against him was allowed to bring it forward; while the priests set forth his merits, and the people by their murmurs or applause decided whether he should be allowed the honour of sepulture or not. Diodorus assures us that there were many instances of its being withheld[1]. On the other hand, an eminently virtuous and popular prince received a kind of deification. Acts of homage were performed to him in subsequent generations, and his name was inscribed as a charm on amulets[2].

The account which Diodorus gives of the influence of these laws and customs in producing virtue and moderation in the kings of Egypt, must be regarded as describing rather the effect designed than the invariable result. The Jewish Lawgiver prescribed that each sovereign should make a copy of the Law, " that it might be with him, that he might read therein all the days of his life, and learn to fear Jehovah his God, to keep all the words of the law and to do them[3];" yet it is doubtful if a single king of Israel or Judah complied with this injunction, and it is certain that even the living voice of the prophets was unable to prevent them from "lifting up their hearts above their brethren, and turning aside from the commandments." The daily homily read to the Egyptian monarchs on the duties of sovereignty would degenerate into a form. The praises bestowed in public prayers on the virtues of a reigning sovereign

---

[1] Diod. 1, 72, *ad fin.*
[2] Rosellini, Mon. Stor. 3, 79-84.
[3] Deut. xvii. 18.

are mere customary compliments. The details of Egyptian history exhibit instances of tyranny; and a king who could command the military power might break through the restraints of morality and religion. In both cases however it would be unjust to deny to the legislation the merit of a noble aim, in framing a standard of duty for the sovereign, and providing the means of its being constantly held up before his eyes. The failure to produce conformity with the standard belongs to all codes, ethical or political. Yet the general testimony of antiquity affirms that Egypt was distinguished among ancient nations, not only for the wisdom of its laws, but the obedience paid to them. The instances of internal revolution are few and late. After we have re-trenched some thousand years from its history, for false and exaggerated chronology, the long duration of the monarchy remains unexampled. The union of priestly sanctity, military power and monarchical authority in one person, gave the government a degree of stability which could not belong to forms of polity in which these powers were dissociated or hostile. At the same time the influence of the sacerdotal order, who were almost the sole possessors of knowledge, stamped it with a character of mildness and humanity, as in the Middle Ages the influence of the Church tempered the rigour of feudalism. It substituted religious awe for constitutional checks and sanctions in the mind of the monarch, and by this sentiment more effectually controlled him, as long as religion and its ministers were respected. Had the authority been exclusively in the hands of the priests, it might have sunk into that imbecility to which a purely sacerdotal administration tends; but the intimate union of the civil power, the military and the hierarchy, appears to have secured to the people a government at once energetic, enlightened and humane.

The earliest account remaining of the Egyptian monarchy, in the history of Joseph, exhibits a court and household with minute gradations of rank and function, and the monuments have added a long list of officers, who ministered to the state and luxury of the sovereign. The king always appears surrounded by numerous military and sacerdotal attendants. Men of high rank, and even princes of the blood, formed his train, screening him from the heat, or cooling him and chasing away the flies with a feather-fan. Besides these personal attendants on the sovereign, there was a numerous body of public functionaries, whose titles and duties have been revealed to us by the inscriptions in their tombs. They show that the government was thoroughly organized in its administrative department, no branch of public service being without its chief. The extent and magnificence of the palaces of Thebes attest the splendour in which the monarch lived; but as the royal state was kept up and the expenditure in peace and war maintained out of the produce of the land, a third of which was allotted to the king, the people do not appear to have been heavily taxed, if at all, in the ordinary course of affairs[1]. It is not probable, however, that such

---

[1]. The πρόσοδοι and ἀποφορή which Herodotus (2, 109) speaks of as imposed by Sesostris in proportion to the land, appear to be only the *rent* paid for the crown lands under another name. Τοὺς

works as the building of the Great Pyramid could be carried on, without levying oppressive taxes, as well as exacting forced labour, and the sovereigns who engaged in them were the objects of popular detestation[1]. The military expeditions would in modern times have been the cause of enormous expense; but ancient warfare supported itself by plunder and exaction, and large tributes were paid by conquered nations.

Nowhere in the ancient world was the number of temples so great as in Egypt, nor the revenue of the priests so ample, nor their influence in the whole social system so predominant. All the events of Egyptian life were intimately blended with religion, and a series of festivals spread itself over the whole year. Every nome had a tutelary god, whom it worshiped with especial honour; every city and town one or more temples. The Egyptians were the authors, as the Greeks believed[2], both of the doctrines and the ritual of polytheism, and had carried both to the utmost limits of refinement and subdivision. The priests lived in abundance and luxury. The portion of the soil allotted to them, the largest in the threefold division[3], was subject to no taxes[4]; and they were so abundantly supplied with the means of subsistence that it was unneces-

ἰδιώτας, διὰ τὴν ἐκ τῶν προσόδων εὐπορίαν, οὐ βαπτίζουσι ταῖς εἰσφοραῖς. (Diod. 1, 73.)

[1] Herod. 2, 128.
[2] Herod. 2, 50. Σχεδὸν πάντα τὰ οὐνόματα τῶν θεῶν ἐξ Αἰγύπτου ἐλήλυθε ἐς τὴν Ἑλλάδα. 58. Πανηγύρις ἄρα καὶ πομπὰς καὶ προσαγωγὰς πρῶτοι ἀνθρώπων Αἰγύπτιοί εἰσι οἱ ποιησάμενοι.

[3] Diod. 1, 73.
[4] This appears not to have been the case in the Ptolemaic times. See the Inscription of Rosetta, in which the priests return thanks to the king for decreeing that they should pay no more than in the first year of his father's reign. (Line 16 of the Greek.)

sary for them to expend their private property[1]. The registers of the temples, of which some fragments have been preserved, show that contributions of various kinds were made to them, though they are not sufficiently precise to enable us to say whether they were dues or voluntary offerings. Their life[2] was the reverse of ascetic. The shaving of the head and body every other day, the cold ablution twice in every day and twice in every night, the use of flax and papyrus instead of woollen and leather[3], in the climate of Egypt were luxuries, not penances and restrictions. The endless variety of rites which they practised[4] served to fill up their time, for which the majority of them, not being initiated into science, would have little occupation. Their numbers were very great; instead of a single priest or priestess attached to each temple, as among the Greeks, a long series of subordinate ministers discharged those multiplied functions in which their religion consisted. Herodotus declares that no female could fill a sacerdotal office[5], though it is evident from his own accounts, as well as from the sculptures and documents[6], that they might be engaged in duties connected with the temples[7]. The office was strictly hereditary. In the temples of the principal gods there was a high-priest, and

---

[1] Herod. 2, 37.

[2] Occasionally they practised rigid abstinence (ἐν ταῖς ἁγνείαις), and did not even allow themselves salt as a provocative of appetite. (Plut. Is. et Osir. p. 352.)

[3] Herod. 2, 37.

[4] Ἄλλας θρησκίας ἐπιτελέουσι μυρίας ὡς εἰπεῖν λόγῳ. (Her. ibid.)

[5] Herod. 2, 35. Ἱρᾶται γυνὴ μὲν οὐδεμία οὔτε ἔρσενος θεοῦ οὔτε θηλέης. But he himself (2, 55) speaks of a female as ἀμφιπολεύουσαν ἱρὸν Διός. See vol. i. p. 452.

[6] Champollion-Figeac, Egypte, L'Univers Pittoresque, 115.

[7] The priestesses mentioned in the Rosetta Stone belonged to the worship of the deified Ptolemies, not the ancient gods of Egypt.

XIV.] CONSTITUTION AND LAWS. 39

if we take literally the statement made by the priests of Vulcan to Hecatæus and Herodotus, the son had succeeded to the father for 340 generations[1]. To the priests alone polygamy was forbidden[2], and this restriction is confirmed by the monuments.

The reverence in which the sacerdotal order was held was not the result of their sacred character only, but of their superior knowledge and education, which comprehended, besides divination and augury, all the human sciences. Their superior skill in geometry and arithmetic, so important in a country whose revenues were raised by a tax on land proportioned to its extent[3], and where changes in the form and area of the fields were frequently produced by the action of the river, gave them a considerable control over property.

It does not appear that the practice of medicine was confined to them. The army was attended by physicians[4], who can scarcely have been priests. The general appearance and costume of the physicians represented in the grottos of Benihassan[5] would lead us to refer them to a low rank in society. No sepulchral inscription has yet been found in which this profession is mentioned, nor has the hieroglyphic character for physician been ascer-

---

[1] Herod. 2, 143, where however ἀπεδείκνυσαν παῖδα πατρὸς ἕκαστον ἑωυτῶν ἐόντα can hardly express a literal fact, especially if we consider the monogamy of the priests. Compare Her. 1, 7, where a similar expression only denotes generally an hereditary succession.

[2] Diod. 1, 80. Comp. Her. 2, 92.

[3] Herod. 2, 109. Εἴ τινος τοῦ κλήρου ὁ ποταμός τι παρέλοιτο, ἐλθὼν ἂν πρὸς τὸν βασιλέα ἐσήμαινε τὸ γεγενημένον· ὁ δὲ ἔπεμπε τοὺς ἐπισκεψομένους καὶ ἀναμετρήσοντας ὅσῳ ἐλάσσων ὁ χῶρος γέγονε, ὅκως τοῦ λοιποῦ κατὰ λόγον τῆς τεταγμένης ἀποφορῆς τελέοι.

[4] Diod. 2, 82.

[5] See vol. i. p. 345. Wilkinson, Manners and Customs, 3, 393.

tained. The embalmers were a part of the physicians[1], but the priests, whose profession required such scrupulous purity, cannot be supposed to have defiled themselves with the touch of dead bodies; and the embalmers are expressly said by Herodotus[2] to have been artisans who plied in public. But all medical practice was carried on in Egypt according to certain established formulas, contained in ancient books. Six of the forty-two treatises attributed to Hermes were devoted to medicine, and the pastophori, a special but inferior order of the priests, studied them[3]. To the precepts contained in these books the practitioners of medicine seem to have been obliged to conform, and thus the sacerdotal order would possess a complete control over the practical branches of the art. So under the Jewish Law, the Levites had to decide on all medical questions which had a bearing on religion[4], such as leprosy, but do not appear to have been in other respects the physicians of the people. In Europe during the Middle Ages, the knowledge of medicine was nearly confined to the clergy, if we except the Jews on the one hand, and the leeches who practised upon the vulgar on the other. The selection and examination of victims, the care of the sacred animals, the rigorous attention to their own health and purity which their office imposed, could not fail to give the Egyptian priests a considerable portion of medical knowledge, besides what the books of Hermes contained.

[1] Gen. 1. 2.
[2] Herod. 2, 86. Εἰσὶ δὲ οἱ ἐπ' αὐτῷ τούτῳ κατέαται καὶ τέχνην ἔχουσι ταύτην.
[3] Clem. Alex. Strom. 6,4, p. 758, ed. Pott.
[4] See Leviticus, xiii. xiv.

The more mysterious doctrines of religion, as well as the knowledge of the hieroglyphic character, in later times were reserved to the higher order of the priesthood[1], and this was probably always the case, the functions of the lower ministers being of a practical kind.

According to Ælian[2], the priests were originally judges, the eldest of them presiding. This appears afterwards to have given place to a select tribunal which we shall subsequently describe. But as the ultimate authority must be the written law, and as literature of every kind was in the custody of the priesthood, it is probable that questions of nice interpretation would be referred to them. So among the Jews, when a matter arose too hard for the decision of the inferior judges, recourse was had to the priests and Levites and the chief judge in the last resort[3]. In Europe in the Middle Ages, the highest offices of the law were filled by ecclesiastics, who alone could read ancient writings and pen decrees. Statistical knowledge was carried to greater perfection in Egypt than anywhere else in the ancient world. The whole country had been geometrically measured; every man's tax was fixed, every man's occupation known[4], and the topography of Egypt was the subject of one of the sacred books[5].

---

[1] Clem. Alex. Strom. 5, p. 670, Pott. Οὐ τοῖς ἐπιτυχοῦσι ἀνετίθεντο τὰ μυστήρια ἀλλ' ἢ μόνοις γε τοῖς μέλλουσι ἐπὶ βασιλείαν προϊέναι καὶ τῶν ἱερέων τοῖς κριθεῖσιν εἶναι δοκιμωτάτοις.

[2] Ælian. Var. Hist. 14, 34.

[3] Deut. xvii. 8. "If there arise a matter too hard for thee in judgement, then shalt thou arise and get thee up into the place which the Lord thy God shall choose, and thou shalt come unto the priests, the Levites, and the judge that shall be in those days, and inquire, and they shall show thee the sentence of judgement."

[4] Herod. 2, 177. He refers the law to the reign of Amasis.

[5] Clem. Alex. *ubi supra*.

The military class formed, like the priesthood, an hereditary caste[1]. They were divided into *Calasirians* and *Hermotybians*, names the signification of which has not been ascertained[2]. According to Herodotus, the Calasirians amounted, when their numbers were largest, to 250,000 men, the Hermotybians to 160,000; and if larger numbers are attributed to some of the armies of Egyptian conquerors, we must remember that oriental armies are swollen by a train of unmilitary followers. Each soldier had an allotment of land, of about six acres, free from taxes. Their settlements were almost exclusively in Lower Egypt[3], each body having only one in either Middle or Upper Egypt, namely the nomes of Chemmis and Thebes, while the Hermotybians were established in five nomes of Lower Egypt and the Calasirians in eleven[4]. It was on the side of Asia that the country was most exposed to attack, Nubia having been completely subjugated during the flourishing times of the monarchy; and the abundance and fertility of land in the Delta pointed out this as the part most suitable for the settlement of the soldiery. The facility with which a large force was collected for the pursuit of the Israelites[5], shows that they must have been quartered chiefly in Lower Egypt. All handicrafts were forbidden to them, but in these agriculture was not included, which was an honourable occupation even among those by whom the mechanical arts were

---

[1] Herod. 2, 166.
[2] Jablonsky (Voc. Ægypt. p. 69, 101.) deduces Calasiris from *Helshiri*, Coptic for *youth*; Hermotybian, from *armatoi oube, militare contra*, and he supposes the latter to have been veterans to whom the defence of the country was chiefly entrusted.
[3] Heeren, 2, 134. (2, 2, 578 Germ.)
[4] Herod. *ubi supra*.
[5] Exod. xiv. 5–9.

most despised[1]. In times of peace, a portion of them discharged garrison-duty in the frontier towns of Pelusium, Marea and Elephantine; a detachment to the number of a thousand of each acted as guards to the king, during the space of a year[2]. To these were given, as a daily allowance, five minæ of baked bread or parched corn, two minæ of beef and four *arysters*, or nearly two pints, of wine. In the Egyptian monuments we can distinguish such a body of men having peculiar arms, clothing and ensigns, and specially engaged in attendance on the king[3]. Perhaps other bodies might be stationed in some of the principal towns, where it has been thought that traces of fortified camps might be perceived[4].

Such a class, trained and armed and possessed of property in land, in the midst of a population of priests, agriculturists and tradesmen, must have had a preponderant weight in the social scale. Yet such was the harmony of the different members of the Egyptian state, that we hear for many centuries of no usurpations or rebellions by the soldiery. The military order was closely united with the monarchy. We find in the monuments that the sons of the kings held high posts in the army[5], and this class generally furnished a sovereign to the vacant throne. The Egyptian military system, as it originally existed, was better calculated to preserve order within the state and resist aggression, than the feudalism of the Middle Ages or the universal soldiership of the Greeks. The former was an instrument of oppres-

[1] Diod. 1, 28.
[2] Her. 2, 168.
[3] Rosellini, Monumenti Reali, tav. c. cii. cxxvi.
[4] Champollion-Figeac, Égypte, p. 147.
[5] Rosellini, Mon. Civili, 3, p. 313.

sion, the latter a constant provocative to civil war. Egypt more resembled Rome, in the ages in which the *plebs* was still devoted exclusively to agriculture and furnished legionaries to the army. The commencement of her fall was the encroachment made by the priests in the reign of Sethos, and the king in that of Psammitichus, on the privileges of the military class.

All the rest of the population may be regarded as forming one class, inasmuch as they were excluded from the possession of land, from the privileges of the priestly and military order, and from every department of political life. Among themselves, however, they were divided into a variety of trades and professions, about the number of which the ancients are not agreed, nor is it probable that any one has enumerated them all. The land was cultivated by a peasantry, tenants to the king, the priests and the warriors, whose traditionary knowledge and early training enabled them to carry the art to a much higher degree of perfection than any other nation[1]. The marshy districts of the Delta and the pastures of the valleys, especially of the Arabian chain of hills, maintained large numbers of cattle, the charge of which created another distinct class. The swineherds formed another—a Pariah-caste—to whom alone, of all the Egyptians, access to the temples was denied, and who could only intermarry among themselves[2]. The artificers and the boatmen and steersmen of the Nile were each a separate class. The monuments lead us to

---
[1] Diodor. 1, 74.
[2] Herod. 2, 47. Rosellini, Mon. Civ. 1, 206, mentions a herd of swine belonging to a priest; they were sometimes used in sacrifice, as Herodotus mentions.

conclude that the navigation of the sea was more common than had been previously supposed, yet it hardly belonged to the habits of the nation and was opposed to its religious ideas, according to which the sea-water, swallowing up the Nile, was symbolized in Typhon destroying Osiris. Even the navigators of the river were a disesteemed race[1]. Huntsmen are mentioned in the enumeration of Plato, among whom fowlers would be included[2]; in a country so abundant in streams and fish, fishermen must have been very numerous[3], and therefore probably a distinct class. On the establishment of the Greeks in Egypt, in the reign of Psammitichus, an hereditary body of interpreters was formed for the purpose of commercial intercourse[4], this being the only one of whose origin we have any historical account, and we see that neither conquest nor religion had anything to do with it, but the hereditary transmission of exclusive knowledge.

There can be no doubt that a broad line of social distinction separated all these classes from the three privileged orders. The principle of caste would have been annihilated, if the children of an artificer or a herdsman could have intermarried with those of a priest, a warrior, or a judge. Religious feeling and *esprit de corps* would no doubt close the sacerdotal or military class against a man of low caste, and want of skill would exclude him from the higher departments of art. We find some remarkable

---

[1] Plut. Is. et Osir. p. 363, c. 32.
[2] Plat. Tim. iii. 24.
[3] Herod. 2, 93. Diod. 1, 36. Isaiah xix. 8.
[4] Herod, 2, 154. Παῖδας παρέβαλε (Ψαμμίτιχος) τοῖς Ἴωσι Αἰγυπτίους, τὴν Ἑλλάδα γλῶσσαν ἐκδιδάσκεσθαι· ἀπὸ δὲ τούτων ἐκμαθόντων τὴν γλῶσσαν οἱ νῦν ἑρμηνέες ἐν Αἰγύπτῳ γεγόνασι.

examples of the hereditary descent of high public office. The long succession of the high-priests of Memphis has been already mentioned. Lepsius[1] quotes an inscription in which a chief of the mining works declares that twenty-three of his ancestors had filled the same office before him. But there is no proof that all the sons of a priest became priests, or of a military man soldiers. The higher professions appear to have been open to all of the higher castes, and might even be united in one person, and they might intermarry with each other; so probably might the lower, with the exception of the swineherds. A monument in the Museum at Naples, to one who was himself a general of infantry, records that his elder brother was a chief of public works and at the same time a priest[2]. In India at the present day no caste but the Brahminical is strictly preserved[3], and this includes not only the priesthood, but the higher civil professions.

The funeral monuments of Egypt, which have thrown light on the relations of the privileged orders and shown that they were not separated by such strict rules as had been supposed, give us no corresponding information respecting the lower castes. Priests, warriors, judges, architects, chiefs of districts and provinces, are nearly the only ranks or classes which appear in the inscriptions; we do not find the labourer, the agriculturist, the artist or the physician receiving those funereal honours which

---

[1] Lepsius, Tour to the Peninsula of Sinai, p. 4, Eng. Transl.
[2] Ampère in Revue des deux Mondes, 1848, p. 410. He, as well as Rosellini, *u. s.*, has controverted the common opinion respecting the distinction of castes, from the evidence of the monuments.
[3] Rickards, India, 1, 31. Elphinstone's India, 1, 103.

consist in the representation of the deceased as offering to the gods, and praying for their protection in another world[1]. And this shows the wide interval in social estimation, by which the upper and lower classes in Egypt were separated.

The Greeks, from whom we derive our earliest knowledge of Egyptian institutions, were naturally struck with the rigid distinction of the different orders of society: it had once existed among themselves[2], but was nearly obliterated and forgotten. If it appear to have been less exclusively a distinction of birth than we have been accustomed to suppose, there can be no doubt that it was one of the most important characteristics of Egyptian society. Perhaps a Mohammedan traveller in Europe during the prevalence of feudalism might have described its different orders and their relation to each other in terms not very unlike those which Herodotus applies to the *genea* of Egypt. Custom and sentiment had fixed a nearly impassable barrier between the villain and burgher on one side, and the military chief and feudal lord on the other. The burghers themselves, arranged in crafts and guilds, the entrance to which was jealously guarded, would have appeared to him rather as an aggregate of separate communities than a uniform mass of industrial population, such as our modern cities exhibit. A plebeian would have as little chance of obtaining a maiden of aristocratic blood in marriage, as an Egyptian of low caste of marrying the daughter

---

[1] Ampère, *ubi supra*.
[2] The most natural explanation of he fourfold division of the Ionic population of Attica (Herod. 5, 66) is that the names denote their different occupations.

of a priest or military chief; the executioner or flayer of cattle in Germany could no more have intermarried with a peasant or a burgher, than the swineherd in Egypt. The difference lies in the sanction by which the separation of ranks and professions was guarded; in Egypt it was enforced by religion; in Europe it was counteracted by the genius of Christianity and the celibacy of the clerical order, in which the humblest birth was no disqualification for the highest dignity.

In a country so fertile as Egypt, in which manufactures, art and internal commerce were carried on to such an extent, wealth must have accumulated among those who were engaged in civil life, and have given rise to a class of independent proprietors, not included in any of the *genea*. On the other hand, we find that in large cities a populace forms itself, depending on casual expedients for subsistence, and, as having no definite occupation, equally excluded from the list. Such a class in later times existed in Egypt; Sethos employed it in support of his usurpation[1]; Amasis endeavoured to check its growth by compelling every man to declare his occupation before the magistrate, under penalty of death, if he made a false statement or followed an unlawful mode of life[2]. With the exceptions which have been pointed out, there can be no question that the rule of Egyptian society was[3], that every man should be strictly limited to his

---

[1] Herod. 2, 141. Ἔπεσθαι δὲ οἱ τῶν μαχίμων μὲν οὐδένα ἀνδρῶν, καπήλους δὲ καὶ χειρώνακτας καὶ ἀγοραίους ἀνθρώπους.

[2] Her. 2, 177.
[3] Diod. 1, 74.

hereditary business[1]. The ancients generally admired this limitation, and attributed to it the high perfection which agriculture and art had attained. The father taught his son without grudging whatever he himself knew; the peasant and the artisan followed their proper business without the distraction of politics which engrossed the lower orders in republics. It was a maxim that it was best for one man to do one thing[2], which is undoubtedly true, as far as the perfection of his work is concerned. The effect of such a limitation on the character of the man, and therefore ultimately on the progress of his art, had not been considered.

The great body of the Egyptian people appear to have had no public duties whatever, neither political, judicial nor military; the idea of a *citizen* was unknown among them. This exclusion of all but priests and soldiers from political functions would ensure revolution in any modern government; but the privileged orders were so firmly established by the threefold monopoly of knowledge, sacred and secular, arms, and landed property, that we do not read even of an attempt to disturb them, on the part of the excluded millions, till the last century of the history of the Pharaohs.

The division of Egypt for administrative purposes was very simple. The principal cities, with their environs, and a number of villages dependent upon them, formed a *nome*, as the Greeks called it, over which a prefect or *nomarch* appointed by the

---

[1] The law which Dicæarchus attributes to Sesostris is μηδένα καταλιπεῖν τὴν πατρῴαν τέχνην. Schol. App. Rhod. 4, 272-276.

[2] Aristot. Polit. 2, 8. Ἐν ᾧ ἑνὸς ἔργον ἄριστ᾽ ἀποτελεῖται· δεῖ δὲ μὴ προστάττειν τὸν αὐτὸν αὐλεῖν καὶ σκυτοτομεῖν.

king presided, to superintend the royal revenues and the details of government[1]. The Delta contained ten of these nomes, the Thebaid ten; the intermediate country in later times sixteen, but originally only seven[2]. This corresponds with the arrangement of the Labyrinth[3], which had, as Strabo saw it, twenty-seven halls. This division was attributed to Sesostris, and it is probable that the boundaries of each nome were definitely fixed, when that general survey of the lands took place, which is said to have been made by this sovereign[4]. Commonly, however, authority only regulates and confirms divisions which have been determined by local and accidental circumstances. Religion appears in Egypt to have furnished the original principle of aggregation. Each of the larger cities was the seat of the worship of a peculiar divinity[5], which had been established there by the inhabitants of the district, and the religious usages which flowed from that worship were co-extensive with the nome[6]. Thus throughout the nome of Thebes, of which the ram-headed god was the chief divinity, goats were sacrificed, but not sheep[7]; while in the Mendesian nome, in reverence for the god to whom the goat was sacred, sheep were sacrificed, and not goats.

---

[1] Diod. 1, 54.
[2] Hence the name *Heptanomis*.
[3] Strabo, B. 17, p. 787, 811. Bunsen, Ægypten's Stelle (1, 179, note).
[4] According to Diodorus, 1, 95, Amasis τὰ περὶ τοὺς νομάρχας διέταξε καὶ τὰ περὶ τὴν σύμπασαν οἰκονομίαν τῆς Αἰγύπτου, but this cannot in either case relate to the first establishment.
[5] Her. 2, 42.
[6] Heeren (2, 108, 112, Eng.) supposes that the temples were foundations by priestly colonies from Meroe, and that they established the worship of the local god in each district. The language of Herodotus implies that the people of the nome established the temple.
[7] Her. *u. s.*

The number of the nomes ultimately amounted to fifty-three, but among them were reckoned the Greater and Lesser Oasis, and the Oasis of Ammon. They were again subdivided into *toparchies*, of whose extent we are not informed. Delegates from the nomes, chosen according to station and character[1], assembled at intervals at the splendid palace of the Labyrinth, near the Lake Mœris. Each delegation was accompanied by the priests and priestesses of its chief temple, and was lodged in its appointed place, among the 3000 apartments which the Labyrinth included. Sacrifices and gifts were made to the gods, and doubtful questions of jurisdiction settled. If the halls in the Labyrinth were, as Herodotus says[2], only twelve in number, only the larger nomes can have sent delegates, and some pre-eminence on the part of twelve of them appears to be implied in the establishment of a *Dodecarchia* or government of twelve kings, after the usurpation of Sethos.

We have no distinct information as to the mode in which justice was ordinarily administered in Egypt. Probably the nomarch and the toparch exercised a jurisdiction in matters of police and causes of minor importance. To judge is also reckoned among the functions of the king[3]. In the monarchies of the East it is an attribute inseparable from royalty, and the authority of all inferior tribunals is only a delegation from the prerogative of the Sovereign. Such is indeed the theory, though not the origin, of our own judicial system. The

---

[1] Strabo, 17, p. 811, with Tyrwhitt's emendation of ἀριστίνδην.
[2] Her. 2, 148.
[3] Diodor. 1, 76.

principal court of judicature was composed of thirty persons, chosen for their merit from the three most celebrated cities of the kingdom, Thebes, Memphis, and Heliopolis—ten from each. As these cities were also the most remarkable for the number and learning of the sacerdotal order, it has been generally taken for granted that the judges belonged to this caste. That they were of sacerdotal families appears, from what has been already said on the subject of castes, very probable, but hardly ministering priests, since each one had duties to perform in the temple to which he was attached. Ælian, by saying that *originally*[1] the judges were priests, implies that in later times it was otherwise. These thirty chose a president from among themselves, in whose place the city by which he had been sent furnished another. Probably therefore the original selection had been made by the cities. Their salaries were paid by the king. All proceedings were carried on in writing, that the decision might not be influenced by the arts of oratory, nor the stern impartiality of law be overcome by personal supplication. A collection of the laws in eight volumes lay before the judges; the plaintiff or accuser declared in writing how he had been injured, cited the portion of the law on which he relied, and laid the amount of his damages, or claimed the penalty which in his view the law awarded. The culprit or defendant replied in writing, point by point, denying the fact alleged, or showing that his act had not been unlawful, or that the penalty claimed was excessive. The plain-

---

[1] Var. Hist. 14, 34. Δικασταὶ τὸ ἀρχαῖον παρ' Αἰγυπτίοις ἱερεῖς ἦσαν.

tiff having rejoined, and the defendant replied again, the judges deliberated among themselves. A chain of gold and precious stones was worn by the president, to which an image of Thmei, the goddess of Truth, was attached, and he pronounced sentence by touching with this image the plaintiff's or defendant's pleadings[1]. We are not told how the facts were established, and indeed the whole account suggests the idea of a Court of Appeal, rather than of primary jurisdiction.

From the complex state of society in Egypt, more strikingly evinced by its monuments than even by the accounts of ancient writers, we may conclude that the laws were numerous. Yet few of them have been handed down to us, and no document of this kind has been hitherto deciphered from the remains of Egyptian antiquity. The character of the legislation therefore must be gathered from the general testimony of the ancient world, or by analogy from a few specimens which remain. The tradition that Lycurgus, Solon, and Plato[2], had borrowed from Egypt the laws of their real or imaginary states, is a proof of the high estimation in which they were held, whatever historical value it may possess. Their wisdom and humanity may be inferred from the correspondence which has been remarked between the Egyptian and the Jewish institutions.

---

[1] The resemblance of this ornament to the *Urim* and *Thummim* worn by the Jewish high priest has been noticed by all writers on Jewish or Egyptian antiquities. Yet the use was very different; one was an official chain, probably with a seal attached to it; the other answered the purpose of an oracle (Exod. xxxix. 10; Lev. viii. 8; Num. xxvii. 21). Nor is there any etymological ground for deriving *Thummim* from the Egyptian *Thmei*, although the Seventy may have been influenced by the Egyptian usage in rendering it by 'Αλήθεια.

[2] Diod. 1, 69, 96, 98.

If this be explained as by Spencer[1], who thinks that certain laws and usages to which the Jews had become accustomed, were adopted into the Mosaic Law, the highest sanction is given to them. If, with his great opponent Witsius[2], we believe that they were copied by the Egyptians from Abraham, and from his descendants, subsequently to their expulsion and the giving of the Law from Sinai (a much less probable supposition)[3], the inference as to their character will be the same.

The criminal law of Egypt was mild and equitable[4]. The wilful murder of a slave was punished with death, like that of a freeman; the exposure of infants was forbidden, nor was the mother allowed to be executed with an unborn child. False accusation (we may presume where a malicious purpose could be shown) was punished with the same penalty as would have fallen on the accused if convicted; and perjury with death. A thousand lashes were inflicted on an adulterer, mutilation of the nose on an adulteress. A parent who had killed his child was compelled to sit three days and three nights, under the guard of a public officer, embracing its body. It was a capital offence not to have assisted one who was slain by violence, the legislator presuming complicity where there had been no effort to prevent murder. Even the neglect to give information of a robbery was punished by stripes and

---

[1] See his great work De Legibus Hebræorum, p. 903, "Monendum est institutorum Mosaicorum partem multo maximam e consuetudine aliqua quæ apud Ægyptios aut alias e vicinia gentes inveteraverat dimanasse."

[2] Witsii Ægyptiaca, lib. 2, c. 1, § vii.

[3] Πατρίοισι χρεώμενοι νόμοισιν οἱ Αἰγύπτιοι ἄλλον οὐδένα ἐπικτέωνται (Her. 2, 79, 91).

[4] Diod. 1, 77, 78.

three days' imprisonment without food. Some of their punishments however were cruel; others appear to us fantastic, from an attempt to carry out strictly the *lex talionis*. Such was the punishment inflicted on a violator of female chastity: one who gave intelligence to an enemy had his tongue cut out; an adulterator of the standard currency[1], a falsifier of weights and measures, a public scribe who had forged or mutilated public writings, had his hand cut off. A grave has been found near Saccara, apparently of such criminals, as the hands and feet have been cut off at the joints[2]. It is probable that in the times of the Pharaohs[3], as well as of the Ptolemies, the working of the gold-mines of the Arabian Desert was one of the punishments of criminals. The labour was cruelly severe, and was exacted by the scourge; in the low and winding passages in which they wrought, the miners were compelled to assume painful and unnatural postures in order to carry on their work[4]. Their complaints could excite no sympathy, for guards were placed over them who did not understand their language. Children, women and old men were employed in different operations, and neither infirmity nor disease procured a respite, while there remained any strength which blows could compel them to exert[5].

---

[1] The Egyptians had no stamped coin, but used rings of metal in exchange.

[2] Perring in Vyse on the Pyramids, 3, 38.

[3] Compare Agatharchides ap. Phot. ccl. 11, p. 1342, whom Diodorus follows. He says that the mines had been wrought in the earliest times, but the working had been interrupted by the incursions of the Ethiopians.

[4] Πολλαχῶς πρὸς τὰς τῆς πέτρας ἰδιότητας μετασχηματίζοντες τὰ σώματα. (Diod. 3, 14.)

[5] Οὐ τυγχάνει συγγνώμης οὐδ' ἀνέσεως ἁπλῶς οὐκ ἄῤῥωστος, οὐ πεπηρωμένος οὐ γεγηρακὼς, οὐ γυναικὸς ἀσθένεια. (Ibid.)

Sabaco the Ethiopian introduced the practice of employing criminals on public works, instead of putting them to death.

A singular law prevailed in regard to thieves[1]. They were organized under a chief, with whom their names were enrolled, and to whom everything stolen was brought. Those who had been robbed applied to him, and obtained back their property on payment of a fourth of the value. This amounts in fact to impunity for any one who was willing to make restitution on payment of one-fourth, and probably nowhere has stolen property been so cheaply recovered. The law has been converted by later authorities[2] into a general permission of theft in Egypt.

The most sanguinary part of the Egyptian law was that which protected the sacred animals, as already mentioned[3]. It is probable, however, that the fanaticism, of which Diodorus witnessed an example, was one mode of expressing national animosity, and that it had not existed in such intensity before the Persian conquest. The law of sacrilege in Christian countries has been equally severe and inhuman; nor would a Jew, suspected of an act of disrespect towards the rites and emblems of the Church, have fared better at the hands of the multitude, than the Roman who fell a victim to the fury of an Egyptian mob.

The condition of females, according to Diodorus[4],

---

[1] Diod. 1, 80.
[2] Aulus Gellins, 11, 18, quoting "Aristo jureconsultus."
[3] Herod. 2, 65. Cicero, N. D. 1, 29, includes the dog and the crocodile among the animals whom it was a capital crime to kill. (Diod. 1, 72.)
[4] Diod. 1, 27.

was singularly favourable to the weaker sex, the prerogatives of a queen being greater than those of a king, and the husband engaging in the marriage contract to obey the wife in everything. These statements are rendered suspicious by being connected with the mythic sovereignty of Isis. The marriage of brothers and sisters was allowed[1]. Herodotus, contrasting the manners and customs of Egypt with those of other countries, remarks, that the women went to market and carried on retail trades, while the men sat in the house, occupied at the loom[2]. This, however, indicates no superior privilege on the part of the Egyptian women; it is only a proof that weaving was in Egypt an art requiring great skill and long practice[3], not as in Greece a part of domestic economy. The other circumstances which Herodotus mentions, as contrasts with Greek customs, are rather proofs of the depressed condition of the female sex. Women carried burthens on their shoulders, men on their heads, the women of course bearing the heavier weights. Women were excluded from all but menial offices about the temples; to maintain their parents if in want was voluntary with sons, compulsory with daughters. The monuments, as far as they have hitherto been interpreted, afford no

---

[1] This custom was explained by the marriage of Isis with Osiris. (Diod. ibid.) It is said to be confirmed by the monuments, but I doubt if *sister* and *cousin* can be distinguished.

[2] Herod. 2, 35. The Greeks, who despised manufactures, ridiculed the habits of the Egyptians as effeminate (Soph. Œd. Col. 337). The Ionian women were peculiarly sedentary (Xen. Rep. Lac. 1, 3, with Haase's note).

[3]   ......Nam longe præstat in arte,
Et solertius est multo genus omne virile.
              Lucr. 5, 1354, speaking of weaving.

countenance to the statement of Diodorus, though we cannot doubt that the condition of the female sex in Egypt partook of the general character of humanity and refinement which belonged to that country. Polygamy was allowed except to the priests[1], and all children, whether by wives or concubines, were equally legitimate. But even where several wives were taken, one of them, under the title of Lady of the House, enjoyed a superiority in honour and authority over the rest[2]. In the marshy districts of Lower Egypt monogamy prevailed, probably owing to the poverty of the inhabitants, as in Mohammedan countries the lower and even middle classes have usually only one wife.

Of the civil laws of the Egyptians very little is known. Most of those which are specified are attributed to Bocchoris[3], who is supposed to be the Pehor of the monuments, and to have lived a short time before the Ethiopian conquest. One of the most important was, that the goods only of a debtor could be taken, and that the arrest of the person was not allowed, on the ground that his services, whether a soldier, a peasant, or an artisan, belonged to the state. In this respect the Egyptian law was wiser and more humane than that of most of the Grecian states, which secured to a debtor the implements by which he gained his living, yet allowed him by imprisonment to be deprived of the means of using them[4]. Solon introduced the Egyptian practice into the law of Athens. If no written security had been given, a man might clear himself

---

[1] Diod. 1, 80. Herod. 1, 92.
[2] Diod. 1, 79, 94.
[3] Rosellini, Mon. Civ. 3, 137.
[4] Diod. ibid.

from a claim by his oath,—a proof how general was the use of writing for civil purposes among the Egyptians in later times, and a salutary limitation of credit. The interest of a debt was never allowed to amount to more than double the principal,—an ample security for the lender's rights, and a preventive of those violent infringements of the law of debtor and creditor, which, under the names of *Seisachtheia* and *Novæ Tabulæ*, we meet with in Greek and Roman history. By a singular law, passed at a time when there was a great want of circulating medium[1], a man was allowed to pledge the mummies of his forefathers for debt, but was himself deprived of sepulture if he omitted to redeem them before his death. The prohibition appears to have included his descendants, as long as the debt remained unpaid.

[1] Ἐπὶ Ἀσύχιος βασιλεύοντος, ἀμιξίης ἐούσης πολλῆς χρημάτων. (Herod. 2, 136.)

HISTORY OF EGYPT.

HISTORY OF EGYPT.

INTRODUCTION.

AUTHORITIES FOR EGYPTIAN HISTORY.

SECT. I.—GREEK WRITERS.

THE commencement of Grecian intercourse with Egypt is hidden by the darkness of antehistoric times. The warlike expeditions of the Egyptian kings no doubt included Ionia, but the coast of Asia was not then inhabited by Greek settlers, and it is not alleged that Sesostris carried his arms into Hellas proper[1]. The stories of Egyptian colonization in Greece are generally of so late an origin, that we cannot even infer from them the existence of a popular belief[2]. There is, however, one exception. The story of Io, the Argive princess, who was changed into a heifer, and after long wanderings reached Egypt where she gave birth to a god, and herself was worshiped as the goddess Isis, points clearly to the introduction of the worship of Isis or Athor, under the symbol of the heifer, at an early period into Argos. As the worship of the Moon under this symbol appears to have prevailed in Phœnicia, as well as in Egypt, it might have been doubted from which of these countries it was transferred to Argos, but for the circumstance that

---

[1] Herod. 2, 103.
[2] Even Diodorus (1,29) acknowledges the vanity of these pretensions on the part of the Egyptians.

Io is the Coptic name of the Moon[1], and the same term was preserved in the dialect of Argos, without apparent affinity with any Greek root[2]. The story of the migration of Danaus and Ægyptus with their fifty sons and daughters to Argos cannot be traced higher than to the age of Æschylus and Herodotus;· but it was received by the latter as historical, and the existence of the belief is hardly to be explained, unless we admit the general fact of an Egyptian colonization.

We are not sufficiently acquainted with the history of navigation among the Greeks, to assign with any probability the time when they first visited the shores of Egypt. They regarded it as at once a distant and a difficult voyage[3]. Even the life of a traveller who fell into the hands of the savage people inhabiting the marshes near the mouths of the Nile was not safe, for there was a time when the harbour of Pharos was not opened for the admission of strangers[4]. The sacrifice of ruddy-coloured men appears to have prevailed in Lower Egypt in the early ages of the monarchy[5], and the fair and yellow-haired Greeks would be especially the objects of aversion and outrage from their *Typhonian* hue[6]. If they visited Egypt, they appear to have confined themselves to the Canopic mouth of the Nile. To this their mythic traditions refer. Here was the Tower of Perseus[7], and a little further to the east the temple of Hercules, who on his return from

---

[1] Peyron, Lex. Copt. p. 59.

[2] Γάζαν Ἰόνην καλοῦσί τινες ἔνθα βοῦς ἦν ἐν ἀγάλματι τῆς Ἰοῦς· ἤτοι τῆς σελήνης· Ἰὼ γὰρ ἡ σελήνη κατὰ τὴν τῶν Ἀργείων διάλεκτον. (Eust. ad Dionys. Perieg. v. 94.)

[3] Od. δ΄, 483.

[4] Eratosth. ap. Strab. p. 802. Diod. I, 67.

[5] Plut. p. 380. Porphyr. de Abst. p. 199.

[6] Ἔν τισιν ἑορταῖς τῶν μὲν ἀνθρώπων τοὺς πυρροὺς προπηλακίζουσι, διὰ τὸ πυρρὸν γεγονέναι τὸν Τυφῶνα. (Plut. Is. et Osir. p.362 F.) Busiris was one of the places in which the Typhonian superstition prevailed. [7] Herod. 2, 15.

Libya had encountered and slain the inhospitable Busiris[1]. Hither Paris had been driven on his way from Sparta to Troy. Canopus itself was supposed to have derived its name from the pilot of Menelaus, who had sailed thither on his return from Troy and been detained by the anger of the gods[2]. The name of Thon, which appears in the story of Menelaus, was derived from a town of that name, which stood near the Canopic mouth[3], and a place called Heleneins is mentioned in the same locality[4]. The Canopic mouth was the nearest to Greece and the coast of Asia Minor inhabited by Greeks; it gave the most ready access to the interior, and afforded, even in the earliest times of Greek navigation, a deeper and safer anchorage than any of the other channels[5].

The incidental mention of Egypt in the Homeric poems leads us to suppose that the Greeks in general were but little acquainted with it, and least of all with Upper Egypt[6]. The island Pharos, which must then as now have lain close to the coast, is placed by the poet at the distance from it of a day's sail[7]. If this arose from ignorance on

---

[1] Strabo, p. 801. Diod. 4, 27. Her. 2, 113.
[2] Od. δ', 83, 351.
[3] Diod. 1, 19.
[4] Hecatæus apud Steph. Byz. s. voc.
[5] "Ἔχει μὲν οὖν εἰσαγωγὰς τὰ στόματα ἀλλ' οὐκ εὐφυεῖς, οὐδὲ μεγάλοις πλοίοις ἀλλ' ὑπηρετικοῖς, διὰ τὸ βραχέα εἶναι καὶ ἑλώδη· μάλιστα μέντοι τῷ Κανωβικῷ στόματι ἐχρῶντο ὡς ἐμπορίῳ. (Strabo, p. 801.)
[6] The assertion of the Egyptian priests (Diod. 1, 96), that it was recorded in their sacred books that Homer had visited Egypt, deserves no credit.
[7] Νῆσος ἔπειτα τίς ἐστι πολυκλύστῳ ἐνὶ πόντῳ
Αἰγύπτου προπάροιθε (Φάρον δέ ἑ κικλήσκουσι)
Τόσσον ἄνευθ' ὅσσον τε πανημερίη γλαφυρὴ νηῦς
Ἤνυσεν, ᾗ λιγὺς οὖρος ἐπιπνείῃσιν ὄπισθεν.—Od. δ', 354.

No deposition of soil can have filled up this interval; nor is anything gained by making Αἰγύπτου here signify the river Nile, con-

his part, it proves that the coast was not much frequented by navigators; if, as seems probable, it was designed in order to afford a more appropriate scene for the "specious miracle" of Proteus, it presumes ignorance of the true position on the part of his auditors. With the exception of Thebes, only Lower Egypt is alluded to. Menelaus is said in the Odyssey[1] to have received rich presents from Polybus, who dwelt in Thebes, and in aftertimes this Polybus was converted into a king of the 19th dynasty. The exaggerated description of Thebes, and its wealth[2], indicates that it was known from the boastful rumour of the natives rather than from ocular inspection. Egypt's abundance in skilful physicians and medicinal herbs is noticed in the Odyssey, but this too is turned into a tale of wonder in the description of the virtues of the *Nepenthe*[3]. Before the time of Psammitichus, Greeks were not allowed to go beyond the coast of Lower Egypt, and the occasional visits of traders to a single sea-port, inhabited by a people whose language was utterly unknown to them, could furnish no accurate knowledge of the interior, much less any insight into the history of the country.

This state of things was entirely changed in the reign of Psammitichus, who gained his kingdom by means of Ionian and Carian mercenaries (670 B.C.), took them permanently into his pay, and established a body of interpreters, by whose means the Greeks

trary to its obvious meaning; for Pharos is not προπάροιθε any part of the river, and much less than a day's sail from the nearest part of it. In Virgil's time the mouth of the Nile was too well known to be the scene of a tale of wonder, and he transfers it to the Carpathian Sea. (Georg. 4, 387.)

[1] Od. δ', 126.
[2] Il. ι', 381. See vol. i. p. 178.
[3] Od. δ', 220 *seq.*

began to acquire an accurate knowledge of Egypt[1]. Amasis, nearly a century and a half later, allowed them to settle at pleasure in Naucratis. Yet Pindar speaks of Mendes as being "near a cliff of the sea," though there is no cliff on the coast, nor was Mendes near it[2]. The state of Greek literature however has prevented our deriving any benefit from this source, in the interval between the reign of Psammitichus and the Persian conquest. During this time Thales and Pythagoras had visited Egypt, and been initiated into the religion and science of the Egyptians[3], but we have only vague traditions of their travels; for history had not yet come into existence among the Greeks themselves. Still the presence of intelligent foreigners controlled the propensity of the natives to give a marvellous air to everything in their history, and established a chronology moderate, credible and continuous for the period subsequent to the reign of Psammitichus, while before that time, in the works of Herodotus and Diodorus, the history is mythical and extravagant, and the chronology exaggerated, uncertain and fragmentary.

The overthrow of the monarchy of the Pharaohs by Cambyses, coinciding with the commencement of prose history in Ionia, at length laid Egypt completely open to the researches of the Greeks, and preserved the record of them to succeeding times. The philosophers who visited it while the hierarchy retained their power, were probably com-

[1] Herod. 2, 154. Diod. 1, 67.
[2] Παρὰ κρημνὸν θαλάσσας. (Frag. Boeckh. 215.) Comp. Fr. 50, where Egypt is called ἀγχίκρημνος.
[3] Antiphon ap. Porph. de Vita Pyth. Diog. Laert. 8, 3. According to this author, the friendly relations between Polycrates and Amasis obtained for Pythagoras admission first to the Heliopolitan, then to the Memphite, and last of all the Theban priests.

pelled to purchase their initiation into the secrets of science and the mysteries of religion[1] by humble entreaty, and attain it through long preliminary forms[2]; and the jealous sensibility of the multitude, in everything which regarded their religion, would co-operate with the spirit of secresy and monopoly in the priesthood, to render free inquiry dangerous and difficult. The Persian conquest made the professors of a different and hostile religion masters of the country, opened all its approaches, and enabled the Greeks to visit every part of it. The reign of Darius established order and peace throughout the whole extent of the monarchy; Egypt in particular felt the benefit of his firm but tolerant sway. The earliest Greek descriptions of Egypt were probably written during his reign[3]. Cadmus must have written on Egypt, since Diodorus (1, 37) includes him among those who had given fabulous accounts of the Nile. Hecatæus, like Cadmus, a native of Miletus, a city which was the first school of Greek history and geography, was a contemporary of Darius, and had included Egypt among the countries which he described in his *Periegesis* or *Periodos*[4]. Nothing has been quoted from this last work, by which we can judge whether he gave its

---

[1] Diod. 1, 98.

[2] Προστάγματα σκληρὰ καὶ κεχωρισμένα τῆς Ἑλληνικῆς ἀγωγῆς, says Antipho of the trials by which the patience of Pythagoras was tried.

[3] Hippys of Rhegium, who lived ἐπὶ τῶν Περσικῶν (Suid.), is reckoned by Heyne among the writers on Egypt (De Font. Hist. Diod. xxviii.), but no such work is ascribed to him, and he may have mentioned the antiquity of the Egyptian people, and the purity of the air and water incidentally in his other writings. Schol. Ap. Rhod. 4, 262, where the name is written Ἵππων in Schol. Paris.

[4] It was doubtful whether the works which were current under these names in the time of Athenæus and Arrian were genuine. (Arr. 5, 6. Athen. Epit. 2, p. 70.)

history, but the descriptive part must have been minute, since Herodotus has been charged with almost literally copying from him the passages in his second book relating to the phœnix, the hippopotamus and the crocodile[1]. Hellanicus of Lesbos, a few years before Herodotus, either wrote a work entitled Αἰγυπτιακά[2], or at all events introduced many particulars respecting the productions, customs and dogmas of Egypt into some of his voluminous writings. According to the judgement of Photius, it contained much that was mythic and fictitious[3], but it might nevertheless be a faithful account of what he had seen and heard. Phereeydes, who was three years younger than Herodotus, but published earlier, introduced the mention of Egypt into his Ἱστορίαι, in connexion with the attempt of Busiris to sacrifice Hercules[4]. But it does not appear that he had visited this country, and the fragments of his work indicate that be regarded the history of all other nations from the Grecian point of view, and endeavoured to interweave it with the mythic history of the heroic age.

Probably none of these writers, not even Hecatæns, contained a connected history and chrono-

---

[1] Euseb. Præp. Evang. 10, 3, quoting Porphyry περὶ τοῦ κλέπτας εἶναι τοὺς Ἕλληνας.

[2] The title quoted by Athenæus, p. 470 D. 679 F., is not decisive evidence of the existence of a separate work so named, since we find the Αἰγυπτιακά of Herodotus quoted, evidently the Euterpe (Sturz, Hellan. p. 40). Plutarch mentions Hellanicus as writing the name Osiris *Usiris* (Is. et Os. p. 364).

[3] Cod. clxi. p. 339. μυθικὰ καὶ πλασματικὰ πολλά. Two sources, however, are mentioned, Hellanicus and Ælius Dionysius (or Dius), and it does not appear what belonged to each.

[4] Pherecydes, ed. Sturz, pp. 132, 137. Herodotus probably had him in view (2, 45) when he charges the Greeks with repeating idle tales respecting human sacrifices in Egypt.

logy of Egypt. We may regard these as beginning with Herodotus. The Egyptians had revolted from Persia at the close of the reign of Darius (486 B.C.), but had been brought into subjection early in that of Xerxes (484 B.C.), and had again revolted under Inaros king of Libya in 460 B.C. This revolt lasted six years, and the Athenians had assisted the Egyptians with a fleet, which at first was successful and took possession of Memphis, but was subsequently destroyed by Megabyzus[1]. Whether Herodotus visited Egypt during its temporary occupation by the Greeks, or subsequently to the re-establishment of the Persian dominion in 455 B.C., is uncertain. It is evident from his history (2, 99) that at the time when it was *written* they were in possession of it; but many years intervened between his travels, and the publication of his Muses in their present form. In either case it is evident that he was able to pass freely through the country to the borders of Nubia[2], and pursue every investigation which his inquisitive mind suggested. His residence, however, seems to have been chiefly confined to Lower Egypt and Memphis; he visited Thebes, but it was to ascertain whether its sacerdotal traditions agreed with those which he had heard at Memphis, and the reader is surprised that he should have passed over in profound silence its temples, palaces and sepulchres, as well as all the circumstances which give to Upper Egypt a character so different from that of the Delta. Thebes

---

[1] Thuc. 1, 104, 109.   [2] Her. 2, 29.

had suffered especially from the fury of Cambyses[1], yet its buildings remained, and even in its ruins it must have far surpassed every other city of Egypt. He appears to have derived his materials almost entirely from the accounts of the priests[2] and the Greeks settled in the country: he never quotes as authorities the writers who had preceded him, though he sometimes alludes to their mistakes[3]. The information which the priests gave him was communicated orally, except in one instance, in which they read to him from a papyrus a list of 341 kings. In other passages[4] he mentions the purport of inscriptions which had been explained to him.

His history begins with Menes, the founder of the monarchy and of Memphis, succeeded by 330 sovereigns, respecting whom, as they had erected no monuments, the priests had nothing further to relate than that eighteen among them were Ethiopians and one a queen, Nitocris. The next name, and therefore the 331st from Menes, is that of Mœris, the author of the remarkable excavation, for so Herodotus considered it, in the district of Fyoum, which received the overflowings of the Nile. The conqueror Sesostris succeeds to Mœris, and to Sesostris his son Pheron. In the reign of his successor, Proteus, is related the history of the adventures of Paris, Menelaus and Helen in Egypt, followed by the reign of Rhampsinitus the wealthy, with the anecdote of the thief

---

[1] Strabo, p. 816. Diod. 1, 46.
[2] 2, 99, 100, 102, 107, 111, 113, 118, 124, 154. In 2, 142 he quotes as his authorities Αἰγύπτιοί τε καὶ οἱ ἱρέες.
[3] 2, 16.
[4] 2, 125, 136, 141.

who robbed his treasury. After Rhampsinitus come the builders of the pyramids—Cheops, Chephren and Mycerinus, followed by Asychis and Anysis, in whose reign Sabaco the Ethiopian invaded Egypt and kept possession of the throne for fifty years. His evacuation of the kingdom made way for the elevation of Sethos, succeeded by the Dodecarchia, or government of twelve chieftains, whose power Psammitichus put down and consolidated the government in his own hands. With Psammitichus, as we have already observed, we reach a period of ascertained history and definite chronology ; but the effect of the establishment of the Greeks in Egypt is in some degree retrospective, and extends this period as far back as the Ethiopian dominion.

In regard to all that precedes this age, the eighth century before Christ, it is evident, from the inspection of the history of Herodotus by itself, and without comparison with monuments or with any other historical book, that it cannot be accepted as true, either in its facts or its dates. Even the circumstance that after Menes 330 sovereigns are said to have succeeded to each other, without leaving any memorial of themselves in public works, or legislation, or conquest, is sufficient to show that the kings and their chronology are unhistorical. If we suppose, which is not improbable, that Herodotus has mistaken the statement received from the priests, and that the 330 kings were not represented by them as intervening between Menes and Mœris, but are to be added to the eleven who succeeded Mœris, and whose reigns are specially described by him, making 341 for the whole number from Menes to the extinction of the line of the Pharaohs in Sethos, this would not be sufficient to make his history credible. The properly historical information, from Menes to the Ethiopian invasion, is comprised in the single reign of his Sesostris, who appears as a conqueror and a legislator. All the other sovereigns serve only to explain the existence of public works and monuments, or connect themselves with narratives which betray their origin in superstition or popular credulity; nothing is recorded of them analogons to the facts which authentic history preserves respecting the real monarchs of powerful and civilized countries, and which must certainly have been contained in the annals of the Egyptians, the most learned people in their national antiquities[1] of any of the ancient world.

It is also obvious, that a considerable portion of this history has been produced, since the establishment of the Greeks in Egypt, by their earnest desire to connect their own mythic history with that of Egypt. The Egyptian priests were ready to cooperate with them for this purpose; each party having also its separate aim, to exalt the glory of their respective countries. The adventures of Menelaus in Egypt, detailed even to the speeches, occupy about the same space (2, 112—120) as the whole reign of Sesostris (102—111). The Homeric mythe of Proteus, a marine divinity feeding his *phocæ* on the coast of Egypt, and endowed with the

---

[1] 2, 77. Οἱ μὲν περὶ τὴν σπειρομένην Αἴγυπτον οἰκέουσι, μνήμην ἀνθρώπων πάντων ἐπασκέοντες μάλιστα, λογιώτατοί εἰσι μακρῷ τῶν ἐγὼ εἰς διάπειραν ἀπικόμην. Λόγιος is explained by Hesychius as τῆς ἱστορίας ἔμπειρος. Clem. Alex. p. 757, Potter, will show how much even the priests had to commit to memory, although they had a large number of written volumes.

gift of prophecy, which he will only exercise upon compulsion, is transformed into the history of a man of Memphis[1], who succeeds to the throne of Egypt on the death of Pheron, the son of Sesostris. This history Herodotus received, and apparently in undoubting faith, from the priests themselves, who, though they could furnish him nothing memorable to record respecting 330 sovereigns, relate with the minuteness of a contemporary journal the adventures of a Trojan prince, cast upon their shores; adventures trivial in themselves if they ever happened, and little likely to have found a place in sacerdotal annals. But while the Greeks were gratified to find a confirmation of their own history in that of Egypt, the Egyptian priests rejoiced in the opportunity of exhibiting their ancient sovereigns as exercising justice and hospitality towards the Greeks. They had been accused by the Greeks of putting strangers to death; but according to the account given by the priests to Herodotus, Menelaus seized and sacrificed two Egyptian children to obtain favourable winds—an evident allusion to the story of the sacrifice of Iphigenia. It is also obvious that Egyptian mythology and popular anecdote have furnished a considerable portion of what Herodotus has given us for history. To the former class belong the stories of the descent of Rhampsinitus into Hades, and the grief of the daughter of Mycerinus; to the latter the pleasant tale of the thief who was

---

[1] Proteus was worshiped at Memphis, but in the quarter of the Tyrians (Her. 2, 112), and he was connected with the temple of the Foreign Venus. The story was transferred, probably by Phœnician colonization, with the worship of the Cabiri (Her. 3, 37) to Pallene (Virg. Georg. 4, 390). See Kenrick's Egypt of Herodotus, p. 265.

caught in the trap, when endeavouring to rob the treasure-house of Rhampsinitus. Such being the general character of the history, even those parts which do not bear on their face the marks of a mythic or fictitious origin, lose their historical evidence; they are less improbable than the rest, but not more certain.

From a history composed of such materials no chronology can be deduced. Herodotus makes Mœris to have preceded only by 900 years his own visit to Egypt; but as we find in the ascent to Mœris a person of such doubtful historical character as Proteus, we can place no reliance on any portion of the chain. Herodotus besides connects this date of the reign of Mœris with the assurance, that in his time a rise of the Nile of eight cubits was sufficient to inundate the Delta; whereas in the historian's own day a rise of sixteen cubits was necessary for this purpose. This however supposes a rate of variation for the height of the soil and river so different from everything which has been ascertained, that if the fact be admitted the date must be false; and if the fact be incorrect, the authority of those by whom it was related, and from whom the whole chronology is derived, as given by Herodotus, is of no value.

It is evident that a popular history had formed itself in Egypt in the time of Herodotus, having very little connexion with written or monumental authority, of which the leading object had been to satisfy the curiosity of travellers by furnishing, what they always eagerly inquire for, the names of the authors of public works, and some anecdotes respecting them.

Had he derived his history from a class of persons corresponding with those who in modern Europe have the charge, and take on themselves the explanation of public monuments, we should not have been surprised at the vagueness of his chronology and the leaning to the marvellous in his narratives. But he repeatedly appeals to the authority of the priests, who as a body must in this age have retained the knowledge of the hieroglyphical character and an ample religious and antiquarian literature. I can only explain this by supposing that the priests with whom he conversed were of a very subordinate rank and ignorant of the antiquities of their country, who had framed for the use of visitors such a history as would satisfy their curiosity and excite their imagination, without overburthening their memory with names[1]. From the account of Clemens Alexandrinus[2], it should seem that the *interpretation* of the hieroglyphic character was the office only of the *hierogrammateus*, from whom the others learnt by heart what it was necessary that they should know for the execution of their offices. This may help to account for the extraordinary character which the history of Herodotus presents, considered only by itself, and its still more extraordinary aspect, when confronted with the monuments.

[1] The account which the *grammatistes* of the temple of Sais gave to Herodotus (2,28) of the source of the Nile, which he describes as rising between Syene and Elephantine, and flowing half towards Egypt and half towards Ethiopia, proves either that the Egyptians made experiments on the credulity of the Greeks, or that an inhabitant of Lower Egypt, where the Greeks chiefly collected their information, might be very ignorant of the geography of Upper Egypt. The Greeks themselves very rarely reached the southern frontier of the kingdom, much less did they venture into Ethiopia. (Diod. Sic. 1, 37.)

[2] Strom. 6, p. 757.

Egypt remained open to the Greeks, when they were not themselves in hostility with Persia. Philistus, the Syracusan, had probably visited this country, during his long exile, at the beginning of the fourth century B.C. He wrote a work on Egypt in twelve books, and on Egyptian theology in three books, besides a discourse concerning Naucratis[1]. Democritus, about the same time, is said to have spent five years in Egypt, and to have written on the sacred characters of Meroe[2]; but neither of his works nor those of Philistus has more than the titles reached us.

If we are inclined to wonder at the vagueness and inaccuracy of these Greek accounts of Egypt, we must remember, that the monuments in general precede by many centuries the earliest of them, and that a variance between them does not therefore necessarily imply unfaithfulness on the part of the Greeks. Besides this, many obstacles stood in the way of their obtaining accurate information. Ignorant themselves of the language of the country, they had to depend on Egyptian interpreters, who probably possessed only that superficial knowledge of Greek which enabled them to carry on intercourse on the common-place topics of commerce and conversation. The repugnance of the Egyptians for foreign religion and manners must have made them unwilling to receive the Greeks into intimacy, or give them information. Like our own countrymen, they bore themselves towards *barbarians* with the air of conscious superiority, which inflames dislike[3].

[1] Suidas, s. v. Φίλιστος.
[2] Diog. Laert. 9, 49.
[3] See the observations of Sir G. Wilkinson, M. & C. 5, 466.

The priesthood in particular appear to have endeavoured to humble the national pride of the Greeks, by representing everything in their civilization, even their philosophy and science, as derived from Egypt.

The next great event in the history of Egypt is its conquest by Ptolemy, the son of Lagus, in the year 322 B.C., by which a Greek dynasty was established there and in Ethiopia. Many of the Greeks subsequently composed Egyptian histories; but none of them has been preserved, except by quotations in later authors. From a fragment of Dicæarchus, who lived about 300 B.C., it appears as if he had placed Sesonchosis or Sesostris at the commencement of the monarchy, immediately after Horus, whom the Greeks reckoned to have been the last of the gods[1], and 2936 years before the æra of the Olympiads. Such a position of Sesostris is purely arbitrary, and must have been owing to his celebrity as a conqueror—a proof that Egyptian history was still arranged according to popular conception rather than documentary and monumental evidence. Eratosthenes of Cyrene, the chief librarian of the Alexandrian library, a man of extraordinary compass of literary and scientific attainments, had occupied himself with the genealogy and succession of the Theban kings[2] in the reign of the second Ptolemy; but his labours appear to have had little influence upon the popular history, which,

---

[1] Schol. Apoll. Rhod. 4, 272.
[2] Τὴν γνῶσιν φησὶν ὁ 'Ερατοσθένης λαβὼν Αἰγυπτιακοῖς ὑπομνήμασι καὶ ὀνόμασι κατὰ πρόσταξιν βασιλικὴν τῇ 'Ελλάδι φωνῇ παρέφρασεν οὕτως (Syncell. Chronog. p. 91. 171 Dind.). The same author says that Eratosthenes received the names ἐκ τῶν ἐν Διοσπόλει ἱερογραμματέων (p. 147. 279 Dind.).

as it is given by Diodorus, retains the same general character as in Herodotus.

Diodorus visited Egypt in the 180th Olympiad, about 58 B.C.[1] From what sources the portion of his history was derived which differs from Herodotus, we do not know. He had seen Memphis, and probably Thebes; he had read the authors who had written on Egypt in the times of the Ptolemies, and quotes, without professing himself to have read, the annals of the priests. Although not admitting that the Barbarians generally were older than the Greeks, the reputed birth of the gods in Egypt, the high antiquity of astronomical science there, and the fullness and importance of its historical records, led him to begin his Universal History with that of Egypt, and prefix to it a speculation, in historical garb, on the progress of civilization in that country, from the time when the inhabitants lived on the spontaneous growth of the papyrus, next on fish, then on the flesh of animals[2], and lastly on lotus, till a king and queen, Osiris and Isis, discovered the cultivation of grain.

In the history of Diodorus we perceive two changes which had taken place since the time of Herodotus. The father of history, in accordance with the accounts given him by the priests, represents the gods of Egypt as wholly distinct from men[3]. But in the interval between Herodotus and Diodorus the opinion had sprung up among the Greeks that the gods had been illustrious chiefs and warriors, inventors and improvers of the arts and sciences, raised to the rank of divinity through the admira-

---
[1] Hist. 1, 46.
[2] Hist. 1, 9. 43.
[3] 1, 143. See vol. i. p. 351.

tion and gratitude of mankind[1]. Osiris, therefore, who had been to Herodotus a god, answering in the Egyptian pantheon to Dionysus in the Greek, appears in Diodorus as a king of Egypt also, according to some accounts the founder of Thebes, who with a large army traversed the world, to diffuse the blessings of civilization[2]. Another change is the endeavour to connect Egyptian history, not only with Greek history generally, but with the country of the reigning dynasty. Osiris is accompanied by his son Macedo, whom he leaves as king of that region, a fiction by means of which Egyptian pride was flattered with the belief that Egypt had been conquered by princes of its own blood[3]. The celebrated wine of Maronea, or Ismarus in Thrace, which in this age was included in Macedonia[4], was also said to have derived its name from Maro, a follower of Osiris in his Thracian expedition; and Lycurgus, a name occurring in the Iliad[5], is represented as being slain in consequence of his resistance to Osiris. In this age it had become known that beer, a common beverage in Egypt, was used among the barbarous nations, whose climate could not ripen grapes, and this also Osiris had taught them to make[6].

The properly human history of Diodorus begins,

[1] The Egyptians combined the ancient with the modern doctrine, by the supposition that each celestial god had a mortal representative mostly of the same name (Diod. 1, 12, 13).

[2] Diod. 1, 24, 28.

[3] Obvious as this is, the interpreters of hieroglyphics have sought for a *Macedo* among the names of the ancient gods of Egypt (Wilkinson, pl. 44; Young in Supp. to Encyclop. Britt.). Fortunately for the credit of their science, they have *not* found him.

[4] Strabo, Epit. 7, 6, 331. The Greeks on their side alleged that Marea, near Alexandria (Georg. 2, 91), derived its name from the Homeric Maron. (Od. ί, 197. Eust. *ib.*)

[5] ζ, 134.

[6] Her. 2, 77. Diod. 1, 20.

like that of Herodotus, with Menes. The line of his insignificant successors, of whom there was nothing to relate, extends only to fifty-two, occupying a space of 1400 years. After this interval Busiris succeeds, and eight of his descendants, of whom the last, Busiris II., founds the city which the Egyptians call the city of Zeus, and the Greeks Thebes. At this point there is a break in the chronology. Having mentioned the sumptuous temples and other works by which the kings who succeeded Busiris II. had adorned Thebes, he describes at great length the monument of Osymandyas[1]; and when he returns to his history and says that Uchoreus, eighth in descent from *this* king, founded Memphis, it is uncertain whether he means from Busiris or from Osymandyas, probably the former. Mœris, the twelfth in descent from Uchoreus, excavated the lake which bears his name, and erected in it two pyramids, on one of which a statue of himself, on the other of his queen, was placed. Seven generations later lived Sesoosis, whose history has so close a resemblance with that of the Sesostris of Herodotus, as to leave no doubt that they are the same persons. His son of the same name succeeded him, and from the circumstances of his history appears to be the Pheron of Herodotus. After him came, in many generations, whose number is not specified, a succession of kings, who performed nothing worthy of record. Amasis, the next named, alienated the minds of his people by his tyranny, so that, being invaded by Actisanes the king of Ethiopia, Egypt fell with little resistance

[1] 1, 47.

under his dominion. At his death the Egyptians recovered their independence, and chose Mendes or Marus for their king, who built the Labyrinth as a sepulchre for himself. An anarchy which lasted five generations was ended by the election of a man of the common people, called Cetes by the Egyptians, Proteus by the Greeks. The variation in the names is perhaps only apparent; for though Κέτης is said to be Egyptian, its analogy to the Greek Κῆτος[1], whence the Latin *cetus, cete*, leads to the suspicion that it represents the same idea as Proteus, a marine deity, partaking of the form of a fish[2]. The reign of Cetes must be considered in the chronology of Diodorus to answer to the time of the Trojan war. The Remphis who succeeds to Cetes is evidently the Rhampsinitus of Herodotus. In comparing the accounts of these two kings, as given by Herodotus and Diodorus, we see an attempt in the latter to give an historical air and historical probability to that which his predecessor had left in the vagueness of mythe and tradition. The knowledge of the winds possessed by Proteus is ascribed to his intimacy with the astronomers, who were supposed to be capable of predicting the changes of the weather; his transformations, to the custom of the Egyptian rulers to put on the heads of lions, bulls and serpents. Herodotus mentions, but does not account for nor specify, the immense

---

[1] We find the various readings of Κέτνα, Κέτην, Κέτηνα (Diod.1,62), but none seems to represent a true Egyptian name.

[2] The knowledge of the future was for some mythic reason, not necessary to be here inquired into, supposed to belong especially to the marine deities. (Hes. Theog. 233. Apoll. Rhod. 1, 310. Ov. Met. 12, 556. 8, 737.) Κητώ in Hesiod *u.s.* is a daughter of Πόντος and sister of Nereus; Proto (ib. 243) is a daughter of Nereus.

wealth of Rhampsinitus, which was probably connected with his supposed descent into Hades[1]; according to Diodorus he is a Henry VII., rigid in the exaction of his revenues and penurious in his expenditure[2]; he knows also the exact amount of treasure which he left behind him, namely four hundred thousand talents of gold and silver. To Remphis succeed for seven generations kings devoted to luxury and indolence, in consequence of which the records related nothing of them, except that from one of them, Nileus, the river, previously called Ægyptus, took its later name. The cause of the change was the great service which he rendered to his country by the construction of canals, a work which Herodotus ascribes to Sesostris. The seven *fainéans* were succeeded by Chembes; Chephres, or Chabryis; and Mycerinus or Mecherinos, the builders of the pyramids, in regard to whom there is no remarkable difference between Herodotus and Diodorus. After these kings comes Bocchoris, son of Tnephactus, of mean person, but surpassing in talent and wisdom all his predecessors. *Long afterwards* Sabaco the Ethiopian reigned over Egypt, and on his retirement the anarchy took place, which was ended by the establishment of the Dodecarchia, and that after fifteen years by the sole reign of Psammitichus. Incidentally Diodorus also mentions Mneves, the first king who gave written laws to the people, which he professed to have received from Hermes; and Sasyches, who was not only a lawgiver, but the inventor of geometry and astronomy[3].

[1] See vol. 1, p. 401.
[2] Διετέλεσε πάντα τὸν τοῦ ζῆν χρόνον ἐπιμελόμενος τῶν προσόδων καὶ σωρεύων πανταχόθεν τὸν πλοῦτον. (Diod. 1, 63.)
[3] 1, 92.

The variations between Herodotus and Diodorus are too great to allow of their being explained by the causes which produce differences in dates, successions and events, even in histories founded upon documentary evidence. Little stress can be laid upon a want of congruity in names, since we know that the sovereigns of Egypt had two or even three[1]; but the discrepancy here affects every element of history. Sixty reigns at least intervene between Menes the founder of Memphis, according to Herodotus, and Uchoreus, to whom Diodorus attributes its foundation. Herodotus extends the number of the obscure successors of Menes to 330; Diodorus limits them to 52. Herodotus includes in these eighteen Ethiopians; in Diodorus there is no mention of Ethiopian sovereignty till the reign of Actisanes, which corresponds in part with the second Ethiopian dominion in Herodotus, that of Sabaco. The building of the Labyrinth, the reign of Remphis, the erection of the Pyramids, are all placed by the two historians in different relative positions; the Labyrinth, which according to Diodorus was erected five generations before the Trojan War, dates according to Herodotus from the Dodecarchia. Diodorus makes the whole number of native sovereigns of Egypt to have been 470 kings and 5 queens[2]. Herodotus[3] makes them 341 from Menes to Sethos; but as only twenty native princes at most reigned from Sethos to Nectanebus, the accounts cannot be reconciled. The duration of the native monarchy was according to the Egyptians above 4700 years (Diod. 1, 69), according

[1] Διώνυμοι καὶ τριώνυμοι πολλαχοῦ τῶν Αἰγυπτίων οἱ βασιλεῖς εἴρηνται. (Syncell. p. 63 A. 117 Dind.)
[2] 1, 44.
[3] 2, 142.

to the calculation of Herodotus (2, 142) 11,340. These discrepancies are so enormous and so fundamental as to preclude the idea that they can have been superinduced by lapse of time and a variety of narrators on a history originally authentic. Nor have we any ground for stamping one with the character of authenticity to the exclusion of the other. Both appeal to the same authority, the narratives of the priests; Diodorus, it is true, with a more frequent allusion to written documents; but as he could not read them himself, he can give no evidence as to their contents. Both of them appear to owe their origin to the same cause, the desire to connect together a few leading facts in Egyptian history, and assign the most remarkable monuments to their authors. In the age of Diodorus the remains of Thebes attracted more attention than in that of Herodotus, and the history is enlarged by explanations of their origin. Both authors were ignorant of the invasion of the Shepherds; both misplaced the æra of the erection of the Pyramids[1], and by these two great errors disturbed their whole chronology. By transposing Cheops, Chephren and Mycerinus to the blank spaces, which in both historians precede Mœris, as suggested by Lepsius, we bring them into a general agreement with the Egyptian authorities. Upon the whole, the history of Diodorus has the more historical air; its chronology is more moderate, its narratives less mythic; not because it is derived more imme-

---

[1] Diod. 1, 63, says that *some* reckoned the pyramids to be above 3400 years old. This would not be very far from Manetho's reckoning.

diately from historical sources but from its being accommodated to the taste of an age which by arbitrary methods gave an historical character to that which was mythic in its origin

The variations between Herodotus and Diodorus may be conveniently exhibited in a tabular form[1].

HERODOTUS	DIODORUS.
Menes.	Menes.
329 kings among whom are 18 Ethiopians and one queen.	52 kings 1400 years.
	Busiris I.
Nitocris.	7 kings.
	Busiris II. founds Thebes.
	7 kings.
	Uchoreus founds Memphis.
	Ægyptus.
	11 kings.
Mœris.	Mœris.
	6 kings.
Sesostris.	Sesoosis.
Pheron.	Sesoosis II.
	Many generations.
	Amasis.
	Actisanes.
	Marrus.
	Five generations.
	Anarchy.
Proteus.	Proteus or Ketes.
Rampsinitus.	Remphis.
	Seven generations.
	Nileus.
Cheops.	Chembes.
Chephren.	Chephren.
Mycerinus.	Mycerinus.
Asychis.	Tnephactus.
Anysis.	Bocchoris.
	A long interval.
Sabaco.	Sabaco.
Sethos.	
Dodecarchia.	Dodecarchia.
Psammitichus.	Psammitichus.
Neco.	Three generations.
Psammis.	
Apries.	Apries.
Amasis.	Amasis.

The Greek history of Egypt, though it can no longer be received as true, must always be studied.

---

[1] See Lepsius Einleitung, 1 p. 259.

The substantial truth of those parts which are not obviously fabulous was admitted till very recent times. The names of the eminent persons mentioned in it passed into history to the exclusion of those to whom this place belonged. Everywhere in ancient and modern literature we meet with allusions to it. The monuments must be consulted, that we may know what the history of Egypt was; the Greek writers, that we may know what the world has till lately believed it to be. Perhaps the reader who compares the imperfect skeleton of the authentic Egyptian annals with the animated and flowing narrative of Herodotus will regret that the age of simple faith is past[1].

SECT. II.—EGYPTIAN AUTHORITIES.

It was impossible that those among the Egyptian priests who were versed in their own history and antiquities, should be satisfied that they should be so imperfectly represented to the Grecian world as by Herodotus, nor could the enlightened Greek sovereigns of Egypt fail to perceive the inconsistency between his accounts, and the facts which were before their eyes. The establishment of the Greek dominion, therefore, by the conquest of Alexander, soon produced a statement of the philosophy, religion and history of Egypt, from one whose authority could not be called in question. Manetho, the high-

---

[1] Χάρις δ' ἅπερ ἅπαντα τεύχει τὰ μείλιχα θνατοῖς,
'Επιφέροισα τιμὰν καὶ ἄπιστον ἐμήσατο πιστόν
″Εμμεναι τὸ πολλάκις.—Pind. Ol. 1.
But Pindar was a philosopher as well as a poet, and he adds—
'Αμέραι δ' ἐπίλοιποι μάρτυρες σοφώτατοι.

priest of the temple of Isis at Sebennytus in Lower Egypt, in the reign of Ptolemy Lagi (322—284 B.C.), a man of the highest reputation for wisdom[1], and versed in Greek as well as Egyptian lore[2], published various works for the purpose of informing the Greeks, and his History, as it should seem, specially to correct the errors of Herodotus[3]. They have all perished[4], but the respect with which he is spoken of by heathen, Jewish and Christian writers, gives a high value to the fragments and incidental notices which alone remain. The longest and the most important are those from his Egyptian History, which consisted of three books. It was derived partly from the sacred books, and partly, according to his own confession, from popular tradition, not warranted by any written document[5]. Eusebius, in the Preface to his second Book of the Evangelical Preparation[6], speaks of Manetho's works as copious, and this accords with the extracts in Josephus, which relate the expulsion of the Shepherds and of the Jews so much at length, that if the whole Egyptian history were treated with the same fullness, it must have been very bulky—a circumstance which by preventing its transcription may have been

---

[1] Σοφίας εἰς ἄκρον ἐληλακότα ἄνδρα. (Æl. Nat. Hist. 10.16.) He was consulted by Ptolemy respecting the introduction of the worship of Serapis. (Plut. Is. et Os. p. 362.)
[2] Joseph. c. Apion., 1, 14. Τῆς Ἑλληνικῆς μετεσχηκὼς παιδείας.
[3] Eustath. ad Iliad. λ', 480, p.857.
[4] There exists under the name of Manetho an astrological poem, entitled Ἀποτελεσματικά, long admitted to be spurious, and a treatise Βίβλος τῆς Σώθεως, which Syncellus quotes as genuine. It is however proved to be spurious by the epithet Σεβαστός, which the introductory Epistle gives to Ptolemy—the translation of *Augustus*, and never found among the titles of the Ptolemies. It was probably the work of a christian.
[5] Joseph. c. Apion., 1, 14, 16, 26, where Manetho himself distinguishes that which he relates ἐκ τῶν παρ' Αἰγυπτίοις γραμμάτων, and ἐκ τῶν ἀδεσπότως μυθολογουμένων.
[6] P. 44, ed. Viger.

the cause of its reaching us only in extracts and quotations. Josephus declares that he gave his extracts in the very words of Manetho, and they show a ready command of Greek language; they show also the desire to establish a correspondence between Greek and Egyptian history. In conformity with the Argive story, he makes Sethos to be Egyptus and Armais to be Danaus, for which there seems to have been no other ground than the hostile relation of the brothers, the circumstances of the Egyptian history and the Argive legend being in every other respect entirely different.

Although the *History* of Manetho is lost, we have his *Dynasties* tolerably entire. As they consisted of three volumes, the same number with the Books of the History, it is probable that they formed a part of it. They have reached us in a tabular form, but we know not whether they were appended in this form to the continuous history, or whether the Christian writers, by whom they have been preserved to us, extracted and arranged them. The first of these was Julius, a native of Africa, thence generally called Africanus, bishop of Emmaus or Nicopolis in Judæa, a man of learning, research and probity, who wrote in the beginning of the third century[1]. His work consisted of five Books, to which he annexed a *Canon*, or regular series of years, one by one, with the events of each if any were known. His object was to establish synchronisms between the history of the Bible and that of the heathen nations; but especially of the Babylonians and Egyptians, with which the history of the Jews is

---

[1] Routh, Rel. Sac. 2, 221. He concluded his Chronicle with the Emperor Macrinus, A.D. 217. Phot. Myriob. xxxiv. p. 19, ed. Hoesch.

most closely connected. Had we a copy of his work, of which unfortunately only a few fragments remain, we should know very accurately the dynasties of Manetho[1]. But it is not probable that he had read the historical work itself[2]; the notices of facts which he gives are very brief, and seem to have been remarks, appended to a chronological table. His successors certainly knew Manetho only at second-hand, through the medium of Africanus.

The first of these was Eusebius, the bishop of Cæsarea, who, about 100 years later than Africanus, undertook a more comprehensive work of the same kind, which owes all its real value as regards Egyptian history to the use which he made of his predecessor's materials. It consisted of two parts, the first of which was a general introduction with extracts from older chronologers, the second a Canon, such as that of Africanus. This Canon was translated by Jerome, and with the exception of fragments of the introductory part chiefly preserved by Syncellus, was all that was known of it till the discovery of the Armenian version of the whole, in the Library of the Convent of that nation at Venice, in 1820. Eusebius carried much further than Africanus had done the attempt to reduce the chronology of other nations to the standard of the Jews, and to establish a general system of synchronisms for ancient history—an undertaking which could be

---

[1] He says of himself, when he was in Egypt, that he had procured a sacred book by Suphis, king of the fourth dynasty and builder of the Great Pyramid. The remains of Africanus have been collected by Routh, Reliquiæ Saeræ, 2, 245, seq. ed. alt.

[2] Two different recensions of it appear to have existed. Κατὰ τὴν δευτέραν ἔκδοσιν Ἀφρικανοῦ, Syncellus remarks, p. 56, 104, ed. Dind. Routh (2, 384) doubts the fact of a second edition, at least of the whole Chronicle.

effected on no sound principle for times preceding the Olympiads, and he appears not to have scrupled arbitrary and even unfair expedients to attain this end[1].

In the interval between Eusebius and Syncellus, Egyptian chronology had been handled by two monks of that country, Panodorus and Anianus, in the same spirit, the scriptural chronology being made the standard by which the other was corrected. George the Syncellus, a Byzantine monk, of the beginning of the ninth century, wrote a general chronology, which has come down to us in a tolerably perfect state, and was executed with great labour, but little sagacity, and with the same implicit deference to the Jewish authority. He assumes 5500 B.C. as the æra of the Creation, and arranges all his dates accordingly. He repeats with some variations the dynasties of Manetho, not having before him, however, certainly, the original work, but collating the lists of Africanus and Eusebius. Having mentioned the discrepancies between the names and dates derived from Manetho by the ecclesiastical historians, especially in regard to the sovereign under whom Joseph ruled Egypt and Moses led forth the people, he says, "I have therefore deemed it necessary to extract and compare with one another the editions of two of the most celebrated men, Africanus and Eusebius[2]." It is thus at the third hand that we have Manetho's lists, and all that criticism can attempt is, by the compa-

---

[1] Bunsen, Ægyptens Stelle in der Weltgeschichte, 1, p. 118. Syncellus, p. 62, 115, ed. Dind., says, ὁ Εὐσέβιος πρὸς τὸν οἰκεῖον σκοπὸν τοὺς τῆς πεντεκαιδεκάτης δυναστείας παρὰ τῷ 'Αφρικανῷ φερομένους κατὰ τὴν ἑξκαιδεκάτην γεγονέναι λέγει. See also p. 65, 121 Dind.

[2] P. 53, 99, Dind.

rison of Eusebius and Syncellus, to ascertain how they stood in the text of Africanus.

Comparing Manetho with Herodotus, we find that the latter distinctly excludes from the belief of the Egyptians all beings partaking of a human and divine descent[1], and passes from the gods to the reign of the mortal Menes. But Manetho, after the reign of Horus, the youngest of the gods, and before the reign of Menes, the first of mortals, speaks of heroes and *manes* as exercising dominion[2]. This seems an example of the reaction of Greek upon Egyptian mythology. The Greeks interposed between gods and the actual race of mortals—*dæmons*, who were the men of the golden age[3]; *manes*, who were the men of the silver age; and *heroes* or *demigods*, who united the divine and human nature; and the Egyptians were probably unwilling not to have a corresponding period of mythic history. We find no trace of these two classes in the Turin papyrus, nor is any hieroglyphic character answering to them known.

The lists of Manetho comprehend, besides the period of gods, manes and heroes, *thirty* dynasties,

---

[1] Οὐ δεκόμενοι ἀπὸ θεοῦ γενέσθαι ἄνθρωπον (2, 143). Νομίζουσι δ' ὧν Αἰγύπτιοι οὐδ' ἥρωσι οὐδέν (2, 50). Diodorus (1, 44) speaks of heroes, as reigning along with the gods in a period of 18,000 years.

[2] Μετὰ νέκυας καὶ τοὺς ἡμιθέους πρώτη βασιλεία καταριθμεῖται. (Dyn. 1.)

[3] Hesiod, W. and D. 120, 140, 155:—

Αὐτὰρ ἐπεί κεν τοῦτο γένος κατὰ γαῖα κάλυψεν
Τοὶ μὲν δαίμονές εἰσι.

Of the men of the silver age:—

Τοὶ μὲν ὑποχθόνιοι μάκαρες θνητοὶ καλέονται
Δεύτεροι.

Of the heroes:—

Ἀνδρῶν ἡρώων θεῖον γένος, οἳ καλέονται
Ἡμίθεοι.

from Menes downward to the younger Nectanebus. In some of them the names of all the kings are given, with the lengths of their reigns, in years, and the sums of each dynasty; in others the names do not now appear, but the numbers of the kings and sum of their reigns are preserved. The historical facts are very brief; of most of the kings nothing whatever is recorded, and the synchronisms noted appear to be due to the Christian chronologers, rather than to Manetho himself. The sum of all the dynasties varies according to our present sources from 4685 to 5049 years[1]; the number of kings from 300 to 350, and even 500[2]. It is evidently impossible to found a chronology on such a basis, but Syncellus tells us that the number of generations[3] included in the 30 dynasties was, according to Manetho, and to the old Egyptian Chronicle, 113; and the whole number of years, 3555[4]. This number falls much short of what the summation of the reigns would furnish according to any reading of the numbers, but is nearly the same as 113 generations would produce, at an average of 32 years to each[5].

That Manetho would have access to all the documentary and monumental evidence which the temples and public records supplied, we cannot doubt; but that from these it was practicable in the third century before the Christian æra, to deduce a chronology extending backward to the foundation

---

[1] Boeckh, Manetho und die Hundssternperiode, p. 525.
[2] Bunsen, 1, p. 119. Germ. p. 83.
[3] P. 52, 98, ed. Dindorf.
[4] Lepsius (Einleitung, 1, 497) adopts the number 3555, but rejects the 113 generations, which number he thinks to be derived only from the Old Chronicle.
[5] Herodotus (2, 142) reckons a generation at thirty-three years and one-third.

of the monarchy, is by no means probable[1]. The imputation of having wilfully forged names, with which to fill out vacant spaces in the early history of Egypt, has been refuted by the very close conformity between his lists and the monuments,—a conformity which manifests itself at the early period of the erection of the Pyramids. According to Lepsius, of 142 kings of the Old Monarchy, *i.e.* those who reigned before the invasion of the Hyksos, 80 are found on the monuments. But we may reasonably doubt, whether the means existed in his time to fix the date of the reign of Menes, or carry the chronology over the troubled period of the Hyksos; and when we compare him with the mo-

---

[1] Boeckh has endeavoured with great learning and ingenuity to show that the chronology of Manetho is not historical but astronomical. Boeckh makes the sum of all the thirty dynasties to be 5366. This is just the sum of three Sothiac periods, or 4383 years, *plus* 983, the years that had elapsed between 1322 B.C., when the last Sothiac period began, and 339 B.C., the last year of Nectanebus II. and the close of Manetho's thirtieth dynasty. Hence he concludes that Manetho had arbitrarily assumed the historical period of Egypt to have begun with a Sothiac period, and accommodated his chronology to that assumption. He argues the probability of this, from the fact that the mythic age ends with the 17th Sothiac period (24,837 years), whence the historical which succeeds it would naturally begin with another, and the time between Menes and 1322 B.C. be so distributed as to fill up two. But Manetho, as reported by Africanus and Eusebius, makes the time before Menes 24,900 years, and says nothing of the reigns of the gods, manes and heroes occupying a certain number of Sothiac periods. This is derived from the Old Chronicle mentioned before; and there is no evidence that the high priest of Sebennytus admitted any such principle into his chronology of the mythic age. Consequently the presumption that he did so in the historic times falls to the ground. The number 5366 is not obtained without many alterations, which, if not arbitrary, derive their probability only from the supposition that the sum is right. Even were the number certain, it might be merely an accidental coincidence that it admitted of division into two Sothiac periods and 983 years.

The recent work of Lesueur (Chronologie des Rois d'Egypte, 1848), crowned by the French Academy, assumes as its basis the Old Chronicle, which I think Lepsius has satisfactorily shown to be an arbitrary adaptation of Manetho's true dates, at once to the Sothiac period and the Hebrew chronology.

numents, although there is sufficient accordance to vindicate his integrity, there is also sufficient discrepancy to prevent implicit reliance in the absence of monuments. Had the series of monuments, indeed, inscribed with the names of the kings and years of their reigns been ever so complete, it could not alone have furnished a chronology, because the Egyptians do not appear at any time to have reckoned in their public monuments, by an *æra*, like that of the Olympiads, but only to have dated events, as we date acts of parliament, by the years of the king's reign.

Syncellus[1] quotes an Old Chronicle, which he says was in vogue among the Egyptians, in which the period before the 16th dynasty of Manetho is allotted to the gods and demigods with 15 generations of the Cynic circle. It was designed to bring the work of the historical Manetho into conformity with the Sothiac or Cynic period, and comprehends 36,525 years, or 25 of these periods, which were each of 1451 years. The number 25 was the length of the life of Apis[2]. The *Laterculus*, as it is called, of Syncellus, is another arbitrary arrangement of Egyptian chronology, and the Sothis, which professes to be the work of Manetho, is manifestly spurious.

If we suppose that an accurate record of the successive reigns and the length of each was preserved from the very commencement of the monarchy, we might easily deduce the chronology of

[1] P. 51, 95, Dind.
[2] See vol. i. p. 336. Lepsius has very fully investigated the relation in which the spurious works, the Sothis, and the Old Chronicle, stand to the genuine work of Manetho (Einleitung, 1, p. 413–460).

the whole interval from Menes to Nectanebus, by adding together the lengths of all the reigns. But this implies that all the reigns were consecutive; that there either were no joint or rival sovereignties, or that if they existed, only one was fixed on as the legitimate monarch, and his years alone entered in the succession. A history of Great Britain in which the years of the kings of England and Scotland before the Union of the Crowns, or the Stuart and the Brunswick princes since the Revolution, were added together, would present a very false chronology. To deduce an Egyptian chronology, therefore, from the lists of Manetho, we must be assured that his reigns are all strictly consecutive, and that no period has been reckoned twice over. Eusebius in the Armenian version of his Chronicle having urged that it is reasonable to reduce the 20,000 years claimed by the Egyptians to as many months, in order to make them suit with the Hebrew chronology, thus proceeds: "If the length of time is still in excess, we should carefully consider that perhaps several Egyptian kings existed in one and the same age; for they say that Thinites and Memphites reigned, and Saites and Ethiopians and others, at the same time. Other kings also appear to have reigned in other places, and these dynasties to have confined themselves each to its own nome; so that single kings did not reign successively, but one in one place, another in another at the same time." As this is introduced as a last resource for the avowed purpose of reducing the Egyptian to the Hebrew chronology, we cannot regard it as of any authority. No other ancient author gives us reason to suppose, that after the time of Menes, Egypt was divided, except under extraordinary circumstances, the mention of which confirms the belief that unity was the rule of the monarchy. The Greek and Roman writers do not even notice the remarkable exception of the period of the Shepherd Kings, when, according to Manetho, a tributary dynasty (the seventeenth) existed at Thebes, contemporaneous with the Shepherd dynasty which exercised sovereignty at Memphis. In Scripture, also, we find one Pharaoh spoken of as ruling in Egypt, whether in the early age of Abraham, during the oppression of the Jews, in the reign of Solomon, or in the time of the later prophets. It is also difficult to conceive that independent dynasties could co-exist without civil war, or subordinate dynasties without rebellion, neither of which can be traced in the Egyptian annals[1]. Notwithstanding these difficulties, we cannot avoid the conclusion that some great error exists in the numbers of Manetho as they now stand, since the summation of the reigns of his kings exceeds by nearly 1500 years the duration assigned to them.

Eratosthenes, whom we have already mentioned, drew up in the reign of the second Ptolemy[2] a catalogue of Theban kings, which Syncellus has incorporated in his work. According to Apollodorus, from whom Syncellus immediately derived his information, Eratosthenes had received their names from the priests or hierogrammats of Thebes, and at the command of the king had expressed

---

[1] Rosellini, Mon. Stor. 1, p. 98. See Clinton, Fasti Hellenici, *sub*
[2] Eratosthenes was born 275 B.C. *anno.*

their meaning in Greek. These Theban kings are 38 in number, and their united reigns amounted to 1076 years. The name of Theban is that by which he designates them collectively and individually, without any distinction of dynasty, though he notices of the first that he was a Thinite, and of the sixth that he was a Memphite. The Greek interpretations of the Egyptian names have a general conformity with the Coptic language, but the corruption which they have suffered in transcription makes it often impossible to trace it. It appears most probable that the list of Eratosthenes was constructed, though more scientifically, yet upon the same principle as those of Herodotus and Diodorus, that of assigning authors to the most remarkable monuments, and introducing the names of remarkable personages. Thus it includes Menes the founder of the monarchy, the builders of the Pyramids, Apappus who lived 100 years, Nitocris the only queen, Ammenemes the author of the Labyrinth, Mares or Maris, the Mœris of the other Greeks; Phrouro or Neilos, the author of the name of the river. The name of *Theban* kings seems equivalent to *earliest*, the Greeks believing that Egypt was once confined to Thebes[1]. Whence the other names were derived it is difficult to say; they do not appear to be of Greek invention. When we contrast the catalogue of Eratosthenes with the dynasties of Manetho, they appear to have had a common or kindred origin. Both begin with Menes the Thinite, to whom his son Athothis succeeds;

[1] Τὸ δ' ὂν πάλαι αἱ Θῆβαι, Αἴγυπτος ἐκαλεῖτο (Her. 2. 15). Ἀρχαῖον ἡ Αἴγυπτος Θῆβαι καλούμεναι (Arist. Meteor. 1, 14).

the names in Manetho, Suphis Suphis (builder of the Great Pyramid), Mencheres, are in Eratosthenes Saophis, Saophis II. and Moscheres; though Eratosthenes takes no notice of the erection of the Pyramids. Phiops according to Manetho, Apappus according to Eratosthenes, reigns 100 years; in each we have a solitary example of a queen Nitocris, who succeeds at the interval of a single reign the centenarian Phiops or Apappus. The names of *Stammenemes*, *Sistosis*, *Mares*, towards the end of the list of Eratosthenes, do not differ so widely from the *Ammenemes*, *Sesostris*, *Lamares* or *Ameres* of the twelfth dynasty of Manetho, but that the variation may be explained by the corruptions of transcribers and the difficulty of representing Egyptian names in Greek orthography.

It was acutely observed by Bunsen, that where a correspondence exists between the names of Eratosthenes and those of Manetho, it is always in the dynasties which the latter calls Theban or Memphite; and that where the names are lost, the numbers show that there has been no such correspondence in the others. And hence he infers that only those who belonged to the two ancient capitals of Egypt were the true sovereigns of the country, whose reigns give its real chronology; while the others (the Elephantinites, Heracleopolites, Xoites), though called kings, never exercised a real supremacy, and being contemporaneous with the Thebans or Memphites, do not enter into the chronological reckoning. Notwithstanding the ability with which this attempt to reconcile Eratosthenes and Manetho is supported, we cannot feel such confidence in its soundness as to make it the basis of a history. We shall therefore treat the dynasties of the latter as being, what he evidently considered them to be, successive, unless where there is some internal or independent evidence of error; admitting at the same time that no great reliance can be placed on a chronology which professes to ascend to the very commencement of the reign of mortal kings in Egypt. But there appears no evidence that Manetho wilfully tampered with facts known to him, to favour either an astronomical or an historical theory; his system may be baseless, but it is not fictitious.

The authority of all that was written in the Ptolemaic age, or subsequently, whether by natives or foreigners, respecting Egyptian history and chronology, must depend very much on the number and quality of the ancient writings which were extant at that period. Herodotus speaks only of a papyrus, from which the names of 330 kings were read to him by the priests; but it does not appear whether the historical facts which they detailed to him in connexion with some of these names were derived from the same source[1]. The Egyptians were celebrated among ancient nations for their historical knowledge[2], the natural consequence of the number and antiquity of their monuments, the early possession and wide diffusion of the art of writing, and the unchanging, *traditionary* character of all their usages and institutions. According to Diodorus[3] it had been the practice of the priests,

[1] 2, 142. He quotes "the Egyptians and the priests" as joint authorities for these details.
[2] Her. 2, 77. Prisca doctrina pollentes Ægyptii. Apuleius, Metam. xi. p. 764.
[3] 1, 44.

from ancient times, to record and hand down to their successors the stature and qualities of their kings and the events of each reign. We have seen that such records existed in the time of Herodotus; they escaped the devastation of Egypt by Cambyses; for Diodorus[1] mentions that Artaxerxes, when he recovered the dominion of the country from Nectanebus, carried off the records from the ancient temples, which the priests redeemed from Bagoas by the payment of a large sum; and nothing had occurred from this time to the age of Manetho and Eratosthenes, to occasion any violent and general destruction of them. Of their absolute age we can have no evidence; it is hardly to be supposed that contemporaneous documents from the foundation or first reigns of the monarchy existed in the Ptolemaic age; what was read to Herodotus was evidently an historical and genealogical *table*, not a record. And analogy would lead us to suppose, that from time to time the information contained in obsolete and perishing documents would be transcribed and incorporated in new ones, and thus the chain of evidence be prolonged from age to age. In this way it is not incredible, that our historical knowledge of Egypt may be carried far up towards the commencement of the monarchy, allowance being made, first for the gaps which time and periods of internal confusion may have produced, and next for the changes which might take place in the process of transcription. The means of preserving such records were not wanting in the very earliest times; the hiero-

---

[1] 16, 51. Ἀναγραφαί is the title by which the historical annals are usually spoken of. See Bunsen, 1, p. 27. Diod. *u. s.*

glyphic character was in use at the erection of the Pyramids, and the reed-pen and inkstand, and scribes employed in writing, appear among the sculptures in the tombs of Gizeh, which are contemporaneous with the Pyramids themselves[1].

Recently among the papyri in the hieratic character, several properly historical documents have been found; one of the most remarkable is the papyrus of Sallier, which appears to contain a narrative of the wars of Rameses-Sesostris, and to be of the same age. Other fragments of an historical nature relate to the reigns of Rameses IX., and Thothmes III., and Lepsius conjectures that one, from its archaic style, may even belong to the Old Monarchy. None of them have been fully read, but they are received as evidence by those most competent to judge, and may hereafter furnish valuable materials for history[2].

It is probable that the priests of Memphis and Thebes differed in their representations of early history, and that each sought to extol the glory of their own city. How otherwise can we account for it, that while Herodotus makes Menes to be the founder of Memphis, and consequently this capital to be coæval with the monarchy, Diodorus attributes its foundation to Uchoreus, eighth in descent from Osymandyas or Busiris II.? The history of Herodotus turns about Memphis as a centre; he mentions Thebes only incidentally, and does not describe or allude to one of its monuments. Diodorus, on the contrary, is full in his description of

---

[1] See Lepsius, Denkmäler, Abth. ii. , 19.
[2] Lepsius, Einleitung, 1, 53. Select Papyri in the hieratic character from the collection in the British Museum, Lond. 1844.

Thebes, and says little of Memphis. Herodotus went to Thebes, to ascertain whether the accounts of the priests corresponded with what he had heard at Memphis, and he seems to have been satisfied with the agreement; but his visit must have been short and his inquiries superficial, or he would have described Thebes more fully.

Besides properly historical documents, which appear to have been the work of the priests and preserved in the temples, there were others, called in a peculiar sense *sacred* books, from which many materials for illustrating and completing history might be derived. They are enumerated in a passage of Clemens Alexandrinus[1]:—" In the sacred ceremonies of the Egyptians," says he, " first of all the *Singer* comes forth, bearing one of the instruments of music. He must know by heart[2] two of the books of Hermes, one of which contains the hymns of the gods, the other the allotment of the king's life[3]. Next to the singer comes the *Horoscopus*, who carries in his hand a *horologium*[4] and a palm-branch, symbols of astronomy. He, they say, must always have at his tongue's end those of the books of Hermes which are astronomical, being four in number; one of which relates to the arrangement

---

[1] Strom. 6, 4, p. 756, ed. Potter.
[2] Ἀνειληφέναι. See Plut. Agesil. c. 24. Λόγον ἀναγνοὺς ἐν βίβλῳ ὃν ἔμελλε λέγειν ἀναλαβὼν ὁ Λύσανδρος ἐν τῷ δήμῳ.
[3] Ἐκλογισμὸν βασιλικοῦ βίου. There is no authority for rendering ἐκλογισμός *distribution*, yet this seems to be the code by which the occupations of the sovereign were regulated. See Diod. 1, 70. Οὐ μόνον τοῦ χρηματίζειν ἢ κρίνειν ἦν καιρὸς ὡρισμένος, ἀλλὰ καὶ τοῦ πε- ριπατῆσαι καὶ λούσασθαι καὶ κοιμηθῆναι μετὰ τῆς γυναικὸς καὶ καθόλου τῶν κατὰ τὸν βίον πραττομένων ἁπάντων.

[4] Ὡρολόγιον is generally rendered Sun-dial (see vol. i. p. 328); but may it not mean a list of the hours of the day with the influences of the constellations during each (see vol. i. p. 348), according to the analogy of μηνολόγιον, an almanac of the month?

of the stars which appear to be fixed; one respecting the conjunctions of the sun and moon, and her illuminations; the remaining one respecting the risings of the heavenly bodies. Next comes forth the *Hierogrammat*, having feathers on his head and a book in his hand, with a rectangular case (κάνων) in which is contained writing-ink and the reed with which they write. He must know the hieroglyphics, as they are called, and what relates to cosmography and geography, the order of the sun and moon and the five planets, and the topography of Egypt and the description of the Nile; and the enumeration of the furniture of the temples and the lands that have been dedicated to them; and concerning the measures and the sacred utensils. After those already mentioned comes the *Stolistes*, having the cubit of justice[1] and the vessel for pouring libations. He knows all the books which relate to education and to the slaughter of victims. There are ten which have reference to the honour paid to their gods, and comprehend the Egyptian religion, *e. gr.* of sacrifices, first fruits, hymns, prayers, processions, festivals and the like. After all these comes forth the *Prophetes*[2], carrying openly in his bosom the vessel of water, followed by those who carry the loaves which were brought forth[3]. The prophetes,

---

[1] The standard measure of length, like the "Shekel of the Sanctuary," the standard of weight, among the Jews. (Exod. xxx. 13. See vol. i. p. 345.)

[2] Προφήτης in Greek has no reference to *prediction*, as we might suppose from our own use of *prophet*. It was his office to *give forth* the declarations of the god, which might be prophetic or otherwise. (Her. 8, 135.)

[3] Οἱ τὴν ἔκπεμψιν τῶν ἄρτων βαστάζοντες. Offerings of loaves or cakes to the gods are common on the monuments. (Rosellini, Mon. del Culto, tav. xxxiii. 2.) Compare the ἄρτοι τῆς προσφορᾶς, 1 Kings, vii. 48, of the Jewish Sanctuary.

as being the president of the temple, gets by heart the ten books which are called *hieratic*; they contain what relates to the laws and the gods, and the whole education of the priests; for the prophetes among the Egyptians presides also over the distribution of the revenues. The books of Hermes therefore which are absolutely necessary are forty-two; of which the persons already mentioned learn thirty-six by heart, containing the whole philosophy of the Egyptians. The remaining six the *Pastophori*[1] learn by heart, being medical, respecting the structure of the body, and diseases, and instruments, and drugs, and the eyes, and finally female diseases[2]." There is not one among these works, however remote its subject may appear from history, which might not incidentally furnish historical illustration, especially the description of Egypt and the Nile, and the account of religion and the laws connected with it. Since they appear to have been in existence in the age of Clemens, at the beginning of the third century after Christ, it is not beyond hope that a portion of them may yet be found among the many unexamined papyri which have been brought from Egypt, or among the treasures of some hitherto unopened grave. As the names of many of their legislators were preserved[3], historical facts and anecdotes must have been handed down along with them.

The Hieratical Canon of Turin is a chronological

---

[1] The Pastophori were an inferior order of priests, whose duty it was to carry about the shrines (παστοί) or images of the gods on a *bari* or a *feretrum* in solemn processions.

[2] The necessity of learning so much by heart, notwithstanding the copiousness of written books, will explain what Herodotus says of the Egyptians, μνήμην ἐπασκέουσι ἀνθρώπων πάντων μάλιστα. (2, 77.)

[3] Diod. 1, 94.

rather than an historical document[1]. As already mentioned, it begins with the dynasties of the gods, to whom years are assigned by tens of thousands, and from them comes down to Menes, the founder of the monarchy. It contained probably the titular shields of 250 kings[2] in its entire state, and those of 119 are still more or less legible. The difficulty which the discrepancy between Manetho and Eratosthenes has occasioned is not removed, but increased, by the discovery of this document, and from its mutilated state its arrangement is doubtful. There exist also fragments of papyri containing accounts of receipt and expenditure of the date of the 18th and 19th dynasties, which from the occurrence of the names of reigning sovereigns, and the years of their reigns, are valuable as subsidiary to history[3]. The majority of the papyri, however, which have been preserved relate to the theology of the Egyptians, describing the state and changes of the soul after death, for which reason they were so commonly placed in tombs and the cases of the mummies. Even though they contain no properly historical information, by their early date, and the proof which they exhibit of the existence of a theological system in Egypt, fully developed and generally received, they give collateral evidence to the accounts of the high antiquity of its arts and institutions. There appear also to be collections of hymns, from which when

---

[1] It has been published according to his own arrangement of the fragments by Lepsius in his *Auswahl*. The names are given in the hieroglyphic character in Lesueur's *Chronologie*, with fac-similes of the original.

[2] Bunsen's Egypt. Eng. p. 50. Birch, Tr. Roy. Soc. Lit. 1, 201.

[3] Champollion, Lettre à M. le Duc de Blacas, 2, pp. 80, 81, 85, 95.

deciphered light may be thrown on history as well as theology[1].

A passage in Diodorus proves that the Egyptians had popular poetry in which the exploits of their kings were celebrated. Speaking of the reign of Sesoosis, he says, "that not only did the Greek historians differ among themselves respecting him, but even in Egypt the priests and those who celebrated him in song did not agree[2]." As a distinction is here made between the priestly and the poetical literature, these songs must have been something different from those which Clemens describes the Ὠδος or singer as repeating, and several of the circumstances which Diodorus goes on to mention have the air of being such exaggerations as a popular poetical literature deals in. Rosellini has suggested, that in the papyrus of Sallier we have a poetical account of the military exploits of Sesostris; and that the long inscription relating to Rameses IV. at Medinet Aboo is rather a song than an historical narrative[3].

No nation has left in its inscribed monuments such ample materials for history as the Egyptians; the statues of their kings are generally inscribed with their names; the walls of their palaces exhibit their exploits, commonly accompanied with the year of their reigns; works of art executed for private individuals and the tombs of public functionaries frequently contain the name of the reigning sovereign. But we commonly derive no information from these sources as to the succession and relative

---

[1] Lepsius, Einleitung, 1, p. 49, speaks of a collection of such hymns of the age of Rameses IX.
[2] 2, 53. Καὶ τῶν κατ' Αἴγυπτον οἵ τε ἱερεῖς καὶ οἱ διὰ τῆς ᾠδῆς αὐτὸν ἐγκωμιάζοντες, οὐχ ὁμολογούμενα λέγουσιν.
[3] Mon. Stor. iv. 91.

position of the sovereigns, or their absolute place in a general system of chronology. There are two remarkable monuments, however, which appear to give a certain number of kings in the order of their succession, the Tablet of Abydos[1] and the Tablet of Karnak[2]. The building to which the former belonged was built or repaired by Rameses the Great (III.), and he is represented on the monument sitting on his throne and contemplating a double series of twenty-six shields of his predecessors. The lowest line of the monument contains only a repetition of his own name and titles. The conclusion which was at first drawn from this monument, that it exhibited a *regnal* succession of fifty-two monarchs anterior to Rameses the Great, has not indeed been realized, nor has the anticipated correspondence been established between the tablet and the lists of Manetho, except for a few reigns in the later part. Still its information is most important for Egyptian history. The tablet of Karnak is a representation of Thothmes III. offering gifts to a series of sixty-one kings, disposed in four lines around the walls. This sovereign himself is the forty-fourth of the tablet of Abydos, and it might have been expected that we should find here his predecessors on that tablet, which, however, is not the case. But though we have been disappointed in the hope of obtaining from the combination of these two monuments an authentic regnal succession from Rameses the Great upwards, and the tablet of Karnak, like that of Abydos, cannot be brought into exact correspondence with Manetho, there are evidently materials in these monuments

[1] See vol. i. p. 45.   [2] Vol. i. p. 174.

for the construction of history, when their true relation has been ascertained. The grottos of Benihassan and Qoorneh contain some successions, corresponding with a part of the tablet of Abydos, and other short successions are found at Thebes[1], but in none is a perfect correspondence discernible. At Tel Amarna and at Thebes is found a succession of several kings whose names do not agree with any of the dynasties of Manetho, and who are supposed, from their physiognomy and the emblems which accompany them, to belong to a foreign race, professors of a peculiar religion, apparently worshipers[2] of the Sun.

The earliest event in Egyptian history which can be connected with a known date in that of any other country, is the invasion of Judæa by Shishak or Sheshonk in the reign of Rehoboam. As the chronology of the Jewish Scriptures is in this age definite and authentic, we are able to fix the reign of Sheshonk in years before the Christian æra. But this does not enable us to carry backward an exact chronology through all the reigns of his predecessors, owing to the uncertainty and interruption of the successions, both in the MSS. and in the monuments; and in the previous part of the Jewish history, the sovereigns of Egypt are only mentioned by the common name of Pharaoh, which would not suffice for their identification, even if the Jewish chronology itself were in early ages certain. Could we, however, connect one of those astronomical phænomena, whose recurrence is invariable, to however remote a period we ascend, with the

---

[1] Rosellini, M. S. 1, 205. Thebes, 2, 72, 216, 255. Trans.
[2] Wilkinson, Modern Egypt and Roy. Soc. Lit. 2nd series, 1, 140.

reign of any of the old Egyptian kings, we should have a fixed point in the flux of time from which we might reckon upwards and downwards with cousiderable security. Whether any such fixed point is to be found is a matter for subsequent inquiry.

Syncellus, we have seen, assigns 3555 years as the duration of Manetho's thirty dynasties. These being Egyptian years are equivalent to 3553 Julian years[1], and added to 339 B.C., when his 30th dynasty expired[2], give 3892 B.C. as the commencement of the reign of Menes. There is nothing incredible in such an antiquity of the Egyptian monarchy; but from what has been already said, and from what will appear in our further investigations, it cannot be regarded as historically proved.

The following History is divided into Three Books, each comprising a period designated respectively as the OLD, the MIDDLE, and the NEW Monarchy. The first extends from the Foundation of the Kingdom of Menes to the Invasion of the Hyksos. The second, from the Conquest of Lower Egypt by the Hyksos and the Establishment of a dependent Kingdom at Thebes, to the Expulsion of the Hyksos. The third, from the Re-establishment of the Monarchy by Amosis to the Final Conquest by Persia[3]. The Dynasties of Manetho have been employed as subdivisions, according to the text of Africanus, because however doubtful the reading or the numbers may be, no better authority exists.

[1] Lepsius, Einleitung, 1, p. 499.
[2] Boeckh, Manetho und die Hundssternperiode, Abschn. 2, § 18, 19.
[3] These designations are due, I believe, to Bunsen and Lepsius. Heeren, however (Ideen, 2, 2, b. 551, note, Germ.), had clearly distinguished the two first periods; but he subdivides the third into the flourishing period 1500–700 B.C., and the period of decline 700 B.C. to the Persian Conquest.

HISTORY OF EGYPT.

BOOK I.

THE OLD MONARCHY.

MANETHO, according to the Armenian version of Eusebius, having enumerated the gods of Egypt, beginning with Vulcan and ending with Horus[1], says, " these first exercised power among the Egyptians.

	Years.	
Next, the royal authority devolved by continued succession to *Bytis*, in the space of	13,900	which are lunar, of 30 days each.
After the gods heroes reigned	1,255	
Then other kings	1,817	
Then 30 other kings of Memphis	1,790	
Then 10 other kings of This	350	
Then followed a dominion of manes and heroes	5,813	

" The sum amounts to 11,000 years (11,025), which, however, are lunar, of a month each."

Without attempting any other explanation of these successions and numbers than what has been already given[2], we pass to the

First Dynasty.

"After the manes and demigods, the first kingdom

---

[1] Vol. i. p. 357.   [2] Vol. ii. p. 92, 96.

is reckoned to have consisted of eight kings, of whom the first—

		Years.
1. Menes the Thinite, reigned[1]		62
He died, torn to pieces by a hippopotamus.		
2. Athothis, his son, reigned		57
He built the palace at Memphis. He was a physician, and anatomical books of his are in circulation.		
3. Kenkenes, his son, reigned		31
4. Ouenephes, his son, reigned		23
Under him a great famine prevailed in Egypt. He erected the pyramids near Cochome.		
5. Usaphaidos (Usaphais), his son		20
6. Miebidos (Niebaes), his son		26
7. Semempses, his son		18
Under him a great pestilence prevailed in Egypt.		
8. Bienneches, his son		26"
	In all	263

The summation of Africanus makes the total 253; that of Eusebius 252 in Syncellus, and the same in the Armenian, notwithstanding the shortening of the reign of Menes. These discrepancies will not be noticed in future, unless for some special reason.

The word *Dynasty*, which does not occur in the older writers on Egyptian history, appears to be used by Manetho nearly in the same sense as when we speak of the Carlovingian or the Capetian dynasty, as an hereditary succession of sovereigns. On the failure of the line, election was resorted to in Egypt. All the kings of the first dynasty succeeded from father to son; afterwards the mention of their relation to each other is omitted, but the descent appears to have been in the same line till the dynasty was changed.

That Menes of This was the first mortal king of Egypt, is one of the very few points in which all the

---

[1] Eusebius in the Armenian makes his reign 30 years.

THE FIRST DYNASTY.

authorities—Herodotus, Eratosthenes, Diodorus, Manetho—agree. This, or Thinis, was a town in Upper Egypt, giving its name to the nome in which Abydos stood, and not far from that ancient and celebrated seat of the Osirian worship[1]. We know little more of This, but Abydos was next to Thebes in importance among the cities of Upper Egypt. The agreement of the historians ends here; for while Menes is to Herodotus the founder of Memphis as well as of the monarchy, Diodorus attributes to another monarch, living many centuries later, the foundation of Memphis[2] and the performance of the great works which were necessary to restrain the Nile, and obtain an area for the site of the capital. Since their accounts so entirely differ, and we have no decisive reason for preferring one to the other, we may doubt if either of them rests on properly historical authority. According to Herodotus a reign of the gods, according to Diodorus of gods and heroes; according to Manetho of gods, *manes* and heroes, preceded the reign of Menes. This is in fact to confess that nothing historical could be related of preceding times. It is indeed common to say, that the reign of the gods means a reign of the priests, and that a period of sacerdotal sway preceded the monarchical, which Menes established. It is not in itself improbable; but had it been known as an historical fact to the ancients, it would have been handed down to us as such, not

---

[1] Ptol. Geogr. B. iv. c.5. Steph. Byz. de Urb. *s. voc.* Strabo, p. 813.

[2] He says (1, 51) that Memphis was so called from the daughter of the king who founded it. The river Nile, assuming the form of a bull, fell in love with her, and her son, Ægyptus, was a king remarkable for benevolence, justice and worth, from whom the whole country took its name. There seems here some allusion to the worship of Apis.

concealed in this mode of expression[1]. Besides, if the reign of the gods means a reign of the priests, what is the historical equivalent of the reigns of the *manes* and the heroes?

The entire uncertainty of all that precedes Menes may even throw doubt on his own historical reality; for we do not commonly find the darkness of a mythic period succeeded at once by light and certainty. The real founders of great cities in ancient times being generally unknown, it was common to suppose one, bearing the same name as the city itself; and as *Menfis*[2] (Coptic, *Menbe*) appears to have been the orthography of the capital of Lower Egypt, Menes was assumed as the founder. His name, written Mena, is found in a solemn procession, in which the images of the predecessors of Rameses the Great are exhibited[3], on the walls of the Rameseion at Thebes, and therefore, if fictitious, it is of very ancient date. The monument, however, belongs to the 18th dynasty, so that many hundred years must have intervened between the origin of the monarchy and the date of the inscription. The same combination of characters occurs also in the hieratic manuscript of Turin, and is thought with probability to have stood at the commencement of the list of kings, which that papyrus contains. This evidence also

[1]. " On croit que ces demidieux étaient des grands prêtres, qui régnaient au nom des dieux, dont ils mettaient les images ou les momies sur le trône." (Lesueur, Chronologie des Rois d'Égypte, p. 309.)

[2] Tochon d'Annecy, Médailles des Nomes. Eratosthenes interprets the name Menes Διόνιος. Jablonsky, in De Vignoles' Chronology, conjectures Αἰώνιος, which Bunsen adopts, and refers to the root *men, perpetuus*. (Egypten, B. 2, p. 45, Germ. See also his Coptic Vocabulary, 1, p. 573.) Memphis is denoted by hieroglyphics which read *Mennofre*, "abode of good" (Wilkinson, M. and C. 3, 278), or good abode, ὅρμον ἀγαθῶν. (Plut. Is. p. 359.)

[3] Champollion, Lettres d'Égypte, p. 270.

refers to the reign of Rameses the Great[1], and therefore establishes the fact of a belief that Menes had been the founder of the monarchy—a predecessor not only of Memphite but Theban kings[2].

Menes has been considered as identical with Mizraim, who is mentioned (Gen. x. 13) as the father of several African nations. The name Mestraia is hence given by the author of the Laterculus to Egypt. The Old Chronicle speaks of three races as inhabiting Egypt successively, the Auritæ, the Mestræi, and the Egyptians. The Auritæ derive their name from Aeria, the Greek epithet for Egypt, signifying *dark*[3]; and neither name has any historical authority. The termination of *Mizraim*, which is plural, or as commonly pointed dual, is sufficient to show that no real person was intended[4], and that Mizraim stands in the genealogy only as representative of the nation, and as indicative of the relation in which the people of Semitic language considered the Egyptians to stand, towards the common ancestor of the postdiluvian nations. Mizraim therefore has an ethnological, not an historical significance, denoting the origin of a people, not a monarchy. The name itself is unknown to the Egyptians; they called their land *Cham* or *Chemi*[5], an appellation which was also known to the Semitic nations, since Mizraim is described

---

[1] Trans. of Roy. Soc. of Lit. 2nd series, 1, 206.

[2] It deserves to be remarked, that the name of Mnevis, the bull of Heliopolis, consecrated to the Sun and Osiris, is written hieroglyphically *Mena* (Lepsius, Einleitung, 1, 261), and that Diodorus calls Mueves (1, 94) the first legislator of Egypt. Pliny (36, 8, Sillig) speaks of a palace of Mnevis.

[3] Schol. Apoll. Rhod. 1, 280.

[4] Misraim non est nomen hominis; id non patitur forma dualis. (Boch. Geogr. Sacra, lib. 4, c. 24.)

[5] Plut. Is. et Osir. p. 364 C.

as the son of Cham (Gen. x. 6). To endeavour to combine in one historical statement conceptions originating in different countries and from unconnected sources, can lead to no satisfactory result. The name of Mizraim, however, conveys to us important information, since in its dual form it recognizes a double character in the Egyptian people. This cannot have consisted in their living on both sides of the Nile; for that circumstance has never constituted a division in population, language, manners, government, or religion. Egypt is the country which the Nile overflows; Egyptians are the people, who, whether on the eastern or western bank, below Elephantine, drink of its waters[1]. But the distinction of Upper and Lower Egypt exists in geological structure, in language, in religion, and in historical tradition; and to this the dual form of Mizraim evidently alludes, proving its origin in times when the whole valley from Syene downwards was peopled. The name exists also in a singular form, *Metzur*[2], and from its derivation appears to allude to the narrow and compressed shape of the greater part of the country, for which reason Egypt is called by the prophet Isaiah (xviii. 2), " a nation spread out in length[3]."

The great works attributed to Menes, as the founder of Memphis, are fully described by Herodotus[4]; they were necessary preliminaries to the

---

[1] Her. 2, 18. Vol. i. p. 4.
[2] It appears to have been an archaism of poetry, 2 Kings, xix. 24, where for "rivers of besieged places" we should read " rivers of Egypt." (Is. xix. 6; Mich. vii. 12, where a similar correction should be made.)
[3] גוי ממשך. Comp. Boch. Geogr. Sacra, *u. s.* Strabo (17, p. 789) compares it to a long sash or girdle.
[4] 2, 99. See Vol. i. p. 112.

establishment of a capital city in that place. To build a temple and unite the people in the worship of a tutelary god was essential to their coalescence in a community, as in the middle ages the erection of a church. Memphis is sometimes designated[1] as Ptah-ei, " the abode of Ptah." The circumstances added by Diodorus betray a later origin. Thus he says that the Egyptians originally lived on herbs, then on fish, afterwards on the flesh of cattle, and that Isis, or one of their ancient kings called Menas, taught them the use of the lotus and grain[2]. This is not in harmony with another account in the same author, that Menas taught the Egyptians to worship the gods and perform sacrifices; and that he also introduced the use of tables and couches and carpets, and the whole apparatus of civilized luxury. Tnephactus, the father of Bocchoris the Wise, making an expedition into Arabia, was compelled to live one day on the simple fare of the common people, and enjoyed his meal so much, that he denounced a curse on the king who had first introduced luxury; and caused it to be inscribed, in sacred characters, in the temple of Jupiter at Thebes. This, adds the historian, is the principal reason why the glory and honour of Menas have not remained to succeeding times. In this account a double purpose is evident, to point a satire against luxury, and to explain the obscurity in which the history of Menas was involved. The founder of Memphis was certainly not the person who introduced religion among the Egyptians, or taught them the use of grain; but popular tradi-

---

[1] Wilkinson, M. & C. 3, 278.   [2] Diod. 1, 45.

tion, or historical hypothesis in every country, is prone to assume that the commencement of its separate history is also the commencement of civilization, and to disregard the law of development, by attributing the changes of centuries to the life of one man[1].

Eusebius adds to the information of Africanus, that Menes led an army beyond the territories of Egypt, and acquired renown. It does not appear from what source he derived his authority, whether from Manetho or not. Under the first sovereign of the third dynasty it is said that the Libyans revolted. These were probably the border tribes on the east of the Canopic branch of the Nile. They bore impatiently their incorporation with Egypt, whose manners and religion were different from their own[2]. We may suppose that their original conquest and annexation was the work of Menes. In later times the Libyans seem to have assimilated themselves to the Egyptians. The oracle of Amun was established in the Great Oasis, and animal worship prevailed among the Libyans[3]. The Lebahim, who are said to owe their origin to Mizraim (Gen. x. 13), are supposed to be the Libyans[4], but this mode of expression does not always indicate an historical descent.

On the whole, Menes seems to fill nearly the same place in regard to Egyptian history as Romulus to the Roman. The monarchy of Egypt, like that of Rome, must have had a founder; whether in either case bearing a name analogous to

---

[1] Of the song of Maneros, said to be the son of the first king of Egypt, see vol. i. p. 238.
[2] Her. 2, 18.
[3] Strabo, 16, p. 760.
[4] Michaelis, Spic. Geogr. 1, 262.

that of the capital of the kingdom is doubtful. As
Romulus was represented by later historical hypothesis to have established the principal civil institutions and religious rites of the Romans[1], as if he
and his people had sprung out of the earth, instead
of being a colony from the civilized Latins, so
Menes was said to have taught religion to the Egyptians, and introduced the use of grain and even
luxury among them, though he came from This,
the ancient seat of the worship of Osiris, and began
his reign over united Egypt by works which certainly do not indicate the infancy of art. Romulus
vanished by a supernatural death, and was suspected to have been taken off by a hostile political
faction. Menes was said to have been torn to
pieces by a hippopotamus[2], the emblem of crime
in the Egyptian mythology. Such disappearances
may generally be taken as an indication that fiction
has been at work, and when they occur at the very
point where the confines of history and mythology
meet, throw a shade of doubt over the personality
of their subject[3].

The establishment of the capital of Egypt at
Memphis was the first step towards the nation's
assuming a place in history. Insulated in the
Thebaid, it might have continued for ages without

---

[1] Dion. Halic. Ant. Rom. 2, 7–29.

[2] Phot. Bibl. Cod. ccxlii. p. 1047. Ὁ ἱπποπόταμος ἐν τοῖς ἱερογλυφικοῖς γράμμασιν ἀδικίαν δηλοῖ. It was consecrated to Typhon (Plut. Is. et Osir. p. 371 C.), and denoted the Western horizon, as the abode of Darkness, Euseb. Præp. Evang. 3, 12.

[3] This, however, affords no ground for an identification of Menes with the *Menu* of the Indians and the *Mannus* of the Germans, as if he were only another name for the human race. See Buttmann's Mythologus, 2, 239. Menes is not the first man, but only the first mortal king. Menu and Mannus denote simply a human being, but Menes has no such sense in Egyptian.

any reciprocal action between it and the other great nations of the world,—without knowledge of the sea which lay beyond the marshes in which the Nile appeared to be swallowed up,—without means of contact with the civilization which was advancing from Mesopotamia to the shores of the Mediterranean. In this sense its history may be said to begin with Menes, although a long period must have preceded his reign, in which the people was acquiring the capacity of a national existence, and receiving the impress of a national character.

Menes was succeeded by his son Athothis. A name which has been read Athoth appears among the fragments of the Canon of Turin, but the correctness of the reading is doubtful[1]. Of him we are told, that he built the palace at Memphis; that he was a physician, and that books of anatomy written by him were still extant, whether in the time of Manetho or Africanus is doubtful. It is worthy of remark, in connexion with the fame of this early sovereign as a physician and anatomist, that not only was Egypt the most celebrated country in the world for drugs and physicians[2], but that Memphis was the seat of the worship of Æsculapius, and therefore it may be presumed remarkable for the cultivation of the art of medicine[3]. Books on the various branches of the medical art formed part of the sa-

[1] Trans. of Roy. Soc. of Literature, 2nd series, 1, 206. Lesueur, Chronologie, pl. xii. xiii. The letter A is wanting, but it is often prefixed euphonically in Coptic, as in Greek.
[2] Hom. Od. δ', 228. Jerem. xlvi. 11. Herod. 2, 84. See vol. i. p 346.
[3] Amm. Marcell. 22, 14. Memphim urbem frequentem, præsentiaque numinis Æsculapii claram. The Mohammedans consider the subject of the hieroglyphical inscriptions to be the charms and wonders of physic (Vyse, 2, 319).

cerdotal library of the Egyptians[1], all of which was attributed to Hermes or Thoth; and it has been conjectured that the name Athoth hides that of the god, from its signifying "that belongs to Thoth[2]." We seem therefore hardly yet to have quitted the domain of mythology. A great deal of supposititious literature owed its origin to Egypt, and that a divine and royal name should have been given to a work of the Ptolemaic or Roman times would be much less wonderful than that a book should have been preserved through so many centuries.

From the time of Athothis, who built a palace at Memphis, we may consider it as the capital of the Old Monarchy. The occasional residence of the sovereign may still have been in the cities whence the several dynasties took their name, but the hills near Memphis appear to have been their burial-place. He was succeeded, according to Eratosthenes, by another Athothis, according to Manetho by Kenkenes, and here the accordance between the two lists ceases. The reign of Kenkenes was marked by no events; in that of his son and successor, Uenephes, a great famine prevailed in Egypt. Its entire dependence on the rise of the Nile makes famine, when it occurs, more dreadful than in countries which have a greater variety of surface, and derive their moist-

[1] See vol. i. p. 346.
[2] Translated by Eratosthenes Ἑρμογένης. "The Christian Fathers often cite a Hermetic book, in which the second Thoth instructs a scholar who is sometimes called Tat, sometimes Æsculapius. See Cyrill. adv. Jul. p. 83. Augustin. de Civ. Dei, viii. 23. Chron. Pasch. 65, 68. This Tat is placed by Manetho" (rather the author of the spurious Sothis) "among those gods to whom the sacred literature was attributed. He is probably the second Egyptian king Athothis." (Mövers, die Phönizier, 1, 527.)

ure from rain and small streams. Egypt has indeed a remedy against famine, in the exuberance of her harvests in fruitful years, and the power of storing up the grain and pulse which are her chief productions, to supply future deficiencies. Yet we see, from the history of Joseph, that this policy had not been adopted before his time by the Egyptian monarchs. Uenephes is also said to have built the pyramids at Cochome. This mode of interment appears in Egypt not only to have been exclusively royal, but exclusively Memphite, pyramids being scarcely found in Upper Egypt[1], and the great functionaries who lie buried around the pyramids of Gizeh being all deposited in excavations. A regal residence required a regal cemetery, but the pyramids were probably only of brick or rough stones; for the art of building with hewn stone was not introduced till the reign of Tosorthrus of the third dynasty. The site of Cochome is unknown. As all the known burial-places of the Memphite kings, however, were in the Libyan hills, on the western side of the Nile, it is here that we should look for the pyramids of Uenephes. His monuments have yielded to the power of Time, which has been unable to make any impression on the works of Cheops, Chephres and Mycerinus; or they may have been among those numerous ruined and nameless pyramids, whose existence the Prussian expedition has ascertained. It is probable that the method of embalmment was already practised; *Kos* is the word used in the Coptic version

[1] Vol. i. p. 148.

of Gen. l. 2, for the embalmment of Jacob; it is found in several names of places[1], and seems to have entered into the composition of *Kochome*. Indeed the Armenian Eusebius reads "the town (κώμη) of *Cho*[2]." Athothis is said to have been a physician and anatomist. Embalmment in early times was a branch of the medical art; anatomy also does not seem in Egypt to have proceeded beyond such a knowledge of the internal structure as the evisceration which accompanied embalmment would furnish. The bodies of the predecessors of Uenephes having been preserved by this art would be naturally transferred to these receptaeles; for he is said to have raised not one, but several pyramids. In the reign of Semempses it is recorded that Egypt was afflicted with a pestilence; and Eusebius adds that many prodigies accompanied it; agreeably to the experience of all ages, that events unnoticed at other times are understood as significant when the public mind is rendered superstitious by alarm and suffering[3].

---

[1] Champollion, L'Égypte sous les Pharaons, 1, 220.
[2] See Bunsen, Urk. p. 9.
[3] Tacit. Hist. 4, 26. Quod in pace fors seu natura tunc fatum et ira dei vocabatur.

Second Dynasty. Nine Thinite kings.

	Years.
1. BOETHOS (BOCHUS, Euseb.) reigned	38
In his reign a great opening of the ground took place, and many persons perished at Bubastos.	
2. KAIECHOS (CHOOS, Euseb.) reigned	39
In his reign the bulls Apis at Memphis and Mnevis at Heliopolis, and the Mendesian goat, were established by law as gods.	
3. BINOTHRIS (BIOPHIS, Euseb.)	47
In whose reign it was decided that women should have the prerogative of royalty.	
4. TLAS	17
5. SETHENES	41
6. CHAIRES	17
7. NEPHERCHERES	25
In whose reign the Nile is fabled to have flowed eleven days, mixed with honey.	
8. SESOCHRIS	48
Who was five cubits three palms in height.	
9. CHENERES	30
In all	302

This dynasty, like the first, is called of Thinite kings, although Memphis had become the capital. It is not said whose son the founder of the second dynasty was; probably he was descended from a collateral branch. It is evident, however, that though called Thinite, they were supposed to be kings of all Egypt: otherwise it would have been absurd to have dated events, changes of religion and political institutions by their reigns[1].

The mention of the city of Bubastos or Bubastis, which is situated in the Delta, on the Pelusiac branch of the Nile, below Heliopolis[2], as having in these early times a large population, shows that when the priests told Herodotus[3] that in the days

---

[1] Lepsius, however, (Einleitung, 1, p. 489) considers this dynasty contemporaneous with the first.

[2] See vol. i. p. 55.

[3] 2, 4.

of Menes all Egypt, except the Theban nome, was a marsh, and that below the Lake of Mœris nothing had yet appeared above water, they spoke entirely without historical authority. They saw, what Herodotus says was evident to one who only used his own eyesight, and had not been previously informed of it, that the Delta was " acquired land, and the gift of the Nile[1]." But being ignorant of the rate at which such phænomena proceed, and conceiving the commencement of their own special history to be the commencement of everything, they made the formation of the Delta, and the whole country below the Theban nome, the work of thousands of years, to have begun with Menes. With the same ignorance of the rate of progression, they represented to Herodotus that there had been a rise of level in the soil of Egypt below Memphis equal to eight cubits in 900 years[2]. The time of the changes by which the Delta was elevated and laid dry stretches far beyond history, and Menes did not found his capital that he might reign over a marsh.

Such an event as the sudden opening of a chasm in the ground, and the consequent destruction of a great multitude of people, would be regarded as a prodigy, and therefore be preserved in the Egyptian annals, scanty as they are. Egypt is not very subject to earthquakes, and the chasm is more probably to be attributed to the undermining of a part of the city by the Nile, on the bank of which it stood. A similar chasm in the Forum at Rome filled the minds of the people with superstitious terror, and it was believed that nothing less than the self-devo-

---

[1] Her. 2, 4, 5.   [2] Her. 2, 13.

tion of Curtius could have averted the omen and closed the abyss[1]. Though the story of the expiation may be false, the terror was real.

The reign of Kaiechos is distinguished by the establishment of the worship of Apis at Memphis, Mnevis at Heliopolis, and the Mendesian goat at the town of that name. We have here a more decisive evidence that Lower Egypt, in the early times of the Old Monarchy, was in a state not materially different from that in which it was known to the Jews and the Greeks. Mendes stood not far from the sea[2]; the Delta therefore, even to its extremity, must have been already firm and dry. It is not the introduction of animal worship among the Egyptians, as sometimes supposed, that is here recorded; *that* lies far beyond the commencement of history; but specially the establishment of the worship of the bull and the goat in the three cities mentioned. Lower Egypt was the principal seat of this superstition. Among other things attributed to Menes, he was said to have introduced the worship of the bull[3]. Basis, the sacred bull of Hermonthis in the Thebaid, is never mentioned by the older writers, and appears to have been an object of merely local reverence, while Apis was passionately worshiped by the whole nation. Every nome had its own animal type of divinity, and abstained from using its flesh for food; but we read of no such extravagant and superstitious homage being paid to the ram at Thebes as to the bull at Memphis. Next to the bull Apis, the cat seems to have been the animal

---

[1] Liv. 7, 6. Plin. 15, 20.
[2] Strabo, 17, p. 802.
[3] Ælian, Hist. Anim. 11, 10.

most superstitiously worshiped by the Egyptians, and the chief temple of the goddess Pasht, to whom it was consecrated, was at Bubastos in the Delta.

A shield has been found by Lepsius in a tomb near the pyramids of Gizeh containing the name *Ke-ke-ou*, which, there can be little doubt, answers to the Kaiechos of Manetho's list[1]. Sethenes, Chaires and Nephercheres have also been identified with some probability[2]. The establishment of the prerogative of royalty on behalf of women in the reign of Binothris, is not connected with the mention of any female succession or claim. History knows only of one queen, Nitocris, and she is not said to have succeeded to the throne by a law of the kingdom, but to have been chosen by a special act of the people, who had put her brother to death[3]. In the monuments only one female appears with the attributes of royalty, Set Amen, Amense or Amesses of the 18th dynasty, who probably reigned as guardian of her son or younger brother. In the lists besides Nitocris, Scemiophris appears at the end of the 12th dynasty, the sister of Ammenemes; and Acencheres of the 18th is called by Josephus daughter of Horus, neither of which is confirmed by the monuments. The specialty of these cases makes us doubt whether the words[4] imply female inheritance, since in such frequent change of dynasty, had there been no Salic law, it is scarcely possible that we should not have found daughters succeeding to the throne. The

---

[1] Bunsen, B. 2, p. 106, Germ.
[2] Lesueur, p. 270, 310.
[3] Her. 2, 100. Τὸν ἀδελφεον ἀποκτείναντες οὕτω ἐκείνῃ ἀπέδοσαν τὴν βασιληίην.
[4] Ἐκρίθη τὰς γυναῖκας βασιλείας γέρας ἔχειν.

words "royal prerogatives" do not necessarily imply more than the monuments exhibit—their exercising regal functions, without being included in the list of sovereigns. Diodorus indeed says, that the queen in Egypt enjoyed greater honours than the king, attributing the distinction to the merits of Isis[1]; in accordance with the practice of a country which allotted greater respect to the female than the male. This appears, however, if the fact be correctly stated, to have been matter of courtesy and sentiment rather than of legal right[2].

In the reign of Nephercheres the Nile was fabled to have flowed eleven days, mixed with honey. As rivers were esteemed divine by the ancients[3], their changes were noted with superstitious apprehension. Whatever affected the Nile, which physically as well as religiously was of vast importance to the Egyptians, would be very likely to be recorded. To have their sacred river changed into blood was one of the humiliations which preceded their permission to the Israelites to depart. Similar changes in rivers are among the omens which have been handed down to us abundantly in the Roman history[4], and the fabulousness[5] of this account of the Nile's flowing mixed with honey is no proof against the historical character of the period and of the sovereigns. The great stature ascribed to Sesochris we shall hereafter see,

---

[1] Diod. 1. 27. Διὰ ταύτας τὰς αἰτίας (the merits of Isis) καταδειχθῆναι μείζονος ἐξουσίας καὶ τιμῆς τυγχάνειν τὴν βασίλισσαν τοῦ βασιλέως.

[2] See what Herodotus says (p. 57 of this vol.) of the *inferiority* of women in Egypt.

[3] Athenag. adv. Gentes, quoted in Voss. de Idol. ii. 78.

[4] See Bryant's observations on the Plagues of Egypt, p. 26.

[5] The expression μυθεύεται τὸν Νεῖλον μέλιτι κεκραμένον ῥυῆναι must belong to Africanus, not Manetho.

has probably been transferred by later authors to Sesostris, whom Herodotus and Eusebius celebrate for his size, though nothing of this kind is asserted by Manetho of the Sesostris of his 12th dynasty.

Third Dynasty. Nine Memphite kings.

		Years.
1. NECHEROPHES (NECHEROCHIS, Eusch.) reigned		28

Under him the Libyans revolted from the Egyptians, and the moon having increased in an extraordinary way, were alarmed and surrendered.

2. TOSORTHRUS (SESORTHOS, Euseb.)	29

He was called Æsculapius by the Egyptians, in reference to his medical art; and he invented building by means of polished stones (ξεστῶν λίθων): he also cultivated the art of writing. [The remaining six did nothing worthy of being recorded, Euseb.]

3. TYREIS	7
4. MESOCHRIS	17
5. SOUPHIS	16
6. TOSERTASIS	19
7. ACHES	42
8. SEPHOURIS	30
9. KERPHERES	26
Total	214

According to Eusebius there were only eight kings in this dynasty, and they reigned, not 214, but 197 years. He specifies the names only of Necherochis and Sesorthus, for so he writes the two first. The revolt of the Libyans, which occurred in the reign of Necherophis, has been explained in speaking of the conquests of Menes; its termination by the terror excited through some unusual appearance of the moon is quite in the character of ancient superstition[1]. The reign of Sesorthos or Tosorthrus,

---

[1] Her. 1, 74, of the eclipse between the Lydians and the Medes, which put an end to the war.

briefly as its events are summed up, was evidently one marked by great improvements in Egypt; he held the same place in the history of medicine in that country as Æsculapius in Greece[1]; and he introduced the use of squared and polished stones in architecture, instead of the rough surfaces and irregular angles of their previous mode of building. The improvement or more extensive practice of the art of writing is naturally connected with this change in building. Writing in its earliest stage in Egypt was hieroglyphic engraving, which could not be practised with facility except on the surface of smoothed stones. And this may have been the reason why both are attributed to the same sovereign.

There is no certain correspondence between the monuments and the names in this dynasty. A shield which has been read Chufu has been found in the grotto of Benihassan, and has been supposed to be the Souphis who stands fifth in the list; it contains, however, one character (the arm and scourge) not commonly found in Chufu, and if it belong at all to this dynasty seems rather to answer to Sephouris, the eighth. A name resembling *Tosorthrus* or *Sesorthus* occurs in the necropolis of Memphis, and another which has been read Aches[2].

---

[1] The expression Αἰγυπτίοις κατὰ τὴν ἰατρικὴν νενόμισται must be that of Africanus, not Manetho, though there is no reason to doubt that the information came from his annals.

[2] Lesueur, p. 311. Lepsius says (Einleitung, 1,551) that only a few dates of months are known to him of this dynasty.

Fourth Dynasty[1].

Eight Memphite kings of another family (seventeen, Euseb.) reigned 284 years (448 Euseb.).

		Years.
1.	SORIS	29
2.	SUPHIS	63

He raised the largest pyramid, which Herodotus says was built by Cheops; he was even a contemner of the gods and [having repented, Euseb.] wrote the sacred book, "which I acquired when I was in Egypt as a very valuable thing," Africanus ["which the Egyptians cherish as a very valuable thing," Eusebius, who adds, "and of the rest nothing worth mention has been recorded"].

3.	SOUPHIS	66
4.	MENCHERES	63
5.	RATOISES	25
6.	BICHERIS	22
7.	SEBERCHERES	7
8.	THAMPHTHIS	9
	Total	284

We may congratulate ourselves that we have at length reached the period of undoubted contemporaneous monuments in Egyptian history. The pyramids and the sepulchres near them still remain to assure us that we are not walking in a land of shadows, but among a populous and powerful nation far advanced in the arts of life. And as a people can only progressively attain to such a station, the light of historical certainty is reflected back from this æra to the ages which precede it. There is, however, extraordinary variance among the ancient

---

[1] According to Bunsen, after 190 years the kingdom of Menes was divided, one branch reigning in Upper, the other in Lower Egypt, the Memphite constituting what he calls the imperial dynasty, alone recognised in the chronology of Eratosthenes. Each of these dynasties came to an end at the same time, 224 years after their establishment, and the kingdom was re-united, 414 years after Menes, under the fourth dynasty. (B. 2, vol. 2, p. 65 foll., Germ.)

authorities, nor is the evidence of the monuments altogether free from difficulty.

We see that Manetho declares Souphis to have been the builder of the Great Pyramid, taking no notice of the building of the Second; and we shall find hereafter that he attributes to Nitocris, a queen of his sixth dynasty, the erection of the Third. Eratosthenes gives in immediate succession Saophis, Saophis II. and Moscheres, but says nothing of the building of the pyramids, as indeed throughout his lists he mentions nothing either of the works or the exploits of the kings. Herodotus says that Cheops built the Great Pyramid, his brother Chephren the Second, and Mycerinus the Third: Diodorus that Chembes or Chemmis built the Great Pyramid, Kephren his brother, or Chabryis his son, the Second, and Mecherinus or Mencherinus the Third. Pliny, after quoting the names of twelve authors who had written on the pyramids, declares that the builders of them were unknown. Till very lately they seemed to give no evidence on behalf of their founders. No inscriptions appeared either within or without; it had grown into one of the commonplaces of morality, that the builders of these stupendous works had been deprived of the fame which they coveted[1]. The Great Pyramid had long been open, and the central chamber contained a sarcophagus, but without a name; Belzoni succeeded in opening the Second, and found a sar-

---

[1] N. II. 36, 12 (17). Qui de his scripserunt sunt Herodotus, Euhemerus, Duris Samius, Aristagoras, Dionysius, Artemidorus, Alexander Polyhistor, Butorides, Antisthenes, Demetrius, Demoteles, Apion. Inter omnes eos non constat a quibus factæ sint, justissimo casu obliteratis tantæ vanitatis auctoribus.

cophagus beneath it; but that also was without an inscription. At length Colonel Vyse in the course of his researches found a way into the chambers already described over the king's chamber, and in two of them discovered shields in the common phonetic character[1]. They are drawn with red paint on the calcareous blocks which form the sides, along with various other marks, supposed to be those of the quarry-men or masons. One of these shields contains four characters which it is agreed should be pronounced *Chufu* or *Shufu*; another is mutilated, but has evidently ended in *fu*, and therefore probably contained the same name. Another chamber contains a shield with the same group[2], but prefixed to it the jug and ram which are found with the figures of the ram-headed god of Thebes, commonly called Kneph, Neph, Cnuphis, Chnoum or Num. Chufu is without violence made to answer to the Souphis of Manetho, the Saophis of Eratosthenes, and the Cheops of Herodotus[3]. And as it is improbable that the same king should be designated in two different ways in the same monument, it has been concluded that there were two of the name of Chufu, one being distinguished by the additional characters of the jug and the ram[4]. Herodotus speaks indeed only of one Cheops; but Eratosthenes mentions a second Saophis, and Manetho a second Souphis. The name of the second has been read Kneph-Chufu, or Chnoum-Chufu,

---

[1] Vyse on the Pyramids, 1, 279. Vol. i. of this work, p. 122.
[2] Lepsius (Denkm. taf. vii.) gives a drawing of an alabaster vase with the banner of a king, the same as Ricci found at Wadi Magara, connected with the name of Chufu. (Rosell. Mon. Stor. iii. 1, 3.)
[3] The final *u* is sometimes omitted in the shield of this king.
[4] See Pl. III. C. 3, at the end of vol. 1.

and it is possible that this additional syllable may have given rise to the name Chembes, which Diodorus attributes to the builder of the Great Pyramid.

It will be seen by recurring to the description of this structure (vol. i. p. 118), that a long straight descent conducts from the opening to a subterranean chamber, in which, however, no sarcophagus or inscription has been found. Now from the analogy of all the other pyramids, we are led to conclude that this was the place in which the interment was originally designed to be made. To this the passage from the opening leads directly. Why it was abandoned, and two chambers constructed in the heart of the pyramid itself, we are not informed, nor can we form any probable conjecture. The lower of these two is traditionally called the Queen's Chamber, but there is nothing which marks it as destined for such a purpose ; and it was not the usual practice of the Egyptians to inter kings and queens in the same monument. It should seem that Herodotus had the subterranean apartment in view, when he spoke of a canal which Cheops introduced from the Nile, by which he insulated his own grave. The actual depth of this apartment below the ground in which the pyramid stands is ninety feet; and though this is still considerably above the highest level of the Nile[1], in the absence of accurate measurements, it might easily be supposed practicable to bring in a canal

---

[1] " On the 23rd of October, 1838, the level of the river (it being High Nile) was 137 feet 3 inches below the base of the Great Pyramid." (Vyse, 2, 148.)

from the river; but this would have been too obviously absurd, if meant of the King's Chamber in the centre of the pyramid, 138 feet above the ground[1]. Diodorus also speaks of (Chembes) Cheops as not being interred in his pyramid, but in some secret place, that his body might not be exposed to the insults of the oppressed people[2]. Now we know that in the time of Strabo, the Great Pyramid was open[3]; probably therefore in the time of Diodorus. But these authors seem to have known nothing of any sepulchral vault except the subterranean; the way to that was open, from the mouth in the side of the pyramid; but all access to the Queen's and King's Chambers was barred by the block of granite which closed the place at which the passage to them diverges; nor do they appear ever to have been seen till a forced passage was made by the Caliphs[4]. The subterranean vault being empty, the tradition of Diodorus had a natural origin. It seems then not improbable that Cheops or Chufu, abandoning his original intention to construct himself a monument *beneath* a pyramid, began the structure which now exists, and that his sarcophagus was placed in what we call the Queen's Chamber. It certainly contained a sarcophagus when this part of the pyramid was opened under the Caliphs[5]. It is in the very centre

---

[1] Vyse, 2, 111.
[2] 1, 64.
[3] Lib. 17, p. 808.
[4] Abdollatif in Col. Howard Vyse, 2, 340.
[5] Edrisi quoted in Vyse, 2, 335. "The alley is ascended until a door is reached near a block of stone by which one ascends towards another sloping alley.—By this door a square room is entered *with an empty vessel in it.*—Returning hence to the place through which one enters, the second alley is ascended. Another square room is then reached—*an empty vessel is seen here similar to the former.*"

of the structure, which may originally not have been carried much higher. His successor, the second Chufu, distinguished by the addition of the ram and jug, appears to have continued his work and constructed for himself the King's Chamber, in which his sarcophagus still remains. The mixture of stones containing the names of the two Chufus in the vacant spaces over the King's Chamber, may be explained by the supposition that the second used some materials which his predecessor had prepared, and which had been marked by his name. It is not surprising, that as both bore the same name, Herodotus and Diodorus should have considered them as one.

The Second Pyramid contains no name in any part of it; but in the adjacent tombs[1] the shield of a king whose name reads *Shafre*[2] has been found, and the figure of a pyramid. In him we recognize without difficulty the Chephren of Herodotus and Diodorus, though there is no corresponding name either in Manetho or Eratosthenes. Diodorus mentions a tradition that he was not the brother, as Herodotus represented him, but the son of Cheops, and that his name was not Kephren, but Chabryis[3]. As there were two Chufus, he might be the son of one and brother of the other; and the difference between Shafre and Chabryis is not so great as to decide that they were not the same person. Herodotus in his account of the Second Pyramid says,

---

[1] The tomb was that of his chief architect, who calls his master, "the great one of the Pyramid" (see Lepsius, Denkmäler, taf. viii. D.). The pyramid is here always represented with a square base, projecting beyond the pyramidal part.

[2] Birch in Vyse, 2, 98.

[3] 1, 64.

that it was inferior to the first in other respects, and also in not containing any subterranean chambers[1]. In fact, however, its only known chamber is subterranean.

The Third Pyramid is assigned by Herodotus and Diodorus to Mycerinus, Mecherinus or Mencherinus[2]. In Manetho, Mencheres immediately follows the second Suphis, but is not mentioned by him as the builder of the pyramid. All doubt on this subject has been removed by the discovery of the coffin[3], inscribed with the name of Menkera. Herodotus calls him the son of Cheops, which is not very probable, if according to his statement the brother of Cheops, Chephren, had reigned after Cheops fifty-six years. The accounts of this king are very inconsistent. According to Herodotus he was a mild and humane monarch, who opened the temples which had been closed for 106 years, and relieved the people of their burdens. And yet he built a pyramid, which, though it fell short of both the others in dimensions, exceeded them in costliness of material and execution[4]. His justice was such that he was more extolled by the Egyptians than any of their kings[5]; yet he was said to have indulged an unnatural passion for his own daughter, who died of grief at the outrage which he offered to her. He was remarkable for his piety, and yet endeavoured to make the oracle of Buto "a liar[6]." These things excite a suspicion that two

---

[1] Herod. 2, 127.
[2] Τινὲς μὲν Χερῖνον leg. Μενχερῖνον. (Diod. 1, 64. Böckh, Manetho, p. 597.)
[3] Vol. i. p. 131.
[4] Her. 2, 129.
[5] Diod. 1, 64.
[6] Θέλων τὸ μαντήϊον ψευδόμενον ἀποδέξαι. (Herod. 2, 133.)

kings of the same name, but very different characters, have been blended in one tradition[1]. In the tablet of Abydos, which here first begins to be legible, we have in the fifteenth shield the evident traces of the name of Menkera; the fourteenth appears to have contained the same name, though little of it is now left; with the addition of the hatchet, which signifies *god*[2]. It had been observed by Lepsius, that the name of Menkera occurs in the Ritual of the Dead[3] as a deceased king, and that it is frequently found on scarabæi which had been used as amulets, and which from the style of their workmanship must have been executed long after his death. This clearly points to a deification of Menkera, or to some cause for which his name was held in special reverence. The same group of characters which is found on the mummy-case in the Third Pyramid is inscribed in red paint on a slab in one of the smaller pyramids of Gizeh, traditionally supposed to be the tombs of queens. The sarcophagus which it contains has no sculpture, and the mummy-case which it once contained has been reduced to dust; but from its small size and the appearance of a tooth which was found in it, it has been concluded that it had received the body of a young female—the wife or daughter of Menkera[4].

The 106 years occupied by the reigns of Chufu

---

[1] Lepsius, Einleitung, 1, p. 309, observes that Psammitichus has the addition *Menkera* in his shield, and supposes that he has been mixed up with Mencheres the builder of the Third Pyramid.

[2] See Wilkinson's copy in the Hieroglyphics of the Egyptian Society, Pl. 98.

[3] It is written in the Ritual (Das Todtenbuch, col. 64), as on the tablet of Abydos, with a single character, *ke*, for "offering;" on the coffin this character is thrice repeated, making the plural *keu*.

[4] Vyse, 2, 48.

THE FOURTH DYNASTY.

and Shafre were regarded by the Egyptians as a period of national oppression and suffering. The people were worn out by forced labours in the quarries and at the pyramids, and the temples were closed, that the celebration of the sacred rites, which occupied so large a portion of the Egyptian year, might not draw off the people from their work. So strong was the hatred with which their memory was regarded, that the common Egyptian was unwilling even to name them, and would gladly have thrown the odium of their erection on a foreign race. In concluding his account, Herodotus observes, that the Egyptians alleged them to have been built by the shepherd Philition, who then fed his flocks in this district. Nowhere else is such a person mentioned, and it has been supposed that in this obscure passage we have an allusion to the Palæstinian Shepherds[1], who, under the name of *Hyksos*, appear subsequently in Egyptian history, oppressing the people for several hundred years, and destroying their temples. The builder of the Great Pyramid was specially the object of popular dislike, which embodied itself in the Greek tale of his compelling his own daughter to prostitution, in order to obtain funds for his work[2]. Manetho admits the impiety of his Souphis[3], but represents him to have also composed "the sacred book," the subject of which is unknown.

Soris, the king whose name stands at the head of

---

[1] Kenrick's Egypt of Herodotus, p. 167.
[2] Her. 2, 126.
[3] Possibly the idea of impiety may have been connected with the erection of a building so lofty that it seemed to invade the skies. Comp. Gen. xi. 4. "Let us make us a tower whose top may reach to heaven."

this dynasty, is thought to be the same with the *Shoure*, whose shield has been discovered in the necropolis of Memphis[1]. In the present state of our knowledge, however, little reliance can be placed on these insulated identifications. What is more important is, that the dominion of Egypt, in the æra of the building of the Pyramids, extended to the northern part of the Arabian peninsula. The motive of the Egyptian kings for establishing themselves here was evidently to obtain possession of the copper-mines, which have been already described[2]. The whole land was called in hieroglyphics *Mafkat*, or the Copper land[3], and the principal mines were at Wadi Magara and Sarabit el Kadim. Large mounds of ore, and masses of scoriæ, attest the extent of the ancient operations. Numerous stelæ record the names of the kings in whose reigns the mines were wrought. Those at Wadi Magara are the oldest. Both the Chufus, Shoure, and a king whose name is found in the pyramid of Reegah, and read Ousrenre or Ranseser[4], are seen in acts of adoration, with dates of their respective reigns. Shonre is represented as in the act of smiting a captive whose hair he grasps, and therefore probably made conquests in this region.

The seventh king in Manetho's list is Sebercheres; this has been corrected by Lepsius into

---

[1] Lesueur, Chronol. p. 271, 311. Birch (Vyse, 3, 22) gives the name Shonre to a king whose shield is found at Abouseir, and read by Lepsius Amchura (Bunsen, B. 2, 99).

[2] Vol. i. p. 61.

[3] See Lepsius, Tour to the Peninsula of Sinai. Comp. Hieroglyph. of the Eg. Society, pl. 41 No.

[4] Birch, in Vyse, 3, 12. 2, 5. The block on which the name is found at Reegah appears to have been taken from some other monument. Among the hieroglyphics is the figure of an obelisk.

Nephercheres[1], and identified with the Nefrukera whose name occurs in the necropolis of Memphis, and on the tablet of Abydos follows that of Menkera. A Nephercheres, however, is actually found in the fifth dynasty of Manetho, who may seem to have a preferable claim.

The glimpse which we thus obtain of the condition of Egypt, in the fifth century after Menes, according to the lowest computation, is far from satisfying our desire for details, but on the other hand it reveals to us some general facts which lead to important inferences. In all its great characteristics it was the same as the Egypt of a thousand years later. It was a well-organized monarchy; the tombs of Gizeh preserve the names and offices of various public functionaries, military and civil. Its religious system was already elaborated and extended throughout the country; the Memphite sovereign, the second Chufu, takes for his difference the hieroglyphic of the tutelary god of Thebes and Elephantine. On the coffin of Menkera we see the same formulary phrases which are familiar to us in so many later funereal inscriptions[2]. The deceased king is identified with Osiris; his regal dignity is indicated by the bee and branch prefixed; the same epithet, "living for ever," is given him, which is assigned to Ptolemy on the Rosetta stone. The system of hieroglyphic writing was the same, in all its leading peculiarities, as it continued to the end of the monarchy of the Pharaohs. We

---

[1] The praenomen Neferkera has been found also on the cover of a small ivory box, now in the Louvre, but it is not probable that it is of such high antiquity (Rosellini, Mon. Stor. iii. 1, 15).

[2] Birch in Vyse, 2, 96.

possess no contemporary manuscripts, but the inscriptions in the pyramids show that the linear hieroglyphic had been already introduced, which prepared the way for the hieratic. As the character of the inkstand and reed-pen is seen in these, we cannot doubt that linen or papyrus was already used as a writing material. We have no statuary of this age, but the hieroglyphics in the tombs are cut with great force and precision. While the present surface only of the pyramids was examined, they might seem a barbarous monument of wasted labour rather than of skill; but the accurate finishing of the masonry with which the passages and even the exterior were lined and cased, and the precise orientation of the whole, show that both art and science had attained to considerable perfection[1].

The relation of the Memphian monarchy to Upper Egypt remains obscure. No mention is even incidentally made of Thebes; a city may have existed there, but not of sufficient importance to be the seat of a rival power to Memphis. Hitherto no trace of the dominion of the Memphian kings has been found at Thebes or elsewhere in Upper Egypt, except some alabaster vases from Abydos, bearing the standard of Chufu; and portable antiquities afford no decisive evidence. But this is no proof of Theban independence, since the fixed monuments of this age are entirely sepulchral; and the Memphian kings and their great officers would be

---

[1] These inferences are fully supported by the drawings from the tombs near the Pyramids contained in the "Denkmäler aus Ægypten und Æthiopien," the fruit of the Prussian expedition under Lepsius; of which the First Part has appeared while this work was passing through the press. The opinion expressed in vol. i. p. 273, of the inferiority of art in this age, must now be somewhat modified.

buried near their own capital. If Thebes has no monuments of Memphian dominion, neither has it any of its own, and it appears probable that till the 12th dynasty of Manetho it continued to be a place of little account.

Fifth Dynasty.

Eight kings from Elephantine[1]. (Thirty-one, Euseb.)

		Years.
1.	USERCHERES reigned	28
2.	SEPHRES	13
3.	NEPHERCHERES	20
4.	SISIRES	7
5.	CHERES	20
6.	RATHURES	44
7.	MENCHERES	9
8.	TANCHERES	44
9.	ONNOS	33
	Total	218

Although the heading says eight kings, nine are mentioned, and the sum agrees with the separate numbers[2].

The supposition that some of the dynasties of Manetho are collateral, is nowhere more probable than in regard to this dynasty of Elephantine kings. No one fact is recorded concerning them. They appear, however, to be a branch of the Memphite dynasty, as the names Sephres, Nephercheres, Mencheres, bear a close analogy to those which

---

[1] Eusebius has transferred here by mistake the names of Othoes and Phiops from the 6th dynasty.

[2] Bunsen, 2, 190 (Germ.), would remove Onnos to the beginning of the 6th dynasty, and supposes that Othoes stands there by a false reading of the transcribers. Onnos, it is true, has 33 years and Othoes 30, but this last number is assigned to Onnos in the Turin papyrus.

we have already found in use among them. Useserkef has been found by Lepsius[1] among the tombs of Gizeh, and he seems to be the Usercheres of Manetho. Although he stands at the head of this dynasty, yet if it were a derivative and dependent line, he might be interred among his ancestors of the Memphite dynasty. Snephres (Snefru), which we may suppose Manetho to have written, instead of Sephres, has also been found at Gizeh[2] and Karnak; and Nephercheres, the third in his list, follows Menkera on the tablet of Abydos, and has been found on alabaster vases from Abydos[3]. The tablet of Abydos, however, does not agree with Manetho; the shields which follow that of Mencheres exhibit different names from his[4], yet names combined out of similar elements, so as to favour the supposition that they contain another derivative, though not royal line[5]. Sesrenre would be the reading, according to Lepsius, of the name usually read *Ousrenre* (see vol. i. p. 312), and this would answer to Sisires, No. 4. Unas or Onas is found in a fragment of the Royal List of Turin, and appears to be the Onnos of Manetho[6]. The phonetic

---

[1] Bunsen, B. 2, p. 180, Germ. Lesueur, p. 312.

[2] Denkmäler aus Ægypten und Æthiopien, altes Reich. Abth. ii. Bl. 2.

[3] Bunsen, 2, 186. He observes that the name is written with a different character from the earlier Nephercheres.

[4] See Wilkinson's copy in Hierogl. of the Egyptian Society, pl. 47. Some of them are no longer legible on the tablet in the British Museum.

[5] Bunsen, *u. s.* p. 188.

[6] Bunsen, 184. He supposes a name beginning with the sign of Thoth to be Tatkeres, which he conjecturally substitutes for Tancheres, eighth in the list. This king is supposed by others to be represented by an inscription at Saccarah, read thus: "The king (Tankera), son of the Sun (Assa)." One character in the first shield, however, is doubtful, and according to analogy, Assa should be the proper name (Lesueur, Chronologie, p. 312).

value of some of the characters in these early shields is uncertain.

If Othoes were the same as Onnos, it would appear that this Elephantine dynasty was brought to a close by a conspiracy of his life-guards, by whom he was murdered, and a new Memphite dynasty succeeded. If, however, the Elephantine was not a sovereign, but a collateral dynasty, then the kings whose names are about to be enumerated must be regarded as the immediate successors of the fourth dynasty, in which the builders of pyramids were included. It is possible that these Elephantine kings may be the Ethiopians of whom Herodotus speaks[1], Elephantine being on the boundary of that country, but the number, eighteen, does not agree.

Sixth Dynasty. Six Memphite kings.

	Years.
1. OTHOES reigned..........................	30
He was killed by his life-guards.	
2. PHIOS	53
3. METHOSUPHIS	7
4. PHIOPS. Beginning to reign at six years old, he continued to	100
5. MENTHESUPHIS............................	1
6. NITOCRIS, the most spirited and beautiful woman of her time, of a ruddy complexion. She erected the Third Pyramid, and reigned...................	12
	203

Eusebius gives only Nitocris by name, but the

[1] 2, 100. "The priests read to me a list of 330 other kings, and in so many generations 18 were Ethiopians." Lepsius considers both the 5th and 6th dynasty as Ethiopian (Einl. 1, 255), and makes them amount together to 15, to which are to be added the three Ethiopian kings of the 25th dynasty. The evidence for these arrangements has not yet been published, nor that on the ground of which he pronounces (517) that the 5th dynasty was not collateral.

number of years is the same. The similarity of the names Phios and Methosuphis and Phiops and Menthesuphis in this list, has given rise to a suspicion that they are really the same. We find in Eratosthenes the following succession:—

	Years.
Apappus	100 within an hour.
A nameless king	1
Nitocris, instead of her husband	6

It would be against all probability that such coincidences should be accidental[1]. The names Apappus and Phiops do not indeed in their actual form appear the same. The hieroglyphics of the king whose name is read Pepi may however be read Apap, and if we retrench the final *s* from Phiops, which was an addition made to give it a Greek termination, we have a name also not very remote from Pepi. The shields of Pepi have been found at Chenoboscion and elsewhere in much greater numbers than those of any preceding king, though not with dates which confirm the account of his extraordinarily long reign[2], the sixteenth year being the highest; nor has any yet been found in Lower Egypt[3], a singular circumstance, as the dynasty is called Memphite. The identification of Pepi with Phiops and Apappus must therefore be considered as still problematical. No other name belonging to this dynasty has been identified hitherto on the monuments. There is a group which reads *Mentopt* or Mentuotep, twice occurring, one of which Bunsen[4] refers to *Mentheophis*,

---

[1] I have already explained (p. 98 of this vol.) the principle on which I believe the list of Eratosthenes to have been compiled.

[2] The long life of Phiops is not more incredible than that of Gorgias of Leontini, who is said (Cic. Sen. 5) to have lived to 107.

[3] Lepsius, Einl. 1, 265.

[4] B. 2, 194. Ark. p. 64, note.

THE SIXTH DYNASTY.

his correction of the Menthesuphis of the lists, and the other to the eighth dynasty. They may belong to the Middle monarchy or the eleventh dynasty. A fragment of the Canon of Turin contains, without a name, the number 90 years as the duration of a reign[1], and from its length there can be little doubt that it refers to Phiops. It is followed by a date of 1 year 1 month, which appears to be that of Menthesuphis.

The figure of Pepi is found in a singular combination with that of another, whose name is read Remai, or Maire. The two princes appear seated on their thrones in the Hall of Assembly, wearing one the crown of the upper, the other that of the lower country; whence Wilkinson concludes[2] that either they were contemporary sovereigns, one ruling at Thebes and the other at Memphis, or that Pepi was the phonetic name of Remai, and that they were the same monarch. This distinction of the names becomes henceforward important and will require to be explained.

In the oldest monuments, as those of the pyramids and tombs of Gizeh, the names of the Egyptian kings are enclosed in oval rings or shields, and each king has only one. The characters included in the shield are phonetic, and express the name of the king as it was pronounced, Mena, Chufu, Shafre, &c. In later times, however, each king has usually two shields; over the first are placed a bee and a branch of a plant[3]; over the second the figure of a vulpanser and the disk of the sun, which are read

---

[1] Lesueur, p. 266.
[2] Manners and Customs, 3, 282.
[3] See Pl. II. vol. 1, Nos. 11, 12, and p. 322.

Son of the Sun. Where two shields are found, the second always contains the name of the sovereign in phonetic characters; thus in the eighteenth and succeeding dynasties it is the name in the second shield which corresponds to the lists of Manetho. The first shield, if there are two, contains always the disk of the Sun or Re, and joined to this two or more characters. Champollion considered the signs included in these shields as symbolical titles, rather than names of the kings; and they are not alphabetical letters, like those of the second shields. They are, however, in one sense phonetic; for the objects and ideas which they represent had of course names in the old Egyptian language, and these, if pronounced, would become a compound name. Thus the two shields in Plate II. 11, 12, read, "The king (*Re-seser-Tmei*, Sun, Guardian of the Truth), Son of the Sun (Amunmai Rameses)." Each king had a combination of these signs, by which he is as readily distinguished from all others as by his phonetic shield; but those of the same family usually preserved a general similarity in their signs. In the case of the two royal figures on the monument of the Cosseir road, the shield on the left, if they are considered to be distinct persons, will be read Remai or Maire; but if the same, then it will be considered as a title of Papi, and explained " beloved of Re," which is the meaning of the word Remai. Such a title, it has been thought, might give rise to second names, as we sometimes call the Ptolemies simply Philadelphus or Epiphanes. Lepsius, however, has observed[1] that he has not found a single indisputable example

---

[1] Einleitung, 1, p. 255.

of the titular shield passing into a proper name[1]; and its phonetic reading is in most cases conjectural.

There is a third way in which the kings of Egypt were distinguished. Each had a standard[2] on which a group of characters is represented, sometimes placed beside the shields, and which serves to discriminate them in the absence of these. On the obelisks, where all their titles are usually set forth, the standard is found immediately under the pyramidion; over it is represented the hawk of Horus, sometimes crowned with the *pschent*, and aecompanied by the uræus or royal serpent and the disk of the sun; the standard itself contains a group of symbolical characters not strictly phonetic, but like those of the titular shield capable of passing into a name, by the pronunciation of the words answering to the objects delineated. An example of this may be seen in Pl. II. No. 15, where the standard of Rameses III. is given. It is surmounted by the hawk of Horus crowned, with the uræus and disk; the banner itself reads, " The strong bull, beloved of Truth." The hawk sometimes appears (ib. 15) as an emblem of royalty, with the character for *gold*, and is called " the golden Horus."

The standard and the titular shield were assumed no doubt by the king on his accession; the phonetic name belonged to him as an individual, but when he ascended the throne he enclosed it within a shield as a mark of royalty. The standard or the titular shield alone is sufficient to distinguish one

---

[1] Bunsen supposes, though with little probability, that Papi, or Phiops Apappus, with the title Maire, is the Mœris of the Greeks, the author of the great works in the Fyoum, B. 2, 209.

[2] Rosellini, Mon. Stor. 1, 156.

king from another; and the phonetic shield is not found on the tablet of Karnak, nor that of Abydos, except in the case of the king by whom it was erected; but it is the phonetic shield which connects them with history. So the armorial bearings of a modern sovereign discriminate him from others; but it is only by the knowledge of his name that his historical place is ascertained.

The sixth name in the list of Manetho is that of Nitocris, whom he describes as a woman of great beauty and spirit, and the builder of the third pyramid. She is no doubt the same as the Nitocris of Herodotus, if identity may be predicated of persons who agree in name, but differ in almost everything else. The Nitocris of Herodotus, after having drowned the Egyptians who had put her brother to death, committed suicide by plunging herself into a pit full of ashes—a mode of destruction common as a punishment among the Persians, but unheard of among the Egyptians. The Nitocris of Manetho is the builder of the third pyramid, a work not to be accomplished in the short interval between her accession and her suicide. Another difficulty is, that we have seen that Mencheres was deposited in the third pyramid, and is therefore to be presumed to have been its builder. This difficulty has been partly removed by the researches of Colonel H. Vyse, and the ingenious combinations of Bunsen. By a reference to the description already given of this pyramid[1], it will be seen, that in a large chamber, which is nearly under its centre, a sarcophagus of red granite had been placed, the

[1] Vol. i. p. 130.

fragments of which are strewed about[1]. The sarcophagus of Mencheres was in an interior and lower chamber, to which a passage led from the larger. This larger chamber, besides the passage by which it is now entered from the exterior, has another going off at the same angle, but which never reaches the exterior. The upper passage had been worked by the chisel from the north or exterior, the lower from the interior; whence Perring concludes that the upper must have been formed first, and the lower cut outward through the pyramid[2]. These appearances have been explained by supposing that Mencheres built a pyramid of much smaller size than the present, of which the entrance was the passage which is now closed up. It would have reached the exterior at about the same height above the ground as the present passage, and the pyramid, if its angle of inclination were the same as that of the present structure, would have a base of 180 feet and a height of 145. In this state Mencheres left his pyramid; Nitocris enlarged it to its actual dimensions, cased it with red granite, and designed at least that her body should be placed in it, but was perhaps frustrated in this purpose by her own suicide or the vengeance of the people. Thus the traditions which ascribed it to Mencheres and to Nitocris would have each a portion of truth.

Another story is related by Herodotus which at first appears simply absurd—that this pyramid was

---

[1] So Bunsen says (B. 2, 168), perhaps from the personal communication of Perring; but Col. Vyse says (2, 81), that these pieces of red granite could not have been fragments of a sarcophagus. The portcullises were of this material, which was also used in the passages.

[2] Howard Vyse, 2, 79. See vol. i. p. 130, of this work.

built by a celebrated Greek courtezan of Naucratis of the times of Amasis or Psammitichus, respecting whom Strabo tells a tale very similar to that of Cinderella and her slipper. As she was bathing, an eagle snatched her shoe from the attendant, and carrying it to Memphis, dropped it in the lap of the king, who was sitting in the open air to administer justice. Charmed with the elegance of the shoe, the king sent through the land to discover its owner, and having found her at Naucratis, made her his queen, and after her death she received the third pyramid as her burial-place[1]. It was acutely observed by Zoega, however, that the courtezan, Rhodopis, had been created by the interpreters out of the queen Nitocris[2]. Both were celebrated for their beauty, and the name Rhodopis or "rosy-faced" is exactly descriptive of Nitocris, who is said to have been "ruddy in complexion."

No such name as Nitocris has been found upon the monuments of this age; but it occurs, written Neitakreti, in the Canon of Turin[3]. If we may venture to combine Herodotus with Manetho, the husband whom she succeeded, and whose death she avenged, was Menthesuphis, who reigned only one year. The following dynasty points to some violent change in the government, to which the death of Nitocris gave occasion.

Seventh Dynasty.

SEVENTY MEMPHITE KINGS, who reigned seventy days .. 70
   (Eusebius, Five Memphite kings who reigned 75 days.
      Arm. 75 years.)

---

[1] Strabo, 17, p. 808.
[2] De Obelisc. p. 390. See also Bunsen, 2, p. 236, Germ.
[3] Lepsius, Einl. 1, 262. Lesueur, p. 313, places it in the eighth dynasty.

Eighth Dynasty.

	Years.
TWENTY-EIGHT MEMPHITE KINGS, who reigned..........	146

(Eusebius, Five Memphite kings, who reigned 100 years.)

Ninth Dynasty.

NINETEEN HERACLEOPOLITAN KINGS, who reigned 409
(Eusebius, Four Heracleopolitan kings, who reigned 100 years.) The first of whom, ACHTHOES, the most atrocions of all who had preceded him, did much mischief to the people of all Egypt, and afterwards fell into madness and was destroyed by a crocodile.

Tenth Dynasty.

NINETEEN HERACLEOPOLITAN KINGS, who reigned 185

Eleventh Dynasty.

SIXTEEN DIOSPOLITAN KINGS, who reigned............	43
After whom AMMENEMES............................	16

"Thus far Manetho brought his first volume, all together 192 kings, 2300 years, 70 days."

The difficulties which this concluding portion of the first volume of Manetho's dynasties offers are very great. The seventy Memphite kings, who reigned seventy days, must have been a temporary government, formed of the chief men of the kingdom, and ruling each for a day; for, as Herodotus (2, 147) observes, the Egyptians could not exist without kingly government. The Roman senators, on the death of Romulus, exercised authority each for five days[1]. The number of seventy

[1] Liv. 1, 17. Rem inter se centum patres, decem decuriis factis, singulisque in singulas decurias creatis qui summæ rerum præessent, consociant; decem imperitabant, unus cum insignibus imperii et lictoribus erat: quinque dierum spatio finicbatur imperium ac per omnes in orbem ibat. Comp. Diod. 1, 66.

days is no doubt correct, for it occurs again in the summation at the end, and can only have arisen here, as the odd number of days is not elsewhere mentioned in giving the length of each king's reign. Eusebius has made a correction, but as it appears arbitrarily, and reads, according to the Armenian version, "five kings who reigned seventy-five years"; but then it would be unexplained how seventy days should appear in the sum of the first volume. Other corrections have been suggested, but they are too arbitrary to be received[1].

There were in Egypt two towns called Heracleopolis[2]. Heracleopolis Magna was situated at the entrance of the valley of the Fyoum, on an island, as the ancients called it, formed by the Nile, the Bahr Jusuf, and a canal. After Memphis and Heliopolis it was probably the most important place in Lower Egypt. Heracleopolis Parva, which is only mentioned in later times, was near Pelusium, in the Sethroite nome, and beyond the westernmost branch of the Delta. If it existed under the Old Monarchy, it was quite insignificant, so that it is not likely its king Achthoes could have inflicted much mischief upon all the inhabitants of Egypt. But if a powerful state sprung up at Heracleopolis Magna, after a revolution at Memphis, which left the government in a feeble condition, it was well adapted by its

[1] Bunsen would transplant twenty (K) from the number of reigns of the eighth dynasty (KZ), which he thinks should be eight instead of twenty-eight, and with Eusebius read five as the number of kings in the seventh. The whole would then stand thus:

Seventh Dynasty.—FIVE Memphite kings, reigned 20 years 70 days.

Eighth Dynasty.—EIGHT Memphite kings, reigned 146 years. (B. 2, p. 248, Germ.)

[2] Strabo, 17, p. 789, 809. Steph. Byz. *s. v.* Champollion, L'Égypte sous les Pharaons, 1, 309, 2, 80. Ptolemy, Geog. 4, 5.

I.]   SEVENTH TO ELEVENTH DYNASTY.   155

position relatively to the Upper and Lower country and the Fyoum, to domineer over them all. With the eighth dynasty Memphis appears to have lost its pre-eminence. It passed first to Heracleopolis, afterwards to Thebes, finally to the towns of Lower Egypt, Tanis, Bubastis, Sais. We hear nothing more of a Memphite dynasty.

The tyranny of the founder Achthoes is absolutely all we know of these two Heracleopolitan dynasties. The text of Africanus assigns to them together the incredible length of 594 years; that of Eusebius 285. To a dynasty reigning here at the entrance of the Fyoum, it seems most natural to assign the commencement of those great works which tradition connected with the name of Mœris. No king of that name has been found in the lists or the monuments; and therefore probably Mœris is the designation of the natural collection of waters at the western side of the Fyoum, the Birket-el-Kerun. The word *Mou* in Coptic signifies *water*, and appears to be the first syllable of this word, which was variously spelt Moiris or Muris by the Greeks. Joined to *res*[1], which denotes *the south* in the same language, it would naturally describe, in contrast with the Mediterranean, this great southern lake, which in its extent, the quality of its waters and the form of its shores, so much resembled the sea, as to suggest the idea that it had been originally a portion of the Mediterranean[2]. The dimensions assigned by Herodotus (2,149) to the lake Mœris (3600 stadia)

[1] The terminations *res* and *ris* are constantly interchanged. Thus we have Uaphris, Sesostris, Sesochris, as well as Mencheres, Ne- phercheres, the origin of both forms being Re or Ra.
[2] Strabo, 1, 50. 17, 809.

cannot have belonged to an excavation in the centre of the Fyoum; nor would any one describe the length of a canal as the perimeter of a lake. It is indeed impossible to reconcile all the accounts which the ancients give us of the lake Mœris; but one circumstance appears decisive: if the Birket-el-Kerun be not the lake Mœris of Herodotus, Diodorus and Strabo, these three eye-witnesses have passed over one of the most remarkable objects in Egypt. There was no doubt also an artificial reservoir in the centre of the Fyoum, which retained the water of the inundation to be dispersed when it was needed over the adjacent country; and Linant has partially traced its embankment[1]. That it was designed to render this service to any other district than the Fyoum is not asserted by the ancients and appears improbable.

If the Fyoum was rendered habitable and fertile by the kings of the Heracleopolitan dynasties, it will be explained how it becomes of so much importance under the twelfth. Sesortasen erected an obelisk and Ammenemes built the Labyrinth there; previously to this time we find no monument and no mention of it in history.

The name Achthoes is the only one preserved in the lists, between Nitocris, the last of the sixth dynasty, and Ammenemes, the last of the eleventh. There is therefore no room for any comparison between the lists and the monuments. Eratosthenes has also no name which corresponds with the monuments in this interval[2].

---

[1] See vol. i. p. 50.
[2] Comp. Bunsen, B. 2, p. 252 foll., who has proposed various corrections of Eratosthenes. In his system the two Heracleopolitan dynasties are collateral.

Achthoes is said to have been killed by a crocodile. This circumstance may have been invented to explain the animosity which the people of Heracleopolis nourished against the crocodile; and their worship of the ichneumon, which was believed not only to destroy its eggs, but even to creep down its throat and eat away its vitals[1]. The mention of this circumstance is an additional presumption that Heracleopolis Magna was the seat of this dynasty.

THE SECOND VOLUME OF MANETHO.

Twelfth Dynasty. Seven Diospolitan kings.

	Years.
1. SESONCHOSIS, the son of Ammenemes, reigned	46
2. AMMENEMES, who was killed by his own guards of the bedchamber	38
3. SESOSTRIS	48
He subdued all Asia in nine years, and part of Europe as far as Thrace (everywhere erecting memorials of his occupation of the nations, engraving masculine emblems on tablets where the men had been valiant, feminine where they had been cowardly), so that he was esteemed by the Egyptians first after Osiris.	
(Eusebius adds, He is said to have been four cubits three palms two fingers in height.)	
4. LACHARES (Lamaris, Eus., Lampares, Arm.)	8
He prepared the Labyrinth in the Arsinoite nome as a tomb for himself.	
5.[2] AMERES	8
6. AMMENEMES	8
7. SCEMIOPHRIS, his sister	4
	160

Until a recent time, this dynasty, notwithstanding

---

[1] Strabo, 17, p. 812.
[2] Instead of Ameres, Ammenemes and Scemiophris, Eusebius has after Lamaris "his successors, years 42."

the completeness of its list of names, appeared to have no confirmation from the discoveries in hieroglyphics. Even its historical character, though marked by so conspicuous a name in the Egyptian annals as that of Sesostris, was hardly established; for this conqueror is known to us from Diodorus and Herodotus, who place him much later in the history. The Labyrinth was another work which might have rescued this dynasty from any doubt of its historical existence, but its remains had not been explored, so as to ascertain the name of its founder; and Herodotus had referred its erection to so late an age as that of the Dodecarchia. Several shields had been discovered bearing the names of kings which began with the letters A M N, but the other characters being unknown, they had not been referred to the Ammenemes whose names recur so often in this dynasty, but to some unknown kings. The monumental evidence indeed seemed to fix them to a later dynasty. Champollion had ascertained the names of several of the kings of the 18th dynasty, beginning with Ahmes or Amosis, whose titular shield is the 40th in the tablet of Abydos[1]. The 17th dynasty consisted of Shepherd kings, who could not be expected to be recorded on an Egyptian monument. The five which preceded Ahmes, it was natural therefore to conclude, must represent the five kings of the 16th dynasty, who were Thebans according to Eusebius. On the obelisks of Heliopolis and the Fyoum, the latter of which bore marks of antique workmanship in the bluntness of the pyramidion

---

[1] Birch, Gall. Brit. Mus. pl. 29.

and the unusual proportions of the height and breadth[1], a name had been read Osortasen, which from the titular shield connected with it, appeared to belong to a sovereign whose name stood first in a succession of four in one of the grottos of Beni-hassan, and the third and fourth of these were the same as the 35th and 36th of the tablet of Abydos. The names corresponding to the 37th, 38th and 39th shields were afterwards discovered, and found to be another Osortasen and two beginning with the letters A M N, followed by the same unknown characters—evidently therefore belonging to one royal family.

Major Felix, to whom, in conjunction with Lord Prudhoe, the discovery of this succession is due, conjectured that these kings were really those of Manetho's 12th dynasty, whose names ought to have been given as those of the 17th, and made the immediate predecessors of Amosis, founder of the 18th. Sir Gardner Wilkinson considered the dynasties between the 13th and 18th to have been interpolated or contemporary in Lower Egypt. Dr. Hincks, in the Transactions of the Royal Irish Academy[3], had also advanced the opinion, that the five names on the tablet of Abydos, which precede the 18th dynasty, constituted the 12th dynasty of Manetho, and that the five dynasties between the 12th and the 18th were either contemporaneous or imaginary. The names, read as they were by the authors of these suppositions, Osortasen and Ammoneith-Thote or Amun-m-gori,

---

[1] Bonomi, in Trans. Roy. Soc. Lit. 8vo, 1, 169.
[2] Manners and Customs, 1, 36.
[3] Vol. 19, P. 2, p. 68.

did not however answer to the names of Manetho. Lepsius had been led, by the circumstance that some of the work of the so-called Osortasen at Thebes had been surrounded by a construction of the kings of the 18th dynasty[1], to conclude that a considerable period must have intervened between this dynasty and that to which he belonged, and one of desolation for Egypt; that consequently he could not have been of the 17th dynasty, but probably lived before the invasion of the Shepherds. The letters of uncertain sound in the shields of the three kings he read *het*, and the whole name becoming thus *Amun-em-het*, there could be little difficulty in identifying it with the Ammenemes of Manetho. The authority for reading the first letter in the shield of Osortasen *O* was very slight; Lepsius considered it as an *S*, and made the name Sesortasen. Thus he had obtained an ascending series, going backward from Amosis[2]; Ammenemes (IV.), Ammenemes (III.), Sesortasen (III.), Sesortasen (II.), Ammenemes (II.), Sesortasen (I.), Ammenemes (I.), and the first five of these corresponded to the five shields (39–35) on the tablet of Abydos, which preceded that of Amosis. It seemed, therefore, impossible to avoid the conclusion, that the tablet of Abydos passed over all the dynasties intermediate between the 12th and the 18th, and connected these immediately with each other. Into the reason for this omission we shall have to inquire hereafter; at present it is sufficient to say, that the coincidences between the names of the shields and those of Manetho's lists are such, that we must re-

---

[1] See vol. i. p. 174.   [2] Bunsen, B. 2, p. 287, Germ.

THE TWELFTH DYNASTY. 161

nounce all attempt at identification if we do not admit them to be the same.

As the lists now stand, however, the coincidence, though striking, is not complete. We have three Ammenemes, but instead of Sesortasen we have Sesonchosis and Sesostris. The latter name does not differ so widely from Sesortasen, but that they may well have been the same, allowance being made for the change which an Egyptian name would undergo, in being adapted to Greek pronunciation. In this case, as the name had become very celebrated among the Greeks, the change to which it had been subjected would be greater than ordinary, and Manetho, who wrote for the Greeks, might adopt the form in which they would recognise the well-known conqueror. The change of Sesonchosis into Sesortosis would, perhaps, be improbable if it stood alone, but ceases to be so amidst so many coincidences. The descending series thus becomes—

1. Ammenemes I. ... Last of the 11th dynasty.
2. Sesortosis I. .... The Sesonchosis or Gesongosis of the MSS.[1]
3. Ammenemes II... Second of the 12th dynasty.
4. { Sesostris or Sesortosis } II..Third of the same dynasty.

Here we find again a variance between the monuments and Manetho; for while they furnish a third Ammenemes, his text reads Lachares or Lamares, who is followed by Ameres. To this Lamares[2], called *Labaris* by Eusebius[3], the building of the

[1] ΓΕΣΟΝΓΟΣΙΣ, the reading of one MS., does not differ very widely from ΣΕΣΟΡΤΟΣΙΣ. See Bunsen, Urk. p. 22, Germ.
[2] The titular shield of Ammenemes III. has been read Ra-n-mat, and it has been supposed that this gave rise to the name Lameres, R and L being interchangeable, but there is no clear example of the titular name finding its way into the lists.
[3] Chron. Can. p. 15, ed. Scalig.

Labyrinth in the Arsinoite nome is attributed, but the unquestionable evidence of the Labyrinth itself declares that Ammenemes was its founder. In Eratosthenes we have Mares or Maris, as the thirty-fifth king, in a position answering generally to the Lamares of Manetho; and according to Diodorus[1], Marus was the name which some assigned to the builder of the Labyrinth. All these names, Marus, Maris, Ammeres, appear to owe their origin to an attempt to connect the foundation of the Labyrinth with the creation of the Lake Mœris. In the form Labaris preserved by Eusebius, and assigned as the founder of the Labyrinth, we have apparently the origin of Lamares, Lamparis, Lachares, and an evident attempt to etymologize the Greek name. The *Imandes* or *Maindes* of Strabo[2] on the contrary appears to be a corruption of Ammenemes, and so also the Mendes of Diodorus (*u. s.*). Dismissing Lamares and Ammeres, we may substitute in their place the two Ammenemes of the monuments. Three reigns, all of eight years, succeeding each other, are certainly not very probable.

Continuing our list, therefore, we have after Sesostris—

    5. Ammenemes III. substituted for Labaris and Ameres;
    6. Ammenemes IV., the Ammenemes of Manetho's list.

This arrangement is conformable to the Turin papyrus, in which we have in succession the titular shields, which are ascertained to belong to Ammenemes I., Sesortasen I., Ammenemes II., Sesortasen II., Sesortasen III., Ammenemes III., Ammenemes IV.[3]

[1] 1, 61.
[2] 17, 811. Epit. p. 1312, Almel.
[3] Bunsen, 2, 299. Lesueur, 316, 317, who give the lengths of the reigns.

According to Manetho, Ammenemes (IV.) was succeeded by his sister Scemiophris, reigning four years. No such person has been discovered in the monuments; but a king, whose name is read Sebeknofre, is found in the Turin papyrus after Ammenemes IV., and on the Karnak Tablet, to whom a reign of 3 years 10 months 24 days is assigned, and it is a probable conjecture of Lepsius that the queen Scemiophris is no other than this king, supposed to be a female from the apparently feminine termination. A third Sesortasen appears in the monuments, who is not mentioned by Manetho. He succeeded the second Sesortasen. Ammenemes, the father of Sesonchosis (Sesortosis I.), was probably the same as the Ammenemes who closes the eleventh dynasty. His name is found in the grottoes of Benihassan, and on two tablets of the Louvre it is conjoined with that of Sesortasen I.[1], whence their joint reign has been inferred. From the investigations of Lepsius and Bunsen it also appears that after the death of Ammenemes I., Sesortasen I. reigned alone for several years, and that in the latter part of his life Ammenemes II. was associated with him in the government[2]. The reign of Sesortasen III. was probably included in that of Sesortasen II., the father having admitted the son to share his power. If the father survived the son, and consequently resumed the sole sovereignty, this would account for the absence of the son's name in Manetho's list.

[1] Rosellini, Mon. Stor. iii. 1, page 46.
[2] Bunsen, B. 2, p. 293. A *stele* in the Museum at Leyden mentions the 43rd year of Sesortasen I. as being also the 2nd of Ammenemes II.

Of Ammenemes, whom, according to this arrangement, we are to call the Second, it is only recorded that he was assassinated by his own officers of the bed-chamber[1].

Sesostris succeeded to Ammenemes II. The resemblance of the names of several Egyptian sovereigns, and the more remarkable coincidence, that three of these appear to have been conquerors, have produced a confusion in the history of Sesostris, which till lately it was impossible to clear up. Four kings of very distant ages,—*Sesochris*, the eighth of the second dynasty; *Sesostris*, the third of the twelfth; *Sethos-Sesoosis-Rameses*, of the nineteenth; *Sesonchis*, of the twenty-second, have all partially contributed to the history of one king, who has been variously placed, according to different hypotheses. The gigantic stature which Herodotus assigns to Sesostris[2] is the historical attribute of Sesochris, who was five cubits and four palms in height[3]. The erection of monuments recording his own victories beyond the limits of Egypt[4] belongs, as far as we know, only to Sesoosis-Rameses, of whom monumental tablets have been found at Nahr-el-Kelb, on the Syrian coast. The erection of two obelisks at Heliopolis[5] again belongs

---

[1] I take the word εὐνοῦχοι in its etymological sense. We have I think no evidence of the prevalence in Ancient Egypt of the practice which prevailed in Assyria and is now common throughout Egypt and Western Asia. That its introduction was attributed to Semiramis is a presumption that it was not an Egyptian custom (Her. 3, 92. Ammian. Marcell. 14, 6. Claud. Entrop. 1, 339). Pliny's Nectabis (36, 13, 2) lived after the Persian conquest. The use of סָרִיס (Gen. xxxvii. 36) is no proof of the custom, the name being used for a great officer, as 1 Sam. viii. 15. Rosellini (M. Civ. iii. 2, 137) thinks that real *evirati* appear in the monuments.

[2] 2, 106. Diod. 1, 55.
[3] See page 124 of this volume.
[4] Herod. 2, 102. Diod. 1, 55.
[5] Diod. 1, 59.

to Manetho's Sesostris, the Sesortasen II. of the monuments, the Sesoosis II. of Diodorus, since the name of this sovereign appears on that which still remains, and they were usually placed in pairs. Another form under which the name of this sovereign and warrior has come down to us, is Sesonchosis, as it stands first in the twelfth dynasty. Had it occurred only there, we might have acquiesced in the correction of *Sesortosis* before mentioned. But the Scholiast on Apollonius Rhodius (4, 272) says that " Sesonchosis, king of all Egypt after Orus, son of Isis and Osiris, conquered all Asia and the greater part of Europe;" adding that Herodotus calls him Sesostris. It is not probable that the same corruption of Sesortosis into Sesonchosis should have taken place here, and therefore we are compelled to believe that this passage exhibits a further confusion of Sheshonk or Sesonchis, the Shishak of Scripture, with Sesostris. Sesonchis was really a great foreign conqueror, and inscribed the palace of Karnak with the representations of numerous sovereigns whom he had led captive. To this Sesonchosis, Dicæarchus, whom the Scholiast appears to follow, ascribes the institution of castes, and of the use of horses for riding—a fresh illustration of the propensity to refer the origin of customs lost in immemorial antiquity to some eminent name. How little chronology was regarded in these matters is evident from the circumstance, that Dicæarchus makes this Sesonchosis to be the successor of Orus, the last of the gods, confounding him with the Menes of the common story. It would be lost labour to endeavour to reconcile such contradictions, and build them up into a chronological system.

The account which is given by Africanus of the conquests of Sesostris may seem to leave no doubt that he is really the hero of the Grecian story. We have already seen, however, that Africanus interposes remarks of his own among the names of the Manethonian lists; and what is said of Sesostris has such a close verbal resemblance to Diodorus, that as Africanus does not appear ever to have seen the work of Manetho, it is probable that he has copied this notice from Diodorus[1].

Since, therefore, the traditions of the Greeks respecting Sesostris either belong to the historical Rameses, or are wholly vague, we cannot venture to attribute to the Sesortasens of the monuments anything which is recorded of Sesostris[2]. The monuments themselves, however, attest the power of the twelfth dynasty. Rosellini dug up near the Second Cataract a *stele*, now preserved in the Florentine Museum[3]; it stood in an edifice raised by Rameses I., on the spot where Sesortasen I. had placed a memorial of his own victories. He is represented upon it standing in the presence of a hawk-headed deity, named Mandoo, who holds in his band a cord to

---

[1] The error with regard to the significance of the emblems which he is said to have inscribed on his *stelæ* is much more likely to have originated with the Greeks or their half-learned interpreters than with a high priest. Such emblems do occur among the hieroglyphics, but in a widely different sense from that attributed to them by Herodotus and Diodorus.

[2] Bunsen (B. 2, p. 309, Germ.) considers Sesortasen II. as the great Sesostris, and supposes him to have conquered Ethiopia as far as the shores of the Red Sea, and crossed into Arabia, and thence to the continent of Asia (Strabo, 16, p. 769).

[3] Mon. Stor. iii. 1, p. 38. Mon. Reali, tav. xxv. 4.

THE TWELFTH DYNASTY.

which are attached shields whose edge represents the battlements of a town, and which are surmounted by the upper half of the human figure, with the hands bound behind. This is the way in which, on the monuments of Egyptian conquerors, their vanquished enemies are usually exhibited[1]. The nations thus led captive appear from the absence of beard to be African, though they exhibit nothing of the negro physiognomy. Five are still extant on the monument, and when perfect it must have exhibited several others. The inscription on the base has not been fully made out, but it appears to record a sacrifice or offering to Mnevis, the white bull of Heliopolis. At Thebes Rosellini found a fragment of a statue of Sesortasen I., which from the manner of its insertion among later construetions, appeared to have been preserved as a relic of some building raised by him, and afterwards destroyed in the devastations of the Shepherds. The tombs of Benihassan are memorials of this dynasty, and in one of them, where a chief of the name of Ammenemes was buried, is an inscription to this king, who is there called " ruler of Upper and Lower Egypt[2]." The obelisk of Heliopolis gives him the same title, along with others of a more mystical kind, but records no historical fact. That of the Fyoum is equally destitute of information, but adds the title " beloved by Ptah." Several funeral tablets have been found in the neighbourhood of Memphis and of Abydos, dedicated to persons who

---

[1] Rosellini reads the names *Kas* or *Kos* (which may be the Cush of Scripture), *Shiameik*, *Soa* and *Shiat*, with two not perfectly legible.

[2] Rosellini, M. Stor. iii. 1, 30.

held office under him; they bear various dates, from the ninth year of his reign to the forty-fourth[1]. Manetho assigns forty-six as the duration of the reign of his Sesonchosis, whom we have supposed to represent Sesortosis I. The occurrence of his name at the copper-mines in the peninsula of Sinai[2] shows that this region still remained in the possession of Egypt.

There is in the grottoes of Benihassan a remarkable picture of the age of Sesortasen II. or Sesostris[3]. The name of the occupant of the tomb has been read Nevopth; and his son, who like the father was of the military caste, is represented as standing to receive a procession of foreigners. They are preceded by a royal scribe, who holds out a scroll, on which is written the sixth year of Sesortasen II., and it is declared that the strangers having been vanquished, they are brought hither to the number of thirty-seven. Such at least appears to be the general sense of the inscription, but the interpretation of the characters is by no means certain. Instead of thirty-seven, only twelve adults and three children actually appear in the procession, and none of them are bound. To the royal scribe another Egyptian succeeds, and is followed by the king of the strangers, who leads an ibex by the horn and bows reverentially. He is uncovered, and wears a tunic of bright colours and an elaborate pattern; in his hand he carries a curved staff not unlike that which is seen in the hand of Osiris. Another stranger follows, of

---

[1] Rosellini, M. Stor. iii. 1, 37.
[2] Wilkinson, Mod. Eg. and Thebes, 2, 406.
[3] See vol. 1, pp. 48, 49. Rosellini, M. Stor. iii. 1, 48. M. R. Tav. xxvi.-xxviii.

humbler rank, leading an ibex. Four men, armed with a kind of club or bow and spear, precede an ass, carrying two children in a pannier, along with an instrument whose use it is not easy to define, but which appears to represent some kind of shield. A boy on foot armed with a lance is followed by four females, and these by another ass with panniers. The whole procession is closed by two men, one of whom carries a lyre and a plectrum, the other a bow and a club. The inscription contains apparently the name of the strangers, but it has not been satisfactorily made out. Their lighter colour and their aquiline noses show that they are neither Egyptians nor natives of a more southern country than Egypt. As they bring no gift but the ibex, it is probable they belong to a pastoral tribe[1], Arabian or Palestinian. They have been thought to represent the migration of Jacob and his family, and certainly the bringing of children in panniers looks like the removal of a family, unless we suppose them to be hostages. But the figure of a prisoner is inconsistent with this idea; and the most probable supposition is, that the picture represents the bringing of tribute, by one of the nations bordering on the Asiatic frontier of Egypt, whom Sesortasen had reduced[2]. Champollion believed them to be Greeks, induced partly by their garments, on which is seen the pattern which we call Greek, and find on the old fictile vases. But nothing else recommends this conjecture, and when we consider the close connexion of Greek with

---

[1] Compare Isaiah lx. 7. "The rams of Nebaioth shall minister unto thee."

[2] Mr. Osburn (Egypt and her Testimony to the Truth of the Bible, pp. 38, 39) reads the name *Jebusites*.

Phœnician art, such a coincidence will not appear surprising.

These grottoes of Benihassan are the best record of the state of manners and art in the flourishing period of the 12th dynasty, when the prosperity of Egypt was about to receive a check by the invasion of the Shepherds. We have already described the architecture of this age, so closely resembling the Doric[1]. The pictures of Egyptian life testify to a state of civilization, in which both the elegant and the useful arts had been carried to a high degree of perfection. It may appear singular that as this dynasty as well as the preceding is called Diospolitan, scarcely any trace of them should be found at Thebes. The fragment of the statue of Sesortasen which has been preserved, however, shows that it was adorned by them.

Whether Sesortasen were the first who made conquests in Nubia depends on the place which we allot to the kings who bear the names of Sebekatep, or Sebekotph, and Nefruatep[2], and are found in the Tablet of Karnak and the Turin Papyrus. If they belong to the eleventh dynasty, which was Theban, Nubian conquest would seem to have begun with them, as the name of Sebekatep occurs at Semne, in the inscriptions which Lepsius supposes to record the rise of the Nile, along with that of Ammenemes[3]. Their place however is doubtful, and they have been reckoned with the kings of the Middle Monarchy[4]. Three kings of the name of Nantef have also been

---

[1] Vol. i. p. 254.
[2] Five Sebekateps and two Nefruateps may be distinguished in the monuments.
[3] Boeckh, Manetho und die Hundssternperiode, p. 627, note[2].
[4] Bunsen, Ægyptens Stelle, Mittleres Reich, pl. iv.

found, who from their place in the Tablet of Karnak[1] and from their sepulture at Qoorneh appear to have belonged to a Theban dynasty, probably the 11th. Sesortasen I. certainly carried his arms into Nubia; under the 18th dynasty, when the monarchy revived in greater splendour than ever, it seems to have been completely incorporated with Egypt, and the banks of the Nile were covered with temples in which their titles are recorded. These facts conclude very strongly against the opinion that civilization descended, either with conquest or the gradual spread of population, along the Nile from Meroe and Nubia to Egypt. It has been supported by the claims of the Theban priests which Diodorus admitted, by the unfounded opinion of the superior antiquity of the remains of Meroe, and perhaps by the fame of the poetical Ethiopians; but is contradicted by the monuments, which show us that Lower and Middle Egypt were the seats of powerful governments before Thebes had attained to any renown, and that Nubia had no civilization before her conquest by Egypt, which began with the 11th or 12th dynasty.

The age of the Labyrinth and the name of the sovereign by whom it was built have been most variously stated by the ancient writers, and nothing but the evidence of the ruins themselves has enabled us to assign with certainty Ammenemes as its founder. Herodotus, we have seen, attributes the building to the twelve kings or chiefs who composed the Dodecarchia; not only making no mention of

---

[1] See Hierogl. of the Egyptian Society, pl. 96. Birch in Gliddon's Egyptian Archæology, p. 80.

any other, but expressly calling them "the original founders[1]." This is in itself very improbable, if we consider how vast was the work, surpassing, as Herodotus says, not only all the works of Grecian architecture, but the Pyramids themselves. It is also in the highest degree improbable that, though after the Egyptian fashion each of these chiefs may have prepared a tomb for himself during his lifetime, they should have been deposited there after Psammitichus had dethroned them. Probably the circumstance that the number of the principal halls was twelve, led to their erection being attributed to these twelve kings. Diodorus gives a different account. He describes, as Herodotus does, the twelve kings as designing to leave a common memorial of themselves in the place which they prepared with all imaginable art for this purpose; and he fixes very precisely on the spot on which the Labyrinth actually stood—the entrance of the Canal into the Lake of Mœris[2]; but he does not call it the Labyrinth. On the contrary, he says[3], that the Labyrinth was built by a much earlier king, who lived long before the building of the Pyramids, by some called Mendes, by others Marrus. Even here, however, we may trace some analogy to the account of Herodotus; Mendes or Marrus was made king immediately after the termination of the Ethiopian invasion under Actisanes; and in Herodotus, the retreat of the Ethiopians is followed by an inter-

---

[1] 2, 148. Φάμενοι θήκας αὐτόθι εἶναι τῶν τε ἀρχὴν τὸν λαβύρινθον τοῦτον οἰκοδομησαμένων βασιλέων καὶ τῶν ἱερῶν κροκοδείλων. These kings can be no other than those whom he has before mentioned— the Dodecarchs, who he says determined to leave the Labyrinth as a memorial of themselves.

[2] 1, 66.

[3] 1, 61.

regnum of the priest Sethos, and then by the builders of the Labyrinth.

Strabo describes the Labyrinth as standing upon a *plateau*, about thirty or forty stadia from the entrance of the canal, and as consisting of the same number of palaces as the nomes of Egypt formerly amounted to[1]. What this number was he does not specify, but from Herodotus and Pomponius Mela we learn that it was twelve[2]. The establishment of an oligarchy of twelve, during the temporary suspension of monarchy, points to such a territorial division previously existing, and probably corresponding to that of the temples of the gods of the second order. One stadium from the Labyrinth stood a pyramid, 400 feet square at the base and of equal altitude, in which, says Strabo, a king named Imandes (Maindes) lies buried. This is the pyramid of Howara, which stands on a desert plain between the Bahr Jusuf and the ravine called Bahr-be-la-ma, which runs down to the north-eastern end of the Lake of Kerun. Its present height is about 106 feet, and its base 300[3]. It is constructed of crude bricks, mixed with straw, and has been originally cased with stone. The sepulchral chamber has been explored by Lepsius, and the discovery of the name of Ammenemes III. has removed all doubt respecting the time and purpose of its erection. He is the same sovereign whose shield occurs everywhere in the ruins of the Labyrinth.

These varying accounts may be partly reconciled by the observation that the pyramid and the laby-

---

[1] B. 16, p. 787, 811.
[2] Psammetichi opus Labyrinthus domos *ter* mille et regias duodecim amplexus. (Pomp. Mela, 1, 9, 65.)
[3] Perring on the Pyr. 3, 83.

rinth are sometimes spoken of as having a common destination, and sometimes discriminated. Strabo discriminates them; the labyrinth was according to him a collection of palaces[1], the pyramid a place of sepulture. Herodotus, on the authority of the inhabitants, speaks of the kings and sacred crocodiles as being interred in the subterranean chambers of the labyrinth; Manetho (or Africanus) says Lamares built *the Labyrinth* as a sepulchre for himself; and Pliny, following Lyceas, calls it the sepulchre of Mœris. It appears quite contrary to Egyptian usages that the same building should be used as a palace and a cemetery. Notwithstanding therefore the tradition of the neighbourhood recorded by Herodotus, the fact of the Labyrinth being at all a place of royal sepulture is questionable. It is however not unlikely that the embalmed crocodiles may have been deposited in the vaults. The name *Petesuchis*, which Pliny gives to the king who founded the Labyrinth 4600 years before his time[2], evidently alludes to this destination of the building; for Suchos was the tame crocodile of the Arsinoite nome, and *Pet* or *Pet-n* occurs frequently in similar combinations[3]. It is not probable that the Labyrinth was all built by a single sovereign; Diodorus[4] speaks of its being left unfinished by its founders, and we have seen reason to conclude that the Pyramids, though attributed by the ancients to a single reign, were not begun and concluded by the same person[5].

---

[1] The Memnoneion of Abydos, which was a palace, was (Strabo, 17, 813) a building in the style of the Labyrinth, only less complex.
[2] Cod. Bamb. Plin. 36, 19 (13).
[3] See vol. i. p. 385, note '.
[4] 1, 66.
[5] No name except that of Ammenemes III. appears to have been discovered by the Prussian Expedition, but only the foundations are left.

The name *Labyrinth* appears to be of Greek origin, and we do not know what word corresponded to it in the ancient Egyptian. It originally denoted a complicated system of passages and galleries[1], such as are found in mines, catacombs and internal quarries. As they were usually of unknown age, mythical personages were assigned as their authors. Those at Nauplia were attributed to the Cyclops[2], that at Cnossus to Dædalus. The last-mentioned is usually supposed to have been a building, like the Egyptian; but no one speaks, as an eye-witness of it; and the story probably originated from the existence of a real labyrinth, excavated in times of unknown antiquity at Gortys in Crete[3]. The idea of perplexity which we associate with the name, and which the mythe represents as the designed end of the construction, was the necessary consequence, in the one case of the multitude of intersecting passages, in the other of the endless succession of apartments, repeating each other. Herodotus describes the Labyrinth of Egypt as the palace of Versailles might be described by one who had been led through it by a guide, and had been at once astonished and bewildered by what he had seen. We can distinguish, however, in his description, *hypostyle halls*, which were roofed by single blocks of stone[4], filling the whole space of the intercolumniations, *closed apartments* adjoining to these, and *porticoes* leading to other roofed apart-

---

[1] Such a gallery was called by the Greeks Λαύρα, from which, pronounced ΛάϜρα, Λάβρα, λαβύρινθος would be formed by a regular analogy. (Wordsworth, Athens and Attica, p. 209. Hoeckh's Creta, vol. 1, p. 62.)
[2] Strabo, 8, p. 369.
[3] Walpole's Travels, 2, 402.
[4] Strabo, p. 811.

ments. The multitude and similarity of these buildings might well make it impracticable for a stranger to find his way through them, especially as the majority of them had no light[1]. Herodotus says they were in all 3000, 1500 above ground and an equal number below. The exactness of this statement rests of course on the fidelity of his guides, who delight in large and round numbers, which are rendered more doubtful by the circumstance that the building was only one story high above the ground. The ruins, which have been explored by the Prussian Expedition, show that the whole was a rectangle of 800 feet by 500. Pliny speaks of this as well as the other Labyrinths as being arched, *fornicibus tecti*; but there is no trace of the use of the arch here or in any other building of this age. It appears to have been chiefly built of a hard white limestone, which has been mistaken for Parian marble[2]; but the fragments of granite which lie scattered about show that this more costly material had also been used for columns, shrines and statues. The white limestone was probably brought from the Gebel-el-Mokattam, where an inscription records the working of a quarry of hard white stone, in the reign of a sovereign of the name of Ammenemes, whose precise place in the series cannot be ascertained, as his distinctive title does not accompany his phonetic name[3].

---

[1] Pliny, N. H. 36, 19 (13). Majore in parte transitus est per tenebras.

[2] Plin. 36, 19, (13) 2. Ægyptius labyrinthus (quod miror equidem) introitu lapide e Pario, columnis reliquis e Syenite, molibus compositis, quas dissolvere ne sæcula quidem possint.

[3] The cornice of the *stele* bears the date "43rd year," and the builder of the Labyrinth reigned only twelve. But this date is no part of the inscription, nor does it express the reign of Ammenemes. (Birch in Vyse, Pyramids, 3, 94. Tourah Quarries, Tablet No. 1.)

THE TWELFTH DYNASTY.

Manetho, according to Africanus, reckoned 2300 years from Menes to Ammenemes I. (see p. 153). If to this we add 160 years for the 12th dynasty, we have 2460 years for the duration of the Old Monarchy. That there is some great error of excess in these numbers cannot be doubted, but they can be corrected only by unauthorized conjecture. Bunsen, taking Eratosthenes for his standard, reduces the Old Monarchy to 1076 years. The question can be settled in no other way than by the discovery of some evidence to show whether any and which of the dynasties of Manetho were contemporaneous.

BOOK II.

THE MIDDLE MONARCHY.

Thirteenth Dynasty.

	Years.
SIXTY DIOSPOLITAN KINGS, who reigned	453

Fourteenth Dynasty.

SEVENTY-SIX XOITE KINGS, who reigned 184

Fifteenth Dynasty.—Of Shepherds.

SIX FOREIGN PHŒNICIAN KINGS, who also took Memphis. They likewise founded a city in the Sethroite nome, advancing from which they reduced the Egyptians into subjection. The first of these who reigned was SAITES 19
From him the Saitic nome was called.
2. BNON 44
3. PACHNAN 61
4. STAAN 50
5. ARCHLES 49
6. APHOBIS 61
                                                        ———
                                                        284

Sixteenth Dynasty.

THIRTY OTHER SHEPHERD KINGS, reigned 518

Seventeenth Dynasty.

FORTY-THREE OTHER SHEPHERD KINGS, AND FORTY-THREE THEBAN DIOSPOLITES. Together the Shepherds and Thebans reigned. 151

BK. II.] THIRTEENTH TO SEVENTEENTH DYNASTY. 179

Eusebius gives these dynasties with very important variations.

Thirteenth Dynasty.

Years.
SIXTY DIOSPOLITAN KINGS, reigned 453

Fourteenth Dynasty.

SEVENTY-SIX XOITE KINGS, reigned 184
[484 in another copy.]
Arm. 434.

Fifteenth Dynasty.

DIOSPOLITAN KINGS, reigned 250

Sixteenth Dynasty.

FIVE THEBAN KINGS, reigned 190

Seventeenth Dynasty.

(FOUR) FOREIGN PHŒNICIAN SHEPHERD KINGS[1] (brothers), who also took Memphis.
First, SAITES reigned 19
   From him the nome Saites was called. They founded a city in the Sethroite nome, advancing from which they subdued Egypt.
2. BNON 40
3. APHOPHIS 14
4. After him ARCHLES 30
                                                                              103

No name is preserved by Africanus or Syncellus from the thirteenth and fourteenth dynasty; consequently we are deprived of the means of comparing them with the monuments. Xois was a town

---

[1] For Ποιμένες ἦσαν ἀδελφοὶ Φοίνικες we should probably read HΣAN Δ̄ (four) ΦΟΙΝΙΚΕΣ. Syncellus complains of the arbitrary manner in which Eusebius had transposed the 15th dynasty into the 17th; his motive was to adapt the Egyptian to the assumed Biblical chronology. (P. 62, 115 Dind.)

of considerable size in Lower Egypt, lying near the centre of the Delta, in an island formed by the Sebennytic and Phatnitic branches of the Nile[1].

The establishment of the Shepherd Kings at Memphis, which is so briefly noticed in the extracts by Africanus, is fortunately related at great length by Josephus in a passage quoted by him from Manetho. Apion the Grammarian, one of those vain pedants whom the school of Alexandria produced in such abundance[2], had attacked the Jews, who were very odious to the Egyptians, and especially to the Alexandrians, in a work on the Jewish history, in which he gave a very reproachful account of the origin of their nation. To this work Josephus replied. In a remarkable Introduction he shows how late was the origin of Greek letters and history, compared with the Egyptian, Babylonian and Phoenician, and opposes to the unfavourable accounts of the Græco-Egyptian Apion, what he considers to be the honourable testimony to the Jewish people, which Manetho had delivered from the Egyptian records. Having described Manetho as a man well skilled in Grecian learning, and who had derived his materials, according to his own declaration, from the sacred records of his country, he thus proceeds with his quotation from the second book of his 'Egyptiaca' (Cont. Apion. 1, 14) :—

---

[1] Champollion, Égypte sous les Pharaons, 2, p. 214, thinks its site was at Sakha, which is the Arabic equivalent of the Coptic *Xeos* and the old Egyptian *Skhoou*. The road from Rosetta to Cairo across the Delta passes through it. (Steph. Byz. *s. v.* Strabo, 17, p. 802.)

[2] "Apion Grammaticus, quem Tiberius Cæsar *cymbalum mundi* vocabat, quum publicæ famæ tympanum potius videri posset, immortalitate donari a se scripsit, ad quos aliqua componebat." (Plin. Præf. H. N.)

" We had once a king called Timæos, under whom, from some cause unknown to me, the Deity was unfavourable to us, and there came unexpectedly from the eastern parts a race of men of obscure extraction, who confidently invaded the country and easily got possession of it by force, without a battle. Having subdued those who commanded in it, they proceeded savagely to burn the cities, and razed the temples of the gods, inhumanly treating all the natives, murdering some of them and carrying the wives and children of others into slavery. In the end they also established one of themselves as a king whose name was *Salatis*; and he took up his abode in Memphis, exacting tribute from both the Upper and the Lower Country, and leaving garrisons in the most suitable places. He especially strengthened the parts towards the East, foreseeing that on the part of the Assyrians, who were then powerful, there would be a desire to invade their kingdom. Finding, therefore, in the Sethroite[1] nome a city very conveniently placed, lying eastward of the Bubastic river, and called from some old religious doctrine[2] Auaris [or Abaris], he built it up and made it very strong with walls, settling there also a great number of heavy-armed soldiers, to the amount of 240,000 men for a guard. Hither he used to come in the summer season, partly to distribute the rations of corn and pay the troops[3], partly to exercise them carefully by musterings and reviews, in order to inspire fear into

---

[1] Syncellus has preserved the true reading; the MSS. and Schol. Plat. Timæus read *Saite*.

[2] Ἀπό τινος ἀρχαίας θεολογίας.

[3] Σιτομετρῶν καὶ μισθοφορίαν παρεχόμενος.

foreign nations. He died after a reign of 19 years. After him another king called *Bnon* reigned 44 years; after him another, *Apachnas*, 36 years and 7 months; then *Apophis* 61 years, and *Jannas* 50 years and 1 month. Last of all *Asses* 49 years and 2 months. And these six were their first rulers, always carrying on war and desiring rather to extirpate the Egyptians. Their whole nation was called *Hyksos*, that is, Shepherd Kings; for *Hyk* in the sacred language denotes King, and *Sos* is a Shepherd in the common dialect, and hence by composition Hyksos. But in another copy it is said, that not Shepherd Kings but Captive Shepherds are designated by the word Hyk; for that on the contrary, Hyk or Hak with the aspirate distinctly means Captives; and this appears to me more credible, and accordant with ancient history. The before-named kings, he says, and their descendants, were masters of Egypt for 511 years.

"After this he says that a revolt of the kings of the Thebaid and the rest of Egypt took place against the Shepherds, and a great and prolonged war was carried on with them. Under a king whose name was Misphragmuthosis, he says that the Shepherds were expelled by him from the rest of Egypt after a defeat, and shut up in a place having a circuit of 10,000 aruræ. This place was called Auaris. Manetho says that the Shepherds surrounded it entirely with a large and strong wall, in order that they might have a secure deposit for all their possessions and all their plunder. Thuthmosis, the son of Misphragmuthosis, endeavoured to take the place by siege, attacking the walls with 480,000 men. Despairing of taking it by siege, he made a treaty with them that they should leave Egypt and withdraw, without injury, whithersoever they pleased; and in virtue of this agreement they withdrew from Egypt with all their families and possessions to the number of not fewer than 240,000, and traversed the desert into Syria. Fearing the power of the Assyrians, who were at that time masters of Asia, they built a city in that which is now called Judæa, which should suffice for so many myriads of men, and called it Jerusalem.

"And in a certain other book of his Egyptiaca, Manetho says that this nation who are called Shepherds are described as Captives in their sacred books. And he says rightly; for the keeping of sheep was the ancient habit of our forefathers, and they were not unnaturally described as Captives by the Egyptians, since our forefather Joseph declares himself to the king of the Egyptians to be a captive, and afterwards at the command of the king sent for his brethren into Egypt. Into these things, however, I will inquire hereafter more accurately."

This is the account which Josephus gives from Manetho of the invasion, reign and expulsion of the Shepherd kings. If we except some evident exaggerations of numbers, such as the host of 480,000 men besieging a city or fortified camp containing 240,000, there is nothing in it which is not quite credible and natural. The nomadic nations have always envied the wealth and luxury which agriculture, commerce and art have procured for their more civilized neighbours; and when these have been weakened by the neglect of military accomplishments, have found it easy to overturn their power and lay waste their country. Such has in fact been the history of Asia; and had it not been for the valour of Ætius in the plains of Chalons, and Charles Martel at Tours, Europe might have been subject for centuries to the sway of "men of unknown extraction from the East, who razed her cities and destroyed the temples of the gods, and carried her children into captivity." If the Hyksos are, as some accounts represented, Arabs, they belonged to the same race as that to which the Hindu, the Parsee and the Christian have been obliged to yield up their lands and their sanctuaries.

How long the war and consequent devastation of Egypt lasted, before Salatis[1] established himself as king in Memphis, we are not told. Africanus must have included in the nineteen years allotted to Salatis the whole period both of his reign and the conquest, as he reckons nothing for an interregnum, or for that of the last king of the preceding dynasty. It seems to have been the maxim of the Egyptian monarchy, that the sovereign never dies. From Menes to Nectanebus the throne appears in the chronological lists always full. The struggle lasted during the reigns of the six first Shepherd kings, after which the Egyptians appear to have made no further attempts at resistance.

If we are to consider all the dynasties of Manetho as strictly successive, and adopt the largest numbers, 937 years (453+484) must have intervened

---

[1] The name Salatis, preserved by Josephus for *Saites*, is supposed to bear an analogy to the Hebrew שלט. "to rule." It occurs Gen. xlii. 6, but the endeavour on the strength of this coincidence to identify Salatis with Joseph is an example of overstraining evidence.

between the 12th dynasty and the invasion of the Shepherds; and again, 953 years (284+518 +151) from that invasion to their expulsion. There are, however, special reasons in this case for admitting them to have been contemporaneous. Manetho does not speak of one king as being at the head of the Egyptians when the Shepherds invaded them, but of "those who commanded in the country[1]," from which we may infer that the unity of the monarchy was already dissolved. Again, when the Shepherds are expelled, it is said that "the kings from the Thebaid *and the rest of Egypt* rose up against them[2]." It seems probable, therefore, that before or in consequence of the invasion of the Shepherds two separate kingdoms were formed, one at Thebes, the other at Xois, which lasted through the whole of the time that the Shepherds maintained themselves in Egypt. Each of them had peculiar local advantages for the establishment of a kingdom, which the invaders might prefer to leave dependent and tributary, rather than attempt to subdue. The Thebaid was remote from Memphis where they fixed their capital, and by retiring into Ethiopia, as Amenophis is said to have done on occasion of a second inroad, the Egyptian kings could easily place themselves beyond the reach of invaders. Xois, on the other hand, was protected by its position amidst the intersecting branches of the Nile, which probably rendered it

---

[1] Καταθαρσήσαντες ἐπὶ τὴν χώραν ἐστράτευσαν καὶ ῥᾳδίως ἀμαχητὶ ταύτην κατὰ κράτος εἷλον, καὶ τοὺς ἡγεμονεύσαντας ἐν αὐτῇ χειρωσάμενοι κ.τ.λ. (Jos. *u. s.* c. 14.)

[2] Μετὰ ταῦτα τῶν ἐκ τῆς Θη-βαΐδος καὶ τῆς ἄλλης Αἰγύπτου βασιλέων γενέσθαι φησὶν ἐπὶ τοὺς ποιμένας ἐπανάστασιν καὶ πόλεμον αὐτοῖς συρραγῆναι μέγαν καὶ πολυχρόνιον. (Jos. *u. s.*)

inapproachable by land forces. When Sabaco and the Ethiopians invaded Egypt, Anysis took refuge in the marshes, and maintained himself for fifty years in an island which he made habitable by laying down ashes in the muddy soil. When Inarus revolted from the Persians (460 B.C.) they reduced without difficulty the rest of the country, but Amyrtæus kept possession of the marshes for several years, perhaps as many as forty[1].

The Theban dynasty lasted 453 years, the Xoite 484, and these numbers are not very different from the 518 or 511 assigned to the dominion of the Shepherds. Africanus indeed appears to make the 16th dynasty last 518 years, besides the 284 of the 15th; but according to Josephus the six kings of the 15th and *their descendants*[2] reigned 511 years. The 17th dynasty of Shepherds and Theban kings represents the period of the struggle, described by Josephus as great and protracted. It lasted for 150 years.

The motive of the Shepherd kings for establishing their place of arms at Abaris, in the Sethroitic nome, is stated, conjecturally, by Manetho to have been the apprehension of invasion from the Assyrians, then predominant in Asia. Another obvious reason was to maintain a connexion with the countries from which they came, and secure a retreat in the event of the Egyptians recovering their independence. The Sethroitic nome was a Typhonian region, and probably the name itself

---

[1] Herod. 2, 140. 3, 15. Thucyd. 1, 110.

[2] Τούτους δὲ τοὺς προκατωνομασ- μένους βασιλέας, τοὺς τῶν ποιμέ- νων καλουμένων, καὶ τοὺς ἐξ αὐτῶν γενομένους κρατῆσαι τῆς Αἰγύ- πτου φησὶν ἔτη πρὸς τοῖς πεντακο- σίοις ἕνδεκα. (Jos. *u. s.*)

II.] THIRTEENTH TO SEVENTEENTH DYNASTY. 187

was allusive to this divinity[1]. Manetho implies that the name Abaris or Auaris had a similar reference[2], but the Egyptian language affords no clue to such an etymology.

Josephus says that in another *book* of the Egyptiaca, or in another *copy* of the passage which we have already transcribed, Manetho explains the name Hyksos as "captive shepherds," not "shepherd kings." To this etymology also the Egyptian language, as we are acquainted with it, gives no support. Indeed the Jewish historian must have calculated upon very uncritical readers, if he supposed that they would believe the Shepherds and his forefathers to be the same. Except their Palestinian origin, and their retreat into Palestine, everything in their history is different. The children of Israel came on the invitation of Pharaoh, a handful of men, into Egypt, and were placed in the land of Goshen, by his appointment, to tend his cattle. When they subsequently multiplied so as to become an object of alarm to the Egyptians, they were subject to cruel persecution and oppression, to which they made no resistance, and even when they were encouraged by Moses to quit the land of their bondage, they never ventured to fight for their liberties. National vanity has often strangely perverted history, claiming conquests which have

---

[1] "Non spernendam censeo observationem viri doctissimi (Marshami) suspicantis tractum illum qui campos Pelusiacos comprebendit et ad lacum usque Serbonidem extenditur, olim Sethroiten dictum, nomen hoc accepisse a Typhone, quem Egyptios lingua sua cognominasse *Seth* infra monebimus. Addere possum *rubicundum* Egyptiis dici *ros*, ex quo conficitur *Sethros* commodissime significare *Typhonem rufum*." (Jablonsky, P. III. p. 65. Comp. vol. i. p. 440.)

[2] This word has been derived from עבר, and connected with the sojourning of the Hebrews.

never been made; but if the Israelites were really the Hyksos of Manetho, they must have foregone the glory of being the conquerors of Egypt, in order to represent themselves as its bondsmen.

Manetho never represents the Hyksos as the same with the Jews, although Josephus artfully slides in the words " our forefathers " into the account which he gives, apparently on Manetho's authority[1]. It is true, Manetho says that the Hyksos, when they retired by treaty from Egypt, established themselves in Judæa and built Jerusalem. But this rather proves them not to have been the Jews; who, instead of building Jerusalem, did not even possess it till the time of David. At their entrance, under Joshua, into Palestine, it was held by the Jebusites, a Canaanitic tribe[2]. Their king was killed in battle; but his people still held the upper city, the place of strength, while the tribe of Judah and Benjamin dwelt around the base. Manetho, therefore, identifies the Shepherds, not with the Jews, but the Jebusites; and Josephus, who had related the facts which I have just mentioned in his 'Antiquities[3],' cannot have been ignorant of the fallacy of his own argument. Theophilus Antiochenus and Tatian, in the second century[4], when they speak of the expulsion of the Jews from Egypt, follow, not Manetho, but Josephus interpreting Manetho. It appears therefore that the ancient and authentic records of Egypt made

---

[1] He repeats the same unfair substitution in cap. 26, with the additional circumstance that they built the Temple.

[2] Josh. x. 1, 23; xv. 63. Judges, i. 21; 2 Sam. v. 6.

[3] Ant. 5, 2; 7, 3.

[4] See the passages quoted in Bunsen's Urkendenbuch, v. vi.

no mention of the Jews, their coming into Egypt, their settlement in Goshen, their bondage, or their Exodus. But there was a popular and traditionary account of them[1] which Josephus has quoted from Manetho, evidently formed under the influence of those feelings of hatred and contempt of which the Jews were the object on the part of their neighbours. It belongs however to the history of the eighteenth dynasty, where it will be particularly considered.

If we could find in the lists or the monuments, the Timæus under whom, according to Manetho, the invasion of the Shepherds took place, we might connect this event with the previous history of Egypt. No such name however is found. He is called Concharis in the Laterculus of Syncellus, a name equally unknown to the monuments. The last king in the list of Eratosthenes is Amuthartaios, and it is probable that this list, as it begins with Menes, the founder of the old monarchy, ends with the king who was reigning when Salatis established himself at Memphis; but between this name and Timaios there is no resemblance[2]. None of the six names of the Shepherd kings preserved by Manetho has been found on the monuments[3], nor is there any monumental or architectural, or even sepulchral trace of the long period of their occupa-

---

[1] Οὐκ ἐκ τῶν παρ' Αἰγυπτίοις γραμμάτων ἀλλ' ὡς αὐτὸς ὡμολόγηκεν ἐκ τῶν ἀδεσπότως μυθολογουμένων (cap. 16).

[2] Bunsen would correct 'Αμουθαρταῖος in Eratosthenes into 'Αμυντιμαῖος, which he substitutes conjecturally for ἦν βασιλεύς HMIN TIMAIOΣ in the extract from Josephus.

[3] A shield which reads Ases is the 4th in the tablet of Karnak, but from its place cannot be Asses, the Hyksos king of Josephus. See p. 144, 182 of this volume.

tion of Egypt. The 39th shield on the tablet of Abydos is that of Ammemenes IV.; the 40th, Aahmes or Amosis, whom Manetho places at the head of the 18th dynasty. So that the whole interval of the Shepherd dominion appears to be passed over, as one of usurpation.

Of the seventy-six tributary kings of Xois, no monuments remain that can be referred to them on satisfactory evidence; though it is by no means improbable that among the many which have not yet had a place assigned them in the series[1], some may belong to this dynasty. The tributary kings of Thebes, however, during the same interval, have been supposed to have a record in the tablet of Karnak and in the papyrus of Turin[2]. Five, as already mentioned, bore the name of *Sebekatep*, and two of *Nefruatep*. Such repetitions, resembling the Louises, Henries and Georges of modern royal families, appear to have been very common among the Egyptian dynasties. It seems upon the whole probable that the Sebekateps lived in the beginning of the thirteenth dynasty, since a monument dated in the reign of one of them speaks of Ammenemes III. as deceased[3]. The whole number of shields is thirty in the second half of the chamber of Karnak, but several are illegible. As the kings of Thebes in the Hyksos period were more than thirty, some cause, to us unknown, must have led to the selection of these. The fragments of the Turin papyrus

---

[1] A long list of these may be seen in Leemans' Monumens Égyptiens portans des Légendes royales, and subsequent discoveries have much increased their number.

See Barucchi Cronologia Egizia. Turin, 1844.

[2] Lepsius, Denkm. taf. i.

[3] Birch in Gliddon's Otia Egyptiaca, p. 82.

II.]   THIRTEENTH TO SEVENTEENTH DYNASTY.   191

show some of the same names as the chamber of Karnak[1], and when entire, this portion of the manuscript appears to have contained sixty-five shields.

The seventeenth dynasty, as it now stands, is apparently corrupt; at least it is improbable that there should be exactly forty-three kings both of the Shepherds and the Thebans, and that in both lines kings should reign on the average only three and a half years. The error, however, appears to be in these numbers, not in the duration of the dynasty. The kings of Thebes declared themselves independent, and cast off their allegiance as tributaries to the Shepherd kings of Memphis. A long and bloody war, or succession of wars, ensued, for a century and a half, which ended in the Hyksos being driven by Misphragmuthosis into Abaris.

Without the testimony of Manetho, we should have been wholly ignorant of this most important event in the history of Egypt. For neither Herodotus nor Diodorus, nor any of the Greek and Latin historians, give any account of it. This is the more remarkable, as the Egyptians had informed them of their subjugation by the Ethiopians, so that national vanity did not carry them so far as to suppress all facts inconsistent with the immemorial independence of their nation. There is indeed a passage before referred to in Herodotus, in which a trace of the invasion of the Hyksos may be visible, but which could never have been so understood without the explanation which Manetho affords. Speaking of the odium in which the

---

[1] Lepsius, Denkm. taf. iv. v. vi. Bunsen's plate v. The names in the shields, which in the papyrus are written in the *hieratic* character, are here transcribed in the hieroglyphic.

memory of the builders of the pyramids was held, he says[1], "that the people did not much like to name them; but even called them the pyramids of the shepherd Philition or Philitis, who fed his flocks in this region at that time." Since the pyramids have been explored, no doubt can remain that they are the work of native kings, and of a much earlier time; yet it is possible that among the various traditions to which their high antiquity had given birth, one may have connected them with the obscurely remembered invasion of the Hyksos, and that the name Philitis may represent Philistim. The scriptural writers certainly attribute a connexion with Egypt to the Philistines[2], who in Amos ix. 7 are spoken of as an immigrant people, like the Israelites themselves; and the name, though confined in the Bible to a small district, was used for the whole country, which thence derived the name of Palestine. The account given by Apollodorus (2, 1, 3), that Ægyptus, the son of Belus brother of Agenor, king of Phœnicia, came from Arabia and conquered Egypt, unhistorical as it is, may have had its origin in the invasion of the Hyksos, who are called both Phœnicians and Arabians, and who settled in Palestine on their expulsion from Egypt[3]. The connexion of the mythe of Isis, Osiris and Typhon with Phœnicia, of the

---

[1] 2, 128.
[2] Gen. x. 14. The *Casluhim* there mentioned are probably the dwellers about the *Mons Casius*, a part of that Typhonian region which the Hyksos occupied. Λίμνη Σίρβωνις καὶ χώρα περὶ ἥν φασι τὸν Τυφῶνα κεκρύφθαι, πλησίον οὖσαν τοῦ πρὸς τῷ Πηλουσίῳ Κα-σίου ὄρους. (Eust. ad Dion. Perieg. 248. Herod. 3, 5.)

[3] "In Agenoris ex Ægypto in Phœniciam migratione videtur latere opinio de communi nescio qua Phœnicum et Ægyptiorum credita origine." (Heyne ad Apollod. 2, 1, 4. Kenrick, Egypt of Herod. 2, 182.)

Tyrian with the Egyptian Hercules[1], and generally of Phœnician with Egyptian civilization, will be best explained by the supposition that the nomad tribes of Palestine were masters of Egypt for several generations, and subsequently returned to the same country, carrying with them the knowledge of letters and the arts, which they were the instruments of diffusing over Asia Minor and Greece. Phœnicia has evidently been the connecting link between these countries and Egypt, which directly can have exercised only a very slight and transient influence upon them.

The narrative of the invasion, the dominion and the expulsion of the Hyksos contains nothing that is incredible; but the duration which is assigned to their sway is certainly startling, not so much because it requires a great extension of Egyptian chronology, as because we do not find in Egypt the traces which we might naturally expect of a dominion said to have lasted six centuries and a half. There are no marks, at least none that have been ascertained, of the city of Abaris, whose walls included a space more than double that of Rome under Diocletian, and not much inferior to that of London at the present day[2]. Although they occupied a country in which pyramids, obelisks, temples and palaces presented themselves on every side, they seem never to have employed the art of their subjects in raising any corresponding memorial of themselves. An equal degree of inertness must have seized on the Egyptians themselves. Under the 12th dynasty, to

[1] Herod. 2, 44.
[2] Joseph. c. Ap. 1, 14, with Bunsen's note, Urkundenb. p. 44.

judge from the descriptions and remains of the Labyrinth, art and skill must have been at a high point of elevation; under the 18th dynasty they showed themselves in unimpaired perfection; but not a single contemporaneous work of art has been found, from the 13th to the 18th dynasty. These things are not sufficient to make us doubt the fact of the invasion and expulsion of the Hyksos; but they may excite a suspicion that the chronology of this period of oppression and confusion is not to be relied on, and that as usual it has been unduly extended[1].

The occupation of Egypt by the Hyksos appears to have been from first to last military. The fortified camp of Abaris, the possession of Memphis and of various other places throughout Egypt which were garrisoned by them, placed the whole country entirely in their power; but the difference of religion, language and institutions would prevent any amalgamation between them and a people so peculiarly inflexible in all these relations as the Egyptians were. Their monarchs took care to preserve the military discipline, on which the maintenance of their superiority depended: from Memphis, where the seat of their government was established, they visited Abaris every summer, and by military exercises and reviews at once kept up the

---

[1] Bunsen extends the dominion of the Shepherds to 929 years (B. 3, p. 48, Germ.), and supposes the fifty-three kings mentioned by Apollodorus (Sync. p. 147. 279, ed. Dind.) to be the Theban kings contemporary with the Shepherds. Lepsius (Einl. p. 520) supposes that Apollodorus began his second list with Amosis, the head of the 18th dynasty and of the New Monarchy, and ended it with Amasis the contemporary of Cambyses. Here the Laterculus of Syncellus ends, and it comprehends in this interval just fifty-three kings.

spirit of the soldiers and made an imposing display of force in the eyes of the natives and foreigners. During the first six reigns a policy of destruction and extermination was pursued; afterwards it should seem that on payment of tribute, the sovereigns of Thebes and Xois were allowed to exercise the powers of royalty, and the people to pursue their labours in peace.

Probably the condition of Greece under the Turks affords the nearest historical parallel to that of the Egyptians under the Hyksos. In both cases a nomadic and military tribe have established themselves among a sedentary and civilized people, whose energies had been impaired; in both, the repugnance occasioned by difference of blood, language and religion has not only prevented any fusion of the two races, but has preserved the hostile feeling between them in undiminished strength, after the cessation of a state of warfare. The Turks have been said to be only *encamped* in Europe, and this was literally true of the Hyksos in Egypt. The number of 240,000, said to have been collected within the walls of Abaris, probably represents the average amount of the Hyksos population, who living on the tribute paid by the Egyptians, followed no other occupation than that of arms, and came in succession to their fortified camp to undergo their military training. The recovery of their country and their capital by the Greeks seemed at one time imminent; had it taken place, their language and religion would have been reinstated with no change from the long predominance of the Turks; the Mosch of the Sultan would have become again the Church of St. Sophia, and the people have re-appeared, after the oppression of four centuries, identical with the subjects of the Palæologi, but regenerated in spirit by the struggle by which their independence was purchased. In such a case it is conceivable that their tables of royal succession might omit all mention of the Mahmouds, Selims and Mustaphas, and pass from the last Constantine to the first Otho. It is true, the period of Turkish sway is not equal to the shortest time at which the dominion of the Hyksos in Egypt has been reckoned. But no nation has ever equalled the Egyptian in the fixedness of its character and institutions. The relations of the Greeks to their Turkish masters might have continued much longer unchanged, had they both been as completely insulated from all foreign influences and political combinations as the Egyptians were.

On the whole, though it is difficult to realize to ourselves a dominion continuing for six centuries and a half, and then terminating with so few traces as the Hyksos left in Egypt, this difficulty is not sufficient to justify us in rejecting the positive testimony of Manetho to events which he could have no motive to feign. We have indeed his testimony only at the second hand, and that not of a wholly trustworthy witness. But though Josephus has certainly perverted, we cannot believe that he invented, his alleged quotation from Manetho. His learned adversary would have easily detected such a fraud.

The confusion and destruction which attended the conquest of the Hyksos, have rendered the chronology of this period of Egyptian history quite uncertain, beyond the reigns of the six kings of the 15th dynasty. We can place no reliance on the assigned length of periods, which furnish us with neither names, nor facts nor monuments, because we have no control over the fictions or the errors of historians. Until this deficiency is supplied, it must remain a fruitless attempt to carry up a connected chain of authentic chronology, through the Middle Monarchy to the termination, and thence to the commencement of the Old, even if the chronology of the latter were better ascertained than it is.

BOOK III.

THE NEW MONARCHY.

Eighteenth Dynasty, according to Africanus.
(Sync. p. 62–72; 115–136, Dind.)

		Years.
1.	Sixteen Diospolite kings, of whom the first was Amos[1], under whom Moses went out of Egypt, as we shall show.	
2.	CHEBROS, reigned	13
3.	AMENOPHTHIS	24
4.	AMERSIS	22
5.	MISAPHRIS	13
6.	MISPHRAGMUTHOSIS[2]	26
7.	TOUTHMOSIS	9
8.	AMENOPHIS	31
	This is he who is thought to be Memnon and the Speaking Statue.	
9.	HORUS	37
10.	ACHERRES	32
11.	RATHOS	6
12.	CHEBRES	12
13.	ACHERRES	12
14.	ARMESSES	5
15.	RAMESSES	1
16.	AMENOPHATH	19

According to Eusebius :—

Eighteenth Dynasty.

1. Fourteen Diospolite kings, of whom the first, AMOSIS, reigned 25

---

[1] Amos should have headed the list of Africanus with the years of his reign, but in consequence of the incidental mention of his name this seems to have been omitted. Syncellus calls his father, Asseth.

[2] By the general consent of critics, ΜΙΣΦΡΑΓΜΟΥΘΩΣΙΣ has been substituted for ΑΛΙΣΦΡΑΓ-ΜΟΥΘΩΣΙΣ in the text of Josephus from Eusebius and Syncellus.

		Years.
2.	CHEBRON	13
3.	AMENOPHIS	21
4.	MIPHRES	12
5.	MISPHRAGMUTHOSIS	26
6.	TOUTHMOSIS	9
7.	AMENOPHIS	31

     He is thought to be Memnon and the Speaking Statue.

8.	HORUS	36 [38]
9.	ACHENCHERSES	16 [12]

     Under him Moses led the Jews in their Exodus from Egypt.

10.	ACHERRES	8
11.	CHERRES	15
12.	ARMAIS, who is also Danaus	5

     Afterwards being exiled from Egypt, and flying from his brother Ægyptus, he comes into Greece, and having made himself master of Argos, rules the Argives.

13.	RAMESSES, who is also Ægyptus	68
14.	AMENOPHIS	40

From the Tablet of Abydos.

It has been already observed that this monument contains no *names* of kings, except Ramses the Great, only the prenominal or titular shields. The researches of Champollion, however, aided and corrected by those of our countrymen and of Lepsius, have ascertained the corresponding phonetic names, and thus we are enabled to present the following series for comparison with the lists of Manetho and Eusebius :—

      1. AAHMES.
      2. AMENOPH (I.).
      3. THOTHMES (I.).
      4. THOTHMES (II.).
      5. THOTHMES (III.).
      6. AMENOPH (II.).
      7. THOTHMES (IV.).
      8. AMENOPH (III.).

9. HORUS.
10. RAMSES (I.).
11. MENEPHTHAH (I.).
12. RAMSES (II.).
13. RAMSES (III.), in whose reign the tablet of Abydos was erected.

The discrepancies are obvious. The Amosis of the lists is evidently the Aahmes of the tablet and monuments, but Chebros appears neither on the tablet nor elsewhere. Amenoph, the second on the tablet, is the third in the lists; Miphres and Misphragmuthosis are again not found on the tablet. Touthmosis of the lists answers to Thothmes of the tablet; but whereas the tablet gives three in succession of this name, the lists present only one. Amenophis II. is found in both, followed, however, on the tablet by a fourth Thothmes and a third Amenoph. In Horus again they agree; but his successor on the tablet is Ramses, in the lists Achencherses or Acherres.

There can hardly be a question which authority is to be preferred. No better evidence than that of a monument, erected by public authority, can be produced in an historical inquiry. Its testimony is liable to no corruption, such as written documents may undergo, from accident or fraud, nor to the variations which are inevitable in oral tradition. It represents the most authentic knowledge of the age in which it was erected, and must therefore take precedence of every other kind of document. It is true that this age may have falsely believed itself possessed of certain knowledge, and such a belief could acquire no additional authority by being recorded on stone. There is no room here, however, for this distinction. The time of the erection of the monument was not much further removed from the reign of Amosis than the present year from the Restoration, and it is incredible that the Egyptians, so learned in their own history and antiquities, should have been in error in regard to the succession of their sovereigns during this period. That Manetho in the age of the Ptolemies, when the tablet of Abydos was extant in its integrity, with the command of numerous other documents, should commit an error on such a point, is indeed strange, but less incredible than an error in the tablet itself. There is in the Rameseion at Thebes a representation of a procession in which the ancestors of Rameses the Great appear, and their succession from Amenoph I. corresponds with that of the tablet of Abydos[1]. Again, we find in a tomb of Qoorneh a succession of four, from Thothmes III. to Amenophis III., in which there is the same correspondence. A procession at Medinet Aboo, similar to the first-mentioned, begins with Amenophis III. and goes on to Ramses IV. This is beyond the limit of the tablet of Abydos, but as far as they are co-extensive they agree[2].

There are some indications of confusion of names in Manetho's list. If we omit Chebros, a name without analogy among those of this dynasty, Amosis is succeeded by Amenoph, according to the tablet; Misaphris, Mephres (Joseph.) or Miphres (Euseb.) and Misphragmuthosis have the appearance of both originating from a title and a phonetic name, Miphra-Touthmosis, or " Thothmes beloved of

[1] Rosellini, Mon. Stor. 1, p. 204.   [2] Rosellini, ibid.

Phre[1]." These will be the Thothmes I. and II. of the tablet; and the Touthmosis of the lists will correspond with the Thothmes III. of the tablet. Amenophis will then occupy the same position in both. But here again occurs a discrepancy. Amenoph II., the vocal Memnon of the lists, is followed on the tablet by Thothmes IV.; but in the lists by Horus, who in the tablet succeeds Amenophis III. After Horus the diversity becomes still greater. He is followed on the tablet by Ramses I., in the lists by Achencherses or Acherres, and the name of Rameses in the shape of Armesses or Armais only appears after Rathos, Chebres and Acherres.

There is a remarkable variation in the lists themselves. According to Africanus, Amenophis I. is succeeded by Amersis, or, according to one MS. Amensis, who does not appear in Eusebius nor on the tablet. Africanus seemed to have gained confirmation from the discovery of a personage named Amense among the royal monuments of the 18th dynasty, with this peculiarity, that the inscriptions in which this figure appears have the feminine termination, article and pronoun, and the title " Beneficent *Goddess*, *Lady* of the World," while the dress, attributes and insignia are those of a male[2]. Hence Champollion devised the hypothesis that Thothmes I. immediately succeeded to Amenophis I.; that his son Thothmes II. followed

---

[1] Thothmes III. actually bears in the monuments the title of *Mei re*, or with the article *Mei phre*, "beloved of Phre." (See Birch, Brit. Mus. P. 2, p. 80.) Although no indisputable example has been found of a title substituted for a name, *Rameses-Meiamoun* affords one of the title being incorporated with the name.

[2] Rosellini, Mon. Stor. 1, p. 222, 223. Champollion, Lettres d'Égypte, xv.

him and died without issue. His sister Amense succeeded him and reigned twenty-one years; her husband, who was named Thothmes, exercised the rights of sovereignty in her name, and was the father of Thothmes III. Amense survived her husband and married for a second, Amenenthes, who also governed in her name, and was not only regent during the minority of Thothmes III., but exercised sovereignty conjointly with him for several years. The shields which contain the title of this supposed Amenenthes have very generally been defaced, and the legend of the second or third Thothmes substituted for them, on a variety of monuments still existing at Thebes. This Champollion believed to have been the effect of the hatred which Thothmes III. cherished towards his stepfather, by whom he had been oppressed during the years of his minority. The name which he read Amenenhe or Amenenthes, is found, as well as that of Amense, on the obelisk of Karnak, along with his image; and if Rosellini may be believed, it exhibits traits unlike those of the sovereigns of this dynasty, and thus favours the supposition that he was a stranger in blood[1].

This ingenious hypothesis has not stood the test of subsequent research. The name Amenset (for such it is, not Amense) is read by Lepsius *Set amen*; and Amenenthe, *Nemt Amen* (Hatusu). This name has feminine affixes, and therefore appears to represent a female sovereign, or at least regent, having the titles " Daughter of the Sun, Beneficent Goddess, Lady of the Worlds." He thus disposes

---
[1] Rosellini, Mon. Stor. 1, 228.

of the relations of the first sovereigns of the 18th dynasty. Amosis, the founder, was succeeded by his son Amenophis, who had a sister, Set Amen, and a brother, Thothmes I. Thothmes I. had a queen Aahmes, whose relation to the founder of the dynasty is uncertain, and who exercised during his reign the functions of a female regent. This Aahmes is the Amersis or Amensis of the lists, the Amessis described by Josephus as the sister of Amenophis, which would make her to be the daughter of Amosis. Thothmes I. had two sons, who reigned successively under the titles of Thothmes II. and Thothmes III. During the reigns of both Thothmes II. and III., the regency was exercised by their sister Nemt Amen. The succession then proceeds, without any further interruption, from father to son, through Amenophis II., Thothmes IV., Amenophis III. and Horus, who appears to have left no male child, as Acherres or Acencheres, the next in the lists, is said by Josephus to have been his daughter[1]. Such is the combination by which Lepsius and Bunsen have endeavoured to reconcile the monuments with the lists. We may adopt it provisionally, with a caution to the reader how uncertain are all such systems in the present state of Egyptian history, and especially without a full knowledge of the evidence on which it is founded. Any other arrangement must be equally hypothetical.

Manetho, in the extracts of Josephus, makes no mention of AMOSIS as bearing part in the long war which preceded the expulsion of the Hyksos and their blockade in Abaris, under Misphragmu-

[1] Bunsen, Dynasty xviii. pl. vii. Ægypten's Stelle, B. 3, p. 78.

thosis. His monuments, however, bear traces of his being engaged in war. A funeral inscription of one of his naval officers, quoted by Champollion-Figeac[1], relates that he entered into his service while the king was residing at Tanis; that battles were fought upon the water; that a part of the troops were detached to the South; that these operations took place in the sixth year of Amosis, and that in the following year he went to Ethiopia to collect tribute. It is to be regretted that the author has not told us where this monument exists, nor by whom it has been read, and therefore we cannot cite it with perfect confidence. There are, however, unquestionable records of his reign. At Semueh in Nubia there is a tablet on the south front of the western temple, in hieroglyphics of an archaic character, over which a subsequent inscription has been cut. The title of Amosis occurs in it, along with that of Thothmes II, and it appears to commemorate the services of one who had been an officer of Amosis[2]. Two tablets in the Louvre contain similar records, extending through the reigns of Amosis and his successors to Thothmes III. Though their import is obscure, and it is scarcely possible that one individual can be relating his own services and their rewards, through so long a period, there appears to be mention made of prisoners taken in war in the reign of Amosis[3].

[1] L'Univers. Égypte, p. 300.
[2] Young, Hieroglyphics of Egyptian Society, pl. 91. Birch, Trans. of Royty Soe. of Lit. 2nd series, 2, 325.
[3] Mr. Birch, to avoid the difficulty of supposing the same individual to have been sixty-four years in service, would reduce the lengths of these kings' reigns; but neither the lists nor the monuments allow this shortening.

The quarry of Masarah, in the Gebel-el-Mokattam, contains a *stele*, on which is a representation of a block of stone, drawn on a sledge by three pair of oxen[1]. Above is an inscription bearing the title of Amosis, along with his queen Nofre-at-are or Nofre-are, and declaring that in the twenty-second year of his reign, the quarries of hard white stone were worked for the repair of the abode of Ptah, and the abode of Amun in Thebes. Such repairs might be undertaken at any time; but if we suppose that the Hyksos had been recently driven into Lower Egypt, the restoration of the temples of Memphis and Thebes, which had suffered from their ravages, would be one of the first acts which a pious sovereign would undertake. There is another inscription of the same import, and of the same year of the reign of Amosis, but less perfect, in the quarries of the Gebel-el-Mokattam[2].

To Amosis succeeded, according to the tablet of Abydos and the other lists which I have quoted, AMENOPHIS I. He was unquestionably a warlike and victorious sovereign. The monument already quoted speaks of captives made in the land of Kesh and also in the North, among an unknown people called Kebak. If these are an Asiatic nation, we may presume that the frontier land of Lower Egypt towards Palestine had been cleared of the Shepherds, as Amenophis could not otherwise have ventured to march into Asia. His presence also in Ethiopia is recorded in a grotto at Ibrim, near

---

[1] Vyse on the Pyramids, 3, 99. Masarah Quarries, Tablet No. 6.
[2] Howard Vyse, Pyramids, vol. 3, p. 94. Masarah Quarries, Tablet No. 8.

Aboosimbel, where he is represented sitting[1] in the middle of a small temple, attended by an officer of state, who holds over him the feather-fan, and two others, fly-flaps. In the collection of Egyptian antiquities made by Mr. Salt, and since transferred to the Louvre, are found several small tablets, resembling in shape the *stele* of an inscription, on which Amenophis I. is represented, grasping captives by the hair, carrying them with their heads downwards, and preparing to destroy them with the curved battle-axe[2]. Some of these are clad in leopards' skins, and are natives of the South; others, from their ample drapery, plainly belong to colder climates. Conventionally they represent the Ethiopian and the Asiatic people, and we may conclude that Amenophis carried on wars successfully against both. These tablets appear to have been designed to be worn as ornaments on the breast; and it is a reasonable inference that a sovereign who was thus honoured must have acquired the affection of his people by some distinguished service; such as the recovery of the ancient dominion of the Sesortasens and Ammenemes over Ethiopia. On another of these tablets the king appears grasping a lion by the tail, either symbolically, or as a record of his prowess in hunting. One of the wives of Amenophis (Aahmes) is always represented black[3]. She

---

[1] Rosellini, M. R. tav. xxviii. 1. He calls the officers *athlophori*, as if the fans were ensigns of victory; but from the mode of carrying them, they appear evidently to be what Champollion called them, fly-flaps. Were they ensigns of victory, it would be somewhat hasty to infer with Rosellini that "they signify the victory which Amenophis had gained over the Hyksos." (Mon. Stor. iii. 1, 74.)

[2] Rosellini, M. Stor. iii. 1, 107. A similar tablet is in the British Museum, and represents Amenophis in a war-chariot (Birch, Gall. of B. M. P. 2, pl. 30).

[3] Rosellini, M. R. tav. xlv.

appears beside her husband, along with another who is of a fair complexion, on a tablet in the British Museum[1]. It is not indeed absolutely certain that the dark lady was the wife of Amenophis; her name is the same as that of the wife of Amosis, and the title of " royal dame," which she bears, is consistent with her having been the widow of the predecessor of Amenophis. In either case, the renewal of relations between Egypt and Ethiopia is equally evident.

Amenophis I. appears from various monuments to have been the object of a kind of posthumous religious worship, different in its kind from the honours which were sometimes paid to deceased monarchs in Egypt. In one of the little chapels, excavated among the quarries of Silsilis, in the reign of Menephthah, Amenoph I., along with Atmoo and another Egyptian deity, receives an offering of incense from the king, and in the tombs of private individuals at Thebes, similar honours are paid to him on the part of the deceased[2]. One of these tombs is of the age of Menephthah I., and it appears from the inscriptions that a special priesthood was instituted to pay these honours to Amenophis. In another inscription he is joined with Amoure, Phre and Osiris, and receives a libation from the priest Amenemoph. In a singular painting in a Theban tomb[3], he is represented with the attributes of Sokari, a character nearly identical with the infernal Osiris, and therefore is painted

---

[1] Birch, Gall. of Ant. 2, pl. 30. The fair-complexioned wife, whose name was *Aahotph*, is also found with Amenophis in a tomb at Qoorneh (Rosellini, Mon. Stor. 1, 212).

[2] Rosellini, Mon. Stor. iii. 1, 82.

[3] Ibid. iii. 1, 98.

black, and in this character he is found depicted in the interior of coffins[1]. In these posthumous honours his wife Aahmes-Nofreare is frequently joined with him. All these circumstances combined lead us to suppose, that the popular tradition in Egypt connected Amenophis with some great service rendered to his country and its religion. He may be regarded as a second founder of the monarchy, having replaced it in the pre-eminence which it had lost by the invasion of the Hyksos.

We have seen that in the lists Chebros is made the successor of Amosis. It has been supposed that this name is the translation of a titular shield, converted into a substantive person. Rosellini[2] conjectures that it has originated from *Shefre*, the title of Thothmes I.; Bunsen[3] from *Neb-rus-ra*, the title of Amosis; but neither conjecture is satisfactory.

The next in succession on the monuments is THOTHMES I. With him appears to have begun the construction of those splendid edifices at Thebes, which still attest the power and civilization of Egypt under the New Monarchy. We have seen that some trifling remains are found there of the works of Sesortasen, who lived near the end of the Old Monarchy; but the great monuments of Luxor, Karnak and Medinet Aboo date from the 18th dynasty. It was natural that Thebes, which had been the refuge

---

[1] Birch, Gallery of Brit. Mus. 2, p. 75.

[2] Mon. Stor. 1, p. 213, note (2). Sharpe refers to Chebros the last shield in the lowest line of the central division of the chamber of Karnak, which is commonly read *Neb-tura*. See Hierog. of Eg. Soc. pl. 96. Sharpe, History of Egypt, Plates, No. 43, 4, 5.

[3] Ægyptens Stelle, B. 3, p. 82.

of the Pharaohs, while the Hyksos held their court at Memphis, or some other town of Lower Egypt, should become the chief capital of the restored race of native kings, the site of their temples, palaces and tombs. Thothmes I. began the construction of the immense pile of the palace of Karnak. About the centre of the great inclosure which comprehended the buildings in their final extension, stood two obelisks, inscribed with the name of this king[1]. We know from other instances that it was not the custom of the Egyptians to place these monuments in open spaces, without connexion with other objects; they stood before the entrance of temples or palaces, and therefore we may conclude that Thothmes, if he did not erect, at least planned some edifice to which these obelisks were an appendage. As far indeed as a plan can be made out, amidst the ruins by which this whole space is encumbered, he actually began a vast square of buildings which Thothmes III. completed[2]. One of the obelisks is still standing, the other has fallen, and is broken to pieces. They were in size rather inferior to the obelisks of Luxor, but in workmanship nearly equal. Only the central line of the inscription belongs to Thothmes I.; the lateral lines were added by Ramses V., according to a practice very common with the Egyptian monarchs. The inscription itself contains no historical information, beyond the fact of a victory over the nations of the Nine Bows, who are commonly understood to be the Libyans, and the erection of

---

[1] See Wilkinson's great Plan of Thebes, Karnak, D., vol. i. p. 173 of this work.

[2] Rosellini, M. Stor. iii. 1, 113, 123. The obelisk is figured, M. R. tav. xxx.

the two obelisks. The rest is occupied by those pompous titles of divine affinity and dominion, which disappoint the decipherer of hieroglyphics, when he hopes to find on these immortal monuments some information worthy of the pains bestowed in preserving their legends to posterity.

A memorial of Thothmes I. is also found on the western side of the Nile at El-Assaseef, a valley lying to the north of the Rameseion[1]. A gate of red granite, of very fine execution, which is still standing amidst the ruins, exhibits his name and title along with those of his successors. Here he appears in conjunction with an Aahmes, the name the same as that of the queen of Amenophis, but apparently a different person. She is described as wife and sister of a king, and as ruler of Upper and Lower Egypt. It has been conjectured that she was the sister of Amenophis, and the Amessis of the lists, in which she immediately follows Amenophis, and regent in the reign of Thothmes I.[2]

The monument already referred to as recording the services of a military officer, who had served in several successive reigns, mentions wars of Thothmes I. in Ethiopia, and also in the land of *Naharaina*[3]. This name occurs in other historical monuments of the 18th dynasty. As Mesopotamia is called in Scripture[4] *Aram Naharaim*, " Syria of the two rivers," it is generally supposed, that the Naharaina of the hieroglyphic inscriptions is Mesopotamia; and it is not incredible, that even in this

---

[1] Vol. i. p. 156.
[2] Bunsen, Ægyptens Stelle, B. 3, p. 79.
[3] Transactions of Roy. Soc. of Lit. 2nd Series, 2, 325.
[4] Genes. xxiv. 10.

early part of the 18th dynasty, Egyptian sovereigns should have encountered the power of the Assyrians on this field. It was through fear of the power of the Assyrians, "who were then predominant in Asia," that the Hyksos, when driven out of Egypt, established themselves in Palestine[1]. The motive of their first king Salatis for fortifying the eastern frontier of Egypt was, that he foresaw the probability of attacks on the part of the Assyrians. That the dominion of Thothmes I. extended as high up the Nile as the island of Argo in Upper Nubia, appears from his name having been found there[2].

It has been already mentioned that, according to Lepsius, the Amense of Rosellini and Champollion is to be read Set Amen, and that she was a daughter of Amosis and sister of Amenophis and Thothmes I. According to the same author, after the death of Thothmes I., the functions of royalty were exercised by Nemt Amen, the sister of Thothmes II., Nemt Amen being the reading which he has adopted for the Amenenthe or Amenenhe of Champollion and Rosellini. The singular circumstance that at El-Assaseef[3] and elsewere this personage is represented with the dress and attributes of a male, yet that feminine prefixes are used throughout the inscriptions, has been explained by the supposition that she exercised sovereignty in her brother's name. That she was the daughter of Thothmes I. appears from the obelisk before the granite sanctuary at Karnak[4]; that she was the sister of Thothmes III., among other evidence from a statue in the British

[1] See before, p. 183.
[2] Vol. i. p. 19.
[3] Vol. i. p. 156.
[4] Rosellini, Mon. Stor. 1, 227.
Birch, Gall. Brit. Mus. P. 2, p. 78.

Museum, in which her name, or rather title, appears to have existed, although subsequently chiselled out, and she is designated as such[1]. The cause of this mutilation can only be conjectured; the most plausible supposition is, that her regency was either usurped or exercised with harshness, and her memory obnoxious to her brother or to the Egyptian people. Sometimes the name of Thothmes II., sometimes of Thothmes III., has been substituted for hers.

The dominion of THOTHMES II. appears to have been not less extensive than that of his predecessor. His name has been found at Gebel-el-Birkel, the Napata of the Romans[2]. In his reign we first find mention of the Royal Son or Prince of Ethiopia, which continues to appear on monuments till the reign of Setei-Menephthah[3], and from which we may infer that during this period Ethiopia formed a viceregal government dependent upon Egypt. The viceroy appears to have been of the blood royal of Egypt. We have scarcely any record of the facts of Thothmes the Second's reign. Of the state of the arts at this period, however, there is extant a most remarkable specimen in the great obelisks of Karnak. They were erected by Nemt Amen in the same central court of that pile of buildings, in which the smaller obelisks of Thothmes I. stood, but far surpass them in magnitude and beauty. One of them is still standing; it is of rose granite and ninety feet in length. Of its execution Rosellini thus speaks[4]:—

---

[1] The title exists, apparently without mutilation, on the pyramidion of the fallen obelisk of Karnak, where Amnura appears, crowning Nemt Amen, designated as a "daughter of the king." It probably escaped mutilation from its elevated position. Birch, Gall. of Brit. Mus. pl. 32.
[2] Wilkinson, M. & C. 1, 52, note.
[3] Lepsius, Einl. 1, p. 320, note ².
[4] Rosellini, M. R. tav. xxxi.-iv.

"All the figures and the hieroglyphics are delineated with such purity and freedom, cut with such art, and relieved within the excavated part with such perfection and precision of outline, that we are lost in astonishment in contemplating them, and wonder how it has been possible to work this hardest of materials, so that every figure seems rather to have been impressed with a seal than engraven with a chisel. The fragments of the companion obelisk which are lying on the ground may be handled; those parts which represent animals in particular are treated with such accuracy of design and finish of execution, as not to be surpassed by the finest cameos of the Greeks." The pyramidion represents Amunre seated, and placing his hand on the head of the king, whom he thus inaugurates. There is a peculiarity in the arrangement of the hieroglyphical inscriptions. The central column is occupied by the customary form of the dedication; but the two lateral columns, which in some obelisks, as that of Heliopolis; are left vacant, in others are filled by inscriptions of subsequent sovereigns, are here occupied more than half way down, with repetitions of the figure of Amunre on one side, on the other of the dedicating sovereign, who offers to the god wine, ointment, milk, perfumes and sacred insignia. The dedication and offering are usually in the name of Nemt Amen, but in some of the compartments the youthful Thothmes III. appears, bringing an offering to the god. The name of Thothmes I. is also found, but he is only referred to as having begun the buildings near which the obelisks were erected. Thothmes II.

nowhere appears[1], whence it seems probable that Nemt Amen set them up during the time in which she exercised the regency on behalf of her younger brother Thothmes III. The name of a much later sovereign, Setei Menephthah, is twice found, but the state of the stone plainly shows that it has been subsequently introduced. The name of Nemt Amen has escaped the mutilation which it has generally undergone, perhaps owing to the beauty of the monument. The fallen obelisk closely resembles its companion, in the subject of the inscription and the figures of the lateral compartments.

The reign of THOTHMES III. is one of the most glorious in the annals of the 18th dynasty. The earliest part of it appears to have been passed under the tutelage of Nemt Amen, whose name is found in an inscription at Wadi Magara of the sixteenth year of his reign[2]. The limits of the dominion of Egypt on the side of Arabia were therefore not reduced; Surabit-el-Kadim, between Ain Moosa and Mount Sinai, contains his name, along with those of Cheops and others of the age of the Pyramids[3]. To the south we find memorials of this monarch at Semueh, a little beyond the Second Cataract. Semueh appears to have been in this age the frontier town of the Egyptian dominions towards Ethiopia, and as such to have been fortified with great care and skill[4]. In later times, after the occupation of Egypt by the Ethiopians, Elephantine

---

[1] Rosellini, Mon. Stor. iii. 1, 164.
[2] Trans. Roy. Soc. Lit. 2, 320. The earliest date of his reign, the fifth year, is found in a papyrus of the Museum of Turin, the oldest known with a precise date. (Champollion-Figeac, L'Univers, Égypte, p. 311.)
[3] Wilkinson, Mod. Eg. & Thebes, 2, 407.
[4] Vol. i. p. 230, note [1].

became the frontier. The traces of the presence of sovereigns of the 18th dynasty further to the south, as in the island of Argo and at Napata, are only occasional, and do not prove a permanent occupation; but between the First and Second Cataracts the frequent recurrence of temples and the remains of towns indicate that this region formed virtually a part of the kingdom of Egypt. Here too, as appears from inscriptions on the rocks, the earliest rise of the Nile was watched and recorded[1]; in later times this was registered by the Nilometer of Elephantine, when that was the beginning of Egypt. The remains at Semueh are partly of the reign of Thothmes III. and partly of Amunoph II. and III., but they exhibit only acts of adoration, and throw no light on political events, except that the absence of the name of Nemt Amen leads to the conclusion that these inscriptions belong to the later part of his reign.

Following the course of the Nile downward from the Second Cataract, we find frequent memorials of Thothmes III. The temple of Amada was begun by him and completed by Amunoph II. and Thothmes IV. He is represented in the act of dedicating a temple and the lands annexed to it to the god Phre[2]. At Ombi he appears on the lintels of a gateway, preserved when the temple was rebuilt by the Ptolemies. He is dedicating the building to the god Sebek or the crocodile, and Nemt Amen is joined with him in this act[3]. A fragment bearing

---
[1] Vol. i. p. 22, note 3.
[2] Rosellini, M. Stor. iii. 1, p. 177. He calls this monarch throughout Thothmes IV.
[3] Rosellini, Mon. di Culto, tav. xxviii.

his title was found by the Tuscan Expedition at Edfoo, which is also of the Ptolemaic times. At Eilithyia his name is also traced, and joined as at Ombi with that of Nemt Amen.

His most magnificent works, however, were those which adorned Thebes, many of which are still extant. There is a mutilated obelisk in the Atmeidan or Hippodrome of Constantinople brought from Egypt by one of the Byzantine emperors, and which is of the reign of Thothmes III.[1] Probably it stood in the central court of Karnak. At first sight the shields which enclose the royal titles might seem to belong to some other sovereign or even sovereigns, for the signs in all are different. But they all contain the three elements[2] which form the title of Thothmes III. on the tablet of Abydos and elsewhere—the disk, the crenellated parallelogram and the scarabæus, and therefore it is probable that the additional signs do not indicate a different sovereign, but only those variations which we know to exist in the titles of kings whose identity is unquestionable. There is only one circumstance which gives this monument an historical significance; among the usual lofty titles of royalty, mention is twice made of the "Land of Naharaim[3]," and in the second instance the figure of a boat and the character for waters lead to the supposition that a naval expedition or a naval combat is intended. The analysis of the hieroglyphics, however, is too

---

[1] It is figured from a drawing of Mr. Cory in the Transactions of the Royal Society of Literature, 2, 228.

[2] A fourth, the waving line or *n*, is often found, always according to Champollion-Figeac (Univers, p. 309) in the hieratic writing.

[3] Col. 1, bottom. Col. 3.

imperfect to afford us exact information, and there is little probability in the supposition that Thothmes III. built a fleet on the coast of the Indian Ocean, and so ascended the Euphrates to attack the Babylonians[1]. The obelisk which Sixtus V. raised up and placed before St. John Lateran at Rome, the loftiest and most perfect in its execution of all that are extant, was set up in the reign of Thothmes III., and in its central column of hieroglyphics bears only his titles; Thothmes IV. added the lateral columns. This act of the dedication of obelisks is represented on one of the walls of the palace of Karnak, on such a scale that the inscriptions on them can be read[2]. They are not identical with those on any obelisk now known, but have a general analogy to that of St. John Lateran. One records the erection of two, the other of three, or it may be an indefinite number of obelisks, which are said to be of granite and resplendent with gold; from which it has been concluded that the pyramidion may have been surmounted with a golden ornament, or gilded as many portions of Egyptian architecture are known to have been[3].

One of the most instructive memorials of the reign of Thothmes III. is a painting in a tomb at Qoorneh, copied by Mr. Hoskins in his Travels in Ethiopia[4]. It represents four principal nations of the earth, bringing their tribute to the king, who

---

[1] Trans. Roy. Soc. Lit. 2, 223.
[2] They were first published by Mr. Burton and repeated from him by Rosellini, M. Stor. iii. 1, 185, 187; Wilkinson, Mod. Eg. and Thebes, 2, 251.
[3] Wilkinson, M. and C. 3, 237.
[4] P. 327, foll. See also Wilkinson, Mod. Eg. and Thebes, 2, p. 234. Manners and Customs, vol. 1, pl. iv. at the end of the volume.

THE EIGHTEENTH DYNASTY. 219

is seated on his throne[1]. Two obelisks of red granite, beside which the various objects are deposited by the bearers, and registered by the royal scribes, probably mark the great court of the palace of Karnak as the scene of the ceremony. The tribute-bearers are arranged in five lines, the first and the third appearing to form part of one procession. A few negroes, having all the characteristic physiognomy of the race, as well as a black colour, are intermingled with men of the same red-brown hue as the Egyptians. They bring only natural productions[2], blocks of ebony, tusks of ivory, strings of coloured stones, ostrich-eggs and feathers, a tree, gold and silver in rings, bags and ingots, and a variety of animals—apes, leopards, an oryx and a giraffe, with cattle and dogs[3]. The name of their land has been read *Pount* or *Phunt*, but this affords

---

[1] Ipse, sedens niveo candentis limine Phœbi,
Dona recognoscit populorum, aptatque superbis
Postibus; incedunt victæ longo ordine gentes,
Quam variæ linguis habitu tam vestis et armis.
Hic Nomadum genus et discinctos Mulciber Afros
Finxerat. Euphrates ibat jam mollior undis,
Extremique hominum Morini, Rhenusque bicornis,
Indomitique Dahæ, et pontem indignatus Araxes.
            Virg. Æn. viii. 720.

What had become in Virgil's time merely poetical ornament had been a fact in the history of the Asiatic and Egyptian monarchies. The *pomps* of the Ptolemies (Athen. lib. 5, 32) were an imitation of the real tribute-bearing processions under the Pharaohs.

[2] Her. 3, 97. Αἰθίοπες οἱ πρόσουροι Αἰγύπτῳ, οἱ περί τε Νύσην κατοίκηνται, ἀγινέουσι δύο χοίνικας ἀπύρου χρυσίου καὶ διηκοσίας φάλαγγας ἐβένου καὶ πέντε παῖδας Αἰθίοπας καὶ ἐλέφαντος ὀδόντας μεγάλους εἴκοσι. The representation of the tribute brought to the Great King at Persepolis, exhibits, besides vases, articles of dress and ornaments, also horses, camels, oxen, mules and sheep. (Niebuhr, Voyage ii. plates 22, 23.)

[3] Among the objects brought in the procession described by Athenæus, u. s., were "26 Indian cattle, 8 Ethiopian, a large white bear, 14 leopards, 16 panthers, 4 lynxes, 1 camelopard and 1 rhinoceros." There were also 2400 dogs, some Indian, some Hyrcanian, some Molossian, and of other breeds.

us no information, as it corresponds with no known name in geography. Those of the third line are specifically called "Nations of the South." From the products which they bring they are evidently inhabitants of the African continent, and of a wide range of country, including the Libyans on the west, the Nubians on the south, and the Ethiopians of the deeper interior. The colour of the men of the second line is not different from that of the Egyptians and Libyans, but their hair is gathered in curls on the front, and divided into two long locks behind, one of which falls on the shoulder. They wear, like the Libyans, only a short kilt round the middle; but while the Libyan is white with a coloured border, that of the third line is of various checks and patterns, closely resembling the drapery of the foreigners who are seen in the tomb of Nevothph[1]. Their offerings are vases of silver and gold of graceful form and elaborate workmanship, and others which resemble, if the representations can be relied upon, the fictile vases of the Greeks and Etruscans. Their name, which is written *Kufa* or Kafa, affords little clue to their locality, but their resemblance to the Egyptians in colour and the advanced state of the arts among them, indicated by the vases which they bring, lead us to conclude that they must belong to the coast of Palestine, which received colonies at an early age from Egypt[2]. The gold and silver vases would suit well with the skill in the toreutic arts attri-

---

[1] P. 168 of this vol.
[2] Gen. x. 14. But the resemblance of Kufa and Caphthor is too slight to found an argument of identity.

buted by Homer to the Sidonians[1]. The Libyans, Egyptians and Ethiopians have naked feet, but these have buskins, reaching half way up the leg, of the same pattern with their kilts. The third company of tribute-bearers, forming the fourth line of the picture, are men of white complexion, with reddish hair and beards. They wear long garments of white cloth, sleeved to the wrists, with the addition of gloves reaching to the elbow; their heads are covered with a close-fitting cap, and everything indicates that they belong to a colder climate than any of the others. Some of them are armed with bows and arrows, and others lead a chariot and horses. Their tribute consists of ring money of gold and silver, coloured woods, precious stones and vases, some of which resemble those brought by the Kufa, but which are in general of less beautiful form and less elaborate workmanship. Their name is *Rot-n-no* or *Lud-n-nu*, but this gives us no precise information of their locality, all comparison with known geographical names being merely conjectural, and it is difficult to fix on any country whose products shall correspond with all the articles of the tribute. The long garments and gloves, with the chariot and horses[2], would suit Northern Media, or the regions near the southern shore of the Caspian; but one of the men carries a tusk of ivory, and leads an elephant and a bear. The range of latitude in which the elephant can live has certainly ascended higher to the north in an-

---

[1] Il. ψ. 741. Od. o. 424.
[2] Birch, Trans. Roy. Soc. Lit. 2, 335, thinks they are the Cappadoeiaus, called also Leuco-Syrians or fair Syrians. This is not improbable. They were δαήμονες ἱπποσυνάων (Dionys. Perieg. 974.)

cient times than at present, but it is difficult to conceive that so great a change has taken place between the times of Thothmes III. and that of the commencement of our knowledge of the zoology of the ancient world, as that elephants should be found in Asia Minor. In the fifth line women, both of this nation and of the people of the South, are introduced, leading their infant children, or carrying them in their arms, or on their shoulders, or in a basket, fastened by a strap to the forehead, a custom which still prevails among the tribes which border the Nile[1].

If there could be any doubt that we have here the representation of a real scene and the evidence of a dominion extending from Nubia to Northern Asia, no such doubt can attach to the monument which is known as the Statistical Table of Karnak[2].

This document is of the reign of Thothmes III., and the inscription placed above it declares its object to be to record the victories of this sovereign. It divides itself into three distinct portions by the dates 29th[3], 30th, and 31st years. As it is mutilated near the beginning, it is not clear in what land the monarch was when the record of his exploits begins, but from the subsequent occurrence of the name of the Tahai[4] and the traces of the obliterated name, it seems probable that they are the people first referred to. It is conjectured that

---

[1] Wilkinson, Mod. Egypt and Thebes, 2, 236, note.
[2] Hieroglyphics of the Eg. Soc. 41. Lepsius, Auswahl, pl. xiii. I quote the former for the facility of reference, as the columns are numbered across as well as vertically. The copy of Lepsius, however, is more exact.
[3] Col. Z b.
[4] Col. V x.

they are the Dahæ, a nomad nation on the northern frontier of Persia[1], or the Taochi mentioned by Xenophon[2] as living between Armenia and Pontus, and maintaining themselves in independence of the Great King[3]. In this case, however, they cannot have brought tribute of frankincense; and the sign which has been so explained must represent some other object. Honey and wine are also mentioned among their tributes, and we know from Strabo[3] that the vine flourished even as far north as Hyrcania, and that these countries were very productive of honey. Their name occurs frequently in monuments recording the victories and expeditions of the Egyptian kings. Two other nations, one called *Vava*, the other *Arutu*, are mentioned in the same inscription, and men, ingots of the precious metals, copper, iron and lead with other metals which cannot be precisely ascertained, 618 bulls, 3636 goats, corn, are all enumerated among the spoils or tribute of the land[4]. This expedition of the 29th year is called the 5th, in reference to some enumeration of which the earlier part is wanting.

In the 30th year of his reign[5], and his sixth expedition, the king is said to have been in the land of the *Rotnno* or *Ludennu*, the same people who appear in the last line of the painting at Thebes already described, and to have taken hostages of

[1] Herod. 1, 125. From their name Δάοι, that of *Davus*, borne by slaves, is supposed to be derived, as *Geta* from another nomad tribe.
[2] Xen. Anab. 4,7,1.5,5,17. From Steph. Byz. s. v. Τάοχοι, it seems probable they were the same people as the Däi or Täi. (Birch, Tr. Roy. Soc. Lit. 2, 330.)
[3] Geogr. B. 2, p. 73.
[4] The cattle enumerated may be regarded as contributions for the use of the army, while serving in the country.
[5] Col. S e.

them and their children. Now in the painting of the Theban tomb, we have seen men and women of the Rotnno nation, led with their children into the presence of the Egyptian scribes. The men are not armed, yet they are not bound, and therefore it is probable that they came as hostages, though it would be too much to infer that these are the very hostages spoken of in the tablet. Forty-two chariots also, "decorated with gold, silver and painting[1]," are among the spoil of the Rotnno; and in the procession in the tomb, we have already described a richly adorned chariot, followed by a yoke of horses, which may be considered as the representative of a larger number.

In the 31st year and on the 3rd day of the month Pachons[2], another expedition is recorded, in which mention is made of 490 captives, who were employed, as far as the imperfect interpretation of the inscription enables us to judge, in felling and carrying timber, and seem to have belonged to the same nation of the Rotnno. The results of the expedition were also the capture, or payment in tribute, of 104 cows, 172 bulls, 4622 goats, and masses of iron and lead[3]. These contributions suit well the countries between the Caspian and the Euxine, which abound in metallic products. The wood might be carried to some branch of the Euphrates, and thence floated to Mesopotamia or Babylonia. The north-eastern part of Asia Minor is also rich in minerals, especially iron; but wood would be conveyed thence with difficulty to any point at which it could be serviceable to the Egyptians,

[1] Col. Q b, c, d.
[3] See vol. i. p. 330.
[2] Col. O.

who, as far as we know, never launched a fleet upon the Euxine.

The following lines on the tablet, owing to the mutilation of the lower part, are very obscure. The 21st (Lepsius) begins with "land of *Nenii*[1]," followed by the mention of setting up a *stele* in Naharaina[2]. The form of this tablet, as represented in the inscription, exactly corresponds with those cut on the rock at Nahr-el-Kelb, bearing the image of Rameses III. The Assyrians continued the same custom, and two of their kings placed a *stele* beside those of Rameses at Nahr-el-Kelb. Darius left a similar record of his expedition against the Scythians, on the shores of the Bosporus[3]. *Nenii* is generally understood to be Nineveh, the capital of Assyria, and the mention of Naharaina, which immediately follows, favours this supposition. The further prosecution of the researches into the remains discovered at Khorsabad and Nemroud may throw light on the relations between Egypt and Mesopotamia. Tablets of ivory in Egyptian style have been found here[4], one of them inscribed with the name of an Egyptian king or god not known from other sources. Such small and portable anti-

---

[1] Hieroglyphics of Egyptian Society, 42, Col. Xb. There is no letter answering to *u*.

[2] The character for *stele* is hardly recognizable in Wilkinson's copy, but is more distinct in Lepsius, taf. xii. 1. 21.

[3] Her. 4, 87. Θησάμενος δὲ καὶ τὸν Βόσπορον στήλας ἔστησε δύο ἐπ' αὐτῷ λίθου λευκοῦ, ἐνταμὼν γράμματα, ἐς μὲν τὴν Ἀσσύρια, ἐς δὲ τὴν Ἑλληνικὰ, ἔθνεα πάντα ὅσαπερ ἦγε. These *stelæ* were not *columns*, as the commentators usually render them, but *tablets*. Hence the use which the Byzantines made of them to build an altar. I see no reason to suppose that such inscriptions marked the frontiers of an empire exclusively. They were naturally placed beside high roads that they might be conspicuous.

[4] Layard's Nineveh, Plates, 89. Birch, Trans. Roy. Soc. Lit. 2nd series, vol. 3. The name is read *Aubnu-ra*.

quities cannot be received as proofs of the occupation of a country, and as far as we can judge, they belong to a much later period of history than the 18th dynasty.

The next column[1] relates to the land of the Tahæ, and makes mention of 260 mares[2], which had been brought thence with gold and silver, both unwrought and in the shape of vases. That which follows enumerates cattle, among the rest 5323 goats, and therefore, though the name of the people is not mentioned, they are probably the same who in a preceding column are said to have furnished a very large number of goats, namely the Rotnno. The next column[3] introduces a people not hitherto mentioned, but whose name frequently occurs in inscriptions. From the ambiguity of the first letter, which stands equally for L or R in the phonetic alphabet, it is doubtful whether it should be read *Lemanen* or *Remanen*. Those who adopt the former suppose the inhabitants of Lebanon to be meant, and derive an argument in favour of their opinion from the circumstance that they are elsewhere represented as felling trees[4], supposed to be the cedars for which this mountain was celebrated. There is nothing in the form of the trees, however, which particularly refers them to the cedars of Lebanon, and in the inscription given by Rosellini, mention seems to be made of building boats on a river, which does not accord with the geography of

---

[1] V. Pl. 42.
[2] Phonetically written *sesem*, with the determinative of the species. See vol. i. p. 197.
[3] Col. Ti.
[4] Rosellini, M. R. tav. xlvi.

Lebanon. Nor do we know that Lebanon was ever used as the name of a nation. Armenia, which has been suggested, would suit the name if read Remanen, and also the operation of felling the trees. The ample clothing of the Remanen also indicates a more northern climate than that of Syria. The following column[1] makes mention of the land of Sankar or Sankal, and Bebel or Baber[2]; the former of which is supposed to mean Singara, and Bebel, Babylon. Singara, Sinjar, is a town near Edessa, inhabited by a tribe of Arabs, whom Pliny calls Rætavi or Prætavi[3]. In connection with both these countries a tribute is spoken of, called *Chesebt*; from the determinative character subjoined to it, it appears to be a metal, but Babylonia was not a metalliferous region, and it cannot be one of the precious metals, the hieroglyphics for which are well known[4]. The next column[5] contains the enumeration of contributions of gold and silver, in vessels and in bulk, and near the bottom, of stone and wood. The lower part of the column is mutilated, but as the next begins with the word Naharaina, followed by the same group of characters as in Col. X., it is thought that the stone and wood were designed for the erection of a stele in Mesopotamia. The land of the Tahæ is again mentioned in Col. O; in connection

---

[1] Col. Sf.
[2] Mutilated in Lepsius' copy, but preserved in Wilkinson's.
[3] H.N. 5, 21. Steph. Byz. Σιγγαρα.
[4] The character which Mr. Birch reads *uten* and Dr. Hincks *mn* (mna) appears to me to represent a coil of metallic rod or wire. The word *chesebt* occurs thrice in this line, twice accompanied by this character, once, before Beber or Bebel, without it. This seems to indicate two different forms under which it was contributed.
[5] Hierogl. of Egypt. Soc. pl. 42, Col. R. Lepsius, l. 26. In Ri Wilkinson's copy has 400, Lepsius 301.

with the 34th year of the king and military operations in the land of *Jukasa*, conjectured to be Oxiana[1], a doubtful appropriation, since it does not appear that Oxus is an Oriental name.

The remaining columns contain in the main only a repetition of tribute similar to the preceding, with a mention of some articles which it is difficult to identify. We find also a people called *Asi*, conjectured to be those of Is, since they appear to bring bitumen, which the springs of that place produce[2]. In others suits of armour are mentioned, brought by the *Kharu*, who appear from other inscriptions to have inhabited Syria. When complete, the whole has comprehended at least fifty-five columns.

There can be little doubt that this is the identical tablet which the priests showed and expounded to Germanicus, when he visited Thebes[3]. Having mentioned the record of the victorious expeditions of Rameses, Tacitus proceeds: "There were also read the tributes levied on the nations, the weight of gold and silver, the number of arms and horses, ivory and perfumes as gifts to the temples, and the stores of corn and other useful products which each nation paid; not less magnificent than are now enjoined by Parthian violence or Roman power[4]." The name of Thothmes is not mentioned by Tacitus, and Rameses has been spoken of immediately before; but his words do not necessarily imply that the tablet of tribute and the record of victories related to the same sovereign.

[1] Birch, *u. s.* p. 359.
[2] Herod. 1, 179.
[3] The expression "structis molibus" shows that obelisks were not meant. Strabo (p. 816) says these records were inscribed on obelisks, and moreover places these obelisks among the royal sepulchres.
[4] Annal. 2, 60.

The Tablet of Karnak is strictly an historical and statistical document. It does not deal in vague ascriptions of a world-wide dominion; its dates are precise, including the month and the day as well as the year of the king; and though we may be unable to identify the countries named, the exactness with which they are enumerated, with the weights and numbers of the objects which they bring, proves that we have before us an authentic record, at least of the tribute *enjoined* upon the nations.

Another remarkable monument of the age of Thothmes III. is the chamber, on the walls of which he is represented making offerings to sixty of his predecessors. It has been already described among the documents of Egyptian history, and it is certainly one of the most important of them, though it has by no means received a satisfactory explanation in all its parts. His name appears to have been held in high veneration by posterity, and is found on a great number of scarabæi and amulets, many of which were probably engraved in subsequent times[1]. Rosellini and others call him Mœris, and suppose him to have been the author of the Lake of Fyoum and the other works connected with it. The epithet *Maire*, beloved of Re, is found connected with his name; but we have seen reason to doubt whether the name of Mœris belongs historically to any king of Egypt, and the works in the Fyoum must be placed in the Old Monarchy.

Besides erecting monuments of stone, Thothmes

[1] Wilkinson, M. and C. 1, 56, note.

III. appears to have been the author of extensive constructions of bricks. Egypt affords abundant material for this manufacture, and a few days' exposure to the sun hardens them sufficiently, unless they are to be subject to the action of water. Bricks bearing his titular shield, the scarabæus, the crenellated parallelogram and the disk of the sun, are more common than those of any other sovereign[1]. There is a tomb at Thebes, the inscriptions of which show, that its occupant, *Roschere*, was "superintendent of the great buildings" in the reign of Thothmes III.: on its walls the operation of brick-making is represented[2]. Men are employed, some in working up the clay with an instrument resembling the Egyptian hoe, others in carrying loads of it on their shoulders, moulding it into bricks, and transporting them, by means of a yoke laid across the shoulders, to the place where they are to be laid out for drying in the sun. The physiognomy and colour of most of those who are thus engaged show them to be foreigners, and their aquiline nose and yellow complexion suggest the idea that they are Jews. Their labour is evidently compulsory; Egyptian taskmasters stand by with sticks in their hands; and though one or two native Egyptians appear among them, we may easily suppose that they have been condemned to hard labour for their crimes. As the foreigners do not resemble any of the nations with whom Thothmes carried on war, and who are well known from the paintings and reliefs of subsequent monarchs,

---

[1] Wilkinson, Manners and Customs, 2, 98. [2] Rosellini, Mon. Civ. tav. xlix.

it is not probable that they are captives taken in war. They can therefore hardly be any other than the Israelites, whom we know from their own history to have been employed in this drudgery. Their oppression began with the accession of the 18th dynasty, and the expulsion of their kindred Hyksos. It was a natural fear, that when any war fell out they should join themselves to the enemies of Egypt and fight against her. The kings of Egypt, therefore, while they endeavoured by a cruel expedient to prevent their increase, and by hard labour to break their spirit, employed that labour to strengthen the frontier on the side of Arabia and Palestine, whence their danger came. The valley of Goshen, which was their place of settlement, was the direct road from Palestine to Memphis[1]. By employing them to build the two fortresses[2], Raameses at the eastern[3], and Pithom at the western extremity of this valley[4], the Pharaohs provided at once a barrier against future invasions and the means of keeping the children of Israel in subjection. Both these objects were important to a sovereign like Thothmes, who, during his Mesopota-

---

[1] Gen. xlvi. 28. During the French occupation of Egypt this same valley, Saba-byar, was assigned to three Arab tribes, driven from Syria. (Bois-Aymé, Mémoires, 8, 111.)

[2] Πόλεις ὀχυράς, Sept. Exod. i. 11. The Egyptian king would hardly have placed "treasure cities" in such a locality, whether we understand money or corn to have been treasured up; but they were excellently adapted for military magazines and garrisons (1 Kings, ix. 19; 2 Chron. viii. 4, Sept.).

[3] See Lepsius, Einleitung, 1, p. 349, on the site of Raameses (Aboo-Kescheib). He attaches, I think, too much importance to the name, as a proof that it was built by Rameses II. A stone with his name has been found there, but the district had the name before the city was built. See Gen. xlvii. 11.

[4] Without the article this would be *Thom*, which in Coptic signifies to close up. (Peyron, Lex. p. 51.) It was not far from Bubastis, and is the Thoum of the Itinerary of Antoninus.

miau expeditions, must have left his country exposed to his neighbours, and whose long absences might tempt revolt. If Roschere were the general superintendent of the great architectural undertakings of Thothmes, and the first who employed the Israelites upon them, it is very natural that we should find a record of it in his tomb, although they may not have laboured in the brick-fields of Thebes.

Thirteen expeditions of Thothmes are referred to in the monument before described, and the thirty-fourth year of his reign; the thirty-fifth has been found by Lepsius. He was succeeded by his son AMENOPHIS II. The memorials of his reign are few, and afford little materials for history. The obelisk at Alnwick Castle, brought by Lord Prudhoe from the Thebaid, is inscribed with his name, but it simply records the fact of his having erected two obelisks in honour of the god Kneph[1]. He continued the buildings at Amada, which Thothmes III. had begun, and appears to have bestowed his labours chiefly on these and other works in Nubia. In a *speos* or excavated chapel at Ibrim, he appears seated with two princes or great officers. One of them, named Osorsate, presents to him the animal productions of the southern regions, lions, jackals and hares, an inscription above specifying their numbers[2]. He also added to the erections of his predecessors at Thebes; but most of his works

---

[1] Trans. Roy. Soc. Lit. 2nd series, 1, p. 171. The surface within the sculptures is nearly flat, not in relief, which is uncommon in works of this age.

[2] Champollion, Lettres d'Égypte, p. 140.

here have perished. There remains a representation of him, in the usual attitude of a conqueror, about to immolate a band of captives whom he holds by the hair; their name however has not been satisfactorily explained. We have no evidence in the monuments of the extent of his Asiatic dominion, but his inscriptions are found at Surabit-el-Kadim, in the Peninsula of Sinai[1].

His son THOTHMES IV. continued the works of his family at Amada, and added a hypostyle hall, which stands in front of them[2]. The hieroglyphical inscriptions, which are very beautifully executed, record his victories over the people of Cush (Ethiopia), but give no other information respecting the events of his reign. This appears, however, not to have been his only war. A stele engraven on a rock of granite, on the right bank of the Nile, opposite to Philæ, records a victory gained by him over the Libyans in the 7th year of his reign, and on the 8th day of the month Phamenoth[3]. At Qoorneh, in a tomb of an officer of his court, the king himself appears seated on a throne, on the base of which are nine foreigners, bound by their necks and arms, in the manner in which captive nations are usually represented on Egyptian monuments. Four only of the nine names are legible; they have not occurred before in the records of Egyptian victories, but some of them are found on later monuments; and they appear all to belong to Asia. From another of these tombs it has been

---

[1] Champollion-Figeac, L'Univers, p. 312. I find those of Amenophis III., but not the second mentioned at this place by Sir G. Wilkinson (Mod. Eg. and Thebes, 2, 406).
[2] Rosellini, Mon. Stor. iii. 1, 205.
[3] Champollion-Figeac, p. 313.

inferred that he built a palace at Thebes, and that it contained an edifice dedicated to Amun-re; but no traces of such a building are now to be found[1].

AMUNOPH, or AMENOPHIS III., the son of Thothmes IV. and his queen Mauthemva, is one of the most celebrated monarchs of the 18th dynasty. We have hitherto found no traces of the permanent occupation of Nubia by the Egyptian kings, higher up the Nile than Semneh, but the temple of Soleh, which stands a degree further south, contains evidence that under Amunoph III. the boundary of the empire extended at least thus far. The remains of this edifice have been already described[2]; thirty-eight, or according to other accounts forty-three, conquered nations are represented there; they have not been exactly copied, but Mr. Hoskins informs us that on one of them he found the name of Mesopotamia[3]. Probably they are chiefly the names of Ethiopian tribes whom he had vanquished in the extension of his frontiers to the South. His name is found on a tablet at Toumbos near the Third Cataract. The lion which now couches at the entrance of the Egyptian Gallery in the British Museum is inscribed with the name of Amunoph III.[4], but it does not appear on any of the buildings there, and the lion may have been brought from Egypt by Tirhakah, by whom the temple seems to have been erected. A scarabæus inscribed with the name of Amenophis III. and his wife Taia speaks of the land

---

[1] Rosellini, p. 212. The person who was buried here had the charge of the sacred *bari* of Amun. See vol. i. p. 459.

[3] Vol. i. p. 20.

[2] Travels, p. 250. Birch (Gall. B. M. p. 84) gives also Sinjar in Mesopotamia.

[4] Vol. i. p. 17.

of *Karoei* or *Kaloei* as the southern boundary of his dominion[1]. If this be Coloe, as has been supposed[2], his conquests must have been carried far to the East as well as the South; for Coloe was within five days' journey of Axum on the Red Sea[3]. The way would thus be prepared for the expedition of Rameses-Sesostris, who is said to have subdued the nations along the Erythræan Sea and crossed the Straits into Arabia[4]. A more full record of the conquests of Amenophis in Ethiopia is found in a fragment of a monolithal granite statue which is now in the Louvre[5]. The prisoners are negroes, and the lotus, which terminates the cord by which they are bound, being the emblem of Upper Egypt, characterizes on monuments all Southern races, as the head of the papyrus, the growth of Lower Egypt, does all nations living to the North of Egypt. There have been originally twenty-six names, of which six are no longer legible, and no resemblance has been found between those which have been preserved and any modern or ancient names of this region, except Kesh, the scriptural Cush. Amenophis may have inherited, as well as conquered dominion over Ethiopia. Those who have compared many of the representations of him affirm, that his own features have something of an Ethiopian cast[6]. On the granite rock of the little island of Beghe, near the

---

[1] Rosellini, M. Stor. iii. 1, 261.
[2] Birch, Gall. B. M. p. 83.
[3] Cellarius, Geogr. Antiq. iv. 8, 27.
[4] Herod. 2, 102. Strabo, 17, p. 769.
[5] Birch in Archæologia, 31, 489-491.
[6] Champollion-Figeac, L'Univers, 317. He says that from the monuments, Mauthemva, his mother, appears to have been an Ethiopian.

Cataract, a figure carrying in his hand what Rosellini calls the ensign of victory, and Champollion a fly-fan, appears doing homage to the titular or prenominal shield of Amenophis III.: over his head is the inscription "Royal Son of the land of Kush, Memes[1]." It seems to have been the custom to grant a virtual or titular governorship of towns and districts to members of the royal family; for we find in the tombs at Suan (Eilithya), mention is made of "royal sons" of this place, during the reigns of the five first kings of the 18th dynasty[2]. The same scarabæus which has been already quoted gives Naharaina as the other limit of the dominions of Amenophis III., agreeing in this respect with the inscription at Semueh.

The quarries of Silsilis, which have supplied the principal materials for the edifices of Egypt, were extensively wrought in the reign of Amenophis III. Two monuments still remain there, which from some cause had not been removed to their destination; they are monolithal shrines, dedicated to Sebek, the crocodile-deity of Ombi: one of them bears the date of the 27th year of the king's reign. He did not continue the works of architecture at Thebes begun by his predecessors of the 18th dynasty, but erected two vast palaces, one on the eastern, the other on the western bank of the Nile. By referring to the description of the remains of Thebes given in the former volume[3], it will be seen that he began the buildings at Luxor and erected the greater part of them. The chambers which yet

---

[1] See p. 213 of this vol.
[2] Champollion, Lettres, p. 198.
[3] Vol. i. p. 156, 172.

remain bear his legends, with the title "Pacificator of Egypt" and "Vanquisher of the Mennahom," an unknown people. In the same place is found a singular representation of his birth, and subsequent education[1]. In the first picture of the series his mother, represented with the attributes of the goddess Athor, but identified by her name *Mauthemva*, stands in the presence of the god Thoth, who holds a roll of papyrus in his hand, and raises the other towards the queen with the action of one who is addressing her. The purport of his address cannot be ascertained, but from the connexion of this with the following scenes, it is probable, that as the Egyptian Hermes he brings a message to the queen from the god of Thebes, announcing her own future maternity. In the second scene this event is near at hand[2], and the queen is led by the god Kneph and the goddess Athor, who stretches the key of life towards her, to the puerperal bed. The chamber in which this is prepared is called *Ma-n-misi*, a name given to the apartment of a temple, in which the mystical birth of the young god, the offspring of the principal deities, is represented[3]. The queen, in the manner of Egyptian women, is resting on the knees and toes, and the goddess Isis behind her holds up her hands, in the attitude of one who is comforting and supporting her. Two goddesses, seated opposite to the queen, are suckling two male

---

[1] Rosellini, Mon. Stor. iii. 1, p. 223, tav. xxxviii.–xl.

[2] "Il profilo del ventre fu evidentemente incurvato oltre il consueto, per dimostrare la gravidanza. Il disegnatore non indicò forse tanto bene questa circostanza nella minor proporzione, come si vede chiara nell' originale." (Rosellini, p. 225.)

[3] Vol. i. p. 255.

children; their finger pointed towards their mouth indicates their childish age[1]; the lock of hair falling on the right side of the head their assimilation to Horus and other youthful deities who are thus characterized[2]. The twofold number does not indicate that Amenophis had a twin brother, but is common where the birth of deities is represented[3]. Beneath the couch are two spotted cows, sacred to Athor[4], who turn complacently round towards the children who are sucking at their udders. In the next scene, Amunre is seen standing and holding in his hand the youthful Amenophis, whom a hawk-headed god has presented to him; he is addressing the child, and declares that he bestows upon him life, stability, purity and happiness, magnanimity and dominion on the throne of Horus[5]. Two figures appear behind carrying the children; they represent the Nile, in the dry season and at the commencement of the inundation, the former being distinguished by the blue colour, the latter by the red-brown[6]. Their introduction here may be only symbolical of the important relation in which the Nile stood to the prosperity of Egypt, or it may be considered as preparing the way for a subsequent representation,

---

[1] Wilkinson, M. and C. 4, 405. Compare vol. 1, p. 422 of Harpocrates.

[2] We see from the Rosetta Stone that the assimilation of a youthful sovereign to Horus was a common flattery. Ptolemy is there called "a god, the son of a god and of a goddess, as Horus the son of Isis and Osiris." (Ros. Inscr. line 10.)

[3] The reader who consults Rosellini's Plates must remember what has been said (vol. i. p. 269) of Egyptian drawing. The four legs of the couch are all seen, and its horizontal seat is represented perpendicularly, so that the queen and goddesses appear to be seated on its turned-up edge.

[4] Wilkinson, M. and C. 4, 489, Plates, 36.

[5] Rosellini, *u. s.* p. 228.

[6] Here, as elsewhere, the figures of the Nile are *androgynous*.

in which two deities, Mandoo and Atmoo, appear pouring the water of the Nile over the king. In the intervening scene we see the goddess *Saf*, the wife of Thoth, and like him presiding over writing, painting and language, to whom the children are presented. Before her kneels a figure with a pot of paint, while the goddess holds a brush or pen ; what she is preparing to write does not appear, perhaps the name and royal title of the child[1], or as Rosellini supposes, the number of years and panegyries that he was to live.

The ceremony of the purification of the young king is preliminary to that of his inauguration; hitherto he has appeared with no emblem of royalty, but now he wears the uræus round his head; hitherto he has been naked, but now he has a short garment fastened round his waist. With this headdress and the crook and scourge in his hands, he is next seen borne on a seat into the presence of Amunre. Having descended from his seat and exchanged the cap bound with the uræus for the royal helmet, he stands holding a bird[2] in his hand before the god, who has placed a collar round his neck. In front of the god are two figures, one of whom bears the red diadem which forms the outer part of the *pschent*, and represents Lower Egypt; the other the white conical cap which represents Upper Egypt. Invested with these he enters into

---

[1] In a subsequent scene Saf says, according to the interpretation of Rosellini, " I establish thy twofold sculpture," *i. e.* thy twofold title, symbolical and phonetic. (p. 238.)

[2] A phœnix, according to Rosellini (p. 238), the emblem of a pure life. If it be a phœnix, length of days, or immortality, would seem a more natural signification.

the full prerogatives of sovereignty. They are, however, laid aside, and the king appears with his helmet only, when he comes in a subsequent scene, conducted by Phre, to kneel before Amunre and receive his benediction[1]. His inauguration endowed him with a sacred character, and he engages immediately after in the performance of solemn religious acts. Crowned with the lower part of the *pschent*, he appears running into the presence of Amunkhem[2] with a vessel of libation in either hand, and leads before the same divinity four living steers, one black, one white, one red and one pied, his head being ornamented, not with a helmet or the pschent, but with the insignia of Osiris-Sokari. The adjoining chambers of the palace of Luxor contain other representations of Amenophis engaged in performing sacred functions, but they do not appear to belong so immediately to his inauguration into the royal and sacerdotal office as those which have been just described.

Besides the palace of Luxor, the long *dromos* of crio-sphinxes which joins it to Karnak[3] was the work of Amenophis III., whose name can yet be traced upon their mouldering remains. But the western bank of the Nile appears to have been adorned with even more stupendous erections than those which we have already described. Of the Amenophion[4], as it has been called, the greater

---

[1] Tav. xli. 1.
[2] See also Wilkinson, pl. 79, 1. This action of running into the presence of a god is explained by Rosellini as emblematic of the completion of a temple (M. Stor. iii. 1, 171, 244), but this is not probable, since the objects brought are very various in different representations.
[3] See vol. i. p. 172.
[4] See vol. i. p. 156.

part is a heap of ruins, but these are sufficient to prove its former extent; and if the two colossal statues[1], which now appear in such striking insulation in the plain of Thebes, once stood at the entrance of a dromos leading to the Amenophion, it is difficult to conceive a more impressive combination.

The northernmost of these statues has connected the name of Amenophis with the Memnon slain by Achilles at the siege of Troy. There is no reason to believe that the mythe of Memnon is of Egyptian origin. In the Odyssey, where he is briefly mentioned[2], for he does not appear in the Iliad, he is introduced only as a hero remarkable for his beauty; his eastern origin may be alluded to in his being made the son of Aurora. He must early have been considered as an Ethiopian, though not so called by Homer; the author of the Theogony (985) makes him king of that country; and Arctinus, one of the first of the Cyclic poets[3], in his Αἰθιοπίς related his arrival at Troy, his death by the hand of Achilles, and the immortality granted to him on the petition of Aurora. As yet, however, Ethiopia appears to have been conceived of as an eastern, not a southern region. Herodotus places the Memnonium at Susa[4]; Æschylus made the mother of Memnon a Cissian or Susian: even in Strabo's time the royal palace there bore this name[5]. But after the Greeks established themselves in

---

[1] See vol. i. p. 157.
[2] Od. δ', 188. λ', 521.
[3] Müller, de Cyclo Græcorum Epico, p. 44, quoting Proclus, Chrestomathia.
[4] 5, 53, 54; 7, 151.
[5] Geogr. 15, p. 728.

Egypt, Ethiopia became to them a definite geographical name, denoting the valley of the Nile above Egypt to the island of Meroe, and eastward to the Erythræan Sea. It was therefore natural that they should seek among the kings of that country, either as ruling in their proper territory or as sovereigns of Egypt, for the original of their Memnon. He had not come alone to Troy; he had led a powerful army (so at least the Greeks believed[1]); no sovereign of Egypt therefore would have fulfilled the conditions of their hypothesis, who had not made conquests in Asia. Now although we have not, probably from accidental causes, the same monumental evidence of campaigns carried on in Asia by Amenophis III. as the tablet of Karnak furnishes respecting his father, we know that at least as far as Mesopotamia the boundaries of his dominion extended; and from the analogy of other reigns we may conclude that this dominion was not maintained without military expeditions. In the passage in which Herodotus describes the tablet erected by Sesostris at Nahr-el-Kelb, and those in Asia Minor on the road from Ephesus to Phocæa, and from Sardis to Smyrna, he says that some persons supposed that these figures represented Memnon, but that they were in error. Whatever Herodotus himself might mean by *Memnon*, those whose opinion he refutes probably meant Amenophis-Memnon; for the monument of Nahr-el-Kelb is so completely Egyptian, that there could be no mistake on that point; but among those who could not read the Egyptian character a question might easily arise,

[1] See Quintus Calaber, lib. 2.

whether Amenophis or Sesostris, both Egyptian conquerors of Asia, were the special object of commemoration on this monument. As some gave the monument of Nahr-el-Kelb to Memnon, others gave the statue at Thebes to Sesostris, a natural confusion between two illustrious names, in an age which had not the means of critical judgement [1].

The word *Memnon* appears to have been a name or epithet of the Ethiopians. Stephanus of Byzantium says, "The Memnones are an Ethiopian nation, a word which, according to Polyhistor, is interpreted fierce or warlike and stern [2]." Agathemerus [3], enumerating the nations who live along the Nile above Egypt, says, "After the Great Cataract westward of the Nile live the Euonymitæ, the Sebridæ, the Catoipi (Cadupi or Catadupi [4], the people of the region of the Cataracts ?), and the Memnones who live close to the island of Meroe, after whom come the Elephant-eating Ethiopians." We conclude, therefore, that Memnones is a real and geographical name; and probably a name of Greek etymology, since it enters into composition with other pure Greek words [5], denoting "the valiant or warlike," a name equally appropriate to the nation and to their chief. *Memnon* is therefore equivalent to an Ethiopian; and as Ethiopian was a name given by the Greeks to all whose complexions were dark-

---

[1] Pausanias, 1, 42, 2. Ἤκουσα δὲ ἤδη καὶ Σέσωστριν φαμένων εἶναι τοῦτο τὸ ἄγαλμα ὃ Καμβύσης διέκοψε.

[2] Ἀγρίους τινὰς ἢ μαχίμους καὶ χαλεπούς. Polyhistor in Steph. Byz. *sub voce* Μέμνονες.

[3] See note to the passage of Steph. Byz. in Berkelius' edition.

[4] Pliny, N. H. 5, 10. 6, 35.

[5] As θρασυμέμνων, Ἀγαμέμνων. Comp. Eust. (ad Il. ε′, 639), p. 591. Δῆλον ὡς καὶ τὸ ἁπλοῦν ὁ μέμνων, καθὰ καὶ ὁ μένων, ἀνδρείους ὑποδηλοῦσι.

ened, whether by an eastern or a southern sun, his mythic genealogy, which made Aurora his mother, is easily accounted for. His pre-eminent beauty, strange as it may seem to us, was also a cousequence of his Ethiopic extraction; for according to Herodotus (3, 114) the Ethiopians were not only the tallest and most long-lived, but the handsomest of the human race.

The fiction of a musical sound, issuing from the statue of Memnon at Thebes at sunrise, appears to be entirely Greek. To the Egyptians it was never anything more than the statue of their king Amenophis[1]; all the inscriptions which record that the sound had been heard are of the Roman times[2]; the name Memnonium was given to the quarter in which it stood, under the Ptolemies, but no monument nor any passage in an author of that age alludes to a vocal Memnon. Cambyses did not need the pretext of its magic music to induce him to mutilate a statue reverenced by the Thebans[3]. As the statue has been silent for centuries, we have no means of ascertaining how the belief in its musical qualities arose; it probably originated in the poetical imagination of the Greeks, favoured by some slight or accidental cause, and the eastward posi-

---

[1] In Syncellus we have after the name of Amenophis Οὗτός ἐστιν ὁ Μέμνων εἶναι νομιζόμενος, καὶ φθεγγόμενος λίθος. "Lemma diversi esse scriptoris a Manethone probat silentium Josephi, ideoque ad Africanum adscribendum." Routh ad Afric. Rel. Sac. 2, 396. The addition is found in the Armenian Version of Eusebius.

[2] See the full collection of them, with the commentary of Letronne, in the Transactions of the Royal Society of Literature, Series i. vol. 1, part 2.

[3] Syncellus. Pausanias mentions the fact, but not the motive. See the passage from Polyænus, vol. i. p. 160, note.

tion of the face of the statue, and was humoured by the art of the Egyptian priests.

The identification of Memnon the Ethiopian with the Theban statue naturally gave rise to historical hypotheses as well as poetical fable. According to Agatharchides[1], the Ethiopians invaded Egypt and garrisoned many of their towns, and by them the so-called Memnonia were completed. Here a false hypothesis is grounded on an historical fact; for though the Ethiopians occupied Egypt, perhaps more than once, it does not appear that they had any share in erecting the buildings called Memnonia. This name was given in the age of Strabo to the remains of a palace at Abydos, and by some also to the Labyrinth[2]. The splendour of the real palace of Amenophis seems to have rendered it a general appellation for a royal building of great extent and magnificence. We know that the palace of Abydos was chiefly the work of Rameses III., the Labyrinth of Ammenemes. The story of an Ethiopian migration or invasion takes a still more definite form, in the statement given in the Chronicon of Eusebius, that the Ethiopians, removing from the river Indus, dwelt on the borders of Egypt[3]. This event being placed under the reign of Amenophis, is evidently intended to be considered as connecting the story of Memnon with his reign, and the date of 1615 years before Christ is assigned to it.

[1] Apud Photium Bibl. p. 1342, ed. Hoesch.

[2] Strabo, 17, p. 813. All the buildings which passed by this name were on the western side of the river.

[3] "Æthiopes, ab Indo flumine consurgentes, juxta Egyptum consederunt." Chron. Hieronym. p. 72, ed. Scaliger.

Like his ancestor Amenophis I., Amenophis-Memnon received divine honours, and a special priesthood, called " the *pastophori* of Amenophis in the Memnoneia," still existed in the Ptolemaic times[1].

The mother of Amenophis, *Mautemva*[2], is represented on the right side of the throne of his statue; his wife, who is seen on the left, was called *Taia*. Her name is joined with his, on the engraved scarabæi of a large size which are frequent in the collections of Egyptian antiquities. One of these, according to the interpretation of Rosellini, commemorates the marriage of the king in the eleventh year of his reign; it has been already quoted, as defining the limits of his kingdom. The other, whose signification is obscure, appears to refer to the performance of some public work[3]. The conjunction of the name of the queen with that of the king on these memorials, indicates a greater participation in the royal power on her part than was common in the Egyptian monarchy. Amenophis appears to have had other children besides Horus who succeeded him on the throne. A stele in the Museum of Florence which bears his title mentions " a royal scribe of the house of the royal daughter *Amenset*[4]," the comptroller, it should seem, of the princess's household.

The tomb of Amenoph III. is the oldest royal sepulchre preserved in the Bab-el-Melook, but is

---

[1] See Papyr. v. vi. vii. in Peyron's Collection.

[2] A monument in the British Museum (Birch, pl. 34) represents her seated on a throne which is placed in an Egyptian boat or *bari*. Her name Mautemva is expressed phonetically by a vulture, *Maut*.

[3] Rosellini (Mon. Stor. iii. 1, 266) thinks the construction of a cistern, but acknowledges the uncertainty of his own interpretation.

[4] Champollion-Figeac, L'Univers, p. 319.

not that which in the Roman times was called the tomb of Memnon. It is of great length, extending, though not in one line of direction, 352 feet, with several lateral chambers[1]. Although now in a state of great decay, the remains of painting on its walls indicate a good style of art. The largest apartment represents a common funeral scene, the passage of the Sun through the inferior hemisphere, the legends being traced in linear hieroglyphics, which approach very nearly to the hieratic character. The tomb of Amenoph III. in its perfect state has been one of the most complete, and Amenophis-Memnon reigned according to Manetho thirty-one years; the thirty-sixth[2] has been found on his monuments, illustrating the remark of Champollion[3], that the most elaborate tombs are those of the sovereigns who had the longest reigns.

He was succeeded by his son, whose name in the lists is HORUS, phonetically expressed by the hawk, the emblem of the god, with the addition of the character which denotes the panegyries or solemn festivals[4]. His monuments commemorate victories obtained over the African tribes. In a grotto near the Second Cataract[5], he is represented in the form of the youthful Horus, suckled by the goddess Anouke[6]. The ram-headed god of Thebes, Kneph or Noum[7], stands by; he, like Anouke, was an object of special veneration between the First and Second Cataract.

---

[1] Wilkinson, Mod. Egypt and Thebes, 2, 215. Champollion, Lettres, 223.
[2] Bunsen, Ægyptens Stelle, B.3, p. 78, Germ.
[3] See vol. i. p. 167.
[4] The whole is read *Hor-mbhai*.
[5] Rosellini, Mon. Stor. iii.1,272. M. R. tav. xliv. 5.
[6] See vol. i. p. 385.
[7] See vol. i. p. 373.

The principal historical monuments of the reign of Horus, however, are in the quarries of Silsilis, which seem to have been extensively wrought for the public works then carried on. A large space on the wall of one of the galleries has been occupied by a scene representing his triumph: much of it has perished, but enough remains to show its purport[1]. He is seated on a throne carried on the shoulders of twelve military chiefs, while two others shade him with fans attached to long spears, and an attendant, keeping his face towards the king as he walks, scatters grains of incense on a censer which he holds out towards him. It is evidently the celebration of a military triumph for a victory over the Africans. Captives, whose features are strongly marked with the negro peculiarities, are led bound by the wrists and neck; and the inscriptions record that the great ones of the land of Cush had been trampled under foot. Both Luxor and Karnak received additions from him. One of the rows of criosphinxes at the last-mentioned place bears his legend, with an inscription declaring that he had made great constructions in the residences of Thebes[2]. The propylæum from which this row leads was also built by Horus, and beside the gate of entrance are seen traces of a gigantic figure of him, engaged in smiting his enemies. The name of *Berber* alone is legible, denoting probably some African race, though it would be hasty to identify it with the Barbaria of Ptolemy, on the eastern coast of Africa, or the modern names of Barabra and Berber[3].

---

[1] Rosellini, Mon. Stor. iii. 1, p. 278. M. R. tav. xliv.

[2] Rosellini, M. Stor. iii. 1, 288.

[3] According to Herodotus, the

The works of sculpture of this age show the high perfection which art had already attained. The Egyptian Museum of Turin contains two admirable statues of Horus, one in a white and crystalline calcareous stone, the other in black granite. On the first the king appears standing beside the god Amonre, who is represented as of colossal size; the hieroglyphics of the latter contain a decree, very analogous in its forms to that of the Rosetta stone, in which the benefits rendered by him to Egypt are enumerated, statues ordered to be erected in the principal temples, and panegyries to be celebrated in his honour, conjointly with the god Phre. His daughter, whose name has been read *Tmauhmot*, sits with Horus on his throne, and the decree ordains that her statue should be placed in the temple along with his[1]. A sphinx with female attributes is carved on the side of the throne, in allusion to her sharing with him the attributes of royalty[2].

The genealogical succession of the kings after Horus is very embarrassing, from the want of harmony between the monuments and the lists. On the tablet of Abydos and the lists in the Rameseion and at Medinet Aboo[3], the next name to Horus is RAMESSU, who is followed by the king whom Champollion and Rosellini call *Menephthah*, Lepsius and

Egyptians called all βαρβάρους who did not speak their own language (2, 158). This may only mean that they designated them by a name implying like βάρβαρος (Strabo, 14, 663) harshness of speech; or they may have used the same *onomatopœia* as the Greeks. *Berber* in Coptic denotes the confused murmur of boiling water, no inapt simile for a foreign speech, which always seems inarticulate to those to whom it is unintelligible. Βράζω or βράσσω, which signifies to *seethe*, also denotes an inarticulate sound. See Hesych. βράζειν, βαβράζειν.

[1] Champollion - Figeac, 321. Compare Rosetta Inscr. translated in Birch, Gall. B. Mus.
[2] See vol. i. p. 137.
[3] Rosellini, Mon. Stor. i. p. 204. iii. 1, 305.

Bunsen, *Seti Merienpthah*; but in the lists we find that Horus was succeeded by Acherres (or as Josephus has it, his daughter Acenchres). These are followed by Rathos (Rathotis), Chebres, Acherres (in Josephus two Acencheres), Armesses (Armais), Ramesses, Amenophath, the first whose name bears any analogy to Menephthah. It would be to little purpose to relate the expedients resorted to for the removal of these difficulties. That a period of civil war or divided reign occurred about this time is evident from the circumstance that the shields of two kings, Amuntoonh or Amuntuanch and a fourth Amenoph, are found mutilated[1]. The explanation which Lepsins has devised of the various facts observed on the monuments is, that besides Horus who succeeded him, Amenoph III. left two sons, Amenoph IV., Amuntuanch, and a daughter, Athotis. The two sons both reigned during the life of Horus, in what relations with him we know not. The shield of Amenophis IV. has not been found further to the north than Hermopolis Magna in Middle Egypt[2], and where found it is always defaced[3]. In like manner the shields of Amuntuanch, which are found chiefly in Ethiopia, are defaced. We may hence conclude that their relations to Horus were hostile. It is evident that he either put down or survived Amenoph IV. and Amuntuanch, as stones marked with their shield are found in buildings at Karnak which Horus erected, and for the name of Amuntuanch has been substituted that of Horus[4]. The

---

[1] Wilkinson, M. & C. 1, 57.
[2] See vol. i. p. 47.
[3] Bunsen, B. 3, p. 88, Germ. Wilkinson, M. & C. 1, 57.
[4] Wilkinson, Mod. Eg. & Thebes, 2, 255.

buildings of Horus contain also stones marked with a royal name, which was read by Wilkinson *Atinre Bakhan*, and by Lepsius *Bech-naten Ra*, in inverted order; and the sculpture of these stones is so fresh, as to show that the buildings of which they are a part were destroyed soon after their erection[1]. This Bech-natenra (sometimes written Bakhan only), hitherto supposed to be an intrusive king, a worshiper of the Sun, Lepsius takes for a queen, the wife and widow of Amunoph IV., and from her name he explains the Acencheres or Kencheres of the lists. The daughter of Amenophis III., whose name is written on a monument *Teti* or *Tati*, and who is called "royal daughter, sister, mother, wife,"[2] is according to him Athothis, the reading of one MS. for Rathotis; her husband, the personage whose tomb Champollion discovered in the western valley of Thebes, and whose name he read *Skhai*[3]. They were, according to Lepsius, the parents of Ramessu, the founder of that long line of princes who fill the 19th and 20th dynasty[4]. Here we find the monuments again coinciding with the lists, and as we follow the former authority only, we shall leave the attempts to reconcile them to be confirmed or overthrown by subsequent research.

Ramessu, the immediate successor of Horus on the tablet of Abydos, appears to be both the

---

[1] Perring (Trans. Roy. Soc. Lit. 2nd Ser. 1, 140) supposes that the figures found at El-Tel, representing the worship of the Sun, are those of the Hyksos kings. All that relates to these Sun-worshipers, to whom Bech-naten Ra belonged, is very obscure. Layard (Nineveh, 2, 211) thinks they may be Assyrians, as the Sun's disk was worshiped at Nineveh.

[2] Bunsen, Neues Reich, pl. viii.

[3] Lettres, 247.

[4] *Ramessu* (born of Ra) is probably the original participial form of the name. (See Bunsen, vol. i. p. 297, Eng. Trans.)

Armesses and the Ramesses, the 14th and 15th of Manetho's 18th dynasty, the consonants in both words being the same. The Armais of Josephus appears also to be the same person with a variation of spelling. Of Ramessu's reign little is known. The second year of his reign is found on a stele dug out by the French and Tuscan expedition[1] from the ruins of a temple near Wadi Halfa, erected by Amenophis II. Ramessu had bestowed gifts upon the priests. The stele, which is dated the 20th of Mechir, in that year, but erected and terminated by his son, speaks of the people of the " Land of the Nine Bows" as being subjected beneath his feet, and commemorates, besides various offerings made by him, " pure men and women of the captives." This description occurs elsewhere on Egyptian monuments. The prisoners are divided into three classes, the first of whom appear to be the ordinary prisoners of war, who were reduced into slavery or employed on public works. The second, called *pure*, which is expressed by the same hieroglyphic character as *priest*, were probably distributed to the different temples, to perform as *hieroduli* the inferior offices of ministration. The third class seem to have been hostages[2].

That the reign of Ramessu was short has been inferred not only from the paucity of his monuments, but from the state of his tomb[3]. It was nearly buried under rubbish, which was cleared

---

[1] Rosellini, Mon. Stor. iii. 1, p. 298.
[2] Birch in Trans. of Royal Society of Literature, 2nd Series, 2. 345.
[3] No. 16 in Wilkinson's enumeration of the tombs in the Bab-el-Melook. Mod. Eg. & Thebes, 2, 214.

away by Champollion, and the tomb itself was found to consist of two corridors, without sculpture, terminating in an apartment decorated with paintings. The granite sarcophagus which once contained the body of the king had no sculpture, but was painted. From the attributes given to Ramessu in the paintings, it appears that some were executed during his lifetime, others after his death[1]. Another presumption that his reign was short arises from the circumstance that Armais or Armesses and Ramesses, whom we believe to be Ramessu, are represented as having reigned together only six years, or according to Josephus, five years and five months.

The name of the successor of Ramessu on the tablet of Abydos has been variously read, and exhibits a diversity which is not common[2]. Champollion at first believed the various forms in which the name is written to represent different kings. One class, in which the figure of Osiris is found united with the syllable EI, he read Osirei. Another, in which a different deity, whom he supposed to be Mandoo, takes the place of Osiris, he read Manduei, and considered him as a successor of Osirei, and both as representing the two Achencheres of Manetho. By local study of the Egyptian monuments he ascertained that the figure of the god Mandoo is very different, but it long remained uncertain how this name was to be pronounced. The divinity represented, a sitting figure with long ears and a head similar to that of a tapir, often occurs on monuments, especially in Nubia.

---

[1] Rosellini, Mon. Stor. iii. 1, 309.
[2] The varieties are given by Rosellini, Mon. Stor. i. 1, tav. ix. 110 a, b, c, d.

The phonetic name was discovered to be Set or Seth. It was observed that the character by which this god is denoted had been chiselled out wherever it occurred in the name of a king[1]. This appearance of hostility, which Champollion first remarked in the Museum at Turin, and found universal in Egypt, led him to conclude that it could be no other than Typhon, the principle of Evil, one of whose Egyptian names was Seth, and thus the name of the king was read *Sethei*, and the effaced figure was supposed to be an ass, which was an emblem of Typhon. The other part of the group was read Phthahmen or Menephtah. It was observed, however, that in the same inscription, and where there could be no doubt of identity, the name of the god Amun was sometimes substituted for that of Pthah[2], which led to the conclusion that neither of these names, nor that of Osiris noticed before, formed a part of the phonetic name, which was pronounced simply *Sethei*. The name of Menephtah, however, has become so current that we shall retain it.

To account for the introduction of such a divinity as Typhon into a royal title, Rosellini supposed that it was adopted by the king to express that he was the destroyer of his enemies; but this leaves unexplained the subsequent obliteration of his figure, which seems to imply that he had become odious after the erection of the monuments on which it is found. Lepsius on the other hand maintains that the figure is not an ass but a giraffe (an animal which is not uncommon in hieroglyphics), and that Seth, whose emblem it is, was originally a benefi-

[1] See vol. i. p. 417, 418.   [2] Rosellini, Mon. Stor. iii. 1, 329.

cent deity, held in high honour by the Egyptians, but that by some revolution in theological opinions he subsequently was identified with the principle of Evil, and his image defaced wherever it was found. The evidence of this hypothesis has not yet been produced. The name *Seth* does not disappear from the Egyptian dynasties, even after the time when the change supposed to be indicated by the obliteration occurred; the priest of Vulcan, who led the Egyptians against Sennacherib, was called Sethos.

SETEI MENEPHTHAH has left a memorial of himself in the temple of Amada in Nubia, built by Thothmes and repaired by him; and at Silsilis, where he excavated one of the small grotto temples in the western rock. But his principal monuments are at Thebes. He began the palace at Qoorneh on the western side of the river, which has been already described under the name of Menephtheion[1], but as it remained scarcely finished at his death, it was completed and decorated by his successors, Rameses II. and III., who give the honour of their own labours to Menephtah. The chief apartment of the palace, forty-eight feet long and thirty-three wide, appears to have been designed as a place of public assembly for civil and judicial purposes. The remains at Karnak are much more important[2]. The north-western wall of the hypostyle hall is divided into compartments which occupy the whole of its vast surface, and covered with figures and hieroglyphics in that peculiar relief which the Egyptian artists practised. Each of them represents some

[1] Vol. i. p. 152.   [2] Vol. i. p. 175, 176.

great military undertaking, in which Menephthah triumphs over five different nations of Asia; and each concludes with a procession in honour of Amun, to whom spoil and captives are presented, in gratitude for his having given the victory to his worshipers. The magnitude of the scale on which these pictures are projected, the spirit of the drawing and the high finish of the execution, show that painting and sculpture, both as mechanical and intellectual arts, had attained to great perfection.

Menephthah had scarcely ascended the throne when he undertook a military expedition against the same nations, over whom the Thothmes and Amenophis had established their dominion. We have no information from monuments of any wars of Horus with Asiatic nations, and the state of division into which Egypt appears to have fallen, both in his reign and that of Ramessu, must have weakened its power over distant countries. One of the compartments of sculpture at Karnak[1] represents him, with a youthful figure, in the first year of his reign, engaged in warfare with a people who are called *Shos* or *Shosu*, and their land *Kanana*. Their features are wholly different from the Egyptians; they have caps on their heads and cuirasses round the body, and have been armed with spears and battle-axes. They are in hasty and disorderly flight before the king, who is pursuing them in his *biga*, and has already pierced many with his arrows. On a hill near stands a fortress, surrounded with a fosse, towards which the fugitives are making their

---

[1] Rosellini, Mon. Stor. iii. 1, 337; Mon. Reali, tav. xlviii. 2.

way;—"fortress of the land of Kanana" is inscribed on the front. Another compartment represents the continuation of this campaign[1]. The king again appears in his chariot, transfixing his enemies with his arrows; three fortresses are seen in the background, the nearest of which is already taken, and has the name of the king inscribed over the gate; the fugitives are making their way towards a mountain covered with wood.

In the same year he carried on war with another people, whose geographical position cannot have been very remote, and whose names may be variously read Remanen or Lemanen, Rotno or Ludnu, owing to the ambiguity of the letters which stand for L or R, T or D in the phonetic alphabet. They have gone forth in chariots to meet the king, but have been utterly routed. Their physiognomy, dress and armour are very different from those of the Shos; they have less pointed features; their heads are covered with a cap, which descends to protect the back of the neck, and is fastened by a band; they wear long garments, with a girdle at the waist, and a deep cape over the shoulders. A fortress is near, on the battlements of which the defenders are standing and holding out their hands, apparently in supplication to Menephthah. In the next compartment the king has descended from his chariot and holds the reins behind him, while he turns to address the chiefs of the defeated people, who supplicate him on their knees. Others of the same nation are felling the trees of a wood, perhaps those which surrounded their fortress and added to

[1] Rosellini, Mon. Reali, tav. xlix. 2.

its strength; for a fortress is seen in the distance, with its gate-posts and architrave falling, as if to indicate that it had been captured and dismantled. The whole concludes with a triumphal procession, in honour of the two campaigns. The king is seen mounting his chariot, lifting two of the conquered nation, who are powerfully grasped in his right arm, while two files, with their hands tied, and bound round the neck by a rope which the conqueror holds, are following him. In a similar way the captive Shos are led in triumph, and three of their heads are fixed on the back of the royal chariot. Egyptians, men and women, come forth to meet him; some kneel, others are standing and lifting up their hands in sign of reverence and welcome; and a company of priests, distinguished by their shorn heads, offer large nosegays of the lotus, the characteristic production of the land [1]. The whole scene is bordered by the Nile, sufficiently marked by the crocodiles with which it is filled; and a palace stands on the bank [2]. The date of the first year of the reign of Menephthah is repeated in the hieroglyphics at this place; a presumption that the scene of the events cannot have been very remote from the frontiers of Egypt. The whole finishes with the presentation of the prisoners of the land of Luden to the Theban triad of gods, Amunre, Maut and Chons, and an offering of vases. The inscription declares them to be fabricated out

---

[1] Rosellini, M. R. tav. xlvi.–l.
[2] A bridge over the stream is here represented, a thing which occurs nowhere else among the Egyptian monuments. It is probably laid over one of the smaller streams of Lower Egypt, where the kings would naturally fix their residence when they were carrying on campaigns in Asia.

of their spoils in gold, silver, copper, and the unknown substance *chesebt*[1], and precious stones. Their devices are emblematic of the event which they record; one of them is supported by figures of captives; on another the head of a prisoner appears as bent down by grief, and in the hieroglyphics above them they are called " images of the chiefs of the strange lands[2]."

No date is found with the scene next represented, in which the king is attacking a fortress, the name of which has been read *Otsch* or *Atet*, situated in the land of Amar or Omar[3]. The people who have been defending it, resemble in their features the Shos, in costume the Remanen. They fight in chariots, and inhabit a mountainous and woody country, through which herds of cattle are flying in consternation at the fray. The king is armed with bow and arrows, and also with a short spear, which serves either to hurl from a little distance, or to stab in close fight. The rest of the events of this campaign are lost by the destruction of the wall; but it appears to have concluded with the usual offering of vases and prisoners to Amunre.

It is probable that the war, which is the subject of the next representation, occurred at a considerably later period of the reign of Menephthah, since his son Rameses appears serving in the campaign[4]. *Tahen* or *Tohen* is the name of the people against

[1] See p. 227 of this volume.
[2] Rosellini, Mon. Stor. iii. 1, p. 333.
[3] Birch in Roy. Soc. Lit., 2nd Series, vol. 2, p. 335. It is conjectured by him to be Haditha on the Euphrates, by Dr. E. Hincks to be Edessa, by Mr. Osburn, Hadashah (Josh. xv. 37), and Amar to be the land of the Amorites. Rosellini compares Omar with Omira, the name which the Euphrates bore previous to its passage through Mount Taurus (Pliny, N. H. 5, 24).
[4] Rosellini, Mon. Stor. iii. 1, 378. M. R. tav. liv.–lvi.

whom it is waged, the Tahai who are mentioned in the account of the statistical tablet of Karnak[1], and who are declared to belong to the Rotno or Ludnu. They wear helmets, from which a strap or strip of metal depends, for the protection of the cheek, and the chiefs are distinguished by two feathers in the helmet. The general of the enemy, who is represented as of an intermediate size between his own troops and the gigantic figure of Menephthah, has been pierced in the breast by one of the king's short spears, and then caught round the neck by his bow; and with the uplifted scimitar in his hand he is preparing to put him to death. In another compartment he appears dismounted from his chariot and about to stab with a short spear a chief who has been also pierced in the breast with an arrow. The captives are as usual led in files to be presented to the god. Among the offerings, besides the customary vases, are bags tied up, probably containing gold dust or precious stones.

The people who are called *Sheto* or *Shetin* are the subject of another of the great historical pictures of the wars of Menephthah. Unlike all those who have been described before, they use cavalry[2] as well as chariots in the field. They are clothed in long tunics, girt round the middle and with sleeves, but these do not descend below the elbow. They have no beard; their heads are covered with a scull-cap which reaches to the shoulders and pro-

---

[1] See p. 222 of this volume.
[2] It is remarkable that the horses have neither saddle nor bridle, in this respect resembling the Numidian cavalry. "Nihil primo adspectu contemtius; equi hominesque paulluli et graciles; discinctus et inermis eques præterquam quod jacula secum portat; equi sine frenis." (Liv. 35, 11.)

tects the back of the neck; the top is ornamented with a tassel, and the side of the neck defended by a strip which extends to the breast. They have square shields with bows. The arrows of the king disperse them, and the war ends with a procession, in which captives and chariots are led before Amunre, who on this occasion is attended by Pasht, Chons and Thmei. With this scene ends the representation of the wars and triumphs of Setei-Menephthah on the wall of the palace of Karnak. They are summed up, as it were, in a vast emblematic picture, in which the king appears of gigantic size, grasping by the hair captives of nine different nations, who are fastened to a stake, and preparing to strike them with a ponderous mace, loaded with a ball of metal at the end, while Amunre stretches out towards him the scimitar or *shopsh*, the emblem of destruction and power [1]. Among these nine nations we recognize distinctly the negro of the interior of Africa; the others, though not so strongly characterized, correspond generally in features and head-dress with the nations already represented as conquered by Menephthah. Naharaina or Mesopotamia is mentioned in an inscription, partly mutilated, above the figure of the king. Elsewhere we have seen the conqueror leading the vanquished nations to the god; but here Amunre himself holds the cords to which their symbolical representations are attached. He is accompanied by a goddess, supposed to be the land of Egypt [2], who also holds

---

[1] Rosellini, Mon. Reali, tav. lvii.–lxi. given with slight variation in Sir G. Wilkinson's Plates, 58, 3, and
[2] The same apparently who is called *Kahi*, i. e. "the land."

three cords. The different tribes or towns (for probably they are no more) are designated by an embattled oval, within which the name is written, and over which is placed a head and shoulders, the cord being fastened round the neck and the arms bound. Of these ovals fifty-six are still legible, and several others obliterated. Among those who belong to the race of Cush, a few names seem to bear some analogy to those known to geography, as the *Barobro*, the *Takrurir*, the *Erk*, supposed to answer respectively to the *Barabra* and *Berber*, the *Dakruri* of Upper Nubia, and *Erchoas* on the Nile[1], but in most of them no resemblance can be traced. Some of the characters do not belong to the general phonetic alphabet, and their sound is unknown. The features of the negro in the group grasped by the king indicate that he came from a country far to the South, unless we are to suppose that tribes of this physiognomy extended further northward in ancient times. The third file led by the god, with the exception of the first oval, is of northern nations[2]. Of those whom the goddess leads, the first oval contains a group of characters which Champollion reads *Nemone*, and supposes to signify shepherds (from the Coptic *Moone*, to feed), and to denote generally foreigners of the North. The next are the Shetin, Naharaina, the Rotnu or Ludun,

---

[1] Rosellini, M. Stor. iii. 1, 421. Birch, Gall. Br. Mus. 2, 89.

[2] This assumes the papyrus-plant, which the second and third ovals contain, to denote the North, as it often does. Rosellini (p. 425) thinks, from its similarity with the character answering to 'Ελληνικοῖς on the Rosetta Stone, that it should be read *Aoninin*, and understood of the Ionians of Asia. I doubt if in this age the Ionians were found on the coast of Asia, and were this reading phonetically correct, should rather connect it with 'Ιόνη, the ancient name of Gaza (Dion. Perieget. 1. 92, with the note of Eustathius).

Upper and Lower, and Sinjar. Of the rest, though many of them are distinctly written, little can be made. Names of places in Palestine have been found in them[1], and nothing is in itself more probable than that conquests in this country should be recorded on the monuments of Egyptian kings; but their identification with biblical names is not sufficiently supported to warrant our proposing them as facts.

There is much probability in the opinion of Rosellini, that we should read the name of the Rotnu, *Ludin*, and that the Lydians are meant; not using this word in the limited sense to which the Greek writers have accustomed us, but as a general name for Asia Minor and its prolongation to the country at the sources of the Tigris and Euphrates. Two wholly different nations are evidently described in Scripture under the name of *Lud*. One of these (Gen. x. 13) is called a son of Mizraim, and is mentioned by Jeremiah with Ethiopia and Libya (xlvi. 9) as an ally of Egypt. The other (Gen. x. 22) is called a son of Shem, and mentioned in connexion with Arphaxad (Arrapachitis in Northern Assyria), and Aram or Syria. This is the position in which a name might be expected to occur which represents the Semitic population of Asia Minor. These Ludim, not the African nation of the same name, appear to be meant in Ezek. xxvii. 10, where they are joined with Persia and Libya as furnishing mercenaries to Tyre. To this Semitic population was probably owing the manifest connexion between the mythology of Lydia and that of

---

[1] Osburn, Onomasticon, Ancient Egypt, p. 156.

Assyria[1], and the early civilization of Lydia, which through the Greek colonies settled on its shores became a source of refinement and culture to all Europe.

We have already described among the sepulchres of Thebes, the tomb and sarcophagus of Setei-Menephthah, discovered by Belzoni in the Bab-el-Melook[2]. It is the most splendid that has hitherto been explored, and the plates to Belzoni's work will give a good idea of the variety and richness of its decorations. It contains a representation which we find repeated with some variation in the tombs of other kings of this and the succeeding dynasty, and which seems designed to express the universality of Egyptian dominion. The god Horus, the symbol of royalty, is preceded by four companies of men, of different colour, physiognomy and costume. The first are plainly Egyptians; the third are blacks; the second white with bushy black hair, blue eyes, aquiline noses and reddish beards; they wear short parti-coloured tunics, with several tassels at the lower extremities. The fourth resemble the people called Rebo in the campaigns of Rameses IV., wearing feathers in their heads, and large cloaks, and having their bodies tattooed. The Egyptians have the name *Rot*, supposed to signify *race*, as if they identified themselves with mankind; the blacks that of *Nahsu*; the third group are called *Namu*, and the fourth *Tamhu*. The Nahsu are represented

[1] Comp. Herod. 1, 7, where Agron, the first of the Heracleid kings of Lydia, is made the son of Ninus the son of Belus. The predecessors of Agron were descended from Lydus the son of Atys, who represents a Phrygian population earlier than the connexion with Assyria.
[2] Vol. i. p. 167.

with variety of dress and physiognomy in the other tombs, but always black; the Namu are elsewhere drawn with an entirely different costume; and the Tambu are made yellow instead of fair, and have ample garments worked in elaborate patterns, instead of the cloaks which half cover their tattooed bodies[1]. The two names therefore appear to be generic, and to comprehend races ethnographically distinct. The people called in the sculptures of the wars of Menephthah, Remenen or Lemenen, and the inhabitants of the land of Omar, belonged to the Namu; the Tohen to the Tambu. In the same way Nahsu is the generic name of the black nations, and Cush the specific name of the Ethiopians. Taken together they appear to have conventionally represented the principal nations known to the Egyptians, and as their wars did not extend to Europe, we must seek the originals in Asia, the Namu in the Semitic nations, the Tamhu in those who dwelt eastward of the Tigris.

The monuments do not afford us data for fixing the length of Setei-Menephthah's reign. The Sethos of the lists is said to have reigned fifty-one or fifty-five years, and the magnitude and elaborate decoration of the tomb of Setei-Menephthah, as well as his recorded conquests, show that his reign cannot have been a short one. The name of one of his queens appears to have been *Twea*, the mother of Rameses II. and III.; of another, *Tsire*[2].

The shields of all the sovereigns hitherto mentioned on the tablet of Abydos contain titles only, and their phonetic names have been ascertained

---

[1] Rosellini, M. S. 4, 228, M. R. tav. clv. &c.   [2] Rosellini, Mon. Stor. 1, 251, 270.

from other monuments. That of the successor of Setei-Menephthah, however, is followed by a shield which contains a phonetic name, and closes the last line but one; this name is Rameses Mei-Amun, and it is repeated along with the titular shield through the whole length of the lowest line. But the titular shield of the lowest line is not exactly the same as the last titular shield of the upper line; it differs from it by the addition of a group of characters which is usually interpreted, "Approved by Re[1]." The lateral column of the tablet, again, exhibits only the shield without the addition. Hence arises the question, do these two titular shields represent two sovereigns, Rameses Meiamun II. and Rameses Meiamun III., or is the addition in the second shield merely a difference, assumed by the same sovereign at a subsequent period of his reign? Such variations, perplexing as they are, appear to have been practised. The obelisk of the Atmeidan, already mentioned, exhibits four several additions to the characters which form the titular shield of Thothmes III.[2], and one of them is this same group, "approved by Re." Again, the same tomb in the Bab-el-Melook was found to contain two shields, one which has, the other which has not the addition "approved by Re;" and hence Major Felix and Sir Gardner Wilkinson were led to the conclusion, that they indicated only one sovereign, Rameses II. The colossal statue which lies reversed at Mitrahenny has on the girdle both shields, one

---

[1] Compare the shields 11, 12 & 13, in the Hieroglyphic Plates, II. vol. 1. No. 12 is the phonetic name belonging to both; no. 13 has the group of characters at the bottom which is read *Sotp-n-ra*, "approved by Ra," which is wanting in no. 11.

[2] See Trans. Roy. Soc. Lit. 2, 228, 2nd Series.

with, one without "approved by Re." At Beitoualli the shield is four times repeated, once with the addition "approved by Re." The processions of the kings at the Rameseion and Medinet Aboo exhibit *only* the shield with the addition[1]. These are strong reasons for believing that only one king is designated by both shields. Yet a great difficulty attends this supposition: the names of their wives and their children are different, and it would be too arbitrary a mode of proceeding to assume a second marriage and the death of the children of the first. Rosellini adds[2], that the physiognomy of the two kings is so different, that even at a distance they can be distinguished by one who is familiar with them. This argument can be appreciated only by those who have seen the monuments of Egypt on the spot; yet the evidence of one who spent so many months among them must be admitted to be of great weight. It is also alleged[3], that in more than one instance the title "approved by Re" has been inserted in a shield in which it had not been originally found, by a cancelling of the previous inscription—an act not likely to have been performed by a sovereign on his own shield, though we find a son using this liberty with the shield of his father. Rosellini assures us also that he has found dates of the reign of Rameses from the second year to the sixty-second, all containing the addition "approved by Re," and it is difficult to conceive that he should before the first of these dates have performed those exploits and executed

---

[1] Rosellini, M. Stor. 1, p. 205. [3] Rosellini, *u. s.* Birch, Gall. B.
[2] Rosellini, M. Stor. 1, 256, 261. Mus. P. 2, p. 91, note 11.

those works, to which the shield without the addition is attached. Where obelisks have been begun by one monarch and finished by another, the central line marks the work of the first. Now the central inscription on three of the faces of the obelisk transported from Luxor to Paris bears the shield without the addition; so does that which remains at Luxor on one of its faces; the others bear the shield with the addition. Without concealing the difficulties which press on either hypothesis, I assume, as most probable according to the present state of the question, that the two shields represent two kings, and I shall proceed to give an account of the monuments which bear their respective names.

To RAMESES II. belong the historical pictures and sculptures of Beitoualli near Kalabshe in Nubia, casts of which, coloured according to the original, may be seen in the British Museum[1]. The sanctuary represents the youthful monarch suckled by Isis and Anouke. The walls of the vestibule exhibit on the left his triumphs over the Ethiopian nations. Mounted in his chariot armed with his bow, and accompanied by two of his sons who are also in chariots, he slaughters and tramples down the negroes who fly in confusion towards a village indicated by its palms. A wounded man, supported by two others, is feebly making his way to a cottage within which the mother is cooking. A child and another female stand beside the door with expressions of sympathy and terror. Conquerors have been fond in all ages of recording the carnage of their battle-

[1] Rosellini, M. R. tav. lxii.-lxxv. Birch, Gall. Brit. Mus. pl. 38. p. 2.

fields, but this is a solitary instance of their completing the picture by an exhibition of the misery which war brings to the cottage-hearth. The fruits of the victory are exhibited in a procession, in which the same productions of Africa, which have been already described in speaking of the reign of Thothmes III., are brought before the king, who is seated under a rich canopy. Immediately before him stands his son, who is introducing into his presence " the royal son of the land of Cush, Anemophth." Rosellini thought that he was brought as a prisoner, but it seems more probable that the two attendants are arraying him in garments of state, previous to his appearance before the king; and that the vase which Rosellini supposed to contain a restorative potion, holds water or perfume. In another part of the procession the same Anemophth brings on his shoulders skins of panthers, rings of gold and exotic plants, and the connection of the different parts of the picture is probably to be conceived of in this way, that having deposited his offerings before the king, he is rewarded by receiving the investiture described above. From his features and dress he is evidently of Egyptian race, and therefore probably of a family which had enjoyed the viceroyalty of Ethiopia since the commencement of Egyptian conquests in that country.

The left side of the vestibule contains representations of the Asiatic victories of Rameses II. The people with whom he is engaged are those whom we have already become acquainted with, in the historical monuments of Setei-Menephthah's reign. In one compartment the king appears mounted in his chariot and pursuing a host of men of yellow complexion, short and peaked beards and a sharp physiognomy, variously armed with scimitars, javelins and throwsticks [1]. In the inscriptions which are legible their name does not occur, but they closely resemble those who on the walls of Karnak are called the *Shos*, and whom we have concluded to be a tribe of Palestine. Next he is seen attacking a fortress, in the upper story of which is a chief whom he grasps by his helmet and is preparing to behead with his scimitar. On the lower story are several figures, in attitudes expressive of distress and consternation. One man holds out a censer towards the conqueror, as if in propitiation of a god; two females are imploring his clemency; a third, with similar purpose, is holding her child from the battlements, from which a man is also precipitating himself. A prince armed with an axe approaches the gate of the fortress to break it open. No name occurs in any part of this scene; but the costume is that of the people whose name is read by Rosellini *Shomui*, by Champollion *Shari* or *Khuru*[2], and supposed to be Syrians. Men of the same nation appear in the next compartment to be brought before the king to receive their doom. He stands on a board beneath which two of them are lying prostrate, and thus literally made *his footstool*; he grasps three by the head, and the prince leads a file of others to him bound. A similar scene is represented in another compartment, where the king holds his scimitar over the head of a kneeling prisoner of Asiatic race. Finally he is seen, seated on his

[1] Rosellini, Mon. Reali, pl. lxvii. [2] See p. 228 of this vol. Vol. i. p. 313.

throne, with a lion having his fore-paws bound couched at his feet. Egyptians, evidently of military rank bearing emblems of victory, stand in order before him, and one of the princes of the blood brings three Asiatic prisoners bound. The inscription appears to be a general summary of the triumphs recorded on both walls, mention being made of victories over the Cushites as well as the Shari[1].

This is the principal historical monument of Rameses II.'s reign; for the obelisks of Luxor contain nothing beyond the customary pompous and mystical phrases. It has been already mentioned, that the tomb in the Bab-el-Melook appears to have been begun, but not carried on far by him. From this and other circumstances it has been concluded that his reign was not long.

He was succeeded by RAMESES III. That he was the brother of his predecessor appears from the Menephtheion[2] already mentioned, in which both of them stand before the figure of Menephthah, and the inscription declares that they have come to render homage to their father[3]. We have seen however that Rameses II. had sons, and therefore we must suppose that they were dead, or what is more probable, that their uncle set them aside and mounted the throne—a proceeding not unsuitable to his energetic character. He may even have dated his accession from his father's death. That Rameses III. is the Sesostris of Herodotus is no longer doubtful. Herodotus says that he had him-

---

[1] Rosellini, Mon. Stor. iii. 2, p. 18.
[2] See p. 255 of this vol.
[3] Rosellini, Mon. Stor. 1, p. 263.

self seen in " Palestine of Syria¹" the tablet which Sesostris set up in commemoration of his conquest. At the mouth of the Nahr-el-Kelb, the ancient Lycus, not far from Beiroot, three such tablets are found, exhibiting an Egyptian king in the customary posture of smiting his enemies. His name is not preserved, but the titular shield is that of Rameses III. with the characters " approved of Re." Further, Herodotus relates that Sesostris on his return to Egypt set up a colossal statue of himself, thirty cubits (forty-five feet) in height, before the temple of Ptah at Memphis. At Mitrahenny we have seen that a colossal statue still exists[2], forty-eight feet in height, bearing not only the titular shield, but the phonetic name of Rameses III. This proof is not so cogent as the preceding, because we are not sure that this is *the* statue of which Herodotus speaks, but even alone it would have furnished a strong argument for the identity of the Sesostris of Herodotus with this king. It does not prove that he was called Sesostris in the Egyptian annals; but it shows that one remarkable circumstance which Herodotus relates of Sesostris is historically true of Rameses III., and justifies our application of the written history, in which no Rameses appears, to the monumental, in which the name of Sesostris is not found. That we should be able to frame from their union a narrative in which every part of both shall find a place, is not to be expected. Diodorus complains that

---

[1] Trans. of Royal Soc. Lit. vol. 3. p. 105, Pl. 1.2. 1st Series. Possibly this may explain the tablets ἐν τῇ Σιριαδικῇ γῇ κειμένων from which, according to Syncellus (p. 40. 73, ed. Dind.), the Pseudo-Manetho in the Sothis professed to have derived his history. The inscriptions in the Wadi Mokuttub are hardly of sufficient antiquity to be referred to.

[2] Vol. i. p. 115.

the Greeks did not agree with one another in what they related of Sesostris (his Sesoosis), nor the priests with those who panegyrized him in song[1] He himself begins his narrative with a circumstance which betrays its own origin in popular and poetical fiction. It is a characteristic of such fictions to represent the birth and earliest years of those who are afterwards to play a distinguished part, as corresponding with their subsequent celebrity. The father of Sesostris collected together all the male children who were born in Egypt on the same day with him, and caused them all to be educated together, that early familiarity might prepare them for friendly cooperation[2]. Their training was such as the future conquerors of the world from India to Thrace might well need; none was allowed to take food in the morning till he had run 180 stadia, at least eighteen miles. While yet a youth he was sent with his companions by his father to undergo a still further hardening in the deserts of Arabia, and subdued its inhabitants, on whom the yoke had never been imposed before. Next he was dispatched to the west, where he subdued also the greater part of Libya. That some reason might appear why his father anticipated such celebrity for his son and educated him accordingly, it was said that Hephaistos appeared to him in his sleep and foretold that the child who was about to be born should be

---

[1] Diod. 1, 53.

[2] Jomard, Description d'Égypte, Mémoires, 9, 151, calculates, that if, when Sesostris was twenty years of age, more than 1700 males, as Diodorus says (1, 54), were living, born on the same day with him, 6800 children must have been born every day of the year, and the whole population of Egypt must have been 72,722,600. The scythe of statistics mows down unmercifully the exuberances of mythology and rhetoric.

the conqueror of the world. On his father's death, either relying on this oracle, or persuaded by his daughter Athyrtis, who was endowed with superior sagacity to all other women, or had acquired her knowledge by divination, he determined to undertake an expedition.

We recognize here plainly enough the exaggerations natural to the story of an heroic conqueror, whose memory has been fondly cherished by the people and celebrated in popular poetry. Herodotus relates no prodigies or incredible facts respecting the childhood of his Sesostris, but he makes his first expedition to be for the subjugation of the people who dwelt on the shores of the Erythræan Sea, that is the Indian Ocean. If he built his fleet of ships of war in some of the harbours on the western side of the Red Sea, and with them passed the Straits of Babelmandeb to subdue the Ethiopians, it is difficult to understand how his further progress could be stopped, as Herodotus says, by shallows. If, however, as Diodorus represents[1], he made a land expedition into Ethiopia, and as he and Strabo say, from that coast entered the Arabian Gulf, he might naturally enough be stopped by shallows, for the sand-banks and coral-reefs make navigation along its shores towards the northern end dangerous in the extreme to all who are not familiar with them. These difficulties were experienced by Ælius Gallus when he undertook his expedition from the head of the Gulf, against the Arabs, in the reign of Augustus; and the tides of the Red Sea, which embarrassed his navigation,

[1] Diod. 1, 55. Strabo, 16, p. 769.

must have been still more formidable to Egyptian sailors in the reign of Sesostris[1]. A fleet for the navigation of this sea would be more easily constructed on the coast of Ethiopia, which abounded with wood, than at Suez, Myos Hormos or Berenice, where no timber whatever is to be found. The subsequent exaggerations of Diodorus, who makes Sesostris conquer the whole sea-coast to India, and even pass the Ganges and reach the Eastern Ocean, do not belong to the poetical fictions of the ancient Egyptians; they indicate the corruption of history from a more recent source—the desire of the priests to exalt the conquests of Sesostris above those of the Macedonians, under whose dominion the land of the Pharaohs had fallen. Diodorus, who assigns him 600,000 infantry, 24,000 cavalry and 27,000 chariots, includes the Cyclades in his conquests; Dicæarchus[2], "the greater part of Europe."

The Greek historians represent Sesostris as of unusually lofty stature; Herodotus, according to the probable meaning of his words, six feet nine inches[3]; and this may perhaps be a cause why he seems to have drawn to himself the fame of the Thothmes and Menephthah, whose names are passed over by them. In the Egyptian battle-pieces the sovereign is always of gigantic size, and to those who could not read their names, they might all pass for one and the same Sesostris[4].

---

[1] Syllæus, who undertook to be his pilot, exposed his fleet to danger ῥαχίαις ἀλιμένοις παραβαλὼν, ἢ χοιράδων ὑφάλων μεσταῖς ἢ τεναγώδεσι· πλεῖστον δὲ αἱ πλημμυρίδες ἐλύπουν καὶ αἱ ἀμπώτεις. (Strabo, 16, p. 780.)

[2] Schol. Apoll. Rhod. 4, 272.
[3] See note on μέγαθος πέμπτης σπιθαμῆς, Kenrick's Egypt of Herodotus, 2, 106.
[4] See p. 164 of this vol.

The historical and other monuments of the reign of Rameses III. far exceed those of any preceding or subsequent sovereign, and correspond with the long reign of upwards of sixty years which the lists and the sculptures agree in attributing to him. The earliest of these records is of the fifth year of his reign. His campaign of this year is partially delineated on the walls of the propylæa of Luxor, but much more fully on those of the temple of Aboosimbel. So numerous are the pictures, that they alone occupy twenty-five plates in the great work of Rosellini[1]. The cost and labour involved in first excavating this temple in the rock, and then covering it with painted sculptures of nearly the size of life, are incalculable; yet they could never be seen, except when explored with artificial light. At the time when this temple was excavated, the valley of the Nile between the two Cataracts was no doubt much better peopled than it has ever since been. But on this site there is no appearance that any town has ever stood; the Nile is close to the front and the desert is behind, whence the sand has poured down in streams, choked up the entrance to the temple, and buried the colossal figure of the king. We can only conjecture therefore that some unrecorded circumstance in the life of Rameses led him to fix on this spot for a record of his gratitude[2].

The pronaos of the temple, into which the traveller first enters when he has worked his way through the sand, is supported by a double row of

[1] Mon. Reali, tav. lxxix. ciii.
[2] Rosellini supposes that here he may have met his queen, by whom the smaller temple was dedicated to Athor, on his return from his expedition. (Mon. Stor. iii. 2, 167.)

eight pilasters, on the front of which stands, like a Caryatid, the figure of Rameses with the attributes of Osiris, thirty feet in height. The walls on the left or south side are divided into several compartments, each of which represents some action of the king; the right is occupied with a single subject, itself comprehending a great variety of actions[1]. The two first on the left side exhibit the victories of the king, accompanied by his three sons[2], one of whom is named Rameses, over the Asiatic nations whose names are already known to us from the sculptures of Setei Menephthah, African victories being also incidentally mentioned in the inscriptions. The artist has apparently had this monument of Menephthah's reign in view, and imitated its composition and arrangement. In the next compartment are seen two files of African prisoners led by the king to be presented to three divinities[3]. These according to the usual theology should be Amunre, Phre, and Maut; but Rosellini has observed a singular piece of flattery in the composition of the group[4]. The figure which should represent Phre has the disk of the sun placed over it, but the features are those of Rameses III. himself, the head-dress is that of a king, and the legend above is, " Discourse of Amun-mai-Ramses, We grant thee life and perfect purity." The African prisoners are coloured alternately brown and black, but it may be doubted whether this is meant to indicate the difference of colour between Nubians and

---

[1] Rosellini, Mon. Stor. iii. 2, 89–119.
[2] Rosellini, u. s. p. 101.
[3] Rosellini, M. R. tav. lxxxiv. v. vi.
[4] Mon. Stor. iii. 2, 117.

negroes; elsewhere we find the Egyptian artists using a contrast of colour for the sake of relief. The features of both the brown and the black men are equally negro, and their costume is the same. In their rude and awkward movements, and the ludicrous expression of constraint and pain in their countenances, the painter has exactly copied the workings of nature as they may be seen at this day in the same people under similar circumstances.

The wall on the right-hand side represents, without divisions, a series of actions in a campaign against the *Sheto* which may be considered as the first military undertaking of Rameses III., as it bears date the ninth of Epiphi, in the fifth year of his reign. The whole composition contains more than eight hundred figures, and the centre is occupied by the camp of the king, the various events of the campaign being exhibited around the four sides[1]. The series begins with an attack made by him on a fortified city standing on a river, branches of which flow around its walls, and serve the purpose of a trench. The enemy, who wear long-sleeved tunics, have generally the head shaven, with the exception of a lock which falls over the back of the neck, and wear mustachios. They fight from chariots, but of much ruder construction than those of the Egyptians, and each chariot carries three persons, a spearman, a charioteer and a shield-bearer. Their shields are of different forms, some square, and apparently made of basket-work, others of wood with incurved sides. The enemy are driven headlong to the fortress, and some of them have been preci-

[1] Rosellini, Mon. Stor. iii. 2, 119, tav. lxxxviii.-ciii.

pitated with their horses and chariots into the river. Mixed with the chariots appear here and there men mounted on horseback; but as they are without armour, and the horses without saddle or bridle, they seem as if they were making their escape from the field on horses which in the conflict had been detached from their harness, or else are acting as messengers[1]. The battle-scene is followed by another, in which the king, seated in his chariot, and surrounded by his guards and officers, sees the amputated hands of his enemies thrown down before him, and their number recorded by scribes. Other scenes of war occupy the borders; they generally resemble those which we have already described. One of them, however, deserves a special notice; two men of the hostile nation are undergoing the bastinade, and from the inscription above them it appears that they are detected spies.

The importance which the Egyptians attached to the events of this campaign is evident from its repetitions at Thebes. The scene represented on the propylæa of the great court of Luxor is the same as that which we have just described[2]. We find again the city round which the river flows assaulted by the Egyptians, and some of the combatants with their chariots and horses precipitated into it. The bastinading of the spies is also repeated, and the centre is occupied, as at Aboosimbel, by a representation of the camp. All doubt of their identity is removed by the date, which is the fifth of Epiphi

[1] The camp which has been already described (vol. i. p. 229) occupies the centre; a lion bound couches in the middle.

[2] Rosellini, Mon. Stor. iii. 2, 222, tav. civ.–cvii.

in the fifth year of the king, Rameses III., the date of that of Aboosimbel being four days later. The Rameseion, on the western bank of the Nile[1], which was his work, repeats, with some variations, the same subject[2]. The city on the river again appears, but it has a double fosse, and a bridge over them connecting it with the main land. The river is full of drowning men and horses; a chieftain has been dragged out on the bank, and his soldiers are endeavouring to restore him to life by holding him with his head downwards. These men have evidently made a sally from the city over the drawbridge, for the purpose of assisting and rescuing their friends whom the Egyptians have driven into the river. In another part of the Rameseion is represented the capture of a second fortress. A scaling-ladder is applied to the walls, two sons of Rameses are ascending upon it, and four others at the base are leading as many bodies of men, who are sheltered by a large wooden coverlet from the stones, lances, and arrows of the besieged. Four other royal princes appear in different parts of the field.

Diodorus Siculus[3], having described, on the authority of the Egyptian priests and the Greek writers who had visited Thebes under Ptolemy Lagi, the fore-courts of the monument of Osymandyas and the colossal statues of the king, his wife and his mother, proceeds:—" Next to the pylon," they say, " is a peristyle hall, more wonderful than the preceding, in which are all sorts of carvings,

---

[1] Vol. i. p. 153.
[2] Rosellini, *u. s.* p. 232, tav. cix.
[3] Hist. 1, 47.

representing the war which he waged with the revolted Bactrians. Against them he made an expedition with 400,000 infantry and 20,000 cavalry, the whole army being divided into four parts, all of which sons of the king commanded. On the first wall the king is represented besieging a fortress surrounded by a river, and encountering some of his enemies, accompanied by a lion who fights fiercely in aid of him. Some of those who expounded the antiquities said that the king had really tamed a lion, which fought for him and put his enemies to flight; others, that being haughtily vain of his valour, he expressed his own character by the figure of a lion. On the second wall captives are represented with their hands cut off, and otherwise mutilated, indicating that their minds were effeminate, and that in their difficulties they had made no vigorous use of their hands. The third wall had carvings of all kinds, and brilliant pictures representing a sacrifice by the king, and a triumph on his return from the war."

There are circumstances in this description which identify the so-called monument of Osymandyas[1] with the Rameseion, and the sculptures of which Diodorus speaks with those which Rosellini has drawn. Such are the river flowing round the fortress, and the four sons of the king. It is true that he also mentions circumstances which are not found here, as the fighting lion, and the mutilation of the captives. But only a part of the original sculp-

[1] No name like *Osymandyas* appears in the lists of Egyptian kings; but *Simandu*, "son of the god Mandu" (see vol. i. p. 394), is the name of one of the sons of Rameses III., and may have been a title of his father. (See Rosellini, Mon. Stor. i. 277.)

tures of the Rameseion remains; and as we have already seen that those of Aboosimbel and Luxor are free copies of the same general subject, we may restore and supply the one from the other; and in one or other all these circumstances are found. If then it be ascertained that all these relate to the same event, we know from Diodorus what that event was; it was reputed to be, according to the Egyptian priests, the campaign of Rameses against the revolted Bactrians. Amidst all the uncertainty which attends the interpretation of the hieroglyphical inscriptions, so much seems to be ascertained, both from the words themselves, and from the comparison of the nations who now appear in the field with those who are seen in the battle-pieces of Setei Menephthah, that this was a second conquest, and that consequently there had been a rebellion. There is no name indeed which bears any resemblance to that of Bactrians; nor is it necessary to suppose that the country bore the same name in the Ptolemaic times as in that of Rameses III. Yet the name is remarkable as it recurs in Tacitus. The priest who acted as guide to Germanicus, related from the monuments of Thebes that Rameses had possessed Libya, Ethiopia, Media, Persia, Bactriana and Scythia, with the territories which the Syrians, Armenians, and their neighbours the Cappadocians inhabit, extending his dominion to the Bithynian sea on the one side, and the Lycian on the other[1]. Now we know from the monuments that the claim of dominion over Libya, Ethiopia, and Syria, was well founded; in

[1] Tac. Ann. 2, 60.

the time of Herodotus its memorials existed in Asia Minor, and may yet perhaps be found there; the valley of the Tigris and Euphrates was familiar ground to the military sovereigns of the 18th and 19th dynasties. Confirmed in so many points, why should not the accounts of the Egyptian priests be believed, when they tell us that Media, Persia and Bactriana were also the scene of the conquests of Rameses? Such were the first conclusions of Champollion respecting the country of the Sheto and the other nations who are represented as warring with Menephthah and his successors; and upon the whole they appear to be the most probable. The expression of Herodotus, that he went through " the whole continent," subduing all whom he met, may be explained by two other passages, in which he uses the same expression, and from which it is evident that it included all Asia, from the shores of the Ægean to the eastern limits of Media and Persia[1].

One of the strong evidences of the wide range which the expeditions of Rameses and other Egyptian sovereigns took in Asia, was the resemblance which the Colchians bore to the Egyptians. Herodotus does not speak from hearsay on this point; he had been among the Colchians, and had made inquiries both from them and the Egyptians. He acknowledges that the resemblance of their dark complexions and crisp hair was not decisive; other

[1] 1, 96. Ἐόντων αὐτονόμων πάντων ἀνὰ τὴν ἤπειρον, ὧδε αὖτις ἐς τυραννίδας περιῆλθον. From the comparison of this passage with the beginning of c. 95, it is evident that "all on the continent" means all who were subsequently included in the dominion of Persia (4, 91). Darius calls himself on the *stele*, which he set up near the Hehrns, Περσέων τε καὶ πάσης τῆς ἠπείρου βασιλεύς.

nations had these peculiarities; but he lays more stress upon their linen manufacture, their whole mode of life, their language, and their practice of circumcision. It was an ancient usage only among the Colchians, Egyptians and Ethiopians; for the Syrians in Palestine (by whom, though ignorant of their distinct nationality, he must have meant the Jews,) and the Phœnicians acknowledged to have learnt it from the Egyptians, and the Cappadocians from the Colchians[1]. Pindar calls the Colchians dark-complexioned, speaking probably according to the received opinion of his contemporaries. The later geographers and Ammianus Marcellinus[2] may have only repeated Herodotus. As we know nothing of the Colchian language, we cannot bring to the test the declaration of Herodotus that they were similar; nor is much stress to be laid upon it, as his knowledge of the Egyptian language was very limited; but the correspondence of their mode of life was a matter in which he could not be mistaken. The Colchians were certainly a civilized and instructed people[3], living among tribes remarkable for their rudeness, and no other source of this superiority appears so natural as a settlement of the soldiers of Sesostris[4]. He remarks that when he inquired of both nations, he found that the Colchians preserved more memory of the Egyptians than the Egyptians of the Colchians. This was natural

[1] Vol. i. p. 448. Her. 2, 103.
[2] 22, 8. Colchos, Ægyptiorum antiquam sobolem.
[3] Bochart, Geogr. Sacr. lib. 4, c. 31.
[4] Ritter, the celebrated geographer, in his "Vorhalle Europäischer Völkergeschichte," denies the Egyptian origin of the Colchians, and derives them from India. One of his proofs will excite a smile at the present day: "the Egyptians," he says, "in early times, according to the unanimous testimony of antiquity, kept themselves to their native country" (p. 40).

under any circumstances; but if Pliny's account be correct, that Sesostris was defeated by Salauces, son of Æetes and king of Colchis, the silence of the Egyptians would be very intelligible[1]. The wealth of Colchis in gold, of which Pliny speaks, and which gave rise to the fable of the fleece, accounts for the Egyptian king's including this remote country in the range of his expedition.

Herodotus does not mention how long the absence of Sesostris lasted. Diodorus makes it nine years, nor is this improbable. Both historians relate that he had made his brother viceroy in his absence, and that on his return his life was exposed to danger at Daphne near Pelusium from his treachery. He invited the conqueror to a banquet in his tent, and when he had fallen asleep under the influence of wine, set fire to a quantity of combustibles which he had piled on the outside. Sesostris awaking and finding his imminent danger, prayed to the gods for the deliverance of himself and his children: his prayer was heard, and he escaped through the flames. To show his gratitude he offered gifts to the other gods, but especially to Hephaistos, as the principal cause of his escape. As related by Herodotus the story is still more portentous. Discovering his danger, he consults with his wife, who advises him to take two of their six children, and make a bridge of them across the flames. He did so, the children were burnt, but Sesostris and his wife escaped. In gratitude for

---

[1] Plin. N. H. 33, 15. Salauces, Æetæ soboles (Cod. Bamb. vulg. Æsubopes), victo Sesostri, Ægypti regi tam superbo, ut prodatur annis quibusque sorte reges singulos e subjectis jungere ad currum solitus, atque ita triumphare.

their preservation he erected statues of himself and his wife thirty cubits high, and of their sons twenty cubits high, before the temple of Hephaistos at Memphis[1]. This tale betrays its origin in an age when Egyptian tradition had begun to be corrupted by a desire to conform to Greek ideas. To the Greeks the Memphian Ptah was the god of fire; and what cause more natural for the erection of the family group in costly statues, than their deliverance from burning? It does not often happen that Diodorus is more moderate and rational than Herodotus; but it is so here. Neither author gives the entire story; Diodorus does not mention the burning of the children, nor Herodotus say that the statues were erected in memory of the escape, but both circumstances are necessary to complete the narrative.

Herodotus and Diodorus describe Sesostris on his return from his long expedition as devoting himself to public works and to legislation. The captives whom he brought back were employed in dragging stones to the temple which he built to Hephaistos, and others which according to Diodorus[2] he erected in the chief city of every nome to its tutelary deity, placing on all of them an inscription purporting that they had been raised by the labour of captives and not of Egyptians.

---

[1] Rameses III. appears to have had twenty-three sons, but four are seen conspicuously on several of the monuments (Rosellini, M. Stor. iii. 2, 240, 265), and this might give rise to the popular opinion that all but four had perished. (Birch, Gall. Brit. Mus. 204.)

Besides Nofre-Atari, who dedicated the smaller temple at Aboosimbel to Athor, he had another wife, Isinofre, who appears along with him in the inscriptions at Silsilis, accompanied by two sons and a daughter. (Rosellini, Mon. Stor. 1, 272.)

[2] 1, 56.

Some of these captives, who had been brought from Babylon, unable to endure the severity of their labour, rose and seized upon a strong post near the Nile and not far from Memphis, to which they gave the name of Babylon, whence they laid waste the neighbouring country. If it were true that they defied the power of the king and at last established themselves here in security, as Diodorus says, this would give us no high idea of the power of the Egyptian monarchy. Tradition, however, varied in regard to the origin of the name; Ctesias derived it from an invasion of Egypt by Semiramis; Josephus with most probability refers it to the invasion of Cambyses[1]. Sesostris raised mounds of earth, to which he removed the inhabitants of those towns which were in danger of being flooded in the inundation of the Nile; cut canals through the whole of Lower Egypt[2], and built a wall, 1500 stadia in length, from Pelusium to Heliopolis, to defend the frontier of Egypt from the invasion of the Syrians and Arabs. According to Herodotus he distributed all the lands of Egypt, assigning to each man his " rood of ground," and laid a land-tax upon them. Even the institution of the law of hereditary occupations was attributed to Sesostris (Sesonchosis) by Dicæarchus and Aristotle[3]. That a reign so long

---

[1] Antiq. Jud. 2, 15.

[2] Diodorus represents this as being done partly to render Egypt inaccessible to cavalry and chariots; Herodotus to supply fresh water to parts remote from the river. The country having been rendered unfit for wheeled carriages by the cutting of canals, it was a natural fiction to attribute to him the introduction of mounted cavalry. Πρῶτον φασὶν αὐτὸν εὑρηκέναι ἵππων ἄνθρωπον ἐπιβαίνειν. (Schol. Apoll. Rhod. 4, 272.)

[3] Pol. 7, 10. Ὁ δὲ χωρισμὸς ὁ κατὰ γένος τοῦ πολιτικοῦ πλήθους ἐξ Αἰγύπτου· πολὺ γὰρ ὑπερτείνει τοῖς χρόνοις τὴν Μίνω βασιλείαν ἡ Σεσώστριος.

and vigorous would witness many improvements in legislation, many works of public utility, we cannot doubt; we know that Rameses III. covered Nubia[1] and Egypt with memorials of his devotion to the gods and his magnificence in building ; but when the raising of the sites of all the cities, the cutting of all the canals, the division of the whole land of the kingdom, the distribution of the people into castes, are attributed to him, we see the tendency of popular history to crowd into one reign the progressive improvements of many. Egypt had been a civilized kingdom long before Rameses III., and those undertakings which are essential to its prosperity and order had probably been the gradual work of several sovereigns.

The hieratic manuscript known by the name of the Papyrus of Sallier, is said to contain an account of a war carried on by Rameses III.[2] with the Sheto in the ninth year of his reign ; but the import of this document is hitherto so little known, that we must content ourselves with indicating the fact, that four years later than the events which have been just described, he was still involved in hostilities with them.

The south wall of the palace of Karnak contains an inscription dated in the twenty-first year of the reign of Rameses and the twenty-first day of Tybi, in which it is recorded that four chiefs of the Sheto came to the tent of his majesty to supplicate for peace, who

---

[1] They are found at Ibrim, Derri, Amada, and Wadi Esseboua.

[2] "Several hieratic papyri, which we still possess, are dated from the Rameseion, and I have found in Thebes the sepulchres of two librarians, father and son, under Rameses Meiamun." (Lepsius, Einleitung, 1, 39.)

III.]   THE EIGHTEENTH DYNASTY.   289

granted it to them on condition of their paying tribute in silver, gems, and balsam or spicery[1]. We learn little from this document respecting the events of this war or revolt. A phrase in the inscription (l. 8 at the end) seems to imply that a battle had been fought in the land of Egypt; but the connexion is not sufficiently clear to warrant the supposition that the Sheto had actually invaded Egypt. It is remarkable that in this document three of the gods of Egypt, and Sut or Sutch, the god of the Sheto, who resembles the figure called Typhon or Seth in the Egyptian monuments, are represented as taking a share in the events of the war and the conclusion of the peace, on behalf of their respective worshipers[2].

This is the latest memorial that has been found of the wars of Rameses III. The temple of Aboosimbel, however, contains a large *stele* evidently later in its erection than the edifice itself, dated the 13th of the month Tybi and the 35th of his reign[3]. Its purport is rather religious than historical. He appears upon it, preparing to smite three foreigners in honour of the god Ptah-Sokari. A long inscription contains the discourse of this divinity to the king, in which he declares that he and the other gods have granted to him that his edifices should be stable as the pillars of heaven, and promise that he shall celebrate many panegyries, that he shall conquer his enemies, and that the rest of the world shall be obedient to him, like the Sheto represented

---

[1] Rosellini, Mon. Stor. iii. 2, p. 268, tav. cxvi.
[2] Rosellini, Mon. Stor. iii. 2, 280, note. This may possibly throw light on the obliteration of the figure of Seth. See vol. i. p. 417.
[3] Rosellini, Mon. Stor. iii. 2, p. 163.

VOL. II.   U

on the walls of this temple. The king in reply boasts of having enlarged and adorned the temple of the god in the habitation of Ptah, that is Memphis, his peculiar dwelling-place. We know from Herodotus and Diodorus what he did for the enlargement and decoration of this temple; the prostrate colossal statue of Mitrahenny bears the image of Ptah and the contemplar goddess Pasht, in the tablet on the breast and the shield on the belt[1]. The quarries of Silsilis contain several *stelæ* in which mention is made of panegyries celebrated by Rameses III. in his 30th, 34th, 37th, 40th and 44th years. The last appears to have been celebrated on a larger scale than usual, the cities of Upper and Lower Egypt being specially mentioned as taking part in them[2].

The smaller temple at Aboosimbel was dedicated by Nofreari[3], queen of Rameses, to the goddess Athyr, and contains chiefly religious inscriptions, but also some in honour of Rameses III., whose victories over the nations of Africa, over the north and the south, are commemorated, but without any precise dates. The face of the rock from which these temples were excavated, also exhibits sculptures of various kinds, and among them some of historical import. One records an act of homage to Rameses III., in the 38th year of his reign, on the part of an Ethiopian prince, Sotekauto[4], holding the

---

[1] Bonomi, in Trans. Roy. Soc. Lit. 2nd Series, 2, 300.
[2] Rosellini, Mon. del Culto, p. 230.
[3] Rosellini, Mon. Stor. iii. 2, 173; Mon. Reali, tav. cxi.
[4] Rosellini, u. s. p. 187. He is called "the living eyes of the king" and "ears of the chamberlains of the royal house." Compare Jul. Poll. ii. 84. Ἐκαλοῦντο δέ τινες ὦτα καὶ ὀφθαλμοὶ βασιλέως οἱ τὰ λεγόμενα διαγγέλλοντες καὶ τὰ ὁρώμενα.

office of basilicogrammat. Neither here, nor in the other numerous examples of such homage, do the persons rendering it exhibit any trace of Ethiopian features or appear in Ethiopian costume. They invoke the gods of Egypt, offer prayers for the Pharaohs[1], and are in every respect Egyptian. Either therefore Nubia between the Cataracts was governed in this age by Egyptian princes, or, as seems more probable from the multitude of temples of that religion, its population was Egyptian. One of these inscriptions on the rocks of Aboosimbel is important, as declaring that Rameses had employed the captives of his Asiatic wars in building the temples of the gods[2].

Aristotle and Strabo inform us that Sesostris undertook, Pliny that he meditated[3], the construction of a canal to join the Nile with the Red Sea. Herodotus, when he relates the similar undertaking of Neco[4], makes no mention of Sesostris, and it is probable that the undertaking has been attributed to him from the celebrity of his name[5].

The tablet which Rameses III. caused to be erected at Abydos, containing the shields of his predecessors, has been already described. Setei Menephthah

---

[1] Rosellini, Mon. Stor. iii. 2, p. 189. Rameses III. added two lateral columns to the inscriptions on the obelisks of Luxor, erected by Rameses II., but they contain no historical information. The colossal statues of granite which (vol. i. p. 171) are attributed to Rameses II. should belong to Rameses III., according to the criterion laid down in p. 268 of this volume.

[2] Diod. Sic. 1, 56. Πρὸς τὰς ἐργασίας τῶν μὲν Αἰγυπτίων οὐδένα παρέλαβε, δι' αὐτῶν δὲ τῶν αἰχμαλώτων ἅπαντα κατεσκεύασε. Διόπερ ἐπὶ πᾶσι τοῖς ἱεροῖς ἐπέγραψεν ὡς οὐδεὶς ἐγχώριος εἰς αὐτὰ μεμόχθηκε. The πᾶσι is an exaggeration.

[3] Meteor. 1, 14. Strabo, lib. 1, p. 38. Plin. N. H. 6, 29.

[4] 2, 158.

[5] Lepsins (Einl. 1, 349) thinks that Sesostris carried his canal only to the eastern extremity of the valley of Goshen.

appears to have been the builder of the temple or palace, the greater part of which is now buried in the sand, and to have begun the temple of Osiris, which his son Rameses III. completed.

Eusebius gives sixty-eight years to Rameses, and his sixty-second is found on a tablet in the British Museum. This collection also contains one of the finest specimens of Egyptian sculpture, in his colossal bust of red granite, the remains of a statue once placed in the Rameseion of western Thebes and removed thence by Belzoni[1].

Mention has been already made of the tomb in the valley of Bab-el-Melook in which the shields of both the second and the third Rameses occur. Rosellini, who entered it with difficulty, found it nearly filled with rubbish, either washed down by torrents or purposely brought in when it was abandoned[2]. It has not been explored to its furthest extremity, but there is no appearance that it was ever elaborately executed, as we might expect in the tomb of so powerful a monarch, and one who reigned so long. Was the great Sesostris content with having covered Egypt with monuments of his magnificence and indifferent to the splendour of his sepulchre, or are we to believe that the Rameseion was his burial-place as well as his palace? Such a combination would be very repugnant to Egyptian usages, and yet the authors whom Diodorus[3] followed distinctly asserted, that the tomb of the sovereign who built the Rameseion lay apart from those of the rest of the kings, and was approached by a flight of steps

---

[1] Birch, Gall. of Brit. Mus. p. 104. Vol. i. p. 154.
[2] Mon. Stor. iii. 2, 284.
[3] 1, 49.

from the palace. It may therefore remain to be discovered.

With Rameses III. we lose the guidance of the Tablet of Abydos, but the procession at Medinet Aboo gives us a royal titular shield, to which it appears from other monuments that the name of MENEPHTHAH II. belongs[1]. Herodotus represents Sesostris as being succeeded by his son Pheron, whose name historians are agreed in considering as a misunderstood *Pharaoh*. Diodorus gives him as successor Sesoosis II., confounding him probably with the next but one in order, Setei Menephthah II. The Rameseion contains the portraits and names and offices of the twenty-three sons of Rameses III.; the thirteenth, Menephthah, bears the addition of *king*, which has evidently been made by a later hand, and subsequently to his accession to the throne. Six princesses, elegantly clothed and with a sistrum in their hands, are figured in the same place[2]. No properly historical monuments of his reign exist; he appears at Silsilis in acts of adoration to various divinities[3], among the rest the Nile, who was worshiped with especial honour at this place, where he seems to issue again as from a second source. Nor does any great building appear to have been erected by this king; when his name is found, it is on trifling additions made to the works of preceding monarchs. The fourth year is the highest date that has yet been found on his monu-

---

[1] Instead of the phonetic characters for Ptah, the last syllable is expressed by the figure of the god. (Rosellini, Mon. Stor. 1, 204. Lin. iv. 12.)

[2] Rosellini, Mon. Stor. i. 275, 6, 7. iii. 2, 297.

[3] Rosellini, Mon. Stor. iii. 2, 298.

ments. His tomb in the Bab-el-Melook is 167 feet in length, and has been ornamented with great care in the portions near the entrance, and one piece of sculpture still remains of which the colours are as brilliant as when they were first laid on[1]. Menephthah, crowned with a splendid head-dress, and clad in a long transparent robe fringed at the bottom, stands before the hawk-headed god Phre, who promises him length of days upon the throne[2]. This is a sufficient proof of the custom of excavating the tomb during the lifetime of the king. The name of the successor of the Rameses, who, according to Eusebius, reigns sixty-eight years, according to Josephus sixty-six, and who must therefore be Rameses-Sesostris, is in Africanus, Amenophath, who reigns nineteen years. Removing the A, which may have been prefixed as in Armesses, Menophath approaches closely to Menephthah. With him the 18th dynasty of Manetho concludes.

To the reign of this Menephthah it appears probable that we are to refer the commencement of a Sothiac cycle. It has been already stated that the 1461 years of which it was composed, having run out in 139 A.D., must have begun in 1322 B.C.[3] If therefore we could ascertain in what year of what king of Egypt it began, we should have a fixed point for our chronological reckonings. Now a passage in the writings of the Alexandrian astronomer and mathematician Theon, published by

---

[1] Wilkinson, Mod. Eg. & Thebes, 2, 211. Rosellini, Mon. Stor. iii. 2, 306.

[2] Rosellini, Mon. Reali, tav. cxviii. A cast of this sculpture was taken by Mr. Hay, and is in the British Museum. (Birch, Gall. pl. 41.)

[3] Vol. i. p. 333.

Larcher in his Notes to Herodotus, implies that this cycle had one of its beginnings, if not its institution, in the reign of a certain king Menophres[1]. As there is no king in the lists whose name exactly answers to this, Champollion-Figeac conjectured that the king intended was the *Ammenephthes* or *Amenophis* who stands third in the list of the 19th dynasty, and the year of the commencement of the cycle the thirty-second of his reign[2]. Bunsen has given reasons, as convincing as the nature of the evidence allows, for considering Menephthah II. as the king intended[3]. We have thus a fixed point from which we can reckon downward to the reign of Sheshonk, and thence to the Dodecarchy and the close of the monarchy of the Pharaohs, with tolerable certainty, and upwards at least to the commencement of the 18th dynasty. The astronomical ceiling at the Rameseion[4], if erected near the close

[1] Λαμβάνομεν τὰ ἀπὸ Μενοφρέως ἕως τῆς λήξεως Αὐγούστου. Ὁμοῦ τὰ ἐπισυναγόμενα ἔτη αχέ, οἷς ἐπιπροστιθοῦμεν τὰ ἀπὸ τῆς ἀρχῆς Διοκλητιανοῦ ἔτη ρ'· γίνονται ὁμοῦ ἔτη αψέ. "The sum of the years from" (the æra of) "Menophres to the end of" (the æra of) "Augustus is 1605, to which adding the 100 years from the beginning of (the æra of) Diocletian, we have altogether 1705 years." The æra of Diocletian began the 29th of August A.D. 284. (Ideler, Handb. der Chron.1, 163; Champollion-Figeac, Première Lettre à M. le Duc de Blacas, p. 100.) Deducting the 283 years of the Christian æra which preceded it, from 1605, the joint duration of the two preceding æras, we have 1322 B.C. for the commencement of that of Menophres. This is the year in which we know from Censorinus (vol. i. p. 334, note) that a Sothiac cycle began.

[2] Syncellus (p. 103. 193, ed. Dind.) says, Τῷ έ (5th) ἔτει τοῦ κέ (25th) βασιλεύσαντος Κογχάρεως τῆς Αἰγύπτου, ἐπὶ ις' δυναστείας τοῦ Κυνικοῦ λεγομένου κύκλου, ἀπὸ τοῦ πρώτου βασιλέως καὶ οἰκιστοῦ Μεστραίμ τῆς Αἰγύπτου πληροῦνται ἔτη ψ' (700) βασιλέων κέ. Champollion-Figeac joined the words πληροῦνται ἔτη ψ' with τοῦ Κυνικοῦ λεγομένου κύκλου, instead of with βασιλέων κέ, and hence concluded, that the fifth year of Concharis, the last king before the Hyksos, fell in the 700th year of a Sothiac cycle. See Bunsen's Egypt, 1, 221, Eng.

[3] Bunsen, Ægyptens Stelle, B. 3, p. 123.

[4] Vol. i. p. 335. The expression "Rameses II. or III." indicates the doubt whether these sovereigns were the same or different.

of the reign of Rameses-Sesostris, would exhibit the state of the heavens as they appeared in the beginning of that of his successor. The reign of Sesostris was one of the times assigned for the appearance of the Phœnix[1].

After the death of Menephthah we have again difficulties from the want of conformity between the monuments and the lists, and discrepancies among the monuments themselves. In the procession of Medinet Aboo, the next shield to that of Menephthah is SETEI-MENEPHTHAH II., *i. e.* SETHOS, whom the lists make the first of the 19th dynasty. But we find on monuments the shields of two other personages with titles of royalty, whose names read Mai-n-Phre Siphthah[2] and Amun-meses. Siphthah appears at Silsilis making an offering to Amunre, accompanied by an officer of his court, who puts up a prayer for the king; and in another sculpture Siphthah supplicates Amunre that his son, Numei, may sit on the throne after him, a prayer nowhere else found on Egyptian monuments, and from which it has been argued that he felt doubtful of the stability of his own power[3]. At Qoorneh, he is represented on a stele inserted into the wall, receiving from the same god the scimitar, the emblem of military dominion, Setei-Menephthah I., Rameses III., and Aahmes the queen of Amenoph I., standing by[4]. The presence of these persons seems to indicate some genealogical connexion with the 18th dynasty on the part of Siphthah, although we are unable to say what it may have been. His tomb in the Bab-

---

[1] Tacit. Ann. 6, 28.
[2] Rosellini, Mon. Stor. iii. 2, 324.
[3] Rosellini, *u. s.* 329.
[4] Rosellini, *u. s.* 330.

el-Melook[1] is of great length, and ornamented with a variety of sculpture. His wife Taoser, Taosiri, or Taseser, appears frequently making offerings to the gods, sometimes alone, sometimes in company with her husband. As the epithet *Osirian* (μακαρίτης) is subjoined to her name, it is evident that she was deceased when these sculptures were executed. There is no date on any of the monuments of Siphthah, but everything tends to show that he was not admitted as a legitimate monarch of Egypt, though he assumed the title, and had for a time possession of Upper Egypt, so as to prepare himself a sepulchre at Thebes[2]. Of Amun-meses we know still less than of Siphthah, but he seems also to have been an intrusive king, and the circumstance that a change of dynasty took place about this time may account for their appearance in monuments and their exclusion from the lists.

Assuming the end of the reign of Rameses III., or the commencement of that of Menephthah II., to fall in the year B.C. 1322, and that Rameses III. reigned 66 years, we are brought to 1388 B.C. for the date of his accession. There is no certainty in the numbers assigned by the lists to his predecessors; but we know from the monuments that Amenophis III. reigned at least 36 years, Thothmes III. at least 35, and Amosis 22 ; while Rameses I. reigned probably only one or two years. If we allot to the twelve predecessors of Rameses III. twenty years each, we shall be brought to 1628 B.C. as an approximate date for the establishment of the New

---

[1] No. 14 on Sir G. Wilkinson's Plan. Rosellini, *u. s.* 331.

[2] Rosellini, Mon. Stor. iii. 2, 319.

Monarchy. If, however, the kings whom we have distinguished as Rameses II. and III. were one and the same, only eleven reigns intervened between Rameses III. and Amosis.

Nineteenth Dynasty. Seven Diospolitan kings. (Eus. Five.)

	Years.	
1. SETHOS, reigned	51	Eus. 55
2. RAPSACES (Rampses, Eus.)	61	Eus. 66
3. AMMENEPHTHES	20	Eus. 40
4. RAMESES	60	Omitted Eus.
5. AMMENEMNES	5	Eus. 26
6. THUORIS, called in Homer Polybus, the husband of Aleandra[1], in whose time Troy was taken	7	
	204	

"In this same second volume of Manetho are 96 kings, 2121 years."

It could not escape the observation of critics, that the commencement of this dynasty bore a very suspicious resemblance to the termination of the last[2]. We have Rampses reigning 66 years, followed by Ammenephthes, who reigns 40 in the 19th, and Rameses reigning 68, followed by an Amenophis reigning 40, (Euseb.) in the 18th. The names Ramesses, Armesses, Armais, Armaios, Ermaios, if we strike out the vowels, which were not originally expressed, reduce themselves to the same three

[1] In the Armenian Eusebius Thuoris is said to be "vir strenuus ac fortissimus," as if the translator had read ἄλκανδρος ἀνήρ, which is the reading of two MSS. of Syncellus, p. 169 D. 320 ed. Dind.

[2] "Hi ipsi reges, ultimi Dy- nastiæ 18 et primi Dyn. 19, valde mihi sunt suspecti tanquam iidem, bis positi et male in diversos distincti, quum utique eadem sint nomina regum, idem ordo, idem denique spatium regni." (Perizon. Ægypt. Orig. Investig. c. xii. p. 194.)

letters, R, M, S, and therefore probably denote the same name, if not the same person; nor are Rampses and Rapsaces so remote from Rameses as to preclude the possibility of their also being the same. Amenophis, Amenophath, and Ammenephthes so nearly resemble each other, as to excite a similar suspicion, especially as the Amenophath of the 18th dynasty reigns 19 years, Amenophis of the 19th, 19 years and 6 months[1], and Ammenephthes, 20. Again, the Sethos-Rameses of Manetho, quoted by Josephus, is so exactly a counterpart of Sesostris-Rameses, that we cannot hesitate to pronounce their histories to be the same in origin[2]. "Sethos, who is also Rameses," says he, "had a large force of ships and cavalry. He established his brother Armais as administrator of Egypt, and invested him with all other royal authority, only enjoining upon him not to wear the diadem, nor to injure the queen, the mother of his children, and to abstain from the royal harem. He himself having made an expedition to Cyprus and Phœnice, and again to the Assyrians and the Medes, brought them all under subjection, some by force of arms, others without fighting, through terror of his great power; and being rendered proud by his success, he went on yet more boldly, subduing cities and lands that lay towards the East. After the lapse of a considerable time, Armais, who had been left behind in Egypt, began to do boldly just the reverse of what his brother had exhorted him to do. He took the

---

[1] The authors of the Lists have suppressed the odd months everywhere, as we find by comparing them with the quotation from Manetho in Josephus.
[2] Joseph. c. Apion. 1, 15.

queen-mother to himself by force, and did not abstain from the harem[1]; and at the persuasion of his friends he began to wear the diadem, and set himself up against his brother. Sethos was informed of these things by the chief priest, and immediately returned to Pelusium and took possession of his kingdom. And the country was called Aiguptos from his name; for he says that Sethosis was called Aiguptos, and Armais, his brother, Danaus." Here we have evidently the same narrative as in Diodorus and Herodotus respecting Sesostris; the great force of ships and cavalry, the conquest of Hither Asia, the invasion and subjugation of countries lying still further East (the Bactrians of Diodorus), the distinction between the nations who timidly submitted and those who resisted by force of arms, the usurpation of power by his brother, and the resumption of it by Sesostris at Pelusium. The recital of Manetho, it is important to observe, since his authority has been often so lightly treated, is simple and historical; it is in Herodotus and Diodorus that we have it embellished and exaggerated from popular tradition.

The monuments strengthen the suspicion which the lists excite. We have seen that the 62nd year of Rameses III. has been found; but there is no trace of any other king of these dynasties reigning so long. We are therefore led to conclude that the Rameses of the 19th dynasty, who reigns 60 years, and the Rampses, who reigns 66, are one and the same historical personage, Rameses III. of the 18th. The identity of Amenophis and Amme-

---

[1] Comp. 2 Sam. xvi. 20.

nephthes cannot be proved by the same argument, because the monuments, instead of 40, which the lists exhibit, have hitherto furnished us only with 4 years. But only one king has been found whose name can with any probability be read into Amenophath. The Ammenemes, who now stands fifth in the 19th dynasty, is, according to Lepsius and Bunsen, the Amenmeses of the monuments, a contemporary, and rival of Menophthes, the last of the 18th.

Thus, when critically examined, the whole 19th dynasty appears to collapse, and resolve itself into a repetition of the 18th, with the exceptions of Sethos the first, and Thuoris the last name. The Sethos of the extracts from Manetho's history in Josephus is only a synonym of Rameses-Sesostris; the Sethos of the lists and the monuments is Setei Menephthah II. (p. 296). He is called Osirei-Menephthah by Rosellini[1] and Wilkinson, as the figure of Osiris occurs instead of Set in some variations of the shield, namely in the tomb, and among the ruins of Karnak, as well as on some of the sphinxes of the dromos, which were originally placed there by Horus[2]. A sarcophagus with his shield, rudely carved, is found in his tomb in the Bab-el-Melook[3], and these are all the memorials of his reign, which can hardly have extended to fifty-five years, according to the present reading of the monuments. The second is the highest that has been found. According to all appearance, it was both a short and an inactive one.

In the monuments nothing has come to light by

[1] Rosellini, Mon. Stor. iii. 2, 311, 313.
[2] Rosellini, u. s. p. 309.
[3] Rosellini, u. s. p. 314.

which the name Thuoris can be explained. Polybus is not spoken of in Homer[1] as a king of Thebes, but as a rich man by whom splendid gifts were bestowed on Menelaus, while his wife Alcandra (not very consistently with the Herodotean story of Proteus) gave appropriate similar presents to Helena. That we should not find an Egyptian king to answer to every name which the Greeks interwove in their mythology is not surprising; yet as fiction is not wholly arbitrary, we might have expected some apparent reason for the selection of this name. Bunsen would read for *Thuoris*, *Phuoris*. Were this admitted, a probable derivation would be from *Ph'ouro*, which is Egyptian for 'king'[2]. Phuoris would then be a name, like Pheron, inserted in the room of one that had been lost or was unknown. It is in this way that we find Pharaoh used in the earlier Jewish books, while in the later and contemporary history, Shishak, Hophra, Necho are mentioned by name. No such sovereign is found in the procession of Medinet Aboo, nor can we trace any resemblance in the history of Pheron to that of Thuoris. Pheron, the son of Sesostris, loses his sight, either by hereditary disease, or as a punishment for impiously darting his javelin into the Nile when its inundation was exceeding bounds, and recovered it by a remedy prescribed by the oracle. In gratitude to the god and at the command of the oracle, he erected two lofty obelisks to the Sun at Heliopolis[3]. One obelisk remains there, but no doubt had once its companion; it bears the

---

[1] Od. δ', 126.
[2] *Ouro* is the Coptic for 'king,' whence the royal serpent, βασι-λίσκος, is called *Uræus*. (Horapoll. 1, 1.)
[3] Diod. 1, 59. Her. 2, 111.

name of Sesortasen I. Pliny appears to refer to it as set up by a king Mesphres. Others at Heliopolis he attributes to Sothis, in whose name we have perhaps the Sesoosis II. of Diodorus. Elsewhere Pliny[1] gives the name of Nuncoreus to the son of Sesoosis, and says that the obelisk which he erected on the recovery of his sight was in the Circus of the Vatican. There is, however, another name, not indeed in the lists, but in the monuments, for which a place must be found. The tomb of Siphthah already mentioned in the Bab-el-Melook originally exhibited on its walls his shield and that of his wife; but they have been covered with plaster and other inscriptions substituted for them. The name of the king who had thus usurped the sepulchre of another is not clearly made out[2], owing to the number of characters not phonetic with which the shield is filled; but it seems to be *Merir* or *Merira*. His name is also on the granite sarcophagus which remains, though broken. In the procession of Medinet Aboo, his shield follows that of Setei-Menephthah II. We cannot therefore question his royal dignity. Bunsen, on the authority of Sir G. Wilkinson, makes him the father of Rameses III. (IV.), and progenitor of the long line of princes of that name who fill up the 20th dynasty. The same author has also remodeled the two preceding dynasties. He makes the 18th to end with Horus, and the 19th to consist of Ramessu, Setei I., Rameses II., Menephthah, Setei II.

---

[1] N. H. 36, 15.
[2] Rosellini calls him Uerri, or Remerri (Mon. Stor. iii. 2, 317, tav. xiv. 116), where the various shields are given. One of them, 116ª, has the figure which in the shield of Menephthah is pronounced *Set*.

Merira, whom he takes to be the same as Phuoris, he places at the head of the 20th dynasty.

The period of the 18th and 19th dynasties exhibits Egypt in a new relation to the rest of the world. Under the Old Monarchy we cannot trace its dominion beyond the peninsula of Sinai, the northern shores of the Red Sea, the Libyan tribes immediately contiguous to the Delta, and in the 12th dynasty Lower Nubia. With the expulsion of the Shepherds, however, begins a series of foreign wars, which led the armies of Egypt to the verge of the then known world.

Nations seem impelled by their geographical position and their relation to neighbouring countries to seek to expand themselves in certain directions. The first necessity for the Egyptians was to secure the valley of the Nile beyond the Cataracts of Syene. From this quarter their independence was always threatened. Nubia was inhabited by a people nearly allied to the Egyptians in blood, and not inferior in valour or perhaps in civilization; the banks of the Nile offered them an easy road to descend on Egypt, which could, therefore, have no peace or safety unless they were kept in subjection. Possibly this may have been facilitated by matrimonial alliances formed towards the close of the Hyksos period, or by the first sovereigns of the 18th dynasty[1]. However this may be, we find that Thothmes I. had possession of the valley of the Nile, as far south as the island of Argo; and the Egyptians remained masters of this country, as completely as of Egypt itself, during the 18th, 19th and 20th dynasties.

[1] See before, p. 207 of this vol.

THE NINETEENTH DYNASTY.

There was no such motive for attempting conquests towards the West. The sandy desert which borders the Nile on that side offered no temptation to ambition, and was too thinly peopled to be formidable. The Oases were valuable as resting-places for commerce, but for this purpose military possession of them was not necessary. The sea-coast westward from the Canopic mouth is not desert, but is of no extraordinary fertility till you reach the district of Cyrene. The Adyrmachidæ, the immediate neighbours of the Egyptians in the time of Cambyses, had in great measure adopted their customs, and therefore probably lived under their laws, but still retained many barbarous usages[1]. The Giligammæ, who extended thence to the territories of Cyrene, closely resembled them. No mention of the characteristic production of this region, the *Silphium*, has hitherto been found on the Egyptian monuments, nor does any inscribed memorial of Egyptian dominion remain in it. In the name *Nahsi*, applied to the black nations in the hieroglyphical inscriptions, a resemblance has been conjectured to the Nasamones, who dwelt on the coast between Cyrene and the Syrtis, feeding their flocks there, and in the season of dates gathering a harvest of them in the Oasis of Augila: but the Nasamones can scarcely have been more black than the Egyptians, living as they did on the shores of the Mediterranean, and no reliance can be placed on such verbal resemblances. Dominion over Libya is claimed for the kings of Egypt in various inscriptions of the 18th dynasty, but nothing indicates its extent, nor is any

[1] Herod. 4, 168.

nation of Western Africa clearly characterized in the sculptures[1]. Till the settlement of the Phœnician colonies, which falls at a later period, this region appears to have contained no civilized or powerful nation.

Towards Palestine, Syria, Arabia and Mesopotamia, Egypt stood in a very different relation. She had to fear at once the power of the nomadic tribes, which still continued to roam over the desert regions included in these limits, and the civilized communities which had been established in other parts of them. At the commencement of the 18th dynasty she was only just recovering herself from the invasion of one of the former class; the Hyksos had been driven out, but from Palestine they still threatened the frontier. The desert which divides the two countries was but a slight protection to Egypt; it has been passed by many invading armies, and would offer little obstacle to Palestinian or Arabian tribes. Besides these, Palestine contained many warlike nations, " dwelling in cities great and fenced up unto heaven," " children of Anak," whose size and strength disheartened the Israelites and made them shrink from the attempt to conquer their country[2]. They had chariots and horses, and in the equipments and arts of war were not inferior to the Egyptians themselves. The towns on the coast were probably

---

[1] There is a country hieroglyphically designated by "the bows" or "9 bows," over which the Egyptian sovereigns are said to reign. A bow in Coptic is *Phit*, and hence is supposed to stand for *Phut*, which (Gen. x. 6) is the name of an African nation, probably the Mauritanians. (Joseph. Ant. 1,6,2.) But this character of the nine bows occurs where it cannot well be understood exclusively of the Libyans. (See Rosellini, Mon. Stor. 4, 16.)

[2] Dent. ix. 1, 2. Numb. xiii. 31.

already engaged in navigation and commerce: Zidon is mentioned in the dying words of Jacob. Syria and Palestine were not only formidable neighbours to Egypt, but a most enviable possession. From the variety of their soil and surface, they furnish every choice production of the vegetable world; in the level districts, grain, in the more hilly regions, the olive, the vine, the pistachio, and the odoriferous gums, for which the temple service of Egypt made a large demand; on the mountain sides inexhaustible forests for architecture, shipbuilding, and the manufacture of articles of luxury. Hence we find that in all ages the acquisition of Palestine has been coveted by the sovereigns of Egypt. Thothmes I. must have held it, or he could not securely have carried on wars in Mesopotamia. Sesostris has left the record of his conquest on the coast; and the last military exploits of the Rameses appear to have had Palestine for their scene. When the spirit of conquest revived in the 22nd dynasty, we find Sheshonk invading Palestine, and besides Jerusalem and "the fenced cities of Judah," occupying other places in that country[1]. There is again an interval in which Egypt was in a state of weakness and anarchy; but when Psammitichus had united its forces, the schemes of Asiatic conquest were renewed. The danger on this side had become more imminent. In earlier times Egypt appears as the assailant of the Mesopotamian nations; but the Assyrians under their later sovereigns had become a conquering people, and Sennacherib had advanced to the gates

[1] 2 Chron. xii. 4.

of Pelusium. The power of the Assyrians soon after passed into the hands of a people even more warlike, the Babylonians; Neco, who had advanced to the Euphrates, received a total defeat at Carchemish. After this, the Pharaohs renounced their attempts to make themselves masters of the country as far as the Euphrates; but Apries recovered much of the sea-coast of Palestine and of the interior of Syria. Under the Persian power all these countries were united in one monarchy; but no sooner had an independent power been established in Egypt than a struggle for the possession of Syria began on the part of the Ptolemies, which was met by attempts on that of the Seleucidæ to make themselves masters of Egypt. The same struggle has been renewed since the Mohammedan Conquest. The powers which have successively reigned in Egypt, Fatemites, Ayubites, Mamlukes, Turks, have all aimed at the same object, but down to the recent attempt of Mohammed Ali, no permanent union has ever been effected between the two countries.

Even the Pharaohs with all their boastful claims to victory and dominion never could incorporate them with Egypt. If one sovereign appears to have put down all resistance, we find that his successors have soon to combat the same nations. Yet this would be an insufficient ground for calling in question the reality of their expeditions and victories. We are not indeed to receive the accounts of them as literally true; Egyptian sculptures and hieroglyphics were not more veracious than modern gazettes and bulletins; Bel and Nebo may have been thanked for the same events as Amun and Phre; we know that Te Deum has been sung for the same battle, at Vienna and Paris. But it would be the excess of incredulity to suppose that the walls of the temples, palaces and tombs of Egypt could be inscribed with the scenes of imaginary campaigns, and that the diversity of names, physiognomy, costume and armour which appears in them has been devised for the purpose of imposture. The evidence of the Statistical Tablet is still more decisive. Here we have the year, month, and day of the king's reign specified on which his expedition was undertaken; and its fruits in spoil or tribute registered with the most formal minuteness. If such evidence can be rejected, we must renounce all hope of establishing history in these ancient times. Few events of the middle ages are certified to us by such authority.

It may seem incredible that kings of Egypt should be able to carry on wars so far from home as the banks of the Euphrates, and still more the confines of Bactria. This feeling, however, arises from the ignorance in which we have remained till lately of the times of the Thothmes and the Rameses. We have known nothing of the wealth and power of Egypt, its population, its military discipline, the perfection of its arts, and its civil organization. The monuments confirm themselves, for they show that all these existed in the 15th and 16th centuries before the Christian æra; and where they exist, the ambition of conquest is not long absent. The power of a single aggressive monarchy was then not easily resisted; extensive coalitions and alliances were impracticable. The extraordinary stability and regularity of the Egyptian government allowed the sovereigns to be absent from their dominions without danger; the people were not seduced from their allegiance, even in the nine years' expedition of Sesostris. If Cambyses could reign from Media to the confines of Ethiopia and to the Ægean sea, there seems no reason why the sovereigns of the 18th and 19th dynasties of Egypt may not have traversed these countries with their armies, and made them for the time their tributaries.

To this period later writers refer the arrival of the first Egyptian colonists in Greece. Herodotus fully believed in the fact, but he did not connect it with any particular event in Egyptian history. He relates the introduction of the worship of Egyptian deities at Dodona, by a female minister stolen from the temple of Thebes; the flight of the daughters of Danaus from the sons of Ægyptus, and their touching at Rhodes in the way; he attributes to them the introduction of the rites of Ceres into the Peloponnesus, and traces the genealogy of the Dorian kings through Perseus and Danaus to Egypt. Divination, processions and solemn festivals, according to him, all came to Greece from the same source[1]. Neither he nor the Greek writers who followed him appear to have doubted the fact of the extensive influence of Egypt on Greece, nor its having been produced by colonization. The circumstances of the arrival and establishment of Danaus are indeed clearly mythic—the fifty-oared ship, the equal number and marriage of his daughters and his brother

---

[1] 2, 54, 58, 171, 182. 6, 53. The inhabitants of Chemmis claimed Danaus and Lynceus as natives of their city.

Ægyptus' sons, the murder of all but Lynceus by the Danaides[1]. But removing these, there remain the belief of the Greeks that the ancient royal family of Argos was of Egyptian descent—a belief which cannot have sprung up and become national, without a specific cause—and the conviction of Herodotus, who knew both Greece and Egypt well, that the Grecian rites had been derived from Egypt. Some circumstances[2] seem to indicate that Phœnicia was the medium through which the worship of Io was brought to Greece; yet the interval was probably short, as the Egyptian name was preserved. Josephus[3] says that the Egyptians became known to the Greeks through the means of the Phœnicians, who visited Greece for purposes of commerce, and these visits began in the heroic age.

Speaking of the introduction of the Bacchic rites into Greece, Herodotus gives it as his opinion that Melampus, by whom they were taught to the Greeks, had himself derived his knowledge of them through the Phœnicians, namely from Cadmus the Tyrian, and those who came with him from Phœnicia into Bœotia[4]. Indeed there is some reason to believe that *Melampus*, the supposed founder of these Bacchic rites in Greece, and progenitor of a caste of sooth-

---

[1] The number of fifty sons and daughters arose from a mythical propriety. The vessel in which a voyage from Egypt to Greece was performed could not be inferior to a pentecontor, the largest then known. But the heroes of mythology, as the Argonauts, were their own rowers; hence the sons of Ægyptus were fifty, and the Danaides, whom each coveted for a bride, of an equal number. The sons of Ægyptus had served their purpose when one of them had furnished a sovereign to Argos; the rest were disposed of by the daggers of their wives. The Danaides remained.

[2] See p. 63 of this volume.

[3] Φοίνικες κατ' ἐμπορίαν τοῖς Ἕλλησιν ἐπεισπλέοντες εὐθὺς ἐγνώσθησαν, καὶ δι' ἐκείνων Αἰγύπτιοι. (Jos. c. Apion. 1, 12.)

[4] Herod. 2, 49.

sayers, is only another name for Egyptian, and that the Egyptian origin of the Bacchic rites is the fact meant to be expressed, in calling Melampus their author[1]. The Attic worship of Neith, under the name of Athena, has evidently come from the Phoenicians of Bœotia.

In the age of Herodotus historical chronology was not sufficiently cultivated to induce an identification of Danaus with an individual king or prince of Egypt. The Greeks had already connected the war of Troy and the wanderings of Menelaus with Egyptian history, but they contented themselves with turning Proteus into a king of Egypt, and Thone into a guardian of the mouth of the Nile. But when learned chronologers began to synchronize the histories of different countries, it was natural to seek for such illustrious personages as Danaus and Ægyptus, joint founders, through a son and daughter, of the Argive royal family, among the characters of history. The feud of Rameses and the brother whom he made his viceroy, repeated in the story of Sethos and Armais, was one of the few personal anecdotes which the Egyptian records had preserved, and was therefore fixed upon to explain the hostility of Danaus and Ægyptus. Sethosis, says Manetho, was called Ægyptus, and Ermaios (Armais) his brother Danaus[2]. The resemblance, indeed, ceased with this circumstance; but this identification served to make the Macedonian conqueror of Egypt

---

[1] Apollod. Bibl. ii. 1, 4. Αἴγυπτος—καταστρεψάμενος τὴν Μελαμπόδων χώραν ἀφ' ἑαυτοῦ ὠνόμασεν Αἴγυπτον. There appears no sufficient reason for the conjecture of Scaliger, Μελαμβώλον, since Eustathius and the Scholiast on the Prometheus evidently read as we now do. (See Heyne ad loc.)

[2] Joseph. c. Ap. 1, 26.

through Hercules, Perseus and Danaus, a descendant of the most illustrious of the ancient Pharaohs. No regard was paid to the heroic chronology of Greece in these deductions; for Amenophis III., who preceded Rameses the brother of Armais-Danaus by five reigns, was made to be Memnon, a contemporary of the War of Troy, and Thuoris, the successor of Rameses by two reigns, the Polybus under whom Troy was taken.

We must therefore regard these identifications as arbitrary, so far as they relate to persons. Yet there was a good reason for referring the commencement of Egyptian influence upon Greece to this period of history—the 18th and 19th dynasties. Such expeditions as Thothmes, Amenophis and Sesostris undertook, could not be without effect upon all the countries around. Their occupation of Phœnicia and Asia Minor may have caused migrations from these countries to a more western land, the traces of which remained in the Greek religion and manners, though the circumstances are disguised in mythe. Sesostris is said by Herodotus to have crossed into Thrace; Diodorus represents him as conquering the Cyclades; he was the first Egyptian king who built ships of war, and the pentecontor or vessel of fifty oars first appears in Greek mythology, in the story of Danaus and Ægyptus. It is from this time also, namely the fourteenth century before Christ, that something like consistency begins to appear in Grecian history.

Diodorus, in a fragment of his 40th Book, refers the expulsion of the Jews and the emigrations of Danaus and Cadmus to the same age and the same cause. The Exodus, or departure of the Children of Israel from Egypt, falls according to the common chronology about the year 1490 B.C.; but as no king is named, in the account either of their settlement in Egypt or of their departure, we cannot connect the scriptural history with the regnal chronology of the Pharaohs. The time of their residence is distinctly fixed, both in the prophecy of the fortunes of his descendants to Abraham and in the narrative of the Exodus itself. In the former (Gen. xv. 13) God says to Abraham, "Thy seed shall be a stranger in a land that is not theirs, and shall serve them; and they shall afflict them four hundred years. But in the fourth generation they shall come hither again." In Exodus (xii. 40) it is said, "The sojourning of the children of Israel in the land of Egypt was four hundred and thirty years; and at the end of the four hundred and thirty years, even on that very day, all the hosts of Jehovah went out from the land of Egypt." These words are so precise, that no other sense would have been affixed to them than that the sojourning in Egypt lasted 430 years, had not a difficulty arisen from the mention of the fourth generation in the prophecy to Abraham, and the genealogical notices in Exod. vi. 16–19, Numb. xxvi. 58, where Kohath is made the grandfather, and Amram the father of Moses; Kohath being the son of the Patriarch Levi (Gen. xlvi. 11), and having gone down with him into Egypt. The difficulty of stretching out four generations to 400 years was early felt, where it was most natural that a chronological difficulty connected with Egypt should be felt, at Alexandria. Accordingly in the Septuagint Version, made by learned Jews at that seat of Græco-Egyptian science, Exod. xii. 40 reads thus: "The sojourning of the children of Israel, which they sojourned in the land of Egypt *and in the land of Canaan*, was 430 years;" the Samaritan Pentateuch, which so often agrees with the Septuagint against the Hebrew[1], here also follows the Greek Version. Josephus is inconsistent; in one place he reckons the whole period of Egyptian bondage at 400 years[2]; in another[3] he gives 215 years to the sojourning of Abraham and the patriarchs in Canaan, and 215 to the sojourning in Egypt. This reckoning appears to have been adopted by the Jews, who chiefly used the Septuagint, in the age of the preaching of the Gospel, and is the foundation of St. Paul's remark (Gal. iii. 17), "that the promise to Abraham preceded by 430 years the giving of the Law." That the reading of the Septuagint is an arbitrary and uncritical alteration of the text is now generally admitted; it appears to remove one difficulty to create a greater; since the increase of the children of Israel from seventy persons to 600,000 fighting-men in 230 years is incredible. A generation is not to be understood in the prophecy to Abraham in the strict and scientific sense; it evidently means the average period of the life of man, which might fairly be estimated at a century, when 110, 120, 130, and 137 years are assigned as its actual dura-

---

[1] This may perhaps be explained by the fact that the Samaritans appear to have been a considerable body in Egypt (Flav. Vop. Saturninus, c. 8), and may have lived there more harmoniously with the Hellenistic Jews than with the Jews of Palestine, who hated the Hellenists as much as they did the Samaritans.

[2] Ant. 2, 9, 1. Τετρακοσίων μὲν ἐτῶν χρόνον ἐπὶ ταύταις διήνυσαν ταλαιπωρίαις.

[3] Ant. 2, 15, 2.

tion. There is then no sufficient ground for impeaching the purity of the Hebrew text, nor for giving to it any other than its obvious meaning, that the children of Israel dwelt 400 years in Egypt[1]. The words of the prophecy to Abraham do not necessarily imply that their oppression should last so long.

If then the Exodus falls in the 15th century before Christ, and the children of Israel went down into Egypt 400 years before, their settlement must have taken place under one of the dynasties between the 14th and the 18th. The friendly reception which they met with in Egypt, and the facility with which the fertile land of Goshen, lying towards Palestine and Arabia, was assigned to them, is most naturally explained, if we assume that the Pharaoh who raised Joseph to the rank of vizir was one of the Hyksos race. The Hyksos were Phœnician shepherds, therefore, of a Semitic race like the Israelites; and by placing them on the frontier of Asia, they secured themselves a friendly garrison in that vulnerable part of their dominions. It is true that we find no marks of the sovereignty of a foreign race in the account of the settlement of the Israelites. Everything corresponds with the usages, ceremonials and condition of society, as we know them from monuments of the native Egyptians. The native gods are in high honour; the prime-minister receives for a wife the daughter of the chief-priest

---

[1] There still remains the difficulty that Moses is made the great-grandson of Levi. But is it probable that genealogical registers would be preserved with such accuracy, as to make them historical documents, in that interval when the children of Israel had ceased to be a family and had not yet become a nation?

of Re at Heliopolis; the lands of the priests alone escape forfeiture to the crown in the famine. He is invested with the insignia of office with the same ceremonies which were practised at the court of Setei Menephthah[1]. The king has a splendid retinue—a chief captain of the guard, a chief butler and chief baker, magicians and wise men. There is the same marked contrast between Egyptian usages and those of neighbouring nations; they will not eat with a Hebrew any more than they would touch the knife of a Greek[2]; when Jacob dies, forty days are consumed in his embalmment, and seventy more in mourning for him. The language of Egypt was unintelligible to the Hebrews, and as far as we can judge from the disguised fragments which have been handed down to us, was the same as that of the monuments. This would be of great weight were it certain that all the details, as well as the great facts of the narrative, have been derived from contemporary authority. It might also be said, that if the Hyksos had been already established some centuries in Egypt when Joseph was transported thither, they would have adopted the language and manners of the conquered people. Joseph suggests to his brethren that they should call themselves shepherds, in order that the land of Goshen might be assigned to them, adding, "for every shepherd is an abomination to the Egyptians;" and this has been thought to refer to the sufferings inflicted on Egypt by the Hyksos and to prove that they had recently been expelled. But the settlement of an aged man with his children and grandchildren, amounting in all

---

[1] Wilkinson, M. and C. pl. 80. [2] Her. 2, 41.

only to seventy persons, could hardly excite apprehension, however much the Egyptians had suffered from an invasion of a nomad people. We do not know indeed, from other authorities, that shepherds, like swineherds, were an abomination to the Egyptians; but they were of a low caste, and their occupation evidently ranked below that of the cultivator of the soil[1].

The language of the Book of Exodus, "a new king arose who knew not Joseph," points to a change of dynasty, and the commencement of the New Monarchy, rather than the succession of a sovereign of the same family, in whom such ignorance would be incredible; and a long interval must have occurred, of which the historian gives us some general measure by saying that "the children of Israel, after the death of Joseph and all that generation, multiplied and waxed exceedingly mighty and the land was filled with them." Their oppression extended through several reigns, for Pharaoh not being a personal name, its recurrence is no proof that one sovereign is intended throughout. After the expulsion of the Hyksos, the Israelites, who, though not the same, were closely connected with them, naturally became an object of alarm, and the kings of the 18th dynasty endeavoured first to check their increase and then to break their spirit.

In endeavouring to connect the Exodus of the Israelites with the Egyptian history, we must lay

---

[1] Wilkinson, M. and C. 2, 16. "As if to prove how much they despised every order of pastors, the artists both of Upper and Lower Egypt delighted in representing them as dirty and unshaven; and at Beni Hassan and the tombs near the pyramids of Geezah, they are caricatured as a deformed and unseemly race."

out of the account entirely the narrative of the expulsion of the Hyksos by Manetho. It is only by the means of the interpolations of Josephus[1] that it has appeared to describe the Exodus of the Israelites. The authentic chronicles of Egypt contained, as far as we can judge, no notice of their settlement, residence or departure. Nor do the monuments supply the deficiency; except that they appear to have been employed in brick-making in the reign of Thothmes III.[2] But the account which Manetho really gives of the departure of the Jews, though by his own confession derived from unauthentic and fabulous sources[3], deserves attention as exhibiting the popular belief. Josephus having represented Manetho as identifying the Jews with the Hyksos, charges him with falsehood in mentioning Amenophis[4] as the king under whom the Exodus took place, when he had himself declared it to be Tethmosis; but Manetho is liable to no such imputation, and it is Josephus who has sacrificed truth to national pride. This popular account represents the expelled nation, not as foreigners, but as an impure and diseased portion of the Egyptian people. "Amenophis, a pious king, desirous of obtaining a vision of the gods, such as Horus his predecessor had enjoyed, had been exhorted by his namesake Amenophis, an inspired man, to clear the land of all impure persons, and those who laboured under any bodily defect. He accordingly collected them to the number of 80,000, and relegated them

---

[1] See p. 187 of this vol.
[2] See p. 230 of this vol.
[3] See p. 189 of this vol., note[1].
[4] Ἀμενώφιν εἰσποιήσας ἐμβόλιμον βασιλέα. (C. Ap. 1, 26.)

to the quarries eastward of the Nile, along with the separated portion of the other Egyptians. It happened that among the leprous persons, who in virtue of the edict were consigned to this region and condemned to labour, were some learned priests. The soothsayer who had given advice to the king to clear his land, was alarmed when he thought of the hostility which he should bring down on the part of the gods by the violence offered to their ministers, and put an end to his life, leaving behind him a written prediction, that the impure persons would obtain auxiliaries and be masters of Egypt for thirteen years. The king, moved by their sufferings, assigned them as an abode the Typhonian city of Abaris, which had once been occupied by the Shepherds, but was then unpeopled. Here they chose for themselves a leader Osarsiph, one of the priests of Heliopolis. He formed them into a confederacy, whose principle was hostility to the religion of Egypt and opposition to its laws and customs. Having fortified their city they sent for aid to the Shepherds who had been expelled by Tethmosis and then occupied Jerusalem, and invited them to invade Egypt by the promise of re-establishing them in the country from which they had been expelled. Two hundred thousand men obeyed the call, and Amenophis went to meet them with 300,000 men, but thinking that he was acting in opposition to the divine will, withdrew with his forces into Ethiopia, leaving behind him his son Sethos (called also Rameses from Rampses his father), a child of five years old, having first collected together the most honoured of the sacred animals, and warned the priests

THE NINETEENTH DYNASTY.

to bury their images. Here he remained during the fated period of thirteen years, while the inhabitants of Jerusalem and the impure men of Egypt committed all manner of outrages, plundering the temples, mutilating the images of the gods, and compelling the priests to kill and cook the sacred animals. The priest Osarsiph changed his name to Moses when he joined this race. At the end of the thirteen years Amenophis returned with a great force, and with his son Rampses attacked the Shepherds and the impure persons, and pursued them to the borders of Syria."

We cannot recognize in this tale anything that claims even the character of an original historical tradition, disguised and perverted by length of time and national feeling. It might have originated in the age when the Jews began to settle themselves in Egypt, and by the establishment of their monotheistic worship to give offence to the religious feeling of the Egyptians[1], as well as in that of the Exodus; for the fundamental fact which it implies, the religious antagonism of the Jewish and Egyptian people, extended through all times, and found an expression in this form[2]. Beyond this there is scarcely a resemblance to the Scripture narrative. Instead of immigrants, immemorially hostile to the polytheism of Egypt, the founders of

---

[1] Is. xix. 18. Plutarch, Is. et Osir. p. 363, makes Typhon the father of Hierosolymus and Judæus, and all the places connected especially with Typhon were on the eastern side of Egypt.

[2] Chæremon (Jos. c. Apion. 1, 32) makes Moses, whose Egyptian name was *Tisithen*, and Joseph, whose name was *Peteseph*, to be hierogrammats, and the leaders of the 2,500,000 impure persons. According to Lysimachus, Bocchoris was the king who endeavoured to clear his country of impure persons by drowning them.

the Jewish nation are impure Egyptians, and their leader a renegade priest. The bitterness of national and religious hatred and contempt is expressed by representing them as originally a company of lepers, a disease of which we do not read in Scripture before their residence in Egypt, but which seems to have been rife among them afterwards, if we may judge from the anxious precautions of the Law against this disease[1]. The historical narrative and the tale agree in the circumstance that the departure of the Jewish people was accompanied by calamity to the Egyptians, but all the circumstances of that calamity are entirely different. The Amenophis to whom it refers, if an historical personage, must be the Menephthah of the monuments, the father of Rameses-Sesostris; we know his history from these monuments with considerable minuteness, and it is quite inconsistent with the story of Manetho. Probably, however, Amenophis has been introduced into the story, without regard to chronology, from his high reputation for piety[2]. What Jews and Christians regard as an act of cruelty and injustice, the Egyptians considered as the necessary means of obtaining the favour or averting the displeasure of the gods. The king was to be rewarded, according to one account, by a sight of the gods, according to others, by deliverance from pestilence[3], or from the displeasure of Isis[4], or famine[5], if he destroyed or expelled the enemies of the gods.

---

[1] The story of Job that the leprosy was considered as indicating the extremest degree of divine displeasure and consequent guilt.

[2] See p. 208 of this vol.
[3] Diod. Fr. lib. 40.
[4] Chær. ap. Jos. c. Ap. 1, 32.
[5] Jos. u. s. 1, 33.

Popular fable, such as we are dealing with, would naturally fix on an eminent name like that of Amenophis, whose connexion with Ethiopia gave probability to the account of his flight to that country.

Who was the Pharaoh of the Exodus, in the silence of Egyptian monuments and the uncertainty of Jewish chronology, we may never be able to ascertain. The most important fact in reference to the providential character of that event, a crisis in the religious history of the world, is, that Israel was brought out of Egypt, not in a period of its weakness and depression, but when its monarchy was warlike and powerful; and only the strong hand and outstretched arm of Jehovah could have effected its deliverance.

We could not suppose that this event was accomplished by the aid of an auxiliary body of Palestinian Hyksos, without imputing to the author of the book of Exodus a wilful suppression of the truth. But it is possible that the expulsion of the Hyksos under the first kings of the 18th dynasty may not have been so complete, but that a considerable remnant of the population was left behind in the country eastward of the Delta, and that uniting themselves with the Israelites, they may have contributed to produce that great increase of numbers which alarmed the kings of Egypt. It was probably during the close union of Phœnicia with Egypt that the alphabetical character of the former was arranged, and learned by the Israelites. In the preceding part of the history there is no trace of its use; but from the account of the giving of the Law, it is evident that it was known at the Exodus, though probably little diffused among the nation at large[1]. Such an adaptation of the phonetic system of the Egyptians is more likely to have been made by the Phœnicians than by the Jews, and the use of the same alphabet by both may be best explained by their dwelling together in Egypt before they became neighbours in the land of Canaan.

During their residence in Egypt, and probably in consequence of this intermixture, the common people among the Israelites appear to have lost in great measure their belief in the God of their forefathers. When Moses came with a message from him, it is evident that he was not known to them under his distinctive appellation; nor have we any account of their religious history during the whole interval from the settlement in Goshen to the Exodus. Their ancient faith was revived by the mission of Moses and the events of their deliverance, but there are evident marks of the prevalence both of Egyptian and Phœnician superstitions among them, notwithstanding the repugnance which their traditionary usages created between them and the Egyptians[2]. As the land of Goshen bordered on Heliopolis, and was not far removed from Memphis, the chief seats of the worship of Mnevis and Apis, it is not wonderful that in their first distrust of the power of Jehovah, they recurred to the worship of the golden calf. The prophet Amos informs us,

---

[1] The mention of a signet-ring in the history of Judah is no proof of the use of alphabetical characters in the patriarchal times. Though worn only as an ornament, of Egyptian fabric, it would serve, like the bracelets and the staff, to identify the owner, which is all that the story requires. (Gen. xxxviii. 18, 25.)

[2] Exod. viii. 26.

that during their wanderings in the Desert, they neglected the sacrifices of Jehovah for those of Moloch and Chiun[1], Palestinian and Arabian divinities[2], with whom they had probably become acquainted by their intercourse with the Palestinian and Arabian Hyksos.

THE THIRD VOLUME OF MANETHO.

Twentieth Dynasty.

	Years.
TWELVE DIOSPOLITAN KINGS, who reigned	135

[Eusebius in Syncellus (p. 139, Dind.) 178 years. Armen. 172.]

The monuments have fortunately preserved for us the names of the sovereigns of this dynasty, which appear to have been lost in Manetho, from the circumstance of their being all Rameses. According to the reckoning of those who make Rameses II. and III. to be one and the same, Rameses III. will be the first of this dynasty, son of Remerri or Merira, who himself never reigned. According to our arrangement it will begin with Rameses IV. The following is the succession which Lepsius has derived from the monuments:

RAMESES IV.
RAMESES V.
RAMESES VI.
RAMESES VII. } Brothers reigning in succession.
RAMESES VIII.
RAMESES IX.
RAMESES X.
RAMESES XI.
RAMESES XII.
RAMESES XIII.

[1] Amos v. 25. [2] Selden de Dis Syris, c. 6, 14.

The monuments of the reign of Rameses IV. show that the power of the 18th and 19th dynasties had been transmitted unimpaired to the 20th. The pavilion of Medinet-Aboo or Southern Rameseion, exhibits the splendid ceremony of his coronation[1]. In the first compartment the king appears, seated under a canopy, the cornice of which is formed by a row of the royal serpents or *urǣi*. Two figures of the goddess of Truth and Justice stand behind his throne, and cover the back of it with their outstretched wings. Rameses wears his helmet and carries in his hands the emblem of Life, and the hook and scourge, the emblems of Dominion, which serve also to identify him with Osiris. The sphinx and the hawk, symbols of royalty, adorn the side of the throne, which is supported by the figure of a lion and of two captives. The poles on which this canopy is carried are supported on the shoulders of twelve princes of the blood; other attendants carry a broad umbrella and feather-fans. Three priests, distinguishable by their shaven crowns, walk beside the throne, carrying the arms and insignia of the king, and four immediately behind it. They are followed by six more princes of the blood, some with hatchets and some with feather-fans. Military attendants bearing the steps of the throne, and square blocks of wood on which it might be rested, when lowered from the shoulders of the bearers, close the lower line of the procession. In the upper, immediately behind the throne, walk two men in civil costume, who from

---

[1] Vol. i. p. 161. Wilkinson, Manners and Customs, pl. 76.

their attitude appear to be making proclamation[1]; they are followed by princes of the blood, fan-bearers and guards. In front of the throne walk two priests, who turn their faces back towards the king and scatter grains of incense on a censer; a scribe reads from a roll; two more princes of the blood, mixed with priests and military officers, make up the rest of the procession, which is headed by drummers, trumpeters, and players of the double pipe.

The second compartment begins with a libation and burning of incense made by the king, who has descended from his throne, to Amun Khem. The statue next appears carried in procession by twenty-two priests, hidden all but the feet and heads by the drapery of the platform on which the statue is erected. The king walks before the god, having a staff in one hand, a sceptre in the other, and the red crown of the Lower Country on his head. He is preceded by a white bull, before whom a priest burns incense, and a long train of other priests carry standards on which are fixed images of the jackal, the bull, the cynocephalus, the hawk, emblems respectively of Anubis, Apis, Thoth and Horus. The images and shields of some of the predecessors of Rameses are also borne on the shoulders of the priests, but a more complete succession is given afterwards. The king now appears wearing the *Pschent*, which on the Rosetta stone[2] he is described as having put on when he entered the

---

[1] The hand raised towards the mouth is an indication of *rehearsing* in Egyptian pictures.

[2] Καλουμένη βασιλεία ψχεντ, ἣν περιθέμενος εἰσῆλθεν εἰς τὸ ἐν Μέμφει *** τελέσθη τὰ νομιζόμενα τῇ παραλήψει τῆς βασιλείας. (L. 11, 12 from the end.)

temple of Memphis, to perform the ceremonies prescribed on taking the throne. The hieroglyphics in front of the king describe him as putting on the crown of the Upper and Lower countries. Four birds are at the same time let loose by the priests, and the columns of hieroglyphics above them being headed by the symbols of the four cardinal points, it has been ingeniously conjectured by Champollion[1], that the birds were to announce to East, West, North and South, the fact that Rameses IV. was crowned.

In the last compartment the king has laid aside his crown, and with a helmet on his head cuts with a sickle six ears of corn, which a priest binds together and offers to the sacred bull. This ceremony no doubt was emblematical of the relation between the kingly office and agriculture, the great source of the prosperity of Egypt. It was also very appropriate to the character of Amun Khem, who symbolized the productive power of nature. The queen, who was not present at the procession of the statue of Amun Khem, appears in the two last compartments, not however as taking a part in the ceremony, but only as a spectator.

The interior court of the palace at Medinet-Aboo contains an inscription in not fewer than seventy-five columns, bearing date the fifth year of his reign, in which his victories over various nations are commemorated[2]. It is not accompanied by any historical picture, and is in some parts injured by time and in others obscure in its construction; but enough remains and is intelligible to furnish us

[1] Lettres d'Égypte, p. 347.   [2] Rosellini, M. R. tav. cxxxix. cxl.

with the information that the king had already made two expeditions[1], and reduced into submission various nations of Asia, some whose names have occurred in the historical inscriptions of his predecessors, others not mentioned before. Among the former are the Mennahom and the Tohen; among the latter the Mashiosha[2].

The inscription is supposed by Rosellini, from its redundant and tautological style, and the more than usual quantity of flattery to the king which it contains, to be the substance of some poem composed to celebrate the expedition. An embassy from the "men of the great island" is also mentioned, to which the king is said to have "passed like a waterfowl over the waters[3]." This island can scarcely be any other than Cyprus, which, according to Manetho, as reported by Josephus, was a conquest of Sethosis Rameses[4].

Of the next expedition of Rameses IV., undertaken in the eleventh and twelfth years of his reign, we have more ample details in a magnificent series of bas-reliefs on the north-eastern walls of the palace of Medinet-Aboo[5]. The whole progress of a campaign is recorded there. We have first an *allocution* of his army by the king; he stands on a raised platform; the commanders have received their banners and kneel with them in their hands, while others stand at a distance and lift their hands towards him in homage. In another division the arming of the

---

[1] His return from one with his prisoners is mentioned, cols. 40, 41 (Ros. Mon. Stor. 4, 88), but he appears subsequently to have undertaken another.

[2] Supposed by Mr. Osburn to be the inhabitants of *Dar-mesek*, Damascus. (Ancient Egypt, p. 102.)

[3] Cols. 51-53.

[4] Cont. Apion. 1, 15.

[5] Rosellini, Mon. Stor. 4, 14-50; Mon. Reali, tav. cxxiv.-cxxxiv.

troops is represented; bows, quivers, spears, battle-axes and scimitars are piled on the ground, and distributed by the officers to men who come in companies to receive them. The lowest compartment, which perhaps should be considered as the first in order, exhibits the enrolment of the soldiers, performed by a prince of the blood, attended by his officers. Next begins the march. The king in his *biga* is accompanied by his guards, and as Diodorus describes Osymandyas, by a lion; before him is another chariot on which is erected the royal standard, the head of Amun with the disk of the sun. In six lines of hieroglyphics placed above, the god promises to go before him into the land of the enemy, and make him pass victorious through it. This and the following scene represent the march through Egypt; the next exhibits the Egyptians in conflict with their enemies. Their head-dress is different from that of any foreigners whom we have yet found on the monuments; a high cap or helmet, wider at the top than at the base, divided into coloured stripes with disks of metal attached to it, descending on the back of the neck, and fastened beneath the chin. It is not unlike the head-dress of figures on the Persepolitan monuments[1], but in other respects their costume is different. They carry round shields, with spears and short straight swords. The arrows of the king are making havoc among them; they fly in all directions, and some of them appear to have seized on an Egyptian chariot, of which the driver had been killed, to aid in their escape. They were probably a people of nomadic life; for in the

[1] Wilkinson, M. and C. 1, 367.

rear are waggons with solid wheels and bodies of wickerwork, drawn by oxen, containing their women and children. Their name, which was read *Tokari* by Sir G. Wilkinson, is read *Fekkaroo* by Champollion and Rosellini[1], but no name in ancient geography has been found by which it can be explained. The Egyptians were aided in this campaign by a body of foreign auxiliaries, who must have been taken permanently into their service, as they form a part of the army when it sets out on its march, and have previously appeared among the troops of Rameses III. They have a helmet of a very peculiar shape, a horned crescent being fixed on the top, with the addition of a stem surmounted by a ball[2]. Their name is written *Shairetaan*, with an addition which shows them to have been a maritime people, and though at times in alliance they were at other times in hostility with Egypt.

The next scene represents a lion-hunt; one of these animals lies in the agonies of death under the feet of the royal horses; another pierced with three arrows is taking refuge among the water-plants, which indicate the vicinity of a river. Remembering the allusions of the Jewish prophets to the lions which harbour on the banks of Jordan, and are driven out by the swelling of its waters[3], we can hardly avoid the conclusion that Rameses was now on his progress through Palestine. If this be the case, it will be somewhere on the coast of Palestine,

---

[1] Osburn makes them *Ekronites*, i.e. Philistines. (Anc. Egypt, p. 107, 140.)

[2] Rosellini, Mon. Stor. iii. 2, 135; Mon. Reali, tav. ci. He calls them "royal guards," but they were evidently not Egyptians. Osburn considers them as Sidonians. (Anc. Egypt, p. 119.)

[3] Jer. xlix. 19; l. 44.

or a country not very distant, that we should seek for the scene of the next transaction—a naval fight between the Egyptians and the nation whom they had just before defeated by land. It is the only representation of a naval battle remaining among the Egyptian monuments[1]. The Egyptian vessels have both oars and sails, those of the enemy sails only, and they differ in their build; the prow of the Egyptian vessel is the head of a lion, of the other that of a water-fowl; the opposite end is armed with a spike. The rowers are protected by a raised bulwark which runs along the side; the combatants assail each other with arrows from a distance, or board and fight hand to hand when the vessels are in contact. The Egyptians as usual are completely victorious; one of the enemies' ships has been upset and is sinking; another has grounded, and the crew are endeavouring to escape. But the king and a body of archers are stationed on the shore; the fugitives are slain or made prisoners, and are marched off bound under the convoy of Egyptian soldiers. It is remarkable that among the crew of the hostile vessels are many of the same nation, distinguishable by their helmets with the horns and disk, who serve in the army of Rameses. We need not, however, suppose that some change of policy had converted them from allies into enemies; Greeks were found fighting against Greeks in the armies of Persia.

In the next compartment the king appears, having laid aside his arms, in his civil costume, and again harangues his soldiers, and distributes arms and insignia to the officers as rewards of merit. The

[1] Vol. i. p. 230.

hands of the slaughtered enemies are told out before him and their numbers recorded by the scribes, and the prisoners led up, some fettered by the arms and others by the wrists. The presentation of the captives to the triad of Theban gods, Maut, Amun and Chonso, closes the series; but here, besides the Fekkaroo, prisoners of another people are introduced, the *Rebo*, against whom Rameses IV. carried on wars. This people have been incidentally mentioned in the inscription which records the expedition of Rameses III. in his fifth year against the Sheto, whose neighbours they must have been. The walls of the second court of the palace of Medinet-Aboo give the details of this or some other war of Rameses IV. against them. Probably the war occurred at some later period of his reign; for in the presentation of the prisoners to Amun, the Fekkaroo and Rebo appear both as prisoners, whereas in the campaign represented in the inner court, the Fekkaroo are acting as auxiliaries against the Rebo. From their costume we should suppose the last to be the inhabitants of a somewhat colder climate, as in addition to tunics they wear long upper vests, crossed by bands of a different colour, open below and fastened on by a strap over the shoulder. This garment appears sometimes to have been of leather. The head is covered with a close-fitting cap, and adorned with feathers; but in war they wore a helmet or cap fastened by a strap beneath the chin. Their physiognomy also indicates a northern race; the eyes are blue, the nose aquiline, the beard red. Occasionally we find the limbs tattooed. The slaughter made of them was great;

3000 hands, according to the inscription, are poured out before the king[1], as he sits on his chariot after the battle to receive the returns; and an equal number in three other compartments, indicating that 6000 had been slain. Besides these, 1000 appear to have been made prisoners. As the conclusion of the whole, the king returns to Egypt and presents his captives to Amunre and Maut.

The sixteenth is the latest year of Rameses IV. that has been found on the monuments, and the lists give only the duration of the whole dynasty; but from the extent of the works executed in his reign, and the size and magnificence of his tomb, we may presume that it was of more than the average length. He appears originally to have destined for himself a tomb at the very entrance of the Bab-el-Melook, but to have abandoned his design, when the excavation had been carried but a short way, and chosen a spot further on in the valley[2]. It had been known as the Harper's Tomb, long before the discovery of the hieroglyphics assigned it to Rameses IV., Bruce having copied two remarkable figures of harpers which one of the apartments contains. Its whole extent is 405 feet; not, however, to that direct depth in the mountain, the line of direction having been diverted to avoid interfering with an

---

[1] This and another kind of mutilation which the bodies of the slain had undergone are inaccurately represented by Diodorus as if performed on the living prisoners. Ἐν δὲ τῷ δευτέρῳ τοίχῳ τοὺς αἰχμαλώτους ὑπὸ τοῦ βασιλέως ἀγομένους εἰργάσθαι τά τε αἰδοῖα καὶ τὰς χεῖρας οὐκ ἔχοντας· δι' ὧν δοκεῖν δηλοῦσθαι διότι ταῖς ψυχαῖς ἀνανδροι καὶ κατὰ τὰς ἐν τοῖς δεινοῖς ἐνεργείας ἄχειρες ἦσαν (1,48). This is part of his description of the tomb of Osymandyas, in which various buildings appear to be confounded.

[2] According to Sir G. Wilkinson, Rameses III. began the tomb, and his legend can still be traced near the entrance beneath that of Rameses IV. (Mod. Eg. and Thebes, 2, 207.)

adjoining tomb. The principal hall contained the sarcophagus of the king, but it had long been rifled. It is of red granite, and is covered with inscriptions which have been filled up with a green enamel. The sarcophagus itself, seven feet in depth and fourteen in length, is in the Louvre, the cover at Cambridge.

The queen of Rameses IV. is not named, though she is represented in the scene of the Coronation; but on the jambs of a door in the Valley of the Queens, the shield of Rameses VI. appears on one side, and on the other that of "the royal mother, ruler of the world, *Ise*." She must therefore have been the queen of Rameses IV.[1] It is probable that his three brothers, one of whom ascended the throne before and two after him, were also her sons; some at least of the numerous other princes of the blood who appear in the procession at his coronation must have been children by his concubines. That he maintained a harem we know from the representations in some of the smaller apartments of his pavilion at Medinet-Aboo, where he is seen among them, playing at a game of draughts or chess[2]. Ten princes appear with their names in one of the courts of the palace; the inscriptions of the four first of these have received additions, as they successively came to the throne; the rest are qualified simply as princes.

We found a temporary agreement between the authentic and monumental history of Egypt, and the legendary history as it was received by Herodotus, in the reign of Rameses III., his Sesostris.

---

[1] Rosellini, Mon. Stor. 4, 119. [2] Rosellini, Mon. Civ. 3, 116; Mon. Reali, tav. cxxii. 2, 3.

It disappears again in that of his successor, whom he calls Pheron, and of whom he expressly says that he undertook no expedition. The interpolation of Proteus after Pheron among the kings of Egypt, in order to connect its history with that of the Iliad and Odyssey, shows how little regard was paid to truth in framing this legendary tale. It is therefore useless to seek among the successors of Rameses III. for the Rampsinitus of Herodotus who surpassed in riches all his successors, and built himself a treasure-house, from which the sons of the architect ingeniously contrived to abstract a portion of his wealth by means of a moveable stone. The name appears to contain that of Rameses, which is spelt among other varieties *Rampses* in Manetho; but the story of his descent into Hades, and his playing at dice there with Ceres, so clearly discloses the unhistorical character of the accounts which Herodotus received, as to deter us from any attempt to place him in relation with really historical personages[1]. Diodorus having related the blindness of Sesoosis II., who corresponds with the Pheron of Herodotus, passes over a long line of his successors with the remark that they did nothing worthy of being recorded.

This appears to be true of the successors of Rameses IV. All record of foreign expeditions ceases with his reign. The principal memorials of Rameses V. are the lateral inscriptions of the obelisk which Thothmes I. erected at Karnak. They contain, however, no historical fact. His tomb in the Bab-el-Melook is small; the sarcophagus remains

[1] Herod. 2, 121, 122.

in it, but has been broken¹. Rameses VI. has in several places effaced the name of his brother, as if some hostility between them had preceded his elevation to the throne²; but we have no memorials of his reign, and can only conjecture that it was long, from the unusual amount of labour bestowed on the preparation of his tomb. It is 342 feet in length, descending by a gradual slope to the depth of 25 feet below the ground, and divided into a number of chambers³. The whole surface of the walls and ceilings is covered with a profusion of coloured sculptures of minute size, chiefly astronomical and mythical. One of them is the Judgement-scene before Osiris already described⁴, and the supposed return of a wicked soul to the world. Of Rameses VII. there is absolutely no memorial except his tomb, which is of much less finished execution than that of his predecessor. The sarcophagus is excavated in the rock of the floor to the depth of four feet, and covered with a slab of granite. Rameses VIII. is known only by the occurrence of his shield among those of the other sons of Rameses IV. (III. according to another reckoning) at Medinet Aboo, and on two tablets in the Museum of Berlin. The titular shield contains the figure of the same deity as the phonetic shield of Setei, and it has here also been effaced. From this time it never occurs in the monuments⁵. The shields of the sovereigns of this dynasty are much

---

[1] Wilkinson, Mod. Eg. & Thebes, 2, 212.
[2] Rosellini, Mon. Stor. 4, 118.
[3] Wilkinson, Mod. Eg. & Thebes, 2, 210.
[4] Vol. i. p. 480.
[5] Bunsen, B. 3, p. 118. Rosellini, Mon. Stor. 4, 124.

more crowded with characters than those of the 18th. As these kings were all brothers, it was natural that the reigns of the last should be short. His third year has been found on a monument [1]. Rameses IX. (VIII.) was according to Lepsius the son of Rameses VII. (VI.) He began a temple to Chons on the right bank of the Nile near Karnak, but left it imperfect except the sanctuary [2]; his tomb is small, and appears to have remained unfinished at his death, as the walls of some of the apartments have figures and inscriptions traced upon them, but not sculptured. The tombs of Rameses X., XI., and XII. have also been ascertained. That of Rameses X. is executed with care, and adorned with astrological paintings. The seventeenth year of Rameses XI.'s reign has been found on a papyrus, and the second of Rameses XII.[3]; of Rameses XIII. and XIV. nothing beyond the names is known, which is the more indicative of the inactivity which characterized the last years of this dynasty, because Rameses XIV. reigned at least thirty-three years [4]. Rosellini reckons a fifteenth, by whom a hypostyle hall was added to the temple of Chons at Karnak, founded by Rameses IX.[5]

The dominion of Egypt had long been on the decline, but Amunre addresses the last Rameses in the same magnificent language as his predecessors, and gives him "to put all foreign lands under his feet." The diminution of power in the Egyptian monarchy

[1] Bunsen, Ægyptens Stelle, B. 3, p. 119.
[2] Rosellini, Mon. Stor. 4, 125.
[3] Amenmeses, whom Rosellini, from the position of his tomb, would interpose between Rameses XII. and XIII., has been already placed last but one in the 19th dynasty. See p. 301 of this vol.
[4] Rosellini, Mon. Stor. 2, p. 49.
[5] Rosellini, Mon. Stor. 2, 50. 4, 137. M. R. tav. cxlvi.

since Rameses IV. was probably caused or accompanied by an increase in that of its neighbours. Ethiopia seems to have regained its independence. The Phœnician cities must have been rapidly rising by means of commerce to the prosperity in which we find them in the age of Solomon. The recent discoveries of the antiquities of Assyria excited the hope that by their means light would be thrown on the relations of that country with Egypt, whose sovereigns, from Thothmes I. to Rameses IV., repeatedly invaded Mesopotamia and Assyria. We cannot, however, trace any conformity between their respective histories, as disclosed by their monuments. Those of Khorsabad, Koyunjik and Nemroud are much later than the 18th and 19th dynasties of Egypt. No Egyptian appears among the nations with whom the Assyrians are at war[1]. Yet it is probable that when the invasions of the Pharaohs ceased, perhaps by means of successful resistance to them, the Assyrian monarchy rose in power. The Greek traditions begin with mythe in Semiramis, and end with it in Sardanapalus; but the monarchy which these mythes represent was real, and must have begun in the thirteenth century B.C.[2],

---

[1] We do not find any close resemblance between the Asiatic nations represented in the Egyptian monuments and those who appear in the Assyrian sculptures. A people armed with shields, like those described, p. 278, are seen on the bas-reliefs of Khorsabad, and among the spoil is a chariot, resembling that brought by the Rotno to Thothmes III., p. 221. The Shairetana, p. 331, have many peculiarities in common with the Assyrians of Nemroud; the Tokkari or Fekkaroo, p. 331, in their arms and dress and the shape of their carts drawn by oxen, bear some resemblance to a nation represented in the Assyrian sculptures. (Layard's Nineveh, 2, 493, foll.)

[2] Herodotus (1, 95) says that the Medes revolted from the Assyrians, who had ruled Upper Asia 520 years. This revolt is commonly placed 711 B.C. (Clinton, *sub anno*.)

that is about the time when the power of Egypt declined.

The battle-pieces of the reign of Rameses IV. are not inferior in design to the works of his predecessors, but those who have studied minutely and on the spot the remains of Egyptian art discover an inferiority in the execution. The inscriptions which Rameses V. added to the obelisk erected by Thothmes I. betray even in an engraving their inferiority in execution. In design there could be little difference, art in its application to sacred subjects being so completely submitted to established rules; but we perceive that the style becomes more loaded and elaborate, an indication of the decline of taste.

Twenty-first Dynasty. Seven Tanite kings.

	Years.	
SMENDES, reigned	26	
PSOUSENNES	46	41 Euseb.
NEPHERCHERES	4	
AMENOPHTHIS	9	
OSOCHOR	6	
PSINACHES	9	
PSOUSENNES	14	35 Euseb.
In all 130 years.	114	130

Tanis or Zoan, although its name now appears for the first time in Egyptian history, had long been the most important city on the coast of Egypt [1]. The branch of the Nile on which it stood was the most easterly and the nearest to Palestine and Arabia, with the exception of the Pelusiac. It is spoken

---

[1] See vol. i. p. 56.

of in Scripture as being founded seven years later than Hebron[1]; the precise date of the foundation of Hebron we do not know, but it was one of the oldest towns in Palestine, and is mentioned in the history of Abraham. It is probable that Tanis rose into importance during the wars of the early kings of the New Monarchy with the Hyksos, and their expeditions into Western Asia. Although Thebes continued to be the place in which the splendour of the monarchy was chiefly displayed, and where the sovereigns held their court during intervals of peace, they must have needed a residence in that part of Lower Egypt which was nearest to the scene of their most important operations. That it should be at the same time not very distant from the sea was also necessary, when they established a navy and carried on maritime warfare against Phœnicia and Cyprus. And as the eastern branches of the Nile one after another became silted up, it is probable that even in this age the Pelusiac mouth may have been too shallow to admit ships of war. In the 78th Psalm (vv. 12, 43) the wonders which accompanied the Exodus are said to have been wrought in " the plain of Zoan." This Psalm is probably somewhat later than the age of David, but it proves that this was supposed to have been for the time the residence of the Pharaoh who had " refused to let Israel go." In the age of Isaiah it was still considered as the capital of the Delta; "the princes of Zoan and the princes of Noph" (Memphis) are spoken of[2] as equivalent to the nobles of Egypt. The ambassadors who go down to

---

[1] Numbers, xiii. 22.   [2] Is. xix. 11, 13.

Egypt to form an alliance which implied distrust in Jehovah[1] are described as repairing to Zoan and Hanes, or Heracleopolis[2]; the desolation of Zoan is threatened by Ezekiel, as the consequence of the invasion of Egypt by Nebuchadnezzar. In Strabo's time it was still a large town[3], the capital of a nome; in the age of Titus it had dwindled to an insignificant place[4]. Its ruins attest its ancient importance; its principal temple stood within an area of 1500 feet by 1250, and appears to have been built by Rameses-Sesostris, whose shield is seen in various parts of the ruins. It was adorned with an unusual number of obelisks[5]. Had its remains been explored with the same diligence as those of Middle and Upper Egypt, we should probably have learnt something of the dynasty which took its name from Tanis. But the inhabitants are rude and the air at most seasons of the year pestilential[6], and no traveller has remained here long enough to ascertain what may be buried beneath the mounds of earth which cover the site.

History has preserved no account of the manner in which the sceptre of Egypt passed from the Diospolite dynasty to the Tanite, and the monuments do not supply the deficiency. The temple which Rameses IX. erected to the god Chons exhibits a priest, whose name has been read *Hraihor* or *Pehor*[7], distinguishable by his shaven head and panther's skin, and denominated in his shield " High-priest of

---

[1] Is. xxx. 4.
[2] Champollion, L'Égypte sous les Pharaons, 1, 309. P. 154 of this volume.
[3] Lib. 17, p. 802.
[4] Joseph. Bell. Jud. 4, 11.
[5] See a plan with drawings of some of the inscriptions in Burton's Excerpta Hier. pl. 38–41.
[6] Wilkinson, Mod. Eg. & Thebes, 1, 450.
[7] Rosellini, Mon. Stor. 4, 139.

Amun," who at the same time appears to have performed the functions of royalty. In one compartment of the sculptures Horus places on his head the white cap, and Nebthi the red cap, acts symbolical of his investiture with the dominion of Upper and Lower Egypt. He even appears in a military capacity with the title of Commander of the archers. Another priest, whose name has been read *Pischiam*, appears on the same building, qualified with the titles of royalty. These names do not correspond with any of those in Manetho[1], and we are left to conjecture, that during the time that elapsed after the expiration of the Rameside dynasty, and before the establishment of the Tanite in full authority over Upper as well as Lower Egypt, the High-priests of Thebes assumed the royal style and even military command. It would be agreeable to the practice of Manetho, not to include them in his dynastic lists, but to carry on his chronology by means of the Tanite kings, even though two or three generations elapsed before their authority was acknowledged in Thebes. His omission of the reign of Actisanes, if, as Diodorus represents[2], such an invasion from Ethiopia really took place, may be explained on the same principle. He did not, like Sabaco, found a dynasty.

During a long interval, from the Exodus to the reign of David, there is no mention of Egypt in the Jewish history. The Jews had not consolidated themselves into a nation during the prosperous

---

[1] Bunsen (B. 3, 121) transfers to this dynasty a *Nefrukera* (Nephercheres) and a *Menephthah* (Amenophthis). He also gives *Pianch*, answering to Psinaches.
[2] 2, 60.

times of the 18th and 19th dynasties, and if they occupied Palestine could offer no resistance to the armies of Rameses III. or IV. An incident mentioned in the first book of Kings (xi. 14) might have given us some light into Egyptian history, had its indications been more precise. When Joab, in the reign of David, slaughtered all the males in Edom, Hadad, one of the royal family, made his escape into Egypt, and being hospitably entertained by Pharaoh, received in marriage the sister of his queen Tahpenes. The name of this queen, however, has not been found on any monument, and therefore we are still at a loss respecting that of her husband. During the reign of Solomon an active commerce in horses, chariots, and linen yarn was carried on between Judæa and Egypt. Solomon not only furnished his own armies with horses and chariots from this country, but sold them again to the chiefs of the Hittites and the kings of Syria[1]. The Pharaoh whose daughter Solomon married[2] must have been one of the latest kings of the 21st dynasty: he received as her dowry the town of Gezer in Palestine, which the king of Egypt had recently taken; but the friendship which this alliance established was soon destroyed under the 22nd.

[1] 1 Kings x. 28. Vol. i. p. 196.   [2] 1 Kings ix. 16.

Twenty-second Dynasty. Nine Bubastite kings. (Euseb. *Three.*)

	Years.
SESONCHIS, reigned	21
OSORTHON	15
Three others [omitted by Eusebius]	25
TACELLOTHIS	13
Three others [omitted by Eusebius]	42
	116 Eus. 49

In regard to this dynasty we have no longer to complain of the silence of history and the monuments. The names of Sesonchis, Osorkon and Tacellothis were early recognised by Champollion[1], and the researches of other Egyptologists have recovered the shields of all the nine kings of whom this dynasty was composed. Those of Sesonchis and several of his successors of this dynasty contain a character which does not occur before, the white crown of Upper Egypt, as if to indicate that it had been acquired by them. Bubastis, whence its name is derived, was one of the most ancient cities of Lower Egypt[2]; it is mentioned in Manetho in the second dynasty of the Old Monarchy, and it stood near the Pelusiac arm of the Nile, about twenty miles below the apex of the Delta. In its modern name, *Tel Basta*, we recognize that of the goddess *Pasht*, to whom the principal temple was dedicated—the Artemis of the Greeks. The Hebrews called it from the same goddess *Pi-beseth*[3], which the Septuagint renders *Boubastos,* and the Coptic *Poubast.* In its present abandoned and de-

---

[1] Lettres à M. le Duc de Blacas, P. 2, p. 119.
[2] Vol. i. p. 55.
[3] Ezek. xxx. 17.

solate condition it still exhibits some of the features which are so graphically described by Herodotus[1]. "There is," says he, "in the city of Bubastis a temple very deserving of description; larger and more costly temples exist, but none so pleasant to behold. Except the entrance it is all an island; two canals come from the Nile, not united, but distinct as far as the entrance, and one flows round it on one side, and one on the other. The propylæa are sixty feet high, and adorned with excellent sculptures six cubits in height. The temple being in the middle of the city, one who walks round looks down upon it from all sides; for the city has been raised by accumulations of earth, and the temple remaining as it originally was can be looked into. An outer wall runs round it, with sculptured figures. Within is a grove of very large trees, planted round a large temple (νηόν), in which the image of the goddess is. The length and breadth of the *hieron* is a stadium each way. Near the entrance is a road paved with stone of the length of three stadia, leading eastward through the agora, its breadth 400 feet. Trees reaching to the skies are planted on either side, and it leads to the hieron of Mercury." The temples of Pasht and Thoth can still be traced; the mounds which surround the ancient site are of extraordinary height, rising above the area of the temple.

SESONCHIS (Shishak), the first of this dynasty, is not mentioned by Diodorus, nor according to our present text by Herodotus. A happy conjecture of Bunsen's has restored his name to the commence-

[1] 2, 138.

ment of the 136th section of the Euterpe. "After Mycerinus the priests said that Sasychis became king of Egypt, and built the eastern propylæa of the temple of Vulcan[1]." With Herodotus the time of the building of the pyramids represents the long interval of decline and insignificance which intervened between the illustrious sovereigns of the 18th and 19th dynasty, and the revival of the prosperity of Egypt before the invasion of the Ethiopians.

The reign of Sesonchis is the first which we are enabled to connect, by means of a synchronism, with our ordinary reckoning of the years before Christ, as he is the first Pharaoh who is mentioned by name in the Jewish Scriptures. The jealousy of Solomon having been excited against Jeroboam[2], in consequence of his being prophetically pointed out by Ahijah as the future sovereign of the ten tribes, Jeroboam, to save his life, had escaped into Egypt, in the last years of Solomon's reign, and had taken refuge with Sesonchis, or as the Hebrews wrote the name, Shashaq. The folly of Rehoboam had caused the erection of a separate kingdom of the ten tribes, which had its capital at Shechem. Of this Jeroboam was made king, and set up here the worship of the Egyptian divinities. The country being thus divided by a double schism, political and religious, and a powerful ally to Egypt being secured, Sesonchis made an easy conquest of Jerusalem. He came up in the fifth year after the accession of Re-

---

[1] Μετὰ δὲ Μυκερῖνον γενέσθαι Αἰγύπτου βασιλέα ἔλεγον οἱ ΊΡΕΕΣ ΑΣΥΧΙΝ. The loss of the Σ in such a position would easily occur. (Comp. Wessel. ad Diod. 1, 94.) The Septuagint calls Shishak, Σου- σακίμ. From the mention of his legislation he appears to be the same as the Sasychis of Diodorus (u. s.), though his chronology is entirely confused.
[2] 1 Kings xi. 40.

hoboam with an overwhelming force of chariots and horsemen[1], and an auxiliary body composed of Libyans, Ethiopians, and the Troglodyte tribes who dwelt on the western shore of the Red Sea[2] and Ethiopia. Rehoboam had not neglected preparation; he had built some strong places and fortified others in the kingdom of Judah, had put garrisons in them and victualled them against a siege[3], and had given the command in them to his own sons. Sesonchis, however, speedily reduced all the fenced cities of Judah and Benjamin. Jerusalem appears to have made no resistance, and thus escaped the sufferings of a siege and a storm[4]; but the treasures both of the Temple and the royal palace were carried off, including the golden shields which Solomon had made for the use of his guards on solemn occasions, and placed in the house of the forest of Lebanon. It was part of the threatening of the prophet Shemaiah that Judah should become subject to the king of Egypt, that they might "learn the difference between the service of Jehovah and the service of the kingdoms round about[5]." During the reign of Sesonchis they probably continued in a state of dependence, which, however, was not burdensome, as we are told that "things went well in Judah[6]" during the later years of Rehoboam.

---

[1] Much over-estimated no doubt in 2 Chron. xii. 3 at 1200 chariots and 60,000 horsemen.

[2] Such is the probable meaning of the Sukiim, mentioned 2 Chron. xii. 3. They were skilful slingers and very useful as light troops. (Heliod. Æth. 8, 16.) There was a town on this coast called Suche (Plin. N. H. 6, 34), supposed to be the modern Suakin.

[3] 2 Chron. xi. 5-12. The Book of Kings makes no mention of these preparations.

[4] 2 Chron. xii. 7. "My wrath shall not be poured out upon Jerusalem by the hand of Shishak."

[5] 2 Chron. xii. 8.

[6] 2 Chron. xii. 12.

A monument still remaining on the outer wall of the hypostyle hall at Karnak confirms in a very remarkable manner this narrative from the Jewish Scriptures[1]. Sesonchis (Amunmai Sheshonk) is there represented as usual of gigantic size, preparing to inflict death on a group of prisoners, African and Asiatic, in the presence of Amunre, who holds out a scimitar towards him with one hand, and with the other leads to him a number of foreigners bound. To each of the five cords which he holds in his hand are attached a series of shields surrounded with an embattled edge and surmounted by a head, round the neck of which the cord is passed. Each of the five rows contains thirteen shields, and about half of the sixty-five is legible. The first in the first line contains the lotus, the symbol of the South, with the character for *region*; the second the papyrus, the symbol of the North. The account given in the Book of Chronicles of the various nations composing the expedition of Sesonchis shows that he held Libya and Ethiopia in his obedience when he invaded Palestine, and renders it probable that he might have subdued them in the previous part of his reign. The third shield is composed of the character which has been read Penne or Pone, and is understood to denote the western bank of the Nile, along with the bows which have been already explained as denoting Libya. Among those which remain legible, few have been identified with known geographical names. Champollion supposed "the land of Mahanima" (line 2, 9) to be the Mahanaim[2] of Scripture; "the land of Baith-

---

[1] Rosellini, Mon. Stor. 4, 149; M. R. cxlviii. [2] Gen. xxxii. 2.

oron" (l. 2, 11) and Makto (l. 3, 1) to be Beth-horon and Megiddo, both of which Solomon fortified[1]. Mr. Osburn has since pointed out some others which bear a resemblance to known names in Palestine[2]. Much uncertainty attends these identifications, because it is necessary to assume certain phonetic values for characters which do not occur elsewhere, or only in positions equally ambiguous. There is, however, no uncertainty respecting the most important figure of the whole, the third in the third line, which contains in well-known characters JOUDHMALK, *i. e.* Joudah-Melek, " King of Judah," which being followed by the usual character for *land*, the whole will be read " Land of the King of Judah;" these shields representing not persons but places, symbolized by a figure of their inhabitants. Another figure on the same wall represents the goddess Egypt, who holds in her hand four cords, to each of which seventeen similar shields are attached. The greater part are legible, but none of them have been identified with names known in geography. Since this is the case on a monument of the middle of the tenth century before Christ, we cannot be surprised at the little success which has attended the attempts made to ascertain the nations who are mentioned in the sculptures of sovereigns of the 18th dynasty, the Thothmes, Menephthah and the Rameses. With the exception of a few general designations of the African nations, we meet with none of those with which the earlier monuments have made us familiar—Naharaina, for

---

[1] 1 Kings ix. 15, 17. 2 Chron. viii. 5.   [2] Ancient Egypt, p. 158.

THE TWENTY-SECOND DYNASTY.

example,—or those which we have supposed to describe people inhabiting the countries eastward of the Tigris and north-westward of the Euphrates. Notwithstanding the pompous list of names in the record of the triumphs of Sesonchis, it is not probable that his expedition extended much beyond Palestine. He could not have advanced towards the Euphrates without encountering the power of the Assyrians.

There are other memorials of Sesonchis[1] at Karnak and Silsilis, but being of the religious class they throw no light on the history of his reign. A stele at the latter place bears date in the twenty-first year of his reign, which must have been the last. It speaks of his excavations in these quarries for the purpose of erecting buildings at Thebes[2]. These were carried on by his successors in the Bubastite dynasty[3].

If Sesonchis were the Sasychis of Diodorus and Herodotus, he was celebrated as a legislator as well as a conqueror. To him Herodotus attributes the law[4] which allowed a debtor to raise money by pledging the body of his father, under the condition that if he did not repay the money, neither he himself nor any of his family should be interred, either in the

---

[1] A cuirass of leather, studded with brass scales, bearing the shield of Sheshonk, is figured in M. Prisse d'Avennes' Monumens Egyptiens, Paris, 1846, p. 735. The name, however, will not prove that it was worn by Sesonchis, as a throwstick is figured in the same work, bearing the shield of a queen.

[2] Rosellini, Mon. Stor. 4, 165. Champollion-Figeac, L'Univers, 359.

[3] It would be premature to enter into any speculations respecting the connexion of Egypt and Assyria in this age till the Assyrian monuments are better understood. See Birch, Trans. Roy. Soc. Lit. vol. iii. From Layard's account, it is evident that the Egyptian remains found at Nineveh do not belong to the earliest age of the Assyrian monarchy, as they occur above ruined buildings. Layard's Nineveh, vol. 2, p. 205.

[4] See p. 59 of this vol.

family sepulchre or elsewhere. He was said also to have erected a pyramid of brick, and placed an inscription upon it, in which he claimed for it a superiority over the pyramids of stone. The inscription as given by Herodotus has very little resemblance to a genuine inscription, and was probably the invention of his guides. But it is not at all improbable that Sesonchis, following the example of his predecessor of the 18th century, may have employed his Asiatic captives in brick-making. The sepulchres of the kings, after the last of the Rameses, are no longer found in the Bab-el-Melook; and there is no reason why some of the brick pyramids of Lower Egypt, which have been ascertained by the Prussian Expedition to be nearly double the number previously known, may not have been the tombs of later kings.

If some of them were built after the end of the 19th dynasty, when royal interments ceased at Thebes, we can understand how all of them were referred to that period. Sasychis, according to Herodotus, built the eastern propylæa of the temple at Memphis, and adorned it with sculptures of remarkable size and beauty. These have perished, and the imperfect remains at Karnak afford no criterion of the state of the arts in the reign of Sesonchis. It may be better judged of by the statues of the lion-headed goddess Pasht, which seem to have been multiplied in the reign of this first Bubastite king. One of these is in the Museum of Turin, another in the Louvre, and a third in the British Museum[1]. In regard to its execution Mr. Birch

[1] Gallery of Antiquities, pl. viii.

observes:—" The style is very different from those executed under Amenoph III. in the same collection; the cheeks are more hollow, the limbs more lissom and less strongly developed; the whole of a style of art less pure and grand than that of the 18th dynasty."

A son of Sesonchis appears joined with him in an act of worship at Karnak. His name is Ushiopf[1], or Schuopt, and like the kings mentioned, p. 343, he united with the sacerdotal office the post of captain of the archers. He did not, however, succeed his father.

OSORTHON is the next king in Manetho's list. Where this name occurs again in the 23rd dynasty in Eusebius, it is *Osorcho* in Manetho; and although there is no various reading here, there can be no doubt that the king intended is the Osorkon of the monuments. His shield follows that of Sheshonk in the sculptures of the court at Karnak, which has been called, from having been adorned by them, the Court of the Bubastite kings[2]. It is also found at Bubastis on a fragment of a cornice, and cut on some blocks where originally the shield of Rameses-Sesostris stood[3]. Among the Egyptian antiquities of the Louvre, there is a magnificent vase of alabaster, which contains on one side a dedication by Osorchon to Amunre. It was subsequently employed to receive the remains of a member of the Claudian

---

[1] Rosellini, Mon. Stor. 4, 163.
[2] See vol. i. p. 176. It is marked B. 4. 8, on Sir G. Wilkinson's Map of Thebes. Rosellini, Mon. Stor. 2, 85.
[3] Wilkinson, Mod. Eg. & Thebes, 1, 429. He has not given any facsimile of these shields, and it is possible that they may not all refer to the same Osorkon.

family at Rome, and bears an inscription to this purpose on its opposite side[1].

The Book of Kings gives no account of the relations between Egypt and the kingdoms of Judah and Israel, from the invasion of Shishak till the reign of Hoshea, who made an alliance with Seva, or So, king of Egypt (725 B.C.), in order to throw off the yoke of Salmaneser and the Assyrians[2]. The Second Book of Chronicles, however, records an invasion of Judah by Zerach, the Ethiopian, in the reign of Asa, the grandson of Rehoboam. In the name of Zerach critics have recognized that of Osorchon, the successor of Sesonchis. A war between the two countries was an exceedingly probable event. Abijah, the son of Rehoboam, had gained a great victory over the kingdom of Israel. Asa had raised an army, according to the Book of Chronicles, of 580,000 men, and built several fortified places in Judah. If Egypt had retained a claim of superiority and tribute over Judah from the time of Sheshonk's invasion, these indications of a growing military power would not be overlooked by her. Zerach (941 B.C., Usher) came up with a very numerous army[3] as far as Mareshah in the plain of Judah, but was defeated by Asa and pursued to Gerar on the southern boundary of Palestine. The only difficulty which attends the narrative is, that Zerach is called an Ethiopian (Cushite). No king of the Bubastite dynasty could have been so designated; the works of Osorchon

---

[1] Champollion-Figeac, L'Univers, p. 360.
[2] 2 Kings xvii. 4.
[3] Estimated in 2 Chron. xiv. 9, at a million of men and three hundred chariots.

and his successors at Thebes show that Upper Egypt was in their possession; and therefore if we could suppose a motive for an invasion of Judæa by a sovereign of Ethiopia, it is not credible that he should have marched through Egypt for its accomplishment. On the other hand, chronology forbids the supposition that Zerach could be one of the 25th or Ethiopian dynasty of Egyptian kings, the earliest of whom lived 200 years later than Asa. The reality of the invasion and defeat cannot be called in question; the name Zerach is not very remote from Osorchon, when reduced to its consonants, and the times would very exactly correspond. Rehoboam reigned twelve years after the invasion of Sesonchis; Abijah, his son, three years; the victory of Asa took place in the fifteenth year of his reign[1]. Thus thirty years elapsed between the invasions by Sheshonk and by Zerach, and as Sesonchis reigned twenty-two years and Osorchon fifteen, there is sufficient room for both events. The name of Ethiopian given to Zerach in the Book of Chronicles, which was not written, at least in its present form, till after the Captivity, may be explained by the circumstance that his army, like that of Sheshonk, was composed chiefly of Libyan and Ethiopian troops[2].

The names of the three successors of Osorkon I. are not given by Manetho; Lepsius makes his immediate successor to have been Amunmai PEHOR, who was probably his son. Another son, whose name was Sheshonk, filled the office of high-priest, and is mentioned in a funeral papyrus which ap-

[1] 2 Chron. xv. 10.   [2] 2 Chron. xvi. 8.

pears to have accompanied the mummy of another high-priest of the name of Osorkon, the son of this Sheshonk, and consequently grandson of Osorkon I. Neither of these appear to have ascended the throne. Pehor was succeeded by OSORKON II., and he by SHESHONK II. His shield is distinguished from that of the founder of the dynasty, by the addition of the name of the goddess of Bubastis, Pasht. The name of Takelothis was recovered by Champollion from a fragment[1] of a piece of sycamore-wood, the remainder of which is in the Vatican, on which a priest clad in the leopard's skin is represented, performing an act of adoration to Phre, in behalf of Takelothis' son. It has since been found on the wall at Karnak, and with the date of the twenty-fifth year of his reign. The same inscription mentions the name of his queen Keromama, and of his son and probably successor Osòrchon, who is called high-priest and captain of the archers[2]. Of OSORKON III., SHESHONK III., and TAKELOTHIS II.[3], with whom the dynasty became extinct, no historical fact is recorded.

The relations of Egypt and Judæa appear not to have been friendly, under this and the succeeding dynasty, even when there was not actual war between them. The prophet Joel[4] (iii. 19) threatens Egypt, as well as Edom, with desolation for its violence against the children of Judah, which may have consisted in the forcible seizure of the inha-

[1] Champollion-Figeac, L'Univers, p.361. Champollion le Jeune Lettre à M. le Duc de Blacas, 2, 123.
[2] Rosellini, Mon. Stor. 4, 170.
[3] Bunsen, Ægyptens Stelle, B. 3, p. 135.
[4] His age is uncertain, but from the absence of all mention of Assyria, he is thought to have lived before that power threatened the independence of Palestine.

bitants for slaves. Eusebius in his Canon remarks, under the 23rd dynasty, that after the Phœnicians the Egyptians became masters of the seas, and they probably exercised their dominion piratically, like their predecessors.

Twenty-third Dynasty. Four Tanite kings.

	Years.	
PETUBATIS [Petubastis, Euseb.], reigned ..	40	25 (Euseb.)
In his reign was the first Olympiad.		
OSORCHO [Osorthon, Euseb.]	8	
Whom the Egyptians call Hercules[1].		
PSAMMUS	10	
ZET [omitted by Euseb.]	31	
	89	44

Of this whole dynasty, till lately, no name had been read on the monuments, as no fact is recorded concerning them. Lepsius has found a shield with the name of *Petsepasht*, the Egyptian word whence the Petubastis of Eusebius was derived. The occurrence of the name of the great goddess of Bubastis in that of the founder of the dynasty, leads us to conclude that this family, though called of Tanis, was genealogically connected with the preceding. This is confirmed by the name of the second king Osorchon, which was borne by so many of the 22nd dynasty. A shield at Karnak, containing the name Psemaut, has generally been attributed to Psemmuthis of the 29th dynasty, which arose during an interval of success-

---

[1] This remark, from its turn of expression, is evidently not that of Manetho. It does not appear what ground there was for this identification, as Chon is said to have been the Egyptian name for Hercules. Etym. M. s. v. Χών. Vol. i. p. 384.

ful revolt from Persia[1], a prince who reigned only during a part of the year. Lepsius has given it to Psammus, the third of this dynasty. There remains then only Zet[2], whose name has not yet been found.

The fifth year of Rehoboam, in which Sheshonk invaded Judæa, is generally placed 974 B.C. Between this date and 1322 B.C. we must place the reigns of all the kings from Menephthah (p. 297) to Sheshonk. These three centuries and a half suffice for the events of the history, but their distribution into reigns would be quite hypothetical. The chronological notice, that the first Olympiad fell in the reign of Petubastis, seems to have been transferred hither by mistake. It is not found in Eusebius, and cannot have proceeded from Africanus, who elsewhere places the first Olympiad in the first year of Ahaz[3]. This is too late, as the other is too early.

We obtain no assistance either from Herodotus or Diodorus, in recovering the history of this dynasty. Herodotus knows the name of no king of Egypt, between Sasychis and Anysis, who was reigning at the time of the Ethiopian invasion. Diodorus passes at once from the builders of the pyramids to Bocchoris, and he makes many years to have intervened between him and Sabaco, contrary to the lists, according to which Bocchoris was taken captive and burnt alive by the Ethiopian king.

---

[1] Wilkinson, Manners and Customs, 1, 207; Mod. Eg. & Thebes, 2, 256.

[2] Lepsius, Einl. 1, 256, makes him to be the Sethos of Herodotus.

[3] Fynes Clinton, Fasti, 1, 150, who observes that the year B.C. 776, the admitted æra of the Olympiads, fell in the 33rd year of Uzziah. His reign lasted 51 years; that of his son and successor Jotham, the father of Ahaz, 16.

There are not even any private monuments which throw light on the condition of Egypt during this period. That it was one of decline and decay we may infer from the ascendency which the Ethiopians acquired in the next dynasty, and apparently with little struggle on the part of the Egyptians.

Twenty-fourth Dynasty.

	Years.	
BOCCHORIS of Sais, reigned.............	6	Euseb. 44

In his reign a lamb spoke [1].

The Dynasty of Sais, founded by Bocchoris, may be said to have been in fact prolonged to the time of the Persian conquest, the Ethiopian dynasty being intrusive and the Dodecarchia only temporary. Sais stood near the Canopic branch of the Nile, to which, as the nearest and the most accessible, the traffic of the Greeks was from the first attracted. Naucratis, the only harbour in Egypt to which strangers were admitted, unless under the plea of stress of weather[2], was on the Canopic branch and nearer to the sea than Sais. It is not certain when the Greeks were first allowed to settle in Naucratis. Eusebius in his Canon says[3], that the Milesians, in the reign of Bocchoris, became powerful at sea and built the city of Naucratis. This is not very probable, if literally taken, and is contradicted by He-

---

[1] Probably a portent of the approaching calamities of Bocchoris and his kingdom. So when Psammenitus was about to be dethroned, rain fell at Thebes (Her. 3, 10). According to Ælian, N. H. 12, 3, this lamb, besides speaking with a human voice, had two heads, eight feet, &c.

[2] This is stated by Herodotus (2, 179) as if true of all strangers. Strabo intimates that it was chiefly intended against the Greeks from their piratical habits, 17, 792. The duty of watching the coast and keeping off strangers was committed to the herdsmen, a rude and inhospitable race.

[3] Under Olymp. vi.

rodotus[1], who says the Ionians and Carians under Psammitichus were the first foreigners who were allowed to settle in Egypt. Considering the widespread colonization of the Milesians in the eighth century before Christ[2], there is however nothing improbable in their having established more regular commercial relations with Egypt than Greece had possessed before.

Gradually greater privileges seem to have been allowed them, and hence the variety of accounts respecting the time of their establishment, which Strabo against all probability brings down as low as the revolt of Inaros[3], 462 B.C. The Portuguese at Macao at first only obtained permission to erect sheds for their goods, but by degrees were allowed to build houses, establish a government of their own and erect a fort. The story of the landing of the Ionian and Carian mercenaries in Egypt at the time of the Dodecarchia indicates that *armed* Greeks were a novel sight to the Egyptians[4]; but of course only merchant ships and men in peaceful attire would be admitted to Naucratis. The English, when they first established themselves at Formosa, agreed to deliver up all their guns and ammunition while in port[5]. We do not, however, derive much increase of our knowledge respecting Egypt from the increased resort of the Greeks before the time of Psammitichus. They have not even preserved

---

[1] 2, 154.
[2] Rambach de Mileto, p. 19, 62. Clinton, F. H. 1, 115.
[3] 17, p. 801. According to him they first fortified a place at the Bolbitine mouth, in the reign of Psammitichus; and afterwards removed in the time of Inaros to the Saitic nome, and fortified Naucratis.
[4] Her. 2, 152.
[5] Davis, The Chinese, vol. 1, p. 35.

such tales of wonder as we find in the Homeric legends. The Epic Muse was silent; the Cyclic, if she deserves the name of Muse, was occupied in combining and harmonizing the traditions of the Mythic age. Prose history, scientific geography and astronomy had their birth-place at Miletus; but in a later century.

The name of Bocchoris, which was probably in Egyptian *Pehor*, does not appear on any monument which can be conclusively referred to his reign[1]. His father's name, according to Diodorus, was Tnephachthus, or Gnephachthus, in which we recognize that of the goddess Pasht[2]. Diodorus calls his father king, and relates an anecdote of him which has been mentioned under the reign of Menes. Bocchoris himself is said by Diodorus to have been mean and feeble in body, but to have surpassed his predecessors in ingenuity and wisdom. He attributes specially to him the laws which regulated commercial contracts and the prerogatives and duties of the king[3]. This reputation seems to imply that at his accession he found public and private law in a state of decay, and laboured to renew them. He is celebrated also for the wisdom of his judicial decisions, many of which were handed down by fame even to very late times. A very different account of his character and administration is given by Ælian[4], who says he had obtained a false reputation for the justice of his decisions. To grieve the Egyptians,

---

[1] The Amunse Pehor, whom the earlier Egyptologists identified with Bocchoris, has been removed by Lepsius to the 21st dynasty. See before, p. 342. Bunsen. 3, 135.

[2] Plut. Is. et Osir. 354 B. gives the name Technatis; Athenæus, x. p. 418, Νεόχαβις.

[3] Τοῦτον οὖν διατάξαι τὰ περὶ τοὺς βασιλεῖς πάντα, καὶ τὰ περὶ τῶν συμβολαίων ἐξακριβῶσαι. (Diod. ibid.)

[4] Nat. Anim. 11, 11.

he set a wild bull to attack their sacred Mnevis. As the assailant was rushing furiously on, he stumbled, and entangling his horn in the tree *persea*, Mnevis gave him a mortal wound in the flank. Plutarch[1], while he acknowledges the just decisions of Bocchoris, calls him a man of stern character. Possibly the avarice which Diodorus attributes to him may have been only the unfavourable aspect of a rigid economy, rendered necessary by dilapidated finances. Economy, especially if accompanied by strictness in the levying of taxes, is seldom a popular virtue in rulers. The celebrity which he enjoyed is hardly reconcilable with the short reign of six years, which the lists attribute to him. Eusebius makes his reign to have lasted forty-four years; but this number is suspicious, as being the same which this author attributes both to the 23rd dynasty which precedes and the 25th which follows. The cruel death inflicted by Sabaco on Bocchoris, which appears inconsistent with the humanity ascribed to the Ethiopian conqueror, may be explained, if we suppose that Bocchoris was at first left on the throne in the capacity of a tributary, but revolting, was taken prisoner by Sabaco and then put to death by burning. Herodotus calls the king who was reigning at the time of the Ethiopian invasion, Anysis, and a native of the city of the same name, probably the Hanes of the prophet Isaiah[2], to which, as well as Tanis, the ambassadors of Israel came, seeking an alliance with the king of Egypt, when they were alarmed by the prospect of an Assyrian invasion, in the reign

---

[1] Περὶ Δυσωπίας, p. 529, E.   [2] xxx. 4. See p. 342 of this vol.

of Sennacherib. According to Herodotus, Anysis was not put to death, but took refuge in the marshes of the Delta. He had made a spot of solid ground of a little more than a mile square, by laying down ashes amidst the muddy soil. These ashes were supplied by the friends, who, unknown to the Ethiopians, brought him provisions. On the retirement of the Ethiopians he issued from his retreat, and resumed his power, after an interval of fifty years. These differences are irreconcilable, but on the whole it appears probable that a considerably longer date is to be allowed to the reign of the immediate predecessor of Sabaco than six years.

Twenty-fifth Dynasty, of three Ethiopian kings.

	Years.	
1. SABACO, reigned..................	8	Eusebius 12
He took Bocchoris prisoner and burnt him alive.		
2. SEBICHOS (Sevechos) his son	14	Eusebius 12
3. TARKUS (Tarakos, Eus.)	18	Eusebius 20
	40	44

The word Ethiopian has so wide a meaning, being applied to the Arab of Yemen, to the Abessinian, the native of Sennaar, Darfur and Kordofan, as well as of Nubia and Dongola, that it is necessary to fix its sense more precisely, in order to conceive rightly of the conquest of Egypt by the Ethiopians in the latter part of the eighth century before Christ. The seat of the monarchy of Sabaco and his successors was Napata, whose site and remains have been already described[1]. It extended as far north as to

[1] Vol. i. p. 15.

the island of Argo; the space between that and the Cataracts of Syene must be regarded as a debateable land, which was held by Egypt or Ethiopia according to their relative strength. Under the 18th dynasty we have seen that the valley of the Nile was completely possessed by Egypt, even to the south of the Second Cataract. During the feebleness of the last years of the 23rd and the 24th, it is probable that the Ethiopians had advanced their arms to the very frontiers of Egypt, or even occupied Thebes. How far to the south of Napata the Ethiopian monarchy extended at this time we do not know. It has been commonly supposed that the island of Meroe was its original seat: Herodotus calls the city of Meroe "the metropolis of the other Ethiopians," meaning probably those of the island. No monuments of equal antiquity with those of Napata have been found in any part of the island[1]. Diodorus[2] says that the city of Meroe was founded by Cambyses and named after his mother; but Cambyses never reached so far. In the Persian times the valley of the Nile above the First Cataract was held by the Ethiopians, but as tributaries; the Persian frontier garrison was established in Elephantine. The Ptolemies before Euergetes left Ethiopia in possession of her independence; we find the names of Erkamen (Ergamenes) and Atharaman on the monuments of Lower Nubia[3]. Under the Romans, in the reign of Augustus, Ethiopia appears again as a powerful mo-

---

[1] See vol. i. p. 10.
[2] 1, 33.
[3] Vol. i. pp. 27, 29.

narchy, and Petronius marched to Napata and compelled Candace to submit herself to the emperor.

The Ethiopians of the eighth century before Christ were little inferior in civilization to the Egyptians themselves. They had a system of hieroglyphical writing identical with the Egyptian, though applied to a different language, and therefore not yet deciphered[1]. The power of the priesthood was greater than even in Egypt, and completely ascendant over the monarchy. Both the historical and the prophetic books of the Jews afford evidence of their military power. They bear a part in the invasions of Palestine; they are joined by Isaiah with the Egyptians when he endeavours to dissuade his countrymen from relying on their aid to resist Assyria. In the 87th Psalm (v. 4) Ethiopia is mentioned along with Egypt, Babylon, Tyre and Philistia, as one of the most illustrious nations[2]. Throughout the prophetic writings the Ethiopians are very generally conjoined with Egypt, so as to show that the union between them, produced sometimes by the ascendency of one country, sometimes of the other, was so close, that their foreign policy was usually the same[3]. We are not therefore to consider the subjugation of Egypt by the Ethiopians

---

[1] It is said that Lepsius has ascertained the language of the Ethiopian inscriptions. Chæremon, who wrote on hieroglyphics about the Christian æra, called them *Ethiopic* letters. His explanations accord in general with modern discovery. See Birch's Remarks on the curious fragment of Chæremon, preserved by Tzetzes, Trans. Roy. Soc. Lit. 3, 384.

[2] The meaning of the passage evidently is, that though it was an honour to be a native of Egypt, Babylon, or Ethiopia, it was a greater honour to be a native of Zion.

[3] Is. xx. 5. Nahum iii. 9. Ezek. xxx. 4.

as if they had fallen under the dominion of a horde of Arabs or Scythians. The *blameless* Ethiopians[1] is the earliest epithet which the Greeks applied to them; Diodorus[2] celebrates the moderation of Actisanes, and the account which Herodotus[3] gives of Sabaco's retirement from Egypt proves his humanity and reverence for the gods. The dynasty was changed; the head of it either put to death or driven into the marshes of Lower Egypt; but the order of government appears to have suffered little change. No difference of religion or manners embittered the animosity of the two nations; they had been connected by royal intermarriages; Ammon and Osiris were equally honoured at Thebes and Meroe[4]; and to the inhabitants of Upper Egypt, the Ethiopians would seem hardly so foreign as the people of Sais.

The Egyptian *history* of Herodotus, if we understand by that word a series of facts connected in chronological order, really begins with the invasion of Sabaco. He himself remarks, that the settlement of the Ionians and Carians in Egypt, in the time of Psammitichus, gave the Greeks an accurate knowledge of all its subsequent history, and the effect would naturally extend upwards also. Herodotus indeed considers the same king Sabaco as reigning through the whole fifty years that the Egyptians kept possession of Egypt; but the similarity of two of the names may partly account for this error, which at all events was not his, since the relation of the departure of Sabaco is evidently

[1] Il. a', 423.
[2] 2, 60.
[3] 2, 139.
[4] Her. 2, 29.

formed on the assumption of the identity of the invader with the sovereign who withdrew from the country.

The name of SABACO, written *Shabek*, is found at Luxor, with the usual titles of Egyptian sovereignty, on the internal wall of the propyla raised by Rameses-Sesostris [1]. The sculptures having been injured, or decayed with time, Sabaco renewed them and substituted his own name for that of Rameses; they indicate that Egyptian art still existed in considerable vigour. A *statuette* of the same king, of the stone called *plasme d'émeraude*, is preserved in the Villa Albani at Rome, and his name occurs also as a date on some amulets and small figures from the collection of Anastasy, now in the Louvre. The shield of Sabaco has also been found over a gate of the palace of Karnak, and on some fragments, one of which bears the date of his twelfth year. This, according to Eusebius, was the last of his reign; according to the text of Manetho, with which the summation of the years of the dynasty agrees, he reigned only eight years. The name of the succeeding king, however, Sebechus or Sevechus, is evidently the same as Sabaco, which Manetho probably adopted as one already established in history; and the shield at Karnak which has been attributed to the first Ethiopic king, may with equal propriety be given to the second, as their phonetic names are written in the same characters[2],

[1] Rosellini, Mon. Stor. 2, 107; 4, 175, 177. Champollion-Figeac, L'Univers, p. 363. The name also occurs (Rosellini, 2, 108) on monuments of private persons, who call themselves natives of Cush.

[2] See Bunsen, Plates of 25th Dynasty, Nos. 1 & 2.

and thus the monuments and the lists will be brought into accordance, the date of the twelfth year being allotted to Sevechus.

Diodorus bestows the highest praise on Sabaco, as surpassing in piety and clemency all his predecessors[1]. Herodotus agrees in representing him as having abolished the punishment of death, and substituted for it compulsory labour on public works[2]. They were such as in the more glorious days of the monarchy had been performed by foreign prisoners. The increase in the rise of the Nile since the reign of Sesostris had made it necessary to add to the height of the embankments which prevented the towns of Lower Egypt from being laid under water at the time of the inundation. He also employed culprits in excavating canals. The circumstances of his retirement from Egypt, as related by both historians, indicate that the priests bore subjection to a foreign power impatiently and caballed for its overthrow. He dreamt that a figure standing over him in his sleep, counselled him to collect all the priests in Egypt together and cut them to pieces[3]. Sabaco perceived in this a design on the part of the gods to entice him to the com-

---

[1] His account of Actisanes has the air of being a confused tradition of *this* Ethiopian conquest; the only circumstance which he definitely mentions concerning his reign is, that he did not put criminals to death, but banished them to Rhinocolura on the confines of Syria (1, 60). Diodorus adds, διὰ μέσων αὐτῶν διέλθῃ μετὰ τῆς θεραπείας (1, 65), a circumstance which seems to have been added from the story of Xerxes (Her. 7, 40), who commanded the eldest son of Pythius whom he had endeavoured to beg off from military service, to be cut in two pieces, which were fixed on either side of the line of march.
[2] Herod. 2, 137.
[3] Μέσους διαταμέειν, Her. 2, 139.

mission of an act of impiety which should bring on his ruin. He had been told by the oracles of Ethiopia that he should reign over Egypt fifty years, and being disturbed by the dream, he determined voluntarily to withdraw into Ethiopia. As related of the Ethiopian king who had invaded Egypt, this cannot be true; but the subsequent elevation of a priest of Memphis to supreme power makes it probable that the sacerdotal order of that city, controlled in their ascendency, had placed the Ethiopian sovereigns in the dilemma of yielding to them or undertaking their extermination. No memorials of any of this dynasty except Tirhakah have been found in Lower Egypt, though it is evident from the account of the raising of the mounds that it was subject to Sabaco.

It is related in the Second Book of Kings (xvii. 4), that Hoshea, king of Israel, who had become tributary to Shalmaneser, king of Assyria, had entered into a secret alliance with Seva, the king of Egypt, the SEVECHUS of Manetho[1], and relying on his assistance, "had brought no present to the king of Assyria, as he had done year by year;" for which the king of Assyria put him in prison, and after a three years' siege took Samaria and carried the people captive into Assyria and Media. This, according to the Jewish Chronology, took place in the year 722 B.C., the ninth of Hoshea's reign. The kings of the Ethiopian dynasty would naturally enter into the policy of the native kings of Egypt, which evidently was to uphold the power of Israel and Judah, the only barrier between them-

---

[1] סוא which without the points may be read *Seva*.

selves and the warlike and aggressive empire of the Assyrians. It is probable that the rapid movements of Shalmaneser, who had an ally in the king of Judah, anticipated the aid which Sevechus had engaged to furnish to Hoshea; but the very brief narrative of the Book of Kings gives us no details. Many of the Israelites avoided the captivity which threatened them, by taking refuge in the friendly territory of Egypt, while others even penetrated into Ethiopia, and from this time forward there seems always to have been a considerable body of Jews in the eastern side of Egypt, speaking their own language, practising their own religious rites, and exciting the bigotry of the native Egyptians[1]. The prophet Isaiah[2] anticipates the time when the remnant of the people should be recalled "from Assyria, and from Egypt, and from Pathros (the Thebaid), and from Cush," and in glowing language describes Jehovah as drying up the gulf of the Red Sea, smiting the seven channels of the Nile, and making a highway through the Desert, that they might return without danger or delay.

TIRHAKAH, the Tarcus or Taracus of Manetho, the Tearco of Strabo[3], succeeded Sevechus. His name, written Tarbak or Tarhaka, is found on the internal face of the pylon of a building erected at Medinet Aboo by Thothmes IV.[4] and at Gebel-el-Birkel, with the date of his twentieth year, which, according to Eusebius, must have been the last of his sovereignty over Egypt. Other inscriptions remain in which he is mentioned, but they give us no

[1] Isaiah xix. 18, foll.
[2] xi. 11.
[3] B. 1, p. 61.
[4] Rosellini, M. Stor. 2, 109.

other knowledge concerning him than the name of his queen and of the nurse of his daughter. The Egypto-Ethiopian monarchy must have been very powerful, though Memphis had been given up to Sethos. Strabo speaks of him as rivalling Sesostris in the extent of his foreign expeditions, and as having reached the Pillars of Hercules[1]. These are evident exaggerations, but they prove the historical fame of Tirhakah, and may have had their foundation in an expedition into Western Africa, of which the Phœnician colonies were the object and limit. The narrative of the expedition of Sennacherib against Judæa and Egypt indicates the opinion entertained of his power. The king of Assyria was dissatisfied with the conduct of Hezekiah, who after having paid him a heavy contribution in gold and silver, was meditating defection in hope of aid from Egypt. He had taken all the strong places of Judah, and from Lachish, a town in the plain of Sephela, on the road to Egypt, which he was besieging, he sent a powerful detachment with a threatening message to Hezekiah[2]. The king himself and the inhabitants of Jerusalem were filled with alarm; but Isaiah encouraged them by a prediction, that Sennacherib "should hear a rumour and return to his own land[3]." This rumour was evidently of the march of Tirhakah to the relief of Judæa, the expectation of

[1] B. 1, p. 61; 15, p. 687.
[2] Isaiah xxxvi. xxxvii.; 2 Kings xviii. xix.
[3] The common Translation has, "I will send a blast upon him, and he shall hear a rumour and return to his own land," in which there appears to be a reference to the miraculous destruction of his army. But this is an error. Archbishop Seeker and Bishop Lowth translate the passage, "I will infuse a spirit into him," and explain it, "a spirit of cowardice."

which had emboldened Hezekiah to withdraw the submission which he had recently made. The narrative, however, implies that there was another power in Egypt on which Hezekiah relied; for Sennacherib in his taunting message says, "On whom dost thou trust, that thou rebellest against me? Lo, thou trustest in the staff of this broken reed, on Egypt; whereon if a man lean it will go into his hand and pierce it; so is Pharaoh king of Egypt to all who trust in him." Now we learn from Herodotus that after the retirement of "the Ethiopian" from Egypt, and the resumption of power by the king who had fled into the marshes, Sethos, a priest of Hephaistos, made himself king, probably only of part of Lower Egypt. He treated the warrior caste not only with contempt, but with injustice, endeavouring to deprive them of the lands which preceding kings had allotted to them. The consequence was, that when Sennacherib, whom Herodotus calls king of the Assyrians and Arabians, invaded Egypt, the military refused to march against him. The priest, reduced to despair, went into the sanctuary of his god, and lamented to him his condition. In the midst of his lamentations he fell asleep, and a dream came over him, in which the god appeared to stand beside him and exhort him to fear nothing from an encounter with the Arabians, for that he would send him defenders. Relying on the dream, Sethos marched to meet the enemy, attended by those of the Egyptians who chose to go. But none of the military joined him; his forces were composed of men altogether unused to warfare, tradesmen and artificers, and the loose population of a great city[1]. With such troops Sennacherib might well describe him as a broken reed, and warn Hezekiah of the folly of trusting to his succour. Similar warnings not to trust in the power of Egypt are given by the prophet himself in the thirtieth and thirty-first chapters, which notwithstanding the place in which they now stand, appear to refer to this alliance, and indicate that Lower Egypt was the seat of the power with whom it was made. Sethos encamped, however, near Pelusium, to defend the entrance of Egypt. The narrative of Scripture does not speak of Sennacherib's advancing so far as Pelusium; but both Libna and Lachish were on the way from Jerusalem to Egypt, and it was natural that if he apprehended an attack from that quarter, he should send a portion of his troops to seize Pelusium, which was equally the key of Egypt and of Palestine. He could do it the more safely as he had already reduced the Arabians, who had possession of the south-western coast of Palestine and the Desert, through which an army must pass[2]. No battle, however, ensued; during the night an immense multitude of field mice covered the encampment of the Assyrians and gnawed the strings of their bows and the straps of their shields. Finding themselves thus left defenceless, in the morning they betook themselves to flight, and many were slain by the Egyptians. A statue of Sethos was set up in the temple of Hephaistos, holding a mouse in his hand,

[1] Ἔπεσθαι οἱ τῶν μαχίμων μὲν οὐδένα ἀνδρῶν, καπήλους δὲ καὶ χειρώνακτας καὶ ἀγοραίους ἀνθρώπους. (Her. 2, 141.)

[2] Comp. Herod. 3, 4–10.

with this inscription, "Whosoever looks on me, let him be pious." We can have no doubt from whom Herodotus derived his tale—the priests of the temple of Ptah at Memphis. The mouse was an emblem of destruction[1], and it may be that the narrative of the defeat of Sennacherib's army owed its specific form to this circumstance. We must believe that in the time of Herodotus the temple of Memphis contained such a statue as he describes[2]; but that it was a statue of Sethos, or that the inscription meant what his guides told him, is not equally certain. The Jewish account is more faithful than the Egyptian, inasmuch as it notices the rumour of Tirhakah's expedition, while the Egyptian makes the cause of the Assyrians' retreat wholly supernatural. Pestilence and panic appear to have combined in bringing it about[3]. The flight of Sennacherib probably put a stop to the march of Tirhakah. Whether he ended his days as sovereign of the Thebais, or retired into Ethiopia and continued to reign there, we do not know; but it is evident that the seat of his power must have been in Upper Egypt, when the rumour of his coming could produce such a sudden retreat of the Assyrians.

The two circumstances which characterize the

---

[1] 'Αφανισμὸν δηλοῦντες μῦν ζωγραφοῦσιν ἐπειδὴ πάντα ἐσθίων μιαίνει καὶ ἀχρηστοί. (Horap. Hierog. 1, 50.) The mouse is produced in sudden and extraordinary numbers in Egypt, and causes great destruction. (Æl. Hist. Anim. 6, 41.) The ancients were not satisfied without exaggerating their destructive powers, and the story of their gnawing bowstrings is told of other places. (Strabo, 13, p. 604.)

[2] Καὶ νῦν οὗτος ὁ βασιλεὺς ἕστηκε ἐν τῷ ἱρῷ τοῦ Ἡφαίστου λίθινος. (2, 141.)

[3] "The Assyrian shall fall by a sword, not of man;
Yea, a sword, not of mortal, shall devour him:
And he shall betake himself to flight from the face of the sword,
And the courage of his chosen men shall fail."--Is. xxxi. 8.

reign of Sethos, the usurpation of supreme power by a priest, and the degradation of the military caste, indicate a decay of the ancient constitution of Egypt. That the increase of population in the great towns of Lower Egypt, the consequence of the fertility of the soil and the growth of commerce, should have made the civil element much more important than it had been in the flourishing days of the monarchy, was natural. It was not less natural that this rise of the commercial and working class should be attended with a change in the military system. Widely different as the Calasirians and Hermotybians were in many respects from the Geomori of Athens before the time of Solon, and the Hippeis and Zeugitæ of his constitution, from the original Plebs of Rome and the Feudal army of the Middle Ages—in one respect they all agreed; landed property and military service were conjoined. And all these, in process of time, yielded up their exclusive right to bear arms, and admitted into partnership with them in this function, the mixed multitude whom the progress of society engenders in flourishing towns. At Athens the change was brought about by the rise of its naval power, which transferred the chief strength of the state from the land to the sea. At Rome the cultivators of the soil were not sufficient to supply the demand of a military republic, and employment and pay were needed for the city population. In modern Europe the rise of the cities was everywhere accompanied with a more promiscuous constitution of the military force, and at no long interval with the establishment of mercenary troops.

We know not how the elevation of Sethos took place; but it is evident that he relied on the town population as the instruments of his design of depressing the ancient military body. His power appears to have been exercised tyrannically; for Herodotus speaks of the Egyptians as being *set free* after his reign[1]. He notices no anarchy as supervening upon his death, but his usurpation and his encroachments on the military order render it abundantly probable; and Diodorus informs us that it actually took place[2], and assigns two years as its duration. The nineteenth chapter of Isaiah, written about this time, perhaps towards the close of Sethos' usurpation, foretells a state of complete anarchy and the consequent depopulation and impoverishment of the country, to be succeeded, as anarchy usually is, by the reign of a despotic monarch. "I will set the Egyptians against the Egyptians, and they shall fight every one against his brother, and every one against his neighbour, city against city, and kingdom against kingdom. And the Egyptians will I give over into the hand of a cruel lord, and a fierce king shall rule over them. In that day shall Egypt be like unto women; and it shall be afraid and fear, because of the shaking of the hand of the Lord of Hosts, which he hath determined against it. And the land of Judah shall be a terror unto Egypt; every one that maketh mention thereof shall be afraid in himself." We know of no period in

---

[1] 2, 147. Ἐλευθερωθέντες Αἰγύπτιοι μετὰ τὸν ἱρέα τοῦ Ἡφαίστου βασιλεύσαντα (οὐδένα γὰρ χρόνον οἷοί τε ἦσαν ἄνευ βασιλέος διαιτᾶσθαι) ἐστήσαντο δυώδεκα βασιλέας.

[2] 1, 66. He places it immediately after the retirement of the Ethiopian, and does not mention Sethos.

Egyptian history to which this description is at all applicable, except that which Diodorus designates as the anarchy[1]. The effects which it is described as producing on the condition of Egypt, however, seem to indicate a longer duration than two years, and Diodorus is never a safe guide in chronology.

The invasion of Judæa by Sennacherib took place 713 B.C., and this fixes a date for the reigns of Sethos at Memphis and Tirhakah in the Thebaid and Ethiopia. The chronology of the two centuries and a half between the invasion of Sheshonk and that of Sennacherib, cannot be settled in detail, from the variations in the lists and the chasms in the series of the monuments. Supposing Sheshonk to have invaded Judæa in the beginning of his reign, the 21st dynasty to have lasted 116 years, according to Manetho, the 22nd, 89 years, the 24th, 6 years, and the 25th, 40, these numbers (116+89+6+40) amount to 251, a coincidence sufficiently close to show that Manetho is substantially correct. Eusebius makes them (49+44+44+44) 181 years.

[1] Gesenius on Is. xix. refers the delivery of the prophecy to the time of Psammitichus; but Isaiah began to prophesy in the reign of Uzziah, who died 757 B.C., and cannot have been contemporary with Psammitichus.

Twenty-sixth Dynasty. Nine Saite kings.

AFRICANUS.

	Years.
1. STEPHINATES, reigned	7
2. NECHEPSOS	6
3. NECHAO	8
4. PSAMMITICHUS	54
5. NECHAO II.	6

He took Jerusalem and carried Jehoash the king captive into Egypt.

6. PSAMMUTHIS II.	6
7. UAPHRIS	19

To him the remnant of the Jews fled when the Assyrians took Jerusalem.

8. AMOSIS	44
9. PSAMMECHERITES	6 months.
	150 6 m.

EUSEBIUS.

	Years.	
1. AMMERIS, the Ethiopian, reigned	12	(Arm. 18)
2. STEPHINATHIS	7	
3. NECHEPSOS	6	
4. NECHAO	8	
5. PSAMMITICHUS	45	(Arm. 44)
6. NECHAO II.	6	
7. PSAMMUTHIS II. who is also Psammitichus	17	
8. UAPHRIS	25	
9. AMOSIS	42	
	168	

We find the list of Manetho beginning with three names before that of Psammitichus, whom Herodotus and Diodorus represent as raising himself to the throne when he had put down the Dodecarchia. It seems to have been his principle to admit of no interregnum; he takes cognizance neither of the anarchy of which Diodorus speaks, nor of the subsequent agreement among the chiefs of the principal cities, but makes Stephinates found the 26th dynasty immediately on the cessation of the 25th or Ethiopian. The list of Eusebius gives a fourth Ethiopian king, Ammeris, who is certainly misplaced at the head of the Saitic dynasty, but may have been transposed from the close of the Ethiopian. In this case we must regard the Ethiopian power as continuing to maintain itself at Thebes, while Sethos called himself king at Memphis, and another power, seated at Sais, claimed to be the depositary of legitimate authority. No such king as Ammeres has been found in the monuments of Thebes[1].

We are not informed in what relation this new dynasty of Saite kings stood to Bocchoris the Saite, whom Sabaco deposed and put to death; but in the statement of Herodotus[2], that the blind king who had fled into the island of Elbo in the marshes, when the Ethiopians invaded Egypt, returned when they retired, we may probably trace the fact, that Sais still claimed the sovereignty over the district of Lower Egypt in which it stood, during the whole time of the Ethiopian dominion. Thus Egypt was truly divided, "every one against his neighbour, city against city, kingdom against kingdom," the upper country being under the dominion of the Ethiopians, Sethos ruling at Memphis, and over the country towards the frontiers of Palestine, and the Saitic nome and western mouths of the Nile, near one of which Elbo stood, being under the sway of the princes from whom Psammitichus

---

[1] Bunsen, B. 2, 139. Lepsius has discovered at Thebes a queen *Amnerith*, whose name, he thinks, might give rise to that of Ammeres.
[2] 2, 140.

descended. That hostile relations existed between them and the Ethiopians is evident from the account of Herodotus, that Necho the father of Psammitichus had been put to death by Sabaco[1]. This cannot have been literally true; but we have seen that to Herodotus the name of Sabaco represented the whole Ethiopic dynasty, which, as enlarged by the addition of Ammeres, will occupy the space from Sabaco to Necho. The first act recorded of this dynasty was the putting of Bocchoris the Saite to death; the last, a similar act of violence towards the Saite Necho. This is a reasonable presumption that during this whole time Sais maintained at least a claim of independence, and will explain its subsequent elevation to the supremacy over all Egypt.

The ruins of Ssa, the ancient Sais, attest its former grandeur; the wall of crude brick which surrounded the principal buildings of the city was seventy feet thick, and therefore probably not less than 100 feet in height. It encloses an area 2325 feet in length, by 1960 in breadth, and traces appear in it of the lake in which according to Herodotus the mysteries of Osiris were performed; of the temple of Minerva, and the tombs of the Saitic kings. There are also beyond this enclosure two large cemeteries, one for the interment of the privileged classes, the other of the common people[2]. The site, however, has been very imperfectly explored by modern travellers, and much may remain undiscovered which will throw light on the history of the last dynasty of the independent Pharaohs. The names of Stephinates, Ne-

[1] 2, 152. 1, 183. Champollion, Lettres, 50–
[2] Wilkinson, Mod. Eg. & Thebes, 53.

cepsos and Nechao I. have not yet been found on any monument.

Herodotus, when he resumes the history of Egypt after the reign of Sethos, remarks that from this time forward he shall relate that in which the Egyptians and other nations agree[1]. Previously to this time there was no other testimony to control the accounts which the "Egyptians and the priests" gave of their own history[2]: no Greek had advanced beyond Naucratis, and no record was left even of the imperfect knowledge of Egypt which they might thus have gained. The effect is immediately visible, and we have henceforth a definite chronology, an authentic succession of kings conformable to the monuments, and a history composed of credible facts. He thus relates the circumstances which led to the establishment of the monarchy of Psammitichus:—"Being freed after the government of Sethos the priest of Hephaistos, the Egyptians, who never could live without a king, set up for themselves twelve kings, dividing all Egypt into twelve parts. These kings gave one another mutual rights of intermarriage[3], and entered into an agreement to abstain from all acts of aggression and live in entire friendship. The reason of their binding themselves so strictly was, that when they entered on their several sovereignties, an oracle had declared that whichever of them should offer a libation to Hephaistos with a brazen helmet[4] would be the king

[1] 2, 147.
[2] 2, 142.
[3] Probably agreeing not to marry out of the twelve families.
[4] This is only another form of the same impression on the mind of the Egyptians, produced by subsequent events, that the brazen-armed foreigners were to be the means of overthrowing the Dodecarchia.

of all Egypt. It was to this temple that they all repaired in a body. For a long time all observed faithfully the terms of their alliance. But it happened one day that as they were sacrificing, the chief priest brought out only eleven vessels of libation instead of twelve, and that Psammitichus, who stood last in the row, took off his brazen helmet, received the sacred wine in it, and poured it out in libation. He had no sinister design—all the other kings had helmets and were wearing them at the time. But the oracle was brought to their mind, and though upon examining Psammitichus they found that he was innocent of any evil purpose and therefore would not put him to death, they determined to strip him of the chief part of his power, and confine him to the marshes on the coast[1], from which he was not to go out into any other part of Egypt. In the former part of his life Psammitichus had been an exile in Syria, his father Necho having been put to death by Sabaco; and the people of the Saitic nome had brought him back and replaced him in the sovereignty. Feeling himself to have been treated with great injustice by the eleven kings, he sought the means of being avenged, and sent from his retreat to consult the oracle of Latona at Buto, which had the reputation of being the most truthful in all Egypt. He received in answer from the oracle a prediction ' that he should have retribution on his enemies by means of brazen men appearing from the sea.' That brazen men should come to his aid appeared to him a thing utterly incredible; but not long after, some Ionians and

---

[1] Diod. 1, 66. προστάξαι διατρίβειν ἐν τοῖς ἕλεσι τοῖς παρὰ θάλατταν.

Carians who had sailed on a piratical expedition were driven by stress of weather to the coast of Egypt, and landing in their complete suits of brazen armour began to plunder the country. An Egyptian who had never before seen men in a panoply of brass, hastened into the marshes to Psammitichus with the intelligence that brazen men had come from the sea. He at once recognized the fulfilment of the oracle, engaged the Ionians and Carians in his service by magnificent promises, and with the assistance of the Egyptians who favoured his cause, he defeated the other dodecarchs[1]." It was natural that the authority of an oracle should be pleaded for a proceeding so repugnant to Egyptian feeling as the engagement of a body of foreign mercenaries to fight against native Egyptians, but we can hardly believe that their appearance was accidental as the story represents. It is evident, from the account of Diodorus, that Psammitichus, who by his possession of Sais and of course Naucratis, had the readiest access to the sea, had encouraged the visits of Phoenicians and Greeks[2], and had excited the jealousy of his colleagues not only by the wealth he thus acquired, but by the friendly relations which he had established with foreigners. In regard to mythic times, the tendency of Diodorus and the authors of his age to find historical explanations for everything makes their accounts suspicious. But on the other hand, Herodotus is disposed to attribute to

---

[1] There was another version of the oracle, that Tementhas, one of the dodecarchs, had been warned to beware of cocks, and that Psammitichus, understanding this of the crests of the Carian helmets (Her. 1,171), immediately engaged them. (Polyæn. Strat. 7, 3.)

[2] Ἐκ τε τῆς Ἀραβίας καὶ τῆς Καρίας καὶ τῆς Ἰωνίας μισθοφόρους μεταπεμψάμενος. (Diod. 1, 66.)

dreams, oracles and prodigies what had its origin in political causes. The mention of Carians renders it probable that the Ionians here spoken of were Milesians, whose territory was surrounded by that of the Carians, pirates and rovers from the earliest times. The Milesians had visited Egypt for half a century before the Dodecarchia, and nothing could be more natural than that Psammitichus, a native of Sais, should engage their services, when he had been deprived of his share of the government by the injustice of his colleagues. He had not trusted to Greek mercenaries alone; during his exile under the Ethiopian sway he had formed connexions with the Arabians who border on Egypt and Palestine, and Diodorus tells us that he had sent for them, and that they composed a part of the forces with which he overthrew the dodecarchs. The battle was fought at Momemphis[1] near the Canopic branch of the Nile, and on the shore of the Lake Mareotis. Some of the dodecarchs were slain; the rest escaped into Libya, near the borders of which the battle took place.

According to Herodotus, the dodecarchs while they lived together in peace conceived the wish to leave a joint memorial of themselves, and in fulfilment of this design built a labyrinth[2] near the Lake Mœris, and not far from the town of Crocodilopolis. It is evident from other passages of his history[3] that

---

[1] Called *Panouf* by the Copts, and *Menouf* by the Arabs. (Champollion, Égypte sous les Pharaons, 2, 252.)

[2] In the time of Herodotus it was a *common* name for a building or excavation of a great variety of passages. He does not call it The Labyrinth, but "a labyrinth," "this labyrinth."

[3] For instance, his believing that the Lake Mœris had been excavated and the earth thrown into the Nile. (2, 150.)

he did not possess an aptitude for measuring the proportion between causes and effects, otherwise he would not have attributed such a work to a period of divided power and no very long duration. We know that Ammenemes was the founder of the Labyrinth; its different parts had their several uses—sepulchres of the sacred crocodiles—halls of assembly for the different nomes—temples in which the tutelary gods of each might be worshiped. It is more probable that the story of its having been built by the Dodecarchs originated in the number of the principal courts being twelve, answering either to the months of the year or the chief gods of the Pantheon, or to the original number of the nomes[1]. Diodorus, who ascribes the building of the Labyrinth to Mendes or Marrus, before the Trojan war[2], makes the building begun by the Dodecarchs to be distinct from it, yet apparently on the same site. The Labyrinth was remarkable for the multiplicity of its rooms and passages; the mausoleum of the Dodecarchs for a large peristyle hall, and apartments adorned with pictures, representing the religious rites of the district to which the chiefs severally belonged. The work was left unfinished at the dissolution of the Dodecarchy. Perhaps antiquarian research may show that the remains are of two different ages, and thus justify Diodorus.

PSAMMITICHUS I. (670 B.C.), having established himself in power by means of his foreign allies and a portion of the Egyptian people, fulfilled the promises by which he had engaged them to assist him. He

---

[1] Strabo, 17, p. 787, 811. [2] 1, 61.

allotted them a district on the Pelusiac branch of the Nile, a little nearer to the sea than the city of Bubastis, and allowed them to construct fortifications. His foreign mercenaries and the native Egyptians who had joined him[1] were stationed on opposite sides of the river,—a necessary precaution, as even their engagement in the same service could hardly have prevented hostilities between them; such was the contempt of the Greeks for Egyptian superstition, and the horror of the Egyptians for Grecian usages[2]. As the Phœnicians had borne a part in establishing him on the throne, it is probable that their settlement at Memphis, in what was called the Tyrian Camp, dates from the same time[3]. It was in great measure commercial, or if meant for warlike purposes was a naval station; but that of the Greeks and Egyptians was evidently designed to form a body of troops on whom he might rely for the maintenance of his throne, to which the ancient militia of the country, the Calasirians and Hermotybians, were made to give way. The Ionians and Carians would no doubt receive accessions by fresh immigration; in the reign of Apries they amounted to 30,000 men[4]. Amasis subsequently removed them to Memphis, that they might aid him more effectually against the Egyptians; but their docks, and the foundations of their houses, were still to be seen at their original settlement in the time of Herodotus[5].

[1] Τοῖσι Ἴωσι καὶ τοῖσι συγκατεργασαμένοισι αὐτῷ ὁ Ψαμμίτιχος δίδωσι χώρους ἐνοικῆσαι ἀντίους ἀλλήλων, τοῦ Νείλου τὸ μέσον ἔχοντος· τοῖσι οὐνόματα ἐτέθη Στρατόπεδα. (Her. 2, 154.) Compare τοῖσι μετ' ἑωυτοῦ βουλομένοισι Αἰγυπτίοισι (2, 152).
[2] Her. 2, 41.
[3] Her. 2, 112.
[4] Her. 2, 163.
[5] 2, 154.

Psammitichus also caused Egyptian children to be placed under the instruction of the Greeks, that they might become masters of the language, and they and their descendants became, after the model of Egyptian life, a γένος or hereditary caste of Interpreters. It is important to remark that the Greeks never appear to have acquired the Egyptian language, but to have depended entirely upon native interpreters. Their knowledge might have been much more comprehensive and accurate, had they been able to converse with the inhabitants, to check the accounts which they received from their *dragoman* by their own inquiry, to test the correctness of the popular explanations of names, and cross-question an informant who might be inclined to impose on the ignorance of a stranger. Unfortunately the Greeks in all ages disdained the acquirement of *barbarous* tongues. Herodotus, with all his zeal for knowledge, does not appear in his wide journeyings to have learned more than a chance word or two of the languages of the countries which he visited. For commercial and political purposes they used interpreters, who were commonly not Greeks, but barbarians speaking Greek[1]. No Greek philosopher ever condescended to study another language than his own for ethnographical or philological purposes[2]. The versatile Greek intellect cannot have wanted aptitude for such attainments; but the perfection of their own language in

---

[1] Timesitheus, the Trapezuntian, addresses the Mosynœci in their own language (Xen. Anab. 5, 4), but he was the Proxenus of their nation.

[2] Pythagoras is said (Diog. Laert. 8, 3) to have learnt the Egyptian language.

sound and structure would make those of Asia and Egypt seem harsh and clumsy. The caste of interpreters in Egypt was probably formed from the lowest people; Herodotus places them last but one in his enumeration[1], immediately before the pilots, with whom Egyptians would hold no intercourse[2]; they possessed no knowledge of the character with which the monuments of Egypt were covered; but being compelled to satisfy the curiosity of the Greeks, they gave such superficial explanations as might correspond with their most obvious features. Before the Persian conquest, very few Greeks penetrated into Upper Egypt. Those who came for commercial purposes would be attracted to Sais; those who, like Thales, or Pythagoras, or Solon, sought scientific knowledge, would find it at Sais, Heliopolis and Memphis[3]. The old national feeling of the Egyptians, which had been weakened in Lower Egypt by commercial intercourse, subsisted in all its intensity in the Upper country, where, except the kindred Ethiopian, the face of a stranger was rarely seen.

No monument of any magnitude, bearing the name of Psammitichus, remains in Egypt, but it is evident that the whole of that country was subject to him, as his shield is found in the palace at Karnak and in a little island of granite in the Nile near Philæ. In the quarry of Tourah[4], the design of a monolithal shrine intended to be excavated is traced

[1] 2, 164.
[2] Plut. Is. et Osir. p. 363. Κυβερνήτας οὐ προσαγορεύουσι, ὅτι χρῶνται θαλάσσῃ.
[3] The account of Pythagoras having been recommended by Amasis to the priests of Heliopolis, and by them put off with a reference to the priests of Memphis, and again by them to those of Thebes, rests on the authority of Antipho, recorded by Porphyry.
[4] See vol. i. p. 140. Champollion-Figeac, l'Univers, p. 367.

on the rock in red paint, and the cornice bears the shield of Psammitichus. Works of his reign are found in several of the European museums, but by far the most remarkable record of the state of the arts is the obelisk which stands in the Monte Citorio at Rome. It was brought by Augustus from Egypt as a memorial of its reduction under the Roman power, and set up in the Campus Martius to serve as a gnomon, the length of the shadow on the pavement which surrounded it marking the longest and shortest and all intermediate days of the year[1]. It bears the phonetic and titular shields of Psammitichus I. It is about seventy feet in height; the sculpture, if compared with the work of Thothmes III. at St. John Lateran, or Menephthah and Rameses in the Piazza del Popolo, appears inferior in execution, the figures being less deeply and finely cut. Yet when we consider that nearly 700 years had elapsed between the latest of these sovereigns and Psammitichus, we shall be astonished that art had declined so little. About an equal length of time intervenes between the execution of the obelisk of Psammitichus and those of Vespasian and Titus in the Piazza Navona; but in these the inferiority of execution is obvious; the characters are rather scratched than cut upon the granite, and the design is cumbrous and incorrect. The obelisk appears to have been brought from Heliopolis, but Psammitichus' principal works were intended for the embellishment of Memphis. It is probable that an *epiphaneia* or manifestation of Apis took place about the time of his obtaining the

---

[1] Plin. N. H. 36, 10. Zoega, p. 612.

sovereignty, and to gratify the people of Memphis he built a splendid court in which he might be shown to his worshipers. It was in front of the propylæa of the temple of Ptah[1], which Psammitichus also built, and was surrounded with a colonnade, in which colossal figures, twelve cubits in height, supplied the place of pillars[2]. The priests who had the charge of Apis brought him forth into this court, that he might be offered food by his votaries, and an omen be drawn from his favourable or unfavourable reception of it.

As Psammitichus had obtained the throne by means of foreign mercenaries, he trusted to them for its support, increased their numbers, and gave them precedence in honour above the native troops. This produced discontent and ultimately revolt on the part of the Calasirians and Hermotybians. Its immediate occasion is variously reported. One of his military enterprises was the siege of Azotus or Ashdod. This town, one of the five called in Scripture "cities of the Philistines," appears to have been a place of great size and importance[3], and the key of Palestine to an invading force from the side of Egypt. It included a harbour and an inland fortress[4] like Gaza, which lay a little nearer to Egypt, and in the age of Psammitichus appears to have had the same place in military importance for the attack of Palestine from Egypt, or Egypt from Palestine, as Gaza in the age of Alexander the

---

[1] Strabo, 17, 807.
[2] Sir G. Wilkinson has given a drawing illustrative of it. (Manners and Customs, 1, Frontispiece.)
[3] Τῆς Συρίης μεγάλην πόλιν. (Her. 2, 157.)
[4] Ἄζωτος πάραλος, Ἄζωτος. (Excerpta ex Not. Patriarchat. in Reland. Palæst. 215.)

Great, who did not venture to pass on to Egypt till he had taken it[1]. Azotus belonged to the Philistines, but it was not their power which enabled it to resist so long the arms of Psammitichus. We find from the prophecies of Isaiah[2] that it had been besieged and taken by Tartan, the general of Sargon king of Assyria. This king is not elsewhere named in history, and it is therefore difficult to say whether he preceded or followed Sennacherib; but as we know the succession of Assyrian kings pretty accurately after Sennacherib, the probability is that he was his immediate predecessor, reigning only for a short time. Tartan was in the service of Sennacherib, and was one of the envoys sent by him to Hezekiah when he invaded Judæa and meditated the conquest of Egypt[3]. Probably the Assyrians had ever since kept a garrison in Azotus, and hence the obstinate defence which it made. Herodotus says it lasted twenty-nine years[4], but we can only understand by this, that from the commencement of the siege to the capture twenty-nine years elapsed, and it would be suspended during the invasion of the Scythians. It was in these operations in Syria that, according to Diodorus, who however does not specifically mention the siege of Azotus, Psammitichus offended his Egyptian troops, by allotting to the mercenaries the post of honour in the right wing. Herodotus gives a different account. He says that in the reign of this king garrisons were

---

[1] Arrian, 2, *ad fin*. The strength of Gaza was so great that Alexander's engineers pronounced it to be impregnable.
[2] Isaiah xx.
[3] 2 Kings xviii. 17.
[4] Ἄζωτον ἑνὸς δέοντα τριήκοντα ἔτεα προσκατήμενος ἐπολιόρκεε ἐς τὸ ἐξεῖλε. (2, 157.)

stationed in Elephantine against the Ethiopians, in Daphne near Pelusium against the Arabians and Syrians, and in Marea against the Libyans, to the number in all of 240,000 men. For three years these garrisons were not relieved, and the soldiers having communicated with one another, all revolted from Psammitichus and marched away into Ethiopia. Diodorus calculates their numbers at 200,000. Both authors agree in representing the king as hastening after them and endeavouring to prevail on them to return. But he was unsuccessful. When he implored them not to forsake their country and the temples of their gods, their wives and their children, they all raised a shout, and clattering with their spears upon their shields, declared that while they were men and had arms in their hands, they should never want a country, nor wives and children[1]. According to Herodotus, on reaching Ethiopia they gave themselves up to the king, and he being in hostility with a portion of the inhabitants, assigned their territory to the Egyptians who conquered and took possession of it. "And by their settlement," says the historian, "the Ethiopians became humanized, learning Egyptian manners[2]."

As the Romans garrisoned Elephantine with three cohorts only[3], we cannot readily believe that 240,000 or 200,000 men should have been distributed through three frontier towns of the kingdom of Psammitichus. Neither is it very credible, that, separated by 600 miles, as those at Elephantine were from their

---

[1] Diod. 2, 67.
[2] Τούτων δὲ ἐσοικισθέντων ἐς τοὺς Αἰθίοπας ἡμερώτεροι γεγόνασι Αἰθίοπες, ἤθεα μαθόντες Αἰγύπτια. (Her. 2, 30.)
[3] Sharpe, Egypt under the Romans, p. 14.

comrades at Marea and Pelusium, they should have concerted a revolt which took Psammitichus so much by surprise, that he could not come up with the deserters till they had passed the frontier of Ethiopia. Two hundred thousand men with arms in their hands, aggrieved by spoliation and indignity, would not surely have withdrawn so peaceably from their country. It is evident that Herodotus and Diodorus have taken some old traditionary numbers of the Egyptian militia as representing their force in the reign of Psammitichus. The fact of the dissatisfaction and revolt is unquestionable, but we shall probably be near the truth if we suppose that it was only the troops in garrison on the Ethiopian frontier who migrated. The unobstructed march of 60,000 or 80,000 men from Marea and Pelusium to Nubia is incredible; but if the garrison of Elephantine mutinied and deserted, owing to their being left so long without relief, it might well happen that Psammitichus could not overtake them till they had proceeded far on their way. He may not have been much displeased that the most turbulent of his ancient soldiery had withdrawn so quietly. Peter the Great and Sultan Mahmoud were not able to emancipate themselves from the tyranny of the Strelitzes and the Janissaries, except by their extermination.

The place in which the deserters (Automoli) settled is said by Herodotus to be as remote from Meroe, as Meroe from Elephantine, and along the course of the Nile[1]. Now fifty-six days' navigation

[1] Ἀπὸ ταύτης τῆς πόλιος πλέων, ἐν ἴσῳ χρόνῳ ἄλλῳ ἥξεις ἐς τοὺς Αὐτομόλους, ἐν ὅσῳπερ ἐξ Ἐλε- φαντίνης ἦλθες ἐς τὴν μητρόπολιν τῶν Αἰθιόπων.

up the Nile from Meroe would carry us very far beyond every trace of that Egyptian civilization which Herodotus declares that the Ethiopians received from the Egyptian deserters. In fact no such traces are found further south than lat. 16°, which is within the limits of the island of Meroe itself. The king of the Ethiopians by whom they were received, and who gave them permission to conquer themselves a settlement within his dominions, was probably a successor of Sabaco and Tirhakah, having his capital, not at the Meroe of later geography, but at Napata; nor does it necessarily follow that they proceeded so far as Napata before they received his commands. Diodorus says they took possession of some of the best land in Ethiopia and divided it among them. Eratosthenes, Strabo, Pliny[1], all mention them, but with such variations as to their position, that it is evident they wrote from no certain knowledge. Herodotus tells us that the Automoli bore the name of *Asmach*, which signifies "those who stand on the left hand of the king;" Diodorus attributes their emigration to their displeasure at being posted on the *left* wing in an expedition into Syria[2]; both accounts being probably etymological conjectures, founded on the circumstance that a people called Euonymitæ (*left*), of Egyptian origin, dwelt between Ethiopia and Egypt. We cannot avoid the suspicion that the distance of the country to which they emigrated, as well as their numbers, has been greatly exaggerated, that their real settlement was near the Second

---

[1] Strab. 17, 786. Plin. 6, 30. [2] Her. 2, 30. Diod. 1, 67.

Cataract[1], and that they were referred to a region far south of Meroe, not because any traces of Egyptian civilization were found there, but in deference to the authority of Herodotus. Those from whom he received his account had made no better estimate of the difficulties of a march to a country fifty-six days' sail south of Meroe, than those who represented Darius as having marched from the Danube to the Wolga; and the historian was not the man to correct such tales by applying the tests of time and space.

Psammitichus, relieved by the departure of his discontented troops, applied himself more diligently to the internal arrangements of his kingdom, the collection of taxes, and the cultivation of friendly relations with the Greeks, especially the Athenians. Egypt, formerly the most inhospitable of all countries towards strangers, now opened all her harbours to them[2]. The king caused his own sons to be instructed in Greek learning. The intercourse of Sais and Athens would be promoted by their worship of the same deity, and the opinion ultimately sprung up, though in a much later age, that Cecrops had led a colony from Sais to Athens[3]. It is cha-

---

[1] Pliny, on the authority of Nero's *exploratores*, places the Euonymitæ on the frontier of Ethiopia towards Egypt, between the Second Cataract and the island Gagaudes, probably Argo. Agathemerus places them on the west or left bank of the Nile, above the Second Cataract, adding the name *Sebridæ* as coming next to them. Stephanus Byzantinus says they are an Egyptian nation on the borders of Ethiopia. (Pliny, 6, 35. Steph. Byz. s. v. Εὐωνυμῖται.

Agath. Geog. Min. 2, 5. Μετὰ τὸν μέγαν καταρράκτην ἀπὸ μὲν δυσμῶν τοῦ Νείλου Εὐωνυμῖται, Σεβρίδαι, Κάτοιποι· καὶ πρὸς τῇ Μερόῃ νήσῳ Μέμνονες· μεθ' οὓς Ἐλεφαντοφάγοι Αἰθίοπες.) The Greeks used the names *right* and *left* as we do, in reference to the course of a river. (See Herod. 1, 72. Eust. ad Dion. Perieg. 251.)

[2] Diod. 1, 67.

[3] Müller, Hellenische Stämme und Städte, 1, 106.

racteristic of a time when there was a great increase of intercourse with foreign nations, that a rivalry in antiquity should have existed, which led Psammitichus to make his experiment of educating two new-born children apart from men, and watching to what language their first vocal utterance would belong[1]. Having been suckled by she-goats, the first sound they uttered was *becos*, and this being found to signify *bread* in the Phrygian language, the Egyptians conceded to the Phrygians the honour of priority[2]. Such was the account given to Herodotus by the priests of Memphis of the first attempt made to apply the evidence of language to decide the antiquity of nations. We may smile at the experiment and the inference deduced from it, but till lately philological arguments have been applied to historical questions with not much more diseretion. To obtain a better knowledge of Africa, be trained youths of the Ichthyophagi to explore the fountains of the Nile, and others to examine the Deserts of Libya. They were taught to endure the extremity of thirst, but few survived[3].

It was towards the latter part of his reign that Egypt was threatened by an invasion of the Scythians. Cyaxares, king of the Medes, having defeated the Assyrians in a great battle, was besieging Nineveh, when his own kingdom was overrun by a horde of Scythians. They had driven the Cimmerians before them and entered Media. Cyax-

---

[1] Her. 2, 4. Schol. Apoll. Rhod. 4, 262. Aristoph. Nub. 397. ὦ μῶρε σὺ καὶ Κρονίων ὄζων καὶ βεκκεσέληνε. The Scholiast there refers the story to Sesonchosis, meaning apparently Sesostris, the world-conqueror. (See p. 165 of this vol.)

[2] Her. 1, 104.

[3] Athen. 8, p. 345.

ares encountered them, but suffered an entire defeat, and for twenty-eight years they kept possession of western Asia. They had advanced to the south of Ascalon on the coast of Palestine, on their way to attack Egypt, when Psammitichus met them, and by entreaties and presents prevailed on them to proceed no further. Some of them on their return plundered the temple of Venus Urania at Ascalon, and were punished by the infliction of a disease[1], which, according to Herodotus, accompanied them to their native land, and even cleaved to their descendants in his own time. The invasion of the Scythians took place in 634 B.C.; their occupation of Palestine (according to Eusebius) in 632; their march towards Egypt somewhere about 630 B.C. They must have passed Azotus on their way, and interrupted the siege of that place. The town of Bethshan, in the north of Palestine, is said to have received the name of Scythopolis[2] from their having made it their head-quarters during their occupation of the country. The prophet Zephaniah (i. 14), who lived in the reign of Josiah (630 B.C.), appears to describe them under the appellation of "a people without fear[3]." The desolation which they would cause throughout Palestine is set forth by the prophet in very forcible language[4]:—

[1] The existence of a peculiar θήλεια νοῦσος among the Scythians is certain, as it is described by Hippocrates de Aer. &c. p. 293. Εὐνουχίαι γίνονται, καὶ γυναικεῖα ἐργάζονται καὶ ὡς αἱ γυναῖκες διαλέγονταί τε ὁμοίως, καλεῦνταί τε οἱ τοιοῦτοι ἀνανδριεῖς. They were nevertheless looked on with reverence, because their disease was referred to the immediate power of the divinity. It appears to have been a species of imbecillity allied to Cretinism.

[2] Judges i. 27, in the Septuagint. Βαιθσάν ἥ ἐστι Σκυθῶν πόλις.

[3] Literally, "the people that turns not pale," הגוי לא נכסף.

[4] 'Επὶ μὲν νῦν ὀκτὼ καὶ εἴκοσι ἔτεα ἦρχον τῆς 'Ασίης οἱ Σκύθαι καὶ τὰ πάντα σφι ὑπό τε ὕβριος καὶ

"That day is a day of wrath;
A day of distress and of anguish;
A day of desolation and of destruction;
A day of darkness and of gloom;
A day of clouds and of thick darkness;
A day of the trumpet and of shouting
Against the fenced cities and against the high towers."

The invasion of the cities of the Philistines is specifically mentioned:—

"Surely Gaza shall be forsaken and Ascalon a desolation;
Ashdod shall be driven out at noonday and Ekron shall be rooted up.
The sea-coast shall be dwellings for shepherds and folds for flocks."
(v. 5, 6.)

The prophet anticipates that the flood of invasion would roll forward even to Ethiopia (v. 12), as no doubt it would have done, but for the gifts and supplications by which Psammitichus induced the Scythians to return. Yet it is intimated also that their success should be short-lived and be followed by a great reverse:—

"Gather yourselves together and assemble, O nation that feareth not;
Before the decree bring forth, that your day pass away as chaff;
Before the hot anger of Jehovah come upon you." (ii. 1.)

This also corresponds with history. The Scythians were enervated by their residence in a southern climate, and overpowered by Cyaxares and the Medes. The capture of Nineveh, foretold by the prophet (Zeph. ii. 13), speedily followed the recovery of Median ascendency[1]. A few years later the northern nomad tribes[2] appear to have meditated another and combined invasion of the South,

ὀλιγωρίης ἀνάστατα ἦν· ἥρπαζον περιελαύνοντες τοῦτο ὅτι ἔχοιεν ἕκαστοι. (Her. 1, 106.)
[1] Herod. 1, 106.
[2] Ezek. xxxviii. " Gog, of the land of Magog, Rhos" (the nations dwelling on the Araxes), " Mesech and Tubal" (the Moschi and Tibareni), "Gomer " (the Cimmerians), "Togarmah" (the Armenians).

in which they were to have been joined by Persia, Ethiopia and Libya[1]; its defeat was foretold, but from some cause which history has not explained, it never took place. The prophecy stands insulated among the oracles of Ezekiel, and may have been delivered when the great power of Nebuchadnezzar had alarmed the neighbouring nations both north and south.

The lists represent Psammitichus as reigning fifty-four years, and Herodotus agrees with them : among the papyri of Turin, Lepsius has found the date of his forty-fifth year[2]. He was succeeded (616 B.C.) by his son NECO or NECHAO, the Pharaoh Necho of the Second Book of Kings. His first undertakings, according to Herodotus, were peaceful. To construct a canal which should join the Nile with the Red Sea, and save the troublesome transport by land across the Desert, was a project which would naturally suggest itself to the mind of a king of Egypt, where stupendous works of the same kind existed in the Fyoum and the Delta[3]. We have noticed the tradition that it had been begun by Sesostris[4]. During the French occupation of Egypt this district was carefully explored, and the ancient line of the canal traced. It went off from the Nile in the neighbourhood of the modern town of Belbeis, supposed to represent the Bubastis Agria

---

[1] Ez. xxxviii. 5. xxxix. 1, "Thus saith the Lord God, Behold I am against thee, O Gog, the chief prince of Meshech and Tubal, and I will turn thee back and leave but the sixth part of thee."

[2] Bunsen, Ægyptens Stelle, B. 3, p. 144.

[3] Diodorus (1, 68) omits the reigns of Neco and Psammis, and passes ($ὕστερον\ τέτταρσι\ γενεαῖς$) to that of Apries. He mentions Neco, however, incidentally (1, 33) as the author of the canal.

[4] See page 291 of this vol.

of the Greeks[1], and ran eastward through a natural valley, the Goshen of Jewish history, till it reached the Bitter Lakes, which derive their quality from the saline impregnations of the Desert. The influx of the water of the Nile rendered them sweet, and they abounded in fish and aquatic birds[2]. Issuing from these it pursued a southerly course to Suez. Towards the western end its traces are very visible, notwithstanding the deposit of the Nile, which has partly filled it up; towards the East, where the influence of the Desert is more powerful, it has nearly disappeared. At the junction of the Red Sea, remains of masonry are visible, but they are probably no older than the time of Ptolemy II. Neco is said to have sacrificed the lives of 120,000 men[3] in the attempt to excavate this canal, which after all he left imperfect, being warned, it is said, by an oracle, that he was only labouring beforehand for the benefit of the barbarian[4]. Darius resumed the work, and according to the description of Herodotus, made it of sufficient width to admit two triremes rowed abreast[5]. His language leaves no doubt that in his time it reached the sea[6], though Diodorus[7] says that Darius left it unfinished, because he was informed that it would inundate Egypt with the water of the Red Sea. Since the French

---

[1] Champollion, L'Égypte sous les Pharaons, 2, 56.
[2] Strabo, 17, p. 804.
[3] Her. 2, 158.
[4] Herodotus (4, 42) repeats his assertion of Neco's having left the canal unfinished; a similar motive is said to have rendered Mohammed Ali averse from the re-establishment of this canal. The Caliphs had closed it for this reason.
[5] Pliny, describing it after its completion by Ptolemy, says 100 feet wide, 40 deep (N. H. 6, 33). The whole length is about 90 miles.
[6] Ἐσέχει ἐς τὴν Ἐρυθρὴν θάλασσαν (2, 158).
[7] 1, 33.

occupation of Egypt it has been taken for granted, on the authority of their engineers, that the average height of the sea at Suez exceeds by twenty-seven feet that of the Mediterranean. Subsequent levelings have thrown doubt on this fact, which contradicts the laws of hydrostatics. The fear seems to have been, that the water of the canal and the Bitter Lakes, which the Nile had freshened, should be made salt by the tides[1]. Ptolemy completed the canal and constructed a flood-gate, which excluded the sea-water, except during the time of the passage of a vessel[2]. The object of Neco in attempting to establish a communication with the Red Sea, was to facilitate his design of creating a fleet there ; and this he accomplished, although his canal was never completed. His alliance with the Phœnicians, who were at this time at the height of their naval power, would furnish him with materials for ship-building, which being brought up the Nile, and along the canal, as far as it was finished, might then be transported to the sea. The docks which he constructed for the reception of his ships were still to be seen in the days of Herodotus. From this point began the voyage which, at the command of Neco, the Phœnicians undertook for the circumnavigation of Africa. Herodotus gives the following account of it[3] :—

" I am astonished at those who divided and fixed the boundaries of Libya, Asia and Europe, seeing

---

[1] The rise of the tide at Suez is six or seven feet. Report on Steam Navigation to India, App. p. 23.
[2] Diod. 1, 33.
[3] 4, 42.

they differ in no small degree. For Europe stretches in length far beyond them both, and as to width it does not appear to deserve a comparison[1]. For as to Libya it shows itself to be circumnavigable, except where it borders on Asia; this was first proved, as far as I know, by Neco, king of Egypt. When he gave up excavating the canal that runs from the Nile to the Arabian Gulf, he sent out some Phœnicians in ships, giving them orders on their way back to sail through the Pillars of Hercules into the Northern Sea, and thus return to Egypt. Setting out then from the Red Sea, they sailed on the Southern Sea. As often as autumn returned they landed and sowed the ground in the part of Libya where they chanced to be, and awaited the harvest; and then sailed again when they had reaped it. So two years having elapsed, in the third, doubling the Pillars of Hercules, they came back to Egypt. And they said, what to me is not credible, but may be to some one else, that in sailing round Libya they had the sun on the right hand. In this way Libya was first known. The Carthaginians are the next who affirm it [*to be circumnavigable*] ; for Sataspes, the son of Teaspis, did not circumnavigate Libya, though sent out for this very purpose, but turned back, fearing the length and the dreariness of the navigation."

It is remarkable that Herodotus does not express

---

[1] Herodotus reckoned as a prolongation of Europe what we call Northern Asia, and as it had never been circumnavigated, its breadth from south to north was unknown, but was evidently supposed by him to surpass that of Asia, as he was not aware of the great extension of the peninsula of India. See 3, 45.

the smallest doubt respecting the reality of this circumnavigation; that the Carthaginians confirmed the testimony of the Phœnicians, all whose naval and geographical knowledge they would share; and that in the age of Xerxes, Sataspes was sent out, not to try if Africa could be circumnavigated, but to perform its circumnavigation, as an admitted possibility. Whether the Ophir of the Book of Kings were a port in India, or Sofala on the S.E. coast of Africa, it is evident that the ships of the Phœnicians had for several centuries been accustomed to distant voyages—voyages even of three years' duration, according to the Book of Chronicles[1]. Their ships were large, and so arranged internally as to give the greatest stowage in the smallest space[2]. Major Rennell's researches have shown, that the circumnavigation might be much more easily accomplished from the eastern side of Africa than the western[3], and that consequently the failure of Sataspes, who tried it from the west, and the slow progress of the Portuguese in reaching the Cape, afford no ground for calling in question the truth of Herodotus' account. The time of three years, however, must appear inadequate, when we consider that Scylax occupied two years and ten months in his voyage from Caspatyrus on the Indus to Suez[4].

It may appear extraordinary, that if the fact

---

[1] 2 Chron. ix. 21, which may be admitted as an evidence for the age in which this book was written, if not for the age of Solomon.

[2] Πλεῖστα σκεύη ἐν μικροτάτῳ ἀγγείῳ διακεχωρισμένα ἐθεασάμην.

Xen. Œcon. c. 8, speaking of the Phœnician vessels that resorted to the Piræus.

[3] Geog. of Herod. Sect. xxiv.

[4] Her. 4, 44.

that Africa was a peninsula had once been ascertained, it should have been virtually denied by Plato[1], and expressly by Ephorus[2], and doubted by Polybius[3], who had himself visited the western coast, in a fleet fitted out to explore the traces of the Carthaginian settlements. The art of navigation, however, had greatly declined among the nations bordering on the Mediterranean, between the times of Ephorus and Polybius, and that in which Phœnicia flourished : the voyages made from Egypt under the Ptolemies were directed in the profitable channel of Indian commerce. He might therefore well speak of that as doubtful, of which the evidence was four centuries and a half old, and which had not been confirmed by subsequent voyages. Strabo appears to have entertained no doubt that Africa terminated in a southern cape, though he conceived most erroneously of its form, believing the eastern coast to form a right angle with the northern, and the western to be the hypotenuse of the triangle[4]. He did not, however, believe in the circumnavigation. In speaking of the eastern coast of Africa, he says that no one had advanced more than 5000 stadia beyond the entrance of the Red Sea[5]; and, having perhaps Ephorus in his mind, that those who had coasted Libya where it is washed by the ocean, whether they had

---

[1] In the age of Plato, the Atlantic was believed to be incapable of navigation, owing to the mud produced by the sunk island Atlantis. (Tim. § 6, iii. 25.) If the Atlantic was not navigable, Africa of course could not be circumnavigable.

[2] Plin. N. H. 6, 31. Ephorus auctor est a Rubro mari navigantes in insulam Cernen non posse provehi.

[3] Οὐδεὶς ἔχει λέγειν ἀτρεκῶς, ἕως τῶν καθ' ἡμᾶς καιρῶν, πότερον ἤπειρός ἐστι κατὰ τὸ συνεχὲς τὰ πρὸς τὴν μεσημβρίαν ἢ θαλάττῃ περιέχεται. (3, 38. Plin. N. H. 5, 1.)

[4] 17, p. 825.

[5] 16, p. 769, from Eratosthenes.

set out from the Pillars or from the Red Sea, had turned back after proceeding a certain distance, whence many thought that an isthmus interposed[1]. Such an isthmus Ptolemy lays down, stretching away from the coast of Africa south of the Equator, to the eastern verge of the world. It is impossible to arrive at any decisive conclusion respecting this celebrated voyage[2], the reality of which rests on the strong conviction of Herodotus, an author, in such matters at least, not prone to credulity; and as at all events it was not repeated, if real it had no influence, like the voyages of De Gama and Columbus, on the subsequent history of the world.

" When Neco abandoned his plan of joining the Nile and the Red Sea by a canal, he engaged," says Herodotus, "in military expeditions, and encountering the Syrians with a land force, he conquered them at Magdolus, and after the battle took Cadytis, which is a large city of Syria[3]." Since the death of Sennacherib, Assyria and Babylon had existed as two independent kingdoms, of which Assyria was manifestly on the decline, while Babylon was in the ascendant. The fate of Assyria, threatened by the Medes, had been delayed by the invasion of the Scythians, who had still kept possession of their conquests in Asia, in the early part of the reign

---

[1] Strabo, 1, p. 32.
[2] The Phœnicians alleged that in their voyage round Africa they had the sun on their right hand, that is in the North (Plut. Is. et Osir. p. 363), which only proves at most that they had passed the Equator. Long indeed before reaching the Equator, navigators, whose home was to the North of the tropic of Cancer, must have been struck with seeing the sun in the summer far to the north of them at noon.
[3] 2, 159.

of Neco. On their expulsion (608 B.C.) Cyaxares resumed his enterprise against Nineveh; and about the same time Neco left his kingdom to march to the Euphrates[1]. He seems to have employed his fleet on the Mediterranean to transport his army to some harbour in the north of Palestine, and was thence proceeding inland towards Carchemish. Josiah, who was king of Judah, and held also the ancient territories of Israel[2], induced perhaps by the Assyrians, endeavoured to stop the march of Neco, with the whole force of his kingdom. He would gladly have passed on to the Euphrates unmolested, and earnestly entreated Josiah to abstain from interrupting him; but Josiah was not to be dissuaded, and they met in battle at Megiddo[3] in the plain of Esdraëlon near the foot of Carmel[4]. Josiah had disguised himself before the battle[5], that the royal insignia might not make him a mark for the enemy; but an arrow reached him; he was brought back to Jerusalem and died there. This battle delayed the march of Neco; he took possession of Jerusalem, the Cadytis of Herodotus[6], and advanced as far as

---

[1] 2 Kings xxiii. 29. "In the days of Josiah, Pharaoh Necho, king of Egypt, went up against the king of Assyria to the river Euphrates." Josephus says (Ant. 10, 5), "against the Medes and Babylonians, who had overthrown the power of Assyria."

[2] 2 Kings xxiii. 19. 2 Chron. xxxiv. 6.

[3] Σύροισι ὁ Νεκὼς συμβαλὼν ἐν Μαγδόλῳ ἐνίκησε (Her. 2, 159). Ἀρτάπανός φησι τοὺς Ἰουδαίους ὀνομάζεσθαι Ἑρμιούθ. (Ensch. Præp. Ev. 9, 18.) This is probably אֲרָמִי־יְהוּדָה Arami Jehudeh, Syrians of Judah. Deut. xxvi. 5,

"A Syrian ready to perish was my father." Her. 2, 104.

[4] Reland, Falæst. 893.

[5] 2 Chron. xxxv. 22.

[6] The name seems to mean "the Holy" city. From a comparison of the passages in Herodotus, 2, 159; 3, 5, it appears that no other place than Jerusalem can be meant. Herodotus would not have compared Gaza or Kadesh-Barnea with Sardis. Jerusalem had been known as the seat of a magnificent temple for several centuries, and had enjoyed a reputation for sanctity in much earlier times. See Gen. xiv. 18.

Riblah in Hamath on his way to the Euphrates. The people of Judæa, however, made Jehoahaz, the son of Josiah, king. Neco sent for him to Hamath, deposed and imprisoned him after he had reigned three months, and sent him to Egypt, where he ended his days[1]. At the same time he made his younger brother Eliakim king, changing his name to Jehoiakim, and imposed a tribute of a hundred talents of silver and a talent of gold upon the land[2]. Whether Neco himself returned to Egypt, or remained in Palestine to secure his power there, we are not informed; but four years later he marched to the Euphrates with an army, comprehending, according to the prophet Jeremiah[3], Ethiopians and Libyans as well as Egyptians[4]. Carchemish, or Circesium, where the battle took place in which he was defeated by Nebuchadnezzar, stood on the eastern side of the Euphrates, in the angle, or as the ancients said, the island, formed by its confluence with the Chaboras, which gathers the waters of northern Mesopotamia and discharges them into the Euphrates nearly in N. lat. 35°. It lies in the line of march of an army proceeding from the north of Palestine to northern Mesopotamia, and Neco was on his march to occupy it, when intercepted by

[1] He is the same who, in Jer. xxii. 11, is called Shallum, and of whom the prophet declares that he should never return to his own land. Comp. Ezek. xix. 4.

[2] 2 Chron. xxxvi. 3.

[3] Jer. xlvi.

[4] Such was the tediousness of ancient sieges, that he might have been engaged in operations before Circesium during the interval, but the language of the prophet seems to indicate a recent invasion. Jer. xlvi. 8:—

"Egypt riseth up like a flood,
And his waters are moved like the rivers;
And he saith, I will go up and cover the earth;
I will destroy the city and the inhabitants thereof."

Josiah[1]. If Nineveh still held out against the forces of Cyaxares and the Babylonians, the object of Neco's march might be to relieve that city; if, as seems more probable, it had already fallen[2], he may have deemed it politic to anticipate the hostilities which he could not but foresee, on the part of the power which had thus become predominant in Asia. Carchemish was an important military position. The Euphrates, in this part of its course, is fordable both above and below the influx of the Chaboras[3], and by the possession of Carchemish its passage might be impeded. When Diocletian was strengthening the frontier posts of the Empire in the East, against the inroads of the Parthians into Syria, he erected a strong fortress at Carchemish, which Procopius calls the most remote garrison of the Romans[4]. In the times of Grecian and Roman power it appears to have been a place of little strength, but it would be otherwise when Egypt and Assyria contended on the Euphrates. This is implied in the boast of the king of Assyria (Is. x. 9), " Is not Calno as Carchemish—is not Samaria as Damascus?" and the name itself indicates the existence of a fortification[5].

We have no further account of the battle of Carchemish than that of the prophet, that Nebuchad-

[1] 2 Chron. xxxv. 20.

[2] The capture of Nineveh is usually placed, but not on very certain grounds, in 606 B.C.; the first year of Nebuchadnezzar, which was that of the battle of Carchemish (Jer. xlvi. 1), on the authority of Ptolemy's Canon, in 604.

[3] See Col. Chesney's Map in Parl. Report on Steam Navigation to India.

[4] Cercusium munimentum tutissimum et fabre politum: cujus moenia Abora et Euphrates ambiunt flumina, velut spatium insulare fingentes. Quod Diocletianus exiguum antehac et suspectum muris turribusque circumdedit celsis. (Ammian. Marc. 23, 5.)

[5] *Karaka* in Syriac is a castle. See Cleric. ad 2 Chron. xxxv.

III.]   THE TWENTY-SIXTH DYNASTY.   409

nezzar "smote the army of Neco;" Herodotus makes no mention of it. It is evident, however, that its effect was to strip Neco of nearly the whole of his Asiatic possessions. "The king of Egypt came not again any more out of his land; for the king of Babylon had taken from the river of Egypt unto the river Euphrates all that pertained to the king of Egypt[1]." An immediate invasion by Nebuchadnezzar seemed impending over Egypt as the result of this defeat[2]. According to Berosus[3], Neco himself, whom he calls the revolted satrap of Egypt and Syria, fell into the hands of Nebuchadnezzar, who was not at this time king of Babylon, but viceroy of his father Nabopolassar. But it would neither accord with scriptural nor Egyptian history to suppose that Babylon had previously to this time conquered Egypt and reduced its king to the condition of a satrap. Doubtless Neco returned to his kingdom as Herodotus implies. It marks the ascendency of Greek ideas, that on his return from Syria, either now or after the battle of Megiddo, he dedicated the dress which he had worn to Apollo of Branchidæ, a celebrated oracle in the territory of his Milesian allies[4]. Herodotus says, he reigned sixteen years; the lists only six, a term evidently too short for the undertakings recorded of him. That the number in Herodotus is correct is proved by a

[1] 2 Kings xxiv. 7.
[2] That Jer. xlvi. 13 belongs to this time, not to the period following the captivity of Zedekiah, is evident from v. 15, 16, which speak of a recent great defeat.
[3] Joseph. contra Apion. 1, 19.
[4] Herod. 2, 159. Strabo, 634. A lion is still found among the ruins of Palet (the ancient Miletus), which is said to be of Egyptian style, and may be the record of the connexion between Miletus and Egypt. (Chandler's Travels, p. 170. Müller's Dorier, 1, 225.)

remarkable monument in the Museum at Florence, published by Rosellini[1]. It records that Psammitichus, a priest of Sokari, was born on the first of the month *Paoni*[2], in the reign of Neco—that he lived seventy-one years, four months, six days, and died on the sixth day of the month *Paopi*[3], in the thirty-fifth year of Amasis. If we allow that the authors of the lists in extracting from Manetho have given us round numbers, instead of the exact sum in months and days which they found in the original, the correspondence will be complete[4].

Neco was succeeded (600 B.C.) by his son PSAMMITICHUS II., whom Herodotus calls PSAMMIS. The record of Manetho in Africanus is evidently imperfect; Psammuthis is called the Second, though no other of the name has been mentioned, and therefore we should read, with the aid of Eusebius, " Psammuthis, who is also Psammitichus the Second." His phonetic name is spelt with precisely the same characters as those of his grandfather, but the titular shield has a difference in the middle character. No public building remains erected by him, nor is any large work of art extant of his

---

[1] Mon. Stor. 2, 151; more accurately 4, 197.
[2] The tenth month of the Egyptian year. See vol. i. p. 330.
[3] The second month.

[4] The reckoning will stand thus, supposing Neco to have reigned sixteen years, and the priest to have been born when he had reigned 2 years 9 months and 1 day:—

Residue of his reign	13 years 3 months.
Psammis or Psammitichus II. ...	6 years.
Apries.....................	19 years.
Amasis, to the death of the priest	34 years 1 month 6 days.
	72 years 4 months 6 days.

The excess of one year is accounted for by Bunsen (B. 3, p. 143) by the supposition that the fractions of years have been reckoned as full years.

reign. Fragments of sculpture, however, bearing his name, exist in the citadel at Cairo, and under the base of the column called Pompey's Pillar at Alexandria. The former of these appears to have made a part of some erection in honour of the god Ptah at Memphis; the latter probably belonged to some building at Sais. His titular shield is also found on the obelisk of the Piazza Minerva at Rome, which was executed under his son and successor Apries[1]. The British Museum contains a portion of an intercolumnial plinth inscribed with his name and titular shield, in which he appears offering to the gods, who give him all power and victory, and put all lands under his sandals[2]. He had a daughter, whose name was Nitocris, the same as that of the queen of Psammitichus the First, and derived from Neith, the tutelary goddess of Sais.

Herodotus mentions a single anecdote of the reign of Psammis, which is not otherwise important than as indicating the reputation which Egypt enjoyed among the Greeks for wisdom and equity. The inhabitants of Elis, to whom the administration of the Olympic games belonged, were accustomed to consult the oracle of Jupiter at Ammonium: inscriptions remained there recording the names of the delegates and the answers which they had received; and libations were offered at Elis to the Ammonian gods, Jupiter and Juno, and Mercury who presided over games[3]. Exercising the delicate function of judges between Greek competitors,

[1] Rosellini, Mon. Stor. 4, 198. 2, 136.
[2] Birch, Gall. of Brit. Mus. P. 2, p. 109.
[3] Pausan. Eliaca, 5, 15. Mercury was surnamed Παράμμων.

they would naturally seek to arm themselves with the authority which this ancient and venerated oracle conferred. To ascend the Nile to Terenuthis on the Canopic branch below Memphis and cross the valley of the Natron Lakes, was an easier way of reaching Ammonium than from the sea-coast, provided Egypt were friendly[1]. In going or returning, the delegates from Elis had an audience of Psammitichus, and boasted to him of the perfect equity with which they made their decisions. If we may believe Herodotus, they had come for the sole purpose of inquiring if the Egyptians, the wisest of men, could devise any better method of securing impartiality. The king summoned those who were reputed wisest among them, and they having heard their statement, asked if Eleans were allowed to contend in the games as well as other Greeks. The Eleans replied that they were. Then said the Egyptians, "Your method is entirely unjust; it is impossible that you should not be biassed in favour of one of your own people; and if you have really come to Egypt desirous of attaining to perfect equity, you must henceforth exclude every Elean from the contest." Diodorus with more probability refers the story to the reign of Amasis, and attributes the advice (which was not followed) to the king himself[2].

Towards the end of his reign Psammitichus II. made an expedition into Ethiopia, of which Herodotus[3] does not mention either the purpose or the

[1] Alexander went by Paraetonium and the coast, but found the difficulties so great that he returned by the Natron Lakes. Arrian, 3, 4. See also Minutoli's Travels.
[2] Diod. 1, 95.
[3] 2, 161.

result. His shield is found at the island of Suem, near the Cataracts of Syene. The Greek inscription on the statue at Aboosimbel, which mentions a visit of Psammitichus to Elephantine, may be of this date. It is in the Doric dialect[1], which we should hardly expect to be in use among the Ionian mercenaries of the first Psammitichus; but as Egypt had now been fully opened to the Greeks for half a century, every variety of dialect might be found among them, though Ionians formed the great body of the mercenary troops[2]. If it should still be thought improbable that a Greek inscription should be found in Egypt exceeding in age any in Ionia or Greece itself, there was a third Psammitichus[3], who lived about 400 B.C., a descendant of the ancient kings of that name, to whose reign it may be referred.

Psammitichus II. died almost immediately after his expedition to Ethiopia, and was succeeded (594 B.C.) by UAPHRIS, as the lists write his name, the Apries of the Greeks and the Hophra of Scripture. After the great defeat which Neco suffered on the Euphrates, no attempt had been made by Egypt to recover her ascendency in Palestine and Syria, which appear to have been entirely dependent on Babylon. Jehoiakim, whom Neco had placed on

---

[1] The inscription is as follows:—
Βασιλεος ελθοντος ες Ελεφαντιναν Ψαμάτιχο ταυτα εγραψαν τοι συν Ψιματιχοι τοι Θεοκλος επλεον· ηλθον δε Κερκιος καθοπερθεν ις ο (εις ου) ποταμος ανιη· αλογλοσος (αλλογλωσσος) ***** Αιγυπτιος δε Αμασις εγραφε Δαμεαρχος Αμοιβιχο και Πελεφος Ουδαμο. (Trans. Roy. Soc. Lit. 1, 223.) As the king had only come to Elephantine, while the Greeks and the ἀλλογλώσσος had gone to the Second Cataract, it is evident that it cannot be the expedition of Psammitichus I. (Herod. 2, 151) to overtake his fugitive soldiery. Nor in his reign is it probable that the son of a Greek should have been named Psammitichus.
[2] Her. 2, 163.
[3] Diod. Sic. 14, 35.

the throne of Judæa, had been compelled to submit himself to Nebuchadnezzar, and for three years remained faithful; but at the end of that time, perhaps in hope of assistance from Egypt, he "turned and rebelled against him." The weakness to which Judæa had been reduced, exposed it to invasions from all the neighbouring tribes, Moabites, Ammonites and Syrians, as well as the Chaldees[1]. The king of Babylon himself, it should seem, was engaged elsewhere, probably in establishing his dominion at home. Jehoiakim was succeeded by his son Coniah or Jehoiakin in 598 B.C. He had either made himself king on his father's death, or had been placed on the throne by the people without the approbation of the king of Babylon. An army was immediately sent against him, and the siege of Jerusalem was formed by the lieutenants of Nebuchadnezzar; but appears to have proceeded slowly, till the king himself came, to take the command of the besieging army, when the city speedily surrendered[2]; Jehoiakin was carried captive to Babylon within twelve months from his accession, and his uncle Zedekiah placed on the throne in his stead. Apries had succeeded to his father about four years previously, and the earliest undertakings of his reign were directed to the recovery of that ascendency in Syria and Palestine which Neco had possessed. But Jerusalem being virtually in the power of Nebuchadnezzar, he did not venture at first to attempt an invasion by land. We find that the hopes of the people of Judæa were strongly excited; the prophet Hananiah foretold, that within

[1] 2 Kings xxiv. 1, 2.   [2] 2 Kings xxiv. 10-16.

two years the yoke of the king of Babylon should be broken, and the captive king be restored to his throne. This was the effect of the success which attended the first undertakings of Apries, and a truer prophet warned them that they would prove fallacious. All the nations of Palestine appear to have been alarmed at the growing power of Babylon, and sent emissaries to Zedekiah, tempting him to throw off his allegiance to Nebuchadnezzar. They were also warned by Jeremiah of the fruitlessness of their attempts, by the symbolical act of sending a yoke to the sovereigns when their emissaries returned[1]. Their more immediate danger, however, was from Egypt. Herodotus speaks only of Apries' expedition against Sidon and his seafight with the king of Tyre; but, according to Diodorus, he took Sidon by storm, reduced the whole sea-coast of Phœnicia and defeated the Cyprians, who appear to have been allies, if not subjects[2], of the Phœnicians. Although Gaza and the other towns of South Palestine are not expressly mentioned by either of the Greek historians, it is probably to this time that the prophecy in the 47th chapter of Jeremiah[3] is to be referred; and as the destruction is said to come from the north, it must have been attacked on the return of Apries from

---

[1] Jer. xxvii. In the first verse of this chapter *Zedekiah* should certainly be read for Jehoiakim (comp. v. 3), if indeed the whole verse, which is wanting in the Septuagint, be not an interpolation.

[2] Virg. Æn. 1, 621:—
  ...... Genitor tum Belus opimam
  Vastabat Cyprum et victor ditione tenebat.

Menander (Jos. Ant. 9, 14, 2) represents Elulæus, in the time of Shalmaneser, as reducing the revolted people of Citium into obedience.

[3] "The word of the Lord that came to Jeremiah the prophet against the Philistines, before that Pharaoh smote Gaza."

his campaign against Cyprus and Sidon. After these successes, Apries dispatched an army into Judæa. Zedekiah having violated the oath of allegiance which he had sworn to Nebuchadnezzar[1], and sent ambassadors into Egypt to ask for an auxiliary force of cavalry and infantry[2], the Chaldæans had invested Jerusalem. The tidings of the march of the Egyptian army caused them to raise the siege[3], but they returned, as Jeremiah had foretold, in greater strength, the king himself commanding them[4]; and the troops of Apries, it is probable, retired without a contest. The prophecy of Ezekiel[5], in which the arm of Pharaoh is described as being broken, so that it could never be bound up again to hold the sword, was delivered on occasion of this retreat, when Egypt renounced for ever its attempts to occupy Palestine. Nebuchadnezzar, after a siege of eighteen months, took Jerusalem by storm, and Zedekiah being made prisoner, as he was attempting to escape in disguise by a concealed breach in the wall[6], was deprived of his eyesight, and carried in chains to Babylon. This took place in the eleventh year of Zedekiah's reign, and the seventh of the reign of Apries (587 B.C.). In consequence of the murder of Gedaliah, to whom the government of Judæa had been entrusted by Nebuchadnezzar, many of the Jewish chiefs who had escaped the execution of Riblah[7] fled into Egypt, carrying with

---

[1] 2 Chron. xxxvi. 13.
[2] Ezek. xvii. 15. The embassy to Egypt must have taken place towards the end of the sixth year of Zedekiah, in 592 or 591 B.C.
[3] Jer. xxxvii.
[4] Ezek. xxiv. 2.
[5] Ezek. xxx. 21.
[6] Ezek. xii. 12.
[7] 2 Kings xxv. 21.

them the prophet Jeremiah. He probably finished his days at Daphnæ near Pelusium, foretelling in the last of his prophecies the fate of Apries[1].

After the occupation of Jerusalem the efforts of Nebuchadnezzar would naturally be directed to the reduction of the sea-coast of Palestine and Syria, without securing which it would have been unsafe for him to have attacked Egypt. Tyre was at this time in the height of her commercial prosperity and naval power[2]. Whether in subjection to Egypt in consequence of the victory of Apries, or not, she was evidently hostile to Babylon from a natural jealousy of any power, Egyptian, Jewish, or Chaldæan, by whose ascendency her commerce might suffer, and Nebuchadnezzar almost immediately undertook the siege. Even before Jerusalem was actually taken, but when that event was clearly to be anticipated, the prophet Ezekiel describes Tyre as exulting in the prospect of the increase of her own power by the sufferings of her rival[3], and foretells her destruction. The siege must have begun soon after the capture of Jerusalem; the insular position of Tyre (for the original city on the mainland had been taken by Shalmaneser), the strength of its fortifications, and the command of the sea, enabled it to hold out for thirteen years, as we learn from the Tyrian historians quoted by Josephus[4]. It is clear that the results were not such as the besieging army had expected from success.

---

[1] They appear to close with the 44th chapter. The Fathers (Hieron. adv. Jov. lib. 2. Tertull. Seorpiace viii.) say that Jeremiah was stoned by the people.

[2] See the description in Ezek. xxvi.–xxviii.
[3] Ezek. xxvi. 2.
[4] Cont. Apion. 1. 21.

"Nebuchadnezzar and his troops had served a great service;" their heads had grown bald with the pressure of the helmet, and their shoulders had been galled by the weight of the cuirass; expressions which indicate a protracted warfare; " yet had they no wages for Tyre for the service that they had served against it[1];" and the spoil of Egypt is promised to them as a compensation for this disappointment, which probably arose from the city having surrendered on terms which saved it from being given up to plunder[2]. That an invasion of Egypt actually took place is probable. Megasthenes asserted that Nauocodrosorus (Nebuchadnezzar) had led his army as far as the Pillars of Hercules, and conquered great part of Libya[3]. Unless this is a pure fiction, he must have made conquests to the westward of Egypt, which he could not do without passing through the northern border of that country.

Now the prophecy of Jeremiah[4] implies no more than such a passage, accompanied by the usual outrages of a victorious army. It does not describe a permanent occupation. The prophet declares that "he would spread his pavilion in Tahpenes (Daphnæ), break the images of Bethshemesh (Heliopolis), and

---

[1] St. Jerome on Ezek. xxix. 18, relates that when Nebuchadnezzar had nearly completed his mole to attack the island, the Tyrians put their wealth on shipboard and carried it off: but it is difficult to know whether he is relating a certified fact or expounding the prophecy.

[2] The reign of Ithobalus, the king under whom the siege took place, was followed by that of Baal, which lasted ten years; then followed a period of mixed government of *suffetes*, high priest and king, for eight years, after which two princes in succession were sent for to Tyre from Babylon, to be invested with royalty, which seems to imply some kind of dependence at that time. (Jos. Ant. 9, 14, 2.)

[3] Strabo, 15, 687.

[4] Jer. xliii. 12; xlvi. 13–26.

III.]   THE TWENTY-SIXTH DYNASTY.   419

lay waste Noph (Memphis); that he should array himself with the land of Egypt as a shepherd putteth on his garment, and go forth thence in peace." He might be deterred from attempting the conquest of Middle and Upper Egypt by the power of Apries, or dissuaded by his submission. This explanation, however, will not apply to the prophecy of Ezekiel[1], according to which man and beast were to be cut off from the land, from Migdol to Syene, and Egypt to be desolate for forty years. The remark is often forced upon one who compares prophecy with history, that the prophet, in enlarging upon his theme and carrying it out into details, indulges his own peculiar genius, and obeys in some measure the impulse of his own feeling. The genius of Ezekiel was exaggerative[2] and vehement, whereas the style of Jeremiah is more simple and prosaic. It would be pushing a negative argument too far to deny any invasion of Egypt by Nebuchadnezzar, because it is not mentioned in Herodotus; but to relate its desolation for a long series of years as a fact, would be a violation of all principles of historical criticism. It is certain that from this time there was no hostility between Egypt and Babylon, and there is even reason to think that Nebuchadnezzar married an Egyptian princess.

There is a striking correspondence between the language in which Ezekiel describes the pride of Pharaoh and its humiliation, and the contrast which Herodotus draws between the commence-

---

[1] Ezek. xxix.
[2] "Ezekiel—est atrox, vehemens, tragicus, totus in δεινώσει, frequens in repetitionibus, non decoris aut gratiæ causa, sed ex indignatione et violentia." (Lowth, de Sacra Poesi Hebræorum, Præl. xxi.)

ment and the close of his reign. Next to Psammitichus he had been the most prosperous of Egyptian kings; but the time had arrived when he was destined to misfortune, and according to the historian's philosophy, great prosperity, especially if accompanied with any elevation of mind, was provocative of a reverse[1]. Both the prosperity and the pride of Apries[2] are set forth in strong poetic imagery by Ezekiel: he is likened to a crocodile lying in the midst of the Nile, saying of the river, "It is mine own, I have made it for myself," troubling the waters with his feet, when he rushed forth to seize his prey[3]. It was not, however, from the rival power of Babylon that he was destined to meet with destruction.

The Greek colony of Cyrene had been founded about half a century before this time. The history of its establishment is curiously illustrative of the state of geographical knowledge among the Greeks in the seventh century before Christ. The king of Thera, a small island of the Sporades, had gone to Delphi, probably to consult the oracle respecting the drought under which the island had suffered[4]. The Pythia replied, "that they should go and found a city in Libya." The Theræans were descended partly from the Minyæ, the earliest navigators of Greece[5], partly from the Phœnician companions of Cadmus, yet they knew not in what part of the

---

[1] 1, 34. Μετὰ δὲ Σόλωνα οἰχόμενον, ἔλαβε ἐκ θεοῦ νέμεσις μεγάλη Κροῖσον· ὡς εἰκάσαι, ὅτι ἐνόμισε ἑωυτὸν εἶναι ἀνθρώπων ἁπάντων ὀλβιώτατον.

[2] Ἀπρίεω δὲ λέγεται εἶναι ἥδε ἡ διάνοια, μηδ' ἂν θεόν μιν μηδένα δύνασθαι παῦσαι τῆς βασιληίης· οὕτω ἀσφαλέως ἑωυτῷ ἱδρῦσθαι ἐδόκεε. (2, 169.)

[3] Ezek. xxix. 1, 3; xxxii. 2.

[4] Her. 4, 151, represents the drought as following the first visit to Delphi.

[5] Müller, Orchomenos und die Minyer, 258.

world Libya was. Not daring, even in obedience to an oracle, to go forth on such a blind expedition, they continued to endure the drought, till every tree on the island, save one, had perished. They had again recourse to the oracle, but received for answer only a renewal of the command to colonize Libya, accompanied by a reproach for their neglect of the previous oracle. They knew, however, that Crete lay between it and their own island, and sent thither to inquire whether any Cretan or stranger settled there had ever been in Libya. After wandering through the island they came to the town of Itanus at its eastern extremity, and there found a manufacturer of purple of the name of Corobius. He had been driven, probably while seeking for the shell-fish from which the purple is derived[1], to the island of Platea, now Bomba, between Parætonium and Cyrene. The promise of a reward induced him to return with them to Thera, and thence to sail, accompanied by an exploring party, to Platea. The Therans left him on the island with such a supply of provisions as they calculated would suffice, and returned to Thera to fetch their countrymen. The time fixed for their coming had expired; and Corobius would have perished from want, had not some Samians on their voyage to Egypt been driven to the same island, who, on hearing his story, left him provisions for a year[2]. A colony after some time arrived from Thera, but

---

[1] Zuchis, on the coast of North Africa, near the Syrtis, is mentioned by Strabo as a great seat of the manufacture of purple (17,835).

[2] These Samians, when they left Platea, made for Egypt, but the violence and long continuance of the east wind drove them through the Pillars of Hercules to Tartessus, a mart till then unvisited by Greeks (Herod. 4, 152).

their first settlement was not prosperous, and when two years had elapsed, leaving one of their number on the island, they again visited Delphi, and complained to the Pythia that though they had colonized Libya, they had fared no better. The answer of the Pythia implied that they were mistaken in supposing that the island was Libya[1], and they accordingly removed to a place named Aziris, opposite to it on the mainland, at the opening of the valley which is now called Wadi el Temmineh. Herodotus says, that after remaining here six years they were induced by the promises of a better settlement to let themselves be conducted by the Libyans to Cyrene, and that their guides contrived to lead them by night through the finest part of the country. But it is evident from the exclamation of one of the guides when they arrived at Cyrene, "Greeks, here it is best for you to dwell; for here the skies are pierced[2]," that they had been pining for a land watered by rain, having found that the evil of drought had followed them to their new settlement. Such a land is the Cyrenaica[3]: as the traveller ascends from the Gulf of Bomba towards the elevated plateau on which the city stands, the sandy soil changes to a rich loam; a fine vegetation clothes the hills (the Arabs now call it the Green Mountain); herds of cattle are seen, which the land on

---

[1] Αἰ τὺ ἐμεῦ Λιβύην μηλοτρόφον οἶδας ἄμεινον
Μὴ ἐλθὼν ἐλθόντος, ἄγαν ἄγαμαι σοφίην σευ.—Her. 4, 157.

[2] In the language of Scripture, "the windows of heaven are opened." (Gen. vii. 11. Mal. iii. 10.)

[3] The name was probably Phoenician, and derived from קרן, cornu, like Cerne on the coast of Mauritania. Compare Isaiah, v. 1, where "a very fruitful hill" is literally "a horn, the son of fatness;" ἐν κέρατι, ἐν τόπῳ πίονι. (Sept.)

the sea-coast is unable to support; the olive, the citron, the juniper, the cypress, the pine, grow luxuriantly[1], and there is an abundant supply of water. The whole district produced the Silphium[2], which was so highly prized in ancient pharmacy that it sometimes sold for its weight in silver[3]. The different elevation of the coast, the mountains and the intermediate region, gave the Cyrenians three harvests in the year, one becoming ripe while the other was gathered in[4]. The site of Cyrene was well adapted for the settlement of a flourishing colony. The promontory on which it stands, between the Syrtis and the Bay of Bomba, is the nearest point to Greece of the whole line of the African coast; and there is an excellent harbour at the distance of 80 stadia or 10 miles from the town[5]. The gardens of the Hesperides, as far as they had a prototype in nature, appear to have been hollows in the limestone hills on the western side of the promontory, where orchards of extraordinary productiveness are found.

The establishment of the colony of Cyrene was indirectly fatal to the Saitic dynasty. Under Battus I. its founder, who reigned 40 years, and his son Arcesilaus, who reigned 16, the numbers of the original settlers were not increased by any new immigration. But in the reign of Battus, surnamed

---

[1] Pacho, Voyage dans la Marmorique, p. 83.
[2] It is supposed to be the *Laserpitium Derias* which Pacho observed to grow plentifully in the Cyrenaica, though he nowhere met with it between Egypt and the Bay of Bomba. It was not found westward of the Syrtis (Her. 4, 169). Pliny, N. H. 22, 49, enumerates its virtues, which extended from the dispersion of a dropsy to the cure of corns.
[3] Aristoph. Plut. 925. Plin. N. H. 19, 15.
[4] Herod. 4, 199.
[5] Scylax, 107, p. 234, ed. Klausen.

the Prosperous, an invitation was sent to all the Greeks to come and aid the Cyrenians in colonizing Libya, with a promise of an allotment of land. The Pythia lent her aid, as before, by an oracle which warned against delay[1], and a great multitude soon assembled at Cyrene from Crete, Peloponnesus, and the Cyclades and Sporades[2]. They could not be provided with the land that had been promised them, but at the expense of the native Libyans, who were not only stripped of their territories, but treated with great insolence, according to the common fate of barbarians who presume to defend their rights against the intrusion of a civilized people. They were probably the same Libyan tribe, the Giligammæ, in whose territory the first Theræan settlers had landed. Egypt was interested in preventing the further growth of a power which threatened to encroach on all its neighbours[3]. Adicran, the king of the Libyans, sent to implore aid from Apries, and place himself under his authority. Apries accepted the offer of the Libyans, and sent a large army to their aid; but as he could not venture to employ his Greek mercenaries against their countrymen, it was composed entirely of Egyptian troops. The Cyrenians marched out, and a battle took place at Irasa, now *Ain Ersen*[4], between the Bay of Bomba and Cyrene.

---

[1] Ὅς δέ κεν ἐς Λιβύην πολυήρατον ὕστερον ἔλθῃ
Γᾶς ἀναδαιομένας, μετά οἵ ποκά φαμι μελήσειν.—Her. 4, 159.

[2] Her. 4, 161.

[3] Her. 4, 168. Scylax (106, p. 233 Klausen) extends the Egyptian territory as far as Apis (Boun Ajoubah); but his work was hardly written before the middle of the 4th century B.C.

[4] Ἐς Ἴρασα χῶρον καὶ ἐπὶ κρήνην Θέστην. (Her. 4, 159.) *Ain* means fountain, and in these countries fountains are more permanent than towns. The name is probably also Phœnician עיר‎ urbs. See Gesenius, Ling. Phœn. 1, 424.

The Egyptians had never before encountered Greek arms and tactics; the disproportion in numbers must have been great, but the negligence of their adversaries enabled the Greeks to gain a complete victory, and few of the Egyptian army returned to their own country. It was the first occasion on which the valour and skill of the free Hellenes was matched in a pitched battle against the forces of the great despotic monarchies which had previously ruled the world; the first of a series of victories, which in the course of two centuries and a half made them masters of the ancient territories of Assyria, Babylonia and Egypt.

The news of this defeat and the almost entire extermination of the army produced a revolt in Egypt. Apries, who had probably imagined that he should easily conquer a handful of Greeks, was accused of having sent his troops on an enterprise in which he knew that they must perish, in the hope of governing his kingdom more securely by means of the foreigners. Those who returned, being joined by the relatives of those who had perished, immediately revolted. Apries, on the receipt of this intelligence, sent to them Amasis, one of his officers, who had gained the favour of the king, and been advanced to high office, though of humble origin, by the beauty of a chaplet which he presented to him on his birth-day. While he was haranguing them in order to bring them back to their allegiance, a soldier came behind him, and placed a crown upon his head. He accepted it without reluctance, and prepared to march against Apries. On hearing this, Apries dispatched

Patarbemis[1], an officer of high rank, with orders to bring Amasis alive into his presence. Amasis bade him return with a contemptuous refusal, and when he appeared before Apries, the king ordered his ears and nose to be cut off. The Egyptians who had hitherto adhered to the royal cause, seeing the outrage offered to a man who was highly esteemed among them, immediately joined Amasis and the revolters. Apries was thus left alone with his Carian and Ionian auxiliaries, whose numbers amounted to 30,000. He marched from Sais, where his royal residence was, to meet Amasis, who was advancing from Libya, and the armies encountered at Momemphis, near the borders of the Lake Mareotis. The digression which Herodotus makes at this moment of his narrative[2], to give an account of the castes of Egypt, and especially of the numbers and privileges of the military caste, proves that in his mind this revolt was closely connected with the attempt which the Saitic princes had carried on for three-quarters of a century, to raise up a body of Greek troops, by whose means they might make themselves independent of the ancient soldiery. Their dissatisfaction first manifested itself in the emigration of the Automoli, and most effectually in the revolt under Amasis. That they were still so powerful is a proof that the numbers of the Automoli must have been greatly exaggerated. The auxiliaries were defeated, owing to the superiority in numbers of the Egyptians, and Apries being

---

[1] Hellanicus (Athen. 15, p. 680) called the king himself Partamis, apparently from confusion with Patarbemis.
[2] 2, 164.

taken prisoner, was carried back to Sais to the palace, now become the property of Amasis. For a time he was treated with kindness by his conqueror; but the Egyptians murmured at the indulgence shown to one who had made himself so odious to them. Amasis therefore delivered him into the hands of the people, by whom he was strangled, but allowed to be buried with his ancestors in the splendid temple of Minerva at Sais. To the modes of interment in pyramids practised under the Old Monarchy and in grotto sepulchres by the Theban dynasties, another had been added by the Pharaohs of Sais. The level and alluvial Delta afforded neither hills on which pyramids could be set up, as objects conspicuous from afar, nor rocks in which sepulchres could be hewn. They therefore constructed for their remains vaults within the precincts of the temples, surrounded with pilasters and columns, and opening with folding-doors. The interments of the common people of Sais were made in a large necropolis, of which the remains may still be traced[2]. Apries had reigned, according to Herodotus and Manetho as reported by Eusebius, twenty-five years, and died 569 B.C.

AMASIS or Amosis, was a native of Siouph, a small town in the Saitic nome, and of plebeian birth[3]. Thus another great principle of the ancient constitution of Egypt was infringed, according to which the king must be chosen from the priests

---

[1] Jer. xliv. 30. "Thus saith the Lord, Behold I will give Pharaoh Hophra into the hand of his enemies, and into the hand of them that seek his life."

[2] Champollion, Lettres, p. 50, 52.

[3] Δημότην τὸ πρὶν ἐόντα καὶ οἰκίης οὐκ ἐπιφανέος. (Her. 2, 172.)

or the soldiery. Being a man of the people, he was no doubt supported by them, and at first despised by the higher castes for the meanness of his birth. He admonished them, by a truly oriental mode, a symbolical action, of the folly of valuing men according to their origin, instead of their actual place and use in society. He had a golden foot-bath, in which he and his guests were accustomed to wash their feet before the banquet. This he broke up, and out of the material fashioned a statue of a god, which was erected in a public place, and received the homage of the citizens. Sending for the Egyptians, he pointed out to them to what honour this vessel had been raised, which had formerly served for humble and even dishonourable uses[1]. " My lot," said he, " has been the same : I was once a plebeian ; I am now your king ; and you must honour and respect me accordingly ; " and in this way he gently reconciled them to his yoke. In another respect he innovated upon ancient customs. The court ceremonial of Egypt, arranged by the priests, regulated for the sovereign the employment of all his hours, and when he had given the morning to the dispatch of business, prescribed to him religious duties and moral reading. Amasis did not neglect the duties of sovereignty ; on the contrary he established a strict administration throughout Egypt, and raised it to a high degree of prosperity. But having given the early hours of the day

---

[1] The lively description of Herodotus gives no high idea of the refinement of Egyptian manners. Φὰς ἐκ τοῦ ποδανιπτῆρος τὤγαλμα γεγονέναι, ἐς τὸν πρότερον μὲν τοὺς Αἰγυπτίους ἐνεμεῖν τε καὶ ἐνου- ρέειν καὶ πόδας ἐναπονίζεσθαι. (2, 172.) In a picture at Thebes (Wilkinson, M. and C. 2, 167) is a representation of the effects of wine on *ladies* at a feast.

to business, he devoted the rest to pleasure, drank freely, and unbent his mind in pleasantry with his boon companions. His friends were scandalized at his levities, and thus addressed him: "You do wrong, O king, in making yourself so cheap; you ought to sit gravely in a throne of state, and give the whole day to business; the Egyptians would then know by how great a personage they are governed, and you would be in better repute with them. Your present conduct is quite unkingly." But Amasis replied: "Those who have bows, string them when they want to use them, and unstring them when they have done; for if they were kept always strung they would break, and be useless when they were wanted. And such is the case with man: if he were to attempt to be always serious, and never to relax with mirth, he would insensibly become mad, or lose his faculties. Aware of this, I give part of my day to business and part to amusement[1]." Amasis is the first king of Egypt of whose personal character we have any knowledge; the older Pharaohs have been distinguished by their names, their public acts, and the length of their reigns; but we have known nothing of the *men*. We readily recognize the qualities which made him the favourite of the people and the common soldiers; Julius Cæsar, Henry V., are examples of a youth spent in licentious and even lawless courses, succeeded by a manhood of vigorous activity and

---

[1] Herod. 2, 172. See vol. i. p. 455, the account of the treatment which the different oracles underwent from Amasis after his accession.

equitable and sagacious administration[1]; and the union of severe application to business, with the love of pleasure and a playful humour in the hours of relaxation, has a parallel in Philip of Macedon.

His reign was favoured by external circumstances. The Nile was regular in its rise, and the land yielded abundance to the people; the number of inhabited places exceeded twenty thousand[2]. A friendly alliance was made with Cyrene, and Egyptian prejudice so far set at nought, that Amasis married Ladike, the daughter either of the king of that city, or of an eminent citizen. No danger threatened on the side of Babylon; on the contrary, their relations were friendly, and Amasis, after the power of Cyrus became formidable, entered into an alliance with Nabonadius or Labynetus, the last king of Babylon, for the defence of Crœsus against the Medes[3]. The rapid movements of Cyrus defeated their purpose, and Sardis was taken before the allies of Crœsus could muster. This was in the year 546 B.C. The naval power of the Phœnicians was so much reduced by the war of Nebuchadnezzar against Tyre, that Amasis dispossessed them of Cyprus[4], and made it tributary, which would facilitate his intercourse with Asia Minor. His internal regulations were so judicious, that he is reckoned with Menes, Sasychis, Sesostris and Bocchoris, as one of the great legislators of Egypt. They extended, according to Diodorus, to

---

[1] Παραδέδοται συνετός τε γεγονέναι καθ' ὑπερβολὴν καὶ τὸν τρόπον ἐπιεικὴς καὶ δίκαιος. (Diod. 1, 95.)
[2] Herod. 2, 177.
[3] Herod. 1, 77.
[4] Herodotus says, εἷλε δὲ Κύπρον πρῶτος ἀνθρώπων, but this is evidently a mistake.

III.]   THE TWENTY-SIXTH DYNASTY.   431

the whole administration[1], but only one of them is specified[2]. It obliged every man to declare every year to the chief magistrate of his nome, by what means he lived, and if he could show no honest livelihood, he was to be put to death. It is probably more correctly stated by Diodorus[3], that he who gave a false account of himself, or followed an unlawful calling, was punishable with death. From the general character of the administration of Amasis, we should expect to find him moderating the severity of a penal law. Herodotus says that the law of Solon which was in force in his time and was an excellent law, was borrowed from Egypt; but Solon's law only punished idleness with the loss of civic rights, and that perhaps only if a man had for three successive years been without an honest calling[4].

Amasis at first was not favourably disposed towards the Greeks[5], by whose defeat he had been advanced to the throne, but he continued them in his service, and afterwards removed their quarters to Memphis, that they might be available against the population of the capital. He showed himself also very friendly towards the whole Greek nation. He allowed all who pleased to inhabit the city of Naucratis, and to those who came only for commercial purposes, he gave sites on which they might build altars to their gods. The largest and most illustrious of these factories was that which was called *Hellenion*,

[1] 1, 95.
[2] Herod. 1, 177.
[3] 1, 77.
[4] Petit, Leges Atticæ, p. 520, ed. Wessel. Herodotus himself speaks of Solon's visiting Egypt *after* he had given laws to Athens (1, 30).
[5] Φιλέλλην γενόμενος ὁ Ἄμασις is the expression of Herodotus (2, 177).

founded by the principal states of Asiatic Greece; Chios, Teos, Phocæa and Clazomenæ in Ionia; Rhodes, Cnidus, Halicarnassus and Phaselis in Doris; and the single city of Mitylene in Æolis. These cities enjoyed exclusively the privilege of appointing the magistrates or *consuls* who regulated the commercial concerns of the Hellenion; others claimed a share, but Herodotus emphatically declares that it did not belong to them. Ægina, however, had independently founded a *temenos* of Jupiter, the Samians of Juno and the Milesians of Apollo, their respective chief divinities; and these were probably older than the Hellenion, as the states which founded them were distinguished in navigation earlier than the others. Amasis sent presents to several of the Grecian temples; a gilded image of Minerva with his own picture, to Cyrene; to Lindus, two statues of Minerva in stone, and a linen corslet of wonderful workmanship. According to the description which Herodotus gives[1] of a similar present made to the Lacedæmonians, each thread consisted of 360 filaments clearly to be distinguished. Figures were woven in the pattern of the linen, and it was adorned with gold and cotton[2]. Cotton, being used as a costly material along with gold for the enrichment of the linen, was probably of recent introduction from Ethiopia or India; for it seems not to have been known in Egypt in earlier times[3]. The corslet sent to Lindus remained to the time of Pliny, though nearly destroyed by the curiosity of tra-

[1] Her. 3, 47.
[2] Ἐόντα μὲν λίνεον καὶ ζώων ἐνυφασμένων συχνῶν, κεκοσμημένον δὲ χρυσῷ καὶ εἰρίοισι ἀπὸ ξύλου. (Her. *u. s.*)
[3] Jul. Poll. 7,75. Plin. N.H. 19,1.

vellers, and the examination of it verified the account of Herodotus[1]. Another occasion for displaying his liberality towards the Greeks was offered by the conflagration of the temple at Delphi, which took place 548 B.C. Its restoration was undertaken for the sum of 300 talents by the wealthy family of the Alcmæonidæ, and was to be paid for by a general contribution of the members of the Amphictyonic confederacy. Of this sum one-fourth part was allotted to the Delphians, who, being unable to raise it themselves, wandered throughout Greece and the Grecian settlements, begging for contributions, and visited among the rest their countrymen settled in Egypt. From them they received 20 minæ; from Amasis 1000 talents, about 50,000 pounds weight, of alum. It is obtained in great quantities from the Oases of the Libyan Desert, and this was reckoned the purest of any. It was of extensive use, especially in dyeing, and very costly; in later times the Lipari Islands enjoyed the monopoly of it, and acquired incredible riches, says Diodorus, from this source[2]. More recently it has been a source of great wealth, first to the Turks, and afterwards to the Popes, who for a long time possessed the monopoly[3].

[1] Mirentur hæc (the fact that there were 150 threads in one rope of a hunting-net) ignorantes in Ægyptii quondam regis, quem Amasim vocant, thorace, in Rhodiorum insula ostendi in templo Minervæ ccclxv. filis singula fila constare; quod se expertum nuper Romæ prodidit Mutianus ter Consul, parvasque jam reliquias ejus superesse, hac experientium injuria. (N.H. 19, 1.)

[2] Diod. 5, 10. Murray's Africa (2, p. 67), of the alum found in the Oasis of Shelima. Hamilton's Ægyptiaca, 428; Russegger, Reise (2, 1, 342), of the Oases Chardscheh, El-Dacheh and El-Bacharieh. A Frenchman in partnership with the Viceroy was carrying on the manufacture there on a large scale at the time of Russegger's visit, 1836 (Reise, u. s. p. 53).

[3] Beckmann's Hist. of Inven-

The alliance and friendship of Amasis with Polycrates of Samos is very celebrated, and must belong to the latest part of Amasis' reign. Polycrates (532 B.C.) had made himself master of the whole of that island, having killed one of his brothers and expelled the other, and acquired a degree of power and splendour which no Grecian tyrant ever equalled, except Gelon and Hiero of Syracuse[1]. The Samians, as we have seen, were commercially connected with Egypt, and Polycrates cultivated the friendship of Amasis. For a time uninterrupted success attended his schemes; but they were carried on with little regard for the rights of his neighbours[2], whom he invaded and plundered without scruple. Amasis had marked his prosperity, and on occasion of some new success was so convinced that a dreadful reverse must be preparing for him, that he addressed to him, says Herodotus, the following letter:—"Amasis to Polycrates. It is pleasant to hear of the prosperity of one with whom we are connected in friendship and hospitality. But thy great successes displease me, knowing how envious the divinity is, and it is my wish for those in whom I am interested, that they should succeed in some things and fail in others, and thus experience an alternation of fortune through life, rather than be always prosperous. For I have never yet heard of any one who had been successful in everything, who did not suffer

tions, London, 1846, 1, 196. The ancient *alumen* appears not to have been so well purified as our alum from the sulphate of iron which is mixed with it in nature.

[1] Herod. 3, 125.
[2] Herod. 3, 39, 40.

entire ruin before he died. Take my advice, then, and counteract your prosperity in this way; consider what is the thing you value most and would be most grieved to lose, and throw that away in such a manner that it shall never come back again among men. And if in future good and ill fortune should not alternate with you, adopt the remedy that I suggest." The moral of this letter is that with which Herodotus himself philosophized on history and human life, and it coincides so exactly with the address of Solon to Crœsus, in another part of his work, even to the phraseology[1], as to leave no doubt that he has held the pen for Amasis, as he made himself the spokesman of Solon. Polycrates weighed the advice, and found that there was nothing which it would grieve him more to lose than a costly emerald ring, engraved by Theodorus of Samos[2]. He therefore ordered a pentecontor to be manned, rowed out into the deep sea, and in the presence of all drew his ring from his finger, dropped it into the water, and returned to his palace with a heavy heart. It was a notion of the ancient religions that one who was threatened with an overwhelming calamity by the anger or envy of the gods, might break the force of the blow by voluntarily taking on himself

---

[1] 1, 32. Ἐπισταμενόν με τὸ θεῖον πᾶν ἐὸν φθονερόν τε καὶ ταραχῶδες, ἐπειρωτᾶς ἀνθρωπηΐων πραγμάτων πέρι; 3, 40. Ἐμοὶ αἱ σαὶ μεγάλαι εὐτυχίαι οὐκ ἀρέσκουσι, τὸ θεῖον ἐπισταμένῳ ὥς ἐστι φθονερόν. 1, 32. Χρὴ παντὸς χρήματος σκοπέειν τὴν τελευτὴν κῇ ἀποβήσεται· πολλοῖσι γὰρ δὴ ὑποδέξας ὄλβον ὁ θεὸς προρρίζους ἀνέτρεψε. 3, 40. Οὐδένα οἶδα ὅστις εἰς τέλος οὐ κακῶς ἐτελεύτησε πρόρριζος, εὐτυχέων τὰ πάντα.

[2] Plin. N. H. 37, 1, 2. "Sardonychem eam gemmam fuisse constat; ostenduntque Romæ, si credimus, Concordiæ delubro, cornu aureo Augusti dono inclusam."

some minor evil, and thus compound his debt to Fate. But in this case the composition was refused. Five or six days after, a fisherman who had caught a fish of unusual size and beauty, carried it as a present to Polycrates. When the servants opened it, they found in the stomach the lost ring, and in great joy brought it to their master, who, struck with the ominous character of the event, wrote a full description of all that had happened to Amasis in Egypt. He perceived that the god was bent upon the ruin of Polycrates, and sent a herald to Samos to renounce his friendship, in order, says Herodotus, that when some terrible calamity should befall him, he might not be grieved by thinking of him as his friend. The story of the ring recovered by means of the fish, is one of the traditionary stock of fictions whose origin is not to be traced. Amasis may have had reasons of policy for renouncing the friendship of Polycrates. He aspired to be master of Ionia and the islands[1], and voluntarily offered a naval armament to Cambyses, for the invasion of Egypt, which was on the point of taking place when Amasis died[2]. And though Herodotus has courteously omitted any intimation in the letter, that the abuse of power was a sure means of drawing down retribution, Amasis cannot have been ignorant that Polycrates was guilty of acts of tyranny, very likely to bring about his ruin. The unromantic account of Diodorus is, that Amasis renounced the friendship of Polycrates, on finding that he paid no regard to an embassy which he sent, exhorting him to abstain from his outrages

---

[1] Her. 3, 122.   [2] Her. 3, 44.

on his own fellow-citizens, and on strangers who resorted to Samos[1]. The fulfilment of the augury took place a few years later, when Polycrates was crucified by the Persian Orœtes, into whose power he had put himself, in spite of the warning of dreams and oracles[2].

Like others whom the Greeks classed under the general name of tyrants, Polycrates collected poets and men of letters around him, and is said to have formed a library[3]. One of the most illustrious of these was Pythagoras, a native of Samos, of Phœnician parentage, who is said to have visited Egypt, recommended by Polycrates to the protection of Amasis. Of the wide peregrinations attributed to this philosopher, which reached even to India and Gaul, his residence in Egypt is the best-attested portion. The authors on whom we are compelled to rely for his history lived so long after his own time, and there is so much of mystery and exaggeration in their accounts, that we know not what reliance is to be placed on the stories of the severe trials which the priesthood made him undergo, and his final success in obtaining initiation into all their secrets. But that he had resided long in Egypt, and become acquainted both with their religion and their science, we learn on surer evidence, the character of his own philosophy and institutions. Herodotus all but names him as having derived from Egypt the doctrine of the Metempsychosis, of which we find no trace before in Greek religion or philosophy[4]. His knowledge of medi-

[1] Diod. 1, 95.
[2] Her. 3, 124, B.C. 523.
[3] Athen. Epit. lib. 1, p. 3. Wolf, without reason, throws doubt on this statement (Proleg. cxlv. note 7).
[4] Herodotus speaks of the pro-

cine, and strict system of dietetic rules, lead us to conclude that he had been trained in Egypt, where medicine had attained the highest perfection, and dietary rules had been systematized with the greatest success. His attainments in geometry correspond with the ascertained fact that Egypt was the birthplace of that art. He is distinguished in the history of philosophy for an attempt, happily unsuccessful, because uncongenial to the Grecian mind, to make knowledge a mystery, to obstruct the approach to it by the interposition of long and repulsive discipline, by investing the teacher with a supernatural character to exalt his precepts into oracles, and to place the governing power of the state in the hands of an order who had been separated from their fellow-citizens and inspired with an *esprit de corps* by their education. In these respects the Pythagorean school resembled the Egyptian priesthood of this age, as far as the different circumstances of Greece and Egypt would allow imitation, and there was no other model in the ancient world that he could have copied[1].

Solon must have come to Egypt[2] before the reign

hibition to bury in woollen as belonging to the orgies which were called Orphic and Bacchic, but were really Egyptian and Pythagorean rites (2, 81); but this does not necessarily imply a belief in the transmigration of the soul.

[1] According to Pliny, N. H. 36, 9, Semenpserteus was the name of the king in whose reign Pythagoras came to Egypt. The Bamberg MS. reads *Spemetnepserphreo*, whence Bunsen elicits *Psameticho Nepherphreo*. (Urkundenbuch, p. 85, Germ.)

[2] Herodotus (1, 29, 30) represents him as visiting Egypt after his legislation (594 B.C.), but does not expressly say that he was there in the reign of Amasis, who came to the throne in 570 B.C., although his words (2, 177) seem to imply not only this, but that Amasis was a legislator before Solon. Grote and Niebuhr have remarked that there is an error of forty years in Herodotus' chronology of this period (Grote, 3, 205). There is a similar variation of forty years in the assigned age of Pythagoras. See Pynes Clinton, F. H. vol. 2, p. 9.

of Amasis, if his visit preceded his legislation; a supposition not necessary to account for the similarity between his laws and those of Egypt. Tradition related that he had been the companion of Psenophis, the priest of Heliopolis, and Sonchis, the priest of Sais, two of the most learned of their order, and philosophized with them[1]. His object would be very different from that of Pythagoras, not to dive into religious mysteries, but to learn practical wisdom, such as he might have applied to the benefit of his country on his return, had he not found its liberties overthrown by Pisistratus. If we may believe Plato, however, he brought home thence a wondrous tale of the ancient glories of Athens, in times some thousand years prior to Phoroneus and Niobe and Deucalion's flood, when she had repelled an invasion of the inhabitants of the since submerged island of Atlantis, who had overrun the whole of the west, as far as Egypt and Tyrrhenia[2]. There is much in the story which betrays the desire of the priests of Sais at once to ingratiate themselves with the Athenians, by finding parallels between Attic and Egyptian usages, and to maintain their own superiority; and no historical inference can be drawn from any part of it. Yet the mention of the impossibility of navigating the Atlantic, in consequence of the mud produced by the subsidence of the island, deserves notice, in reference rather to the age of Plato than of Solon. We have seen that after the time of

---

[1] Plut. Sol. 26. Λογιωτάτοις οὖσι τῶν ἱερέων συνεφιλοσόφησε.

[2] Tim. iii. 25, Steph.

Herodotus it became the established opinion that Africa could not be circumnavigated, owing to some obstruction vaguely described. The modern navigator finds neither mud nor shallows nor dead calms, but the seaweed which covers the ocean south of the Azores really does impede navigation, and would have stopped the enterprise of Columbus, had he not skilfully turned the terror of his crew into an encouragement, by representing it as a proof that land was near[1]. Should it hereafter be ascertained that a ridge now covered by the Atlantic ocean once joined the two worlds, the tale of the priest of Sais, or of Plato, will only be an example of a guess curiously fulfilled, like Seneca's prophecy of the discovery of a new world.

Among the temples enlarged or decorated by Amasis, that of Minerva at Sais was particularly distinguished. He erected there propylæa, which, both for height and size and the magnitude and the quality of the stones employed, surpassed all others. These he brought from the quarries of Memphis, as well as the colossal figures and androsphinxes with which the dromos was adorned. A monolithal shrine of granite from the quarries of Elephantine excited the especial admiration of Herodotus. Two thousand men were appointed to bring it down the Nile; from Elephantine to Sais was an ordinary navigation of only twenty days, but in this case three years were occupied, probably because the immense weight made it impossible to float it except during the season of the high Nile. Its height

---

[1] See Grote's Greece, 3, 382, note.

was above thirty feet; its depth, from front to back, twelve feet; its breadth twenty-one[1]. After all the cost and labour bestowed on its extraction and conveyance, it was not erected in the temple of Minerva: as they were drawing it in, the superintendent of the works uttered a groan through weariness of the labour and the thought of the time that had been expended; and Amasis, either because he deemed this ominous, or because one of the workmen had been killed in the process of moving it on levers, would not allow it to be drawn any further. When Herodotus visited Egypt, it remained lying on the ground before the temple. There remains at Tel-et-mai, the ancient Thmuis in the Delta, a monolithal shrine of the granite of Syene, bearing the name of Amasis, of similar form to that which Herodotus describes; but its length is only twenty-one feet nine inches, and its breadth thirteen feet[2]. Amasis erected also a colossus seventy-five feet in height at Memphis, before the temple of Ptah, and two of granite, twenty feet in height, one on each side of the inner sanctuary. One of the same size at Sais was prostrate like the great colossus. Judging from analogy, we may suppose that these were colossal statues of himself, which the Persian conqueror of Egypt threw down, among his other outrages on the memory of Amasis. He also built a large and splendid temple to Isis at Memphis[3]. Inscriptions are found on the rocks at

---

[1] See note on Kenrick's Herod. 2, 175. He gives its measures as it lay on the ground; consequently what he calls the length was the *height*, and so of the other dimensions.

[2] Wilkinson, Manners and Customs, 1, 191; Mod. Eg. and Thebes, 1, 440. Champ. Égypte sous les Pharaons, 2, 114.

[3] Her. 2, 176.

Syene which confirm the accounts of Herodotus respecting the extensive excavations made there by this king for his various public works.

His reign lasted, according to the lists and Herodotus[1], forty-four years; and Rosellini has found a tablet in the quarries of Mokattam, bearing his name and this date[2]. His death took place in the year 526 B.C., when his kingdom was on the point of being invaded by Cambyses, the son of Cyrus.

Cyrus, the grandson of Astyages, and son of the Cyaxares by whom Nineveh was besieged, had united the empire of the Medes with that of the Persians, and reduced Asia Minor, Lydia, and the Grecian colonies into subjection. Babylon alone remained in Western Asia as an independent state. It is remarkable that Herodotus says nothing of the expansion of the power of Babylon in the reign of Nebuchadnezzar, but represents Nitocris, queen of the Babylonians, as alarmed at the growing empire of the Medes, after their capture of Nineveh[3]. It should seem that immediately after this event, accomplished by the alliance of the Medes and Babylonians, the Medes turned their arms towards Lydia, and left Babylon in possession of the greater part of the territories dependent on Nineveh; for

---

[1] 3, 10.

[2] Mon. Stor. 2, 152. It has been said by Sir Gardner Wilkinson (M. and C. 1, 179), that the title *Melek* is given to Amasis in some of his legends. Dr. Wiseman (Lectures on Science and Revealed Religion, page 301) says, that Amasis on his monuments *never* receives the Egyptian titles of royalty, but instead of a prænomen the Semitic title of *Melek*. This is a mistake; Amasis has the usual titles, "Son of the Sun," &c. *Malek* is found over some shields bearing this name, but they may belong to the Amasis mentioned by Herodotus (4, 167), who lived in the reign of Darius. See Sharpe, Hist. of Egypt, plates 190, 191.

[3] Her. 1, 185. Τὴν Μήδων ὁρῶσα ἀρχὴν μεγάλην τε καὶ οὐκ ἀτρεμίζουσαν ἀλλὰ τε ἀραιρημένα ἄστεα αὐτοῖσι, ἐν δὲ δὴ καὶ τὴν Νίνον, προεφυλάξατο ὅσα ἐδύνατο μάλιστα.

III.]   THE TWENTY-SIXTH DYNASTY.   443

the king against whom Cyrus advanced is called, not king of Babylon, but king of Assyria[1]. The name of the queen Nitocris is so entirely Egyptian, that we cannot hesitate to consider her as a daughter of the Pharaohs[2]. The wife of Psammitichus I., and the daughter of Psammis or Psammitichus II., both bear this name[3]. Coupling this circumstance with the absence of all hostility between Egypt and Babylon after the invasion of Nebuchadnezzar[4], it seems probable that Nebuchadnezzar had married an Egyptian princess. The succession of the Babylonian kings is thus given by Ptolemy, whose authority must be considered as the highest:—

		Years.
1.	NABOCOLASSAR (Nebuchadnezzar)	43
2.	ILLOARADAMUS	2
3.	NERIGASSOLASSAR (Neriglissar)	4
4.	NABONADIUS	17

The Nabonadius of Ptolemy is evidently the Labynetus of Herodotus, the Belshazzar of Daniel, and, according to Herodotus, the son of Nitocris. Herodotus calls her husband also Labynetus, which does not agree with Ptolemy; but he appears to have known only two Babylonian kings, both of whom he calls Labynetus[5]. In what relation Illoaradamus (Evilmerodach, Nebuchadnezzar's son) stood to Neriglissar we do not learn from Ptolemy, but Berosus[6] informs us that Neriglissar was husband of his sister, and put him to death. It seems probable therefore that Nitocris was the widow of Nebuchad-

---

[1] Her. 1, 188.
[2] Philostr. Vit. Apoll. 1, 25, calls her a Median.
[3] Rosellini, Mon. Stor. 2, 130, 137.
[4] See p. 419 of this vol.
[5] Labynetus the Babylonian, whom he mentions (1, 74) as making peace between the Lydians and Medes, must be Nebuchadnezzar.
[6] Jos. Apion. 1, 20.

nezzar[1]; that after the death of Neriglissar, who reigned but four years, she was regent, or guardian of her son Nabonadius, and that foreseeing the impending attack of Cyrus, she performed those works which Herodotus describes and praises for the protection of Babylonia against invasion. They are such as might naturally suggest themselves to a native of Egypt. That country had been rendered impracticable for the operations of cavalry by its canals. The Euphrates just above Babylon had previously flowed in a straight channel; she gave it such a winding and interlaced course, that, according to Herodotus (1, 185), in descending in a boat you were brought thrice to the same place, and on the third day were no further advanced than on the first. She raised an embankment along the course of the river, resembling that by which Memphis was protected; and a reservoir like that of Mœris below the city to receive the superfluous waters of the inundation. These works were evidently intended to answer a double purpose, to regulate the operations of the river, and render the country inaccessible and difficult for an invading army. Another of her works was the construction of a bridge, consisting of piers on which planks were laid, for joining the two parts of Babylon on the opposite sides of the Euphrates. We know from the monuments that the Egyptians had constructed such bridges some centuries before this time[2]. All her precautions, however, were unavail-

---

[1] From Jeremiah xxvii. 7, it has been inferred that Nebuchadnezzar's grandson was to lose his power, and Evilmerodach may have been the husband of Nitocris and father of Labynctus. But perhaps "son's son" may only mean a short succession, as Παῖδες παίδων τοί κεν μετόπισθε γένωνται in Homer, an indefinitely long one.

[2] See p. 258 of this vol.

ing; Cyrus defeated the Babylonians in the field, and afterwards captured the city by drawing off the waters of the river, and entering along its bed. This was in the year 538 B.C. No hostility against Egypt[1] followed the conquest of Babylon; the attention of Cyrus was drawn towards the nomadic nations on his north-eastern frontier, and in an expedition against the Massagetæ, he lost his life in the year 529 B.C. He was succeeded by his son Cambyses, who almost immediately began to prepare for an expedition against Egypt.

Twenty-seventh Dynasty. Eight Persian kings.

	Years.	
1. CAMBYSES, in the fifth year of his reign over Persia became king of Egypt, and reigned..	6	
2. DARIUS, son of Hystaspes	36	
3. XERXES THE GREAT	21	
4. ARTABANUS		7 months.
5. ARTAXERXES	41	
6. XERXES	2	
7. SOGDIANUS		7
8. DARIUS, son of Xerxes	19	
	124	4 ,,

No single or personal cause is at all necessary to account for an attack on a wealthy country like Egypt, by a newly-risen and aggressive power such as that of the Medo-Persians, which, according to Herodotus, " would not rest[2]." In all recent encounters between the armies of Egypt and those of the great Asiatic states, Egypt had been worsted, if we except the invasion of Sennacherib, whose defeat the Egyptians themselves regarded as a

---

[1] The assertion of Xenophon in his Cyropædia, 1, 1, that Cyrus conquered Egypt, is generally and justly rejected by historical critics.
[2] Οὐκ ἀτρεμίζουσαν. See note 3, p. 442.

miracle. Popular tradition, however, supplied many such causes. According to that which was most evidently devised in order to soothe the national pride of the Egyptians, Cambyses was the son of Nitetis, a daughter of Apries, whom Cyrus had taken as a secondary wife—whereas, says Herodotus, it is notorious that no son of a secondary wife could succeed to the throne of Persia, and that Cambyses was the son of Cassandane, the daughter of Pharnaspes, a man of the Achæmenid family. The Persian story was, that Cambyses had sent to Egypt to demand in marriage a daughter of Amasis, who, knowing she would be only a secondary wife and not his queen, substituted a beautiful daughter of Apries, and that Cambyses discovering the fraud, was so enraged that he determined to invade Egypt. This story is refuted by chronology. Apries had died more than forty years before, and his daughter[1], though arrayed, as Herodotus says, "in royal vestments and gold," could never have gained the affections of the youthful monarch, as the story implies. Another version was that Nitetis was the wife, not of Cambyses, but of Cyrus. A Persian woman visiting his harem, was struck with the beauty of the children of Cassandane, and praised them greatly to their mother. "Yet would you believe it," said Cassandane, "Cyrus neglects me, the mother of such children as these, to pay honour to an Egyptian interloper[2]." On this, Cambyses,

---

[1] Herodotus calls her ἡ παῖς, but we have before had occasion to observe how little he troubles himself with chronological difficulties.

[2] Τὴν ἀπ' Αἰγύπτου ἐπίκτητον ἐν τιμῇ τίθεται (3, 3).

her elder son, a boy of ten years of age, exclaimed, "Therefore, mother, when I am a man, I will turn Egypt upside down;" and recollecting his promise when he came to the throne, he prepared to invade that country.

Among these various stories, one thing alone appears to have the sanction of Herodotus. An Egyptian, at the request of Cyrus, had been sent to him by Amasis, as the most skilful oculist in the country. This was equivalent to a perpetual separation from his wife and children; and either in revenge, or in the hope of revisiting Egypt, if war should result from the refusal of Amasis, he urged Cambyses to demand his daughter. The demand was probably refused—the Persians said, eluded. It happened about the time when Cambyses was preparing his expedition, that Amasis had given offence to Phanes of Halicarnassus, one of the commanders of his mercenary troops, a man of great valour and ability. He had got on shipboard, intending to join Cambyses, but Amasis, knowing his estimation among his auxiliaries, and his accurate acquaintance with everything relating to Egypt, sent a trireme in pursuit of him. The eunuch who had the command of the vessel overtook and seized him in Lycia, but he made his guards intoxicated, and escaped to Cambyses. The Persian king was then deliberating how he should pass the Desert between Egypt and Palestine, and Phanes not only gave him information on this point, but laid open to him the whole state of Amasis' affairs. This Desert of sand extends from Kan Iones (Jenysus), about five or six hours' travelling to the south-west of Gaza, to Salahieh in Egypt. Along this distance of 107 geographical miles there is no trace of vegetation, nor any water fit for drinking; the first sixty miles, from Kan Iones to the commencement of the Casian Mount at the angle of the coast, are entirely destitute of water[1]. The sands of the Isthmus are loose and shifting[2], and the track was marked by tall poles. The Casian Mount, on which a temple of Jupiter stood, was only a ridge of sandy downs, somewhat higher than the adjacent coast[3]. The sea-coast anciently possessed by the Philistines as far south as Jenysus was at this time in the power of the Arabians, and from Jenysus to the confines of Egypt, of the Syrians of Palestine[4]. The Arabians were Idumeans, who had encroached upon the territory of the Jews[5], and extended themselves from Petra and the Ælanitic Gulf to the Mediterranean. The Syrians, according to the use of that name elsewhere by Herodotus, must have been Jews, some of those fugitives who, as we learn from various passages in the prophets, had settled themselves, at the time of the Captivity, along the frontiers of Egypt, from the neighbourhood of Heliopolis to the sea. The Syriac language was spoken there, even in the days of Jerome[6].

[1] Ἄνυδρὸν δεινῶς. (Her. 3, 5.)
[2] Nisi calami defixi regunt via non repéritur, subinde aura vestigia operiente. (Plin. N. H. 6, 33.)
[3] Strabo, 16, p. 760. Lucan, Phars. 8, 539.
[4] Ἀπὸ Φοινίκης μέχρι οὔρων τῶν Καδύτιος πόλιος, ἥ ἐστὶ Σύρων τῶν Παλαιστινῶν καλεομένων, ἀπὸ ταύτης τὰ ἐμπόρια τὰ ἐπὶ θαλάσσης μέχρι Ἰηνύσου πόλιός ἐστι τοῦ Ἀραβίου, ἀπὸ δὲ Ἰηνύσου, αὖτις Σύρων μέχρι Σερβωνίδος λίμνης. (Her. 3, 5.) By "the boundaries of the city Cadytis" Herodotus probably means Joppa, which was the port of Jerusalem. (Strabo, 16, 759.)
[5] Ezek. xxxvi. 5.
[6] Hieron. ad Is. 19, 18. "Os-

Phanes advised Cambyses to avail himself of the aid of the Idumæans for accomplishing his passage through the Desert. Without their friendship he could have obtained no adequate supply of water[1]: he had an auxiliary fleet of Asiatic Greeks, Ionians and Æolians whom his father had reduced; but the nature of the coast precludes the possibility that an army should be supplied by a fleet accompanying its progress. It is destitute of harbours, and the shore is bordered by shifting sands, which appear firm, but give way under the foot[2]. The Egyptian kings had made no provision for a supply of water in this Desert, whose sands were a better bulwark to their kingdom than any wall or trench[3]. Cambyses entered into a treaty for this purpose with the Idumæans. According to their usage, it was ratified by the representatives of the two contracting parties allowing a vein to be opened with a sharp stone in one of their hands, beside the middle finger. With a shred from the outer garment of each dipped in the blood, the person who officiated then anointed seven stones placed in the midst[4], and called on Dionysus and Urania by the names of Orotal and Alilat to sanction the pledge[5]. Dif-

tracinam et ceteras juxta Rhinocoluram et Casium civitates usque hodie in Ægypto lingua Canaanitide, hoc est Syra, loqui manifestum est." See p. 321 of this vol. note [1].

[1] Herod. 3, 88.

[2] From Strabo (16, 758) it seems as if there were a tide here as in the Syrtes, and several other bays of the Mediterranean, which increased the danger of passing, especially as they were of irregular occurrence. See in Diod. 20, 73 seq. the account of the expedition of Antigonus, and the danger to which his fleet was exposed.

[3] Rennell's Geogr. of Herodotus, 1, 339.

[4] Compare Gen. xxi. 28. "To swear" in Hebrew is literally "to seven" שׁבע. Traces of this practice of taking an oath before a stone were found at Athens. (Poll. Onom. viii. 9, 86.)

[5] Probably the Sun and Moon, who appear from Job xxxi. 26, 27, to have been worshiped in Idumæa, the country of the patriarch.

ferent accounts were given of the manner in which the necessary quantity of water was supplied. It was said that a river had been conveyed through leather hose into three reservoirs on different parts of the line of march. But no such river existed anywhere within reach, and it appears that a great number of camels were laden with water-skins, and driven by the Idumæans to those points in the Desert at which the army of Cambyses would halt. The Book of Job affords a proof that the Idumæans possessed very numerous herds of camels, which in this age were unknown, except as foreign animals, on the western side of the Isthmus of Suez[1]. The Persians immediately took measures to secure a regular passage, by laying down vessels of earthenware beside the track, which were filled with water[2] from the Nile.

Amasis died (525 B.C.) while Cambyses was preparing his expedition[3], and had been embalmed and consigned to the tomb which he had constructed for himself in the temple of Minerva at Sais. His son PSAMMENITUS assembled his Greek and Egyptian forces, and awaited the approach of the Persians in his camp near Pelusium. Before the armies engaged, the Ionians and Carians took a cruel revenge on Phanes, by whose treachery the enemy had been

---

[1] See Ritter, Asien, 13, 757.
[2] This practice the Nabathæan Arabs also used. (Diod. 19, 94.) They buried pots full of rain-water in the Desert, in places known only to themselves. See Rennell, *u. s.*
[3] A passage of Theopompus, preserved by Longinus, sect. 43, and describing the κατάβασις of some Persian king into Egypt, has been referred by Toup (*l. c.*) and Schweighaeuser (ad Athen. 2, 67) to the expedition of Cambyses. But the description evidently belongs to a much later period of the Persian Monarchy, nor is it easy to conceive how the reign of Cambyses should come within the scope of any work of Theopompus, who wrote a History of the latter part of the Peloponnesian war and the reign of Philip.

enabled to pass the Desert. His children, whom he had left behind him in Egypt, were brought out, one at a time, into the space between the camps in view of their father, their throats cut, and the blood, which was received into a goblet, mixed with wine and water, and drunk by the auxiliaries. "And so," says the historian, "they went to battle[1]."

The calamitous issue of the battle had been portended to the Egyptians by the fall of a shower of rain at Thebes[2]; it was obstinate, and attended with great slaughter on both sides, but ultimately the Persians triumphed, and the Egyptians fled in disorder to Memphis. The field remained strewed with skulls in the time of Herodotus, and those of the Egyptians could be distinguished from the Persians by their superior hardness (a fact confirmed by the mummies), the result, as he thought, of the practice of shaving the head from infancy. We read of no outrages or acts of cruelty committed by Cambyses on occasion of his victory; he sent a Mitylenean vessel, with a Persian herald on board, to Memphis to propose a pacification. The Egyptians, as soon as they saw it approaching, rushed down in a body, destroyed the ship, hacked the crew to pieces, and exposed their mutilated limbs on the wall. Cambyses immediately formed the siege of Memphis, which held out for a considerable time, but ultimately surrendered. Ten

---

[1] According to Polyænus (7, 9) Cambyses used a stratagem, placing in front of his line, dogs, sheep, cats, ibises and other animals held sacred by the Egyptians, and thus preventing them from using their missiles against the Persians as they approached.

[2] Her. 3, 10.

days after its capture, 2000 Egyptian youths were led out to be put to death, in reprisal for the 200 men of the Mitylenean vessel whom the people of Memphis had massacred. This was no sudden act of furious revenge on the part of Cambyses; the royal judges had decided that a tenfold retribution must take place. Darius without such provocation empaled 3000 of the most eminent Babylonians[1]. The law of reprisals is terrible in its operation, falling on the innocent instead of the guilty, or at best involving both; but it is the *ultima ratio* which upholds the law of nations, clearly violated by the Egyptians. Herodotus thus relates the scene which passed. I regret the necessity of giving his narrative in any other language than his own:—

"Ten days after Memphis had surrendered, Cambyses brought out Psammenitus, who had been six months king of Egypt, and seating him, exposed to public contumely, in the suburb, along with other Egyptians of the first rank, put his spirit to the proof in this way. Having dressed the daughter of Psammenitus in the garb of a slave, he sent her forth carrying a pitcher to fetch water, and with her the maiden daughters of the chief men, in a similar garb to that of the princess. The other parents, when their children came opposite to where they sat, lifted up their voices and wept at the sight of their afflicted condition; but Psammenitus, though he recognized his daughter, only bent his head towards the ground. When these were gone by, Cambyses made his son pass before him along with 2000 other Egyptians of the same age, gagged,

[1] Herod. 3, 159.

and with ropes round their necks, who were on their way to execution, in reprisal for the Mityleneans who had been put to death at Memphis. The other Egyptians who sat near him wept and lamented as before; but Psammenitus, though he saw them pass, and knew that his son was on his way to death, did as he had done when his daughter went by. But when they all had passed, there happened to come by an aged man, who had been one of his table-companions, now stripped of everything, and begging from the soldiers. On the sight of him Psammenitus burst into tears, and, calling on his friend's name, beat his head in grief. Men had been stationed to watch him, and report his behaviour to Cambyses, who, being astonished, sent a messenger to him with this inquiry,— 'Psammenitus, thy lord Cambyses asks thee why, when thou sawest thy daughter in affliction and thy son going forth to death, thou didst neither weep nor utter any exclamation, but hast shown respect to this beggar, who, as I hear, is no way allied to thee.' Thus Cambyses questioned, and thus Psammenitus replied:—'O son of Cyrus, the misfortunes of my own family were too great for weeping, but the sorrow of my companion deserved tears; on the threshhold of old age he has fallen from great prosperity into beggary.'" The history beautifully illustrates the difference between the misery that closes, and the sympathy that unlocks the source of tears, and the sequel shows that it was not lost on Cambyses. The Persians who were present wept; Crœsus, who had followed Cambyses from Lydia, wept; he himself (it is the

Egyptians who report) felt some touch of pity[1]; he commanded the son of Psammenitus to be spared, and his father to be brought from the suburb to his presence. The son had suffered before the messenger arrived; but Psammenitus was conducted to Cambyses, and for the present lived unmolested in his household.

From Memphis Cambyses went to Sais, and commanded the mummy of Amasis to be brought forth from its repository. It was subjected to various indignities, the hair was plucked off, the body pierced and beaten with stripes. But the process of embalmment had made it so firm, that all this produced little change in it, and Cambyses ordered it to be burnt. This was an act, according to Herodotus, equally abhorrent to the feelings both of Persians and Egyptians; for the Persians, who esteemed fire to be a god, would regard its employment for the consumption of a dead body as a pollution[2]. The Egyptians believed or pretended[3] that it was not really the corpse of their late king which underwent these indignities, but that Amasis, foreseeing the violation of his sepulchre, of which he had been warned by an oracle, had buried a corpse close to the entrance, and commanded his son to inter his own in an interior recess. Such outrages on the remains of the dead are justly reprobated as

---

[1] Her. 3, 14. Ὡς δὲ λέγεται ὑπ' Αἰγυπτίων....αὐτῷ Καμβύσῃ ἐσελθεῖν οἶκτόν τινα.

[2] Ctesias (Pers. § 57. Bähr.) appears to deny this burning of the body of Amasis, but only on the ground that it was not accordant with Persian usage. He does not indeed mention Amasis (the extract in Photius is obscure), but he charges Herodotus with falsehood, and there is no other part of the history to which he can refer.

[3] Αἱ μέν νυν ἐκ τοῦ Ἀμάσιος ἐντολαὶ αὗται οὔ μοι δοκέουσιν ἀρχὴν γενέσθαι, ἄλλως δ' αὐτὰ Αἰγύπτιοι σεμνοῦν. (Her. 3, 16.)

effusions of impotent rage, but they have been too often imitated among Christian nations.

As Egypt was subdued, and apparently incapable of resistance, Cambyses planned three expeditions for the extension and security of his conquests. The people of Libya bordering on Egypt surrendered without a battle, submitted to become tributaries, and sent presents with which Cambyses was satisfied. The people of Cyrene and its colony, Barca[1], did the same; but he either despised their gifts or doubted their sincerity, and flung the 500 minæ of silver which they had sent him in handfuls to his soldiery. He allowed, however, Ladice, the widow of Amasis, to return unmolested to Cyrene, her native city. The Carthaginians were the only other power in Northern Africa from whom Cambyses had anything to fear. They were at this time in the height of their prosperity, predominant over the colonies which they had planted among the Libyan tribes, without a rival in naval power in the western part of the Mediterranean[2], and enriched by an extensive traffic both maritime and inland. They could be reached, however, only by sea, and Persia had no fleet of her own, depending on her Greek subjects and her Cyprian and Phœnician allies[3]; and Carthage being a colony of Tyre, the Phœnicians professed to regard it as an impiety to attack their own children. Cambyses did not think it expedient to attempt to force them, and the rest

---

[1] Her. 4, 160. It had been founded about thirty years before. The remains of walls and sepulchres at *Merge*, about eight miles from Cyrene, which were first discovered by Della Cella, appear to mark its site. (Ritter, Erdk. 1, 942.)
[2] They had defeated the Phocæans in a great naval battle B.C. 536.
[3] Her. 3, 19.

of his fleet not being able alone to cope with the Carthaginians, they escaped being reduced into slavery to Persia.

Nothing has contributed more to procure for Cambyses the character of a frantic madman than his expedition to Ethiopia. Had it been really undertaken against a people living, as Herodotus supposed, where Africa is washed by the southern sea[1] and in revenge for an insulting message, he would have deserved this character. But we must distinguish between the Ethiopia of Egyptian history and the Ethiopia of Greek mythology. The former is better known in this age than in the age of Herodotus. Its seat was in Upper Nubia, Dongola and Meroe, and though we have heard of no invasion of the Egyptian territories by the Ethiopians since the accession of the Saitic dynasty, we have no ground to believe that their power was so decayed as to be no longer formidable to Egypt, especially to Egypt when become a province of Persia, and filled with a discontented population. Sound reasons of policy might therefore induce Cambyses to undertake an expedition against it. The narrative of Herodotus is altogether romantic. Even in the time of Homer the Greek fancy was excited by tales respecting the Ethiopians. They were a blameless race, extending from the rising to the setting sun, devoted to the worship of the gods, and honoured by their special presence. If Homer had any distinct conception of their geographical position, he probably placed them immediately above Egypt, whence he believed them to spread in indefinite ex-

---

[1] Her. 3, 114.

tension to the east and west, wherever there was a rumour of sun-blackened men. But in the age of Herodotus the countries which bordered upon Egypt, though rarely visited by Greeks, were too well known to be the scene of prodigies; the course of the Nile to Meroe was explored and measured; it was believed that the limits of geographical knowledge had been carried forward a thousand miles above Meroe by the settlement of the Automoli. Yet fiction would not for this loose its hold of the Ethiopians; to Herodotus as to Homer they were still "the remotest of men, dwelling on the shores of the ocean[1];" but the ocean was now the southern boundary of Africa, a real sea, though misconceived by Herodotus in regard to its position and direction. The barbarism of the tribes who dwelt to the south of Meroe, and their consequent freedom from the vices of civilization, afforded an opportunity for making them the heirs of that peculiar favour of the gods which their mythic predecessors had enjoyed; they surpass all men in beauty, strength and longevity, and instead of living by laborious culture of the soil, a table covered with flesh was said to be renewed every night by the bounty of their chief god, the Sun.

The first step which Cambyses took in the execution of his enterprise was to send an exploring party into Ethiopia. Where the Ethiopia lay which he was intending to invade, is evident from his choice of spies. Psammitichus, as we have mentioned, had trained a body of the Ichthyophagi, the inhabitants of the eastern coast of the Red Sea, southward of

[1] Il. ψ′, 205; α′, 423. Od. α′, 22.

Berenice, to assist him in seeking the fountains of the Nile, and a chief requisite for this purpose would be a knowledge of the language of the Ethiopians, who occupied the banks of the Nile for more than a thousand miles of its course. They appear to have been permanently established at Elephantine, the frontier town of the two nations and languages, where their services as interpreters would be equally valuable to the Egyptians and Ethiopians[1]. The subsequent proceedings are thus related by Herodotus:—

"When the Ichthyophagi appeared before the king of the Ethiopians, bringing the gifts which Cambyses had entrusted to them (a purple garment, a twisted golden collar and bracelets, an alabaster vase of perfume and a jar of palm wine), they thus spoke: 'Cambyses, king of the Persians, wishing to be on a footing of friendship and hospitality with thee, has sent us to confer with thee, and offers thee as gifts these things, in using which he himself most delights.' The king of Ethiopia, knowing that they had come as spies, replied to them thus: 'The king of Persia has not sent you with these gifts because he values my friendship, but ye are come to spy out my kingdom: nor is he a just man; for if he had been, he would not have desired any other country than his own, nor have reduced to slavery men who had done him no injury whatever. Give him then this bow, and say these words to him,— The king of the Ethiopians advises the king of the Persians not to invade the long-lived Ethiopians

---

[1] Her. 3, 19. The expression of Herodotus, 2, 29, Strabo, 17, p. 818, is ambiguous, but it is probable he meant Elephantine by ἡ νῆσος.

till the Persians can draw with ease such large bows as this, and then to come with superior forces. Till that time, let him thank the gods that they do not put it into the hearts of the Ethiopians to add to their own territory.' Then unstringing his bow he gave it to the messengers of Cambyses. Next, taking up the purple garment, he asked what it was, and how it was made. The Ichthyophagi having told him all about purple and dyeing, he said they were deceitful men and their garments deceitful. Then he inquired about the golden collar and bracelets, and when the Ichthyophagi explained the ornaments, he laughed and said that they had stronger fetters than these, thinking they were meant for fetters. In the third place he inquired about the perfume; and when they told him how it was made and how it was used, he said the same thing as about the purple garment. But when he came to the wine and heard how it was made, being excessively delighted with the draught he inquired on what the king lived, and what was the longest life that a Persian attained. They told him, on bread, explaining the nature of wheat, and that 80 years was the longest term of life that awaited man. ' No wonder, then,' said the Ethiopian, ' if those who live on dirt have such short lives; they would not even have lived so long if they had not kept themselves up with this liquor; in this one thing the Persians have the advantage of us.' The Ichthyophagi in their turn questioned the king about the life and diet of his people, and he said that the majority of them lived to 120 years and some even more; that their food was boiled flesh, and their drink was milk. When they expressed their wonder that the Ethiopians lived so long, he led them to a fountain, which made those who bathed in it sleek as if it had been oil, and had a fragrance like violets, and so light that neither wood nor bodies lighter than wood would swim in it; they all sunk to the bottom. Next they were taken to the prison, where all the prisoners had fetters of gold, and to the table of the Sun."

The view which a barbarian takes of the arts of civilized life always affords a lively contrast, and the opportunity of covert satire on artificial manners. Such is evidently the purpose with which this scene has been described. The king of the Ethiopians treats the dyed garment as a fraud, the perfumed ointment as a corruption of the simplicity of nature[1], and takes the royal ornaments for the collar and fetters of a culprit. In one thing only does he admit the superiority of the Persian—the art of producing wine, everywhere the most irresistible attraction to the savage. There is a certain adaptation in the story to what was known or believed respecting the interior of Africa, but it can only be received as a happy fiction. The Ichthyophagi vanish and re-appear, like theatrical messengers, without any note of time, Cambyses remaining as it should seem at Memphis, while they go to "the ends of the earth" and return[2]. The sole fact on

[1] The rustic served the same purpose of contrast to Virgil, as the king of Ethiopia to Herodotus, or the author of the tale:—

Si non.... varios inhiant pulchra testudine postes
Alba neque Assyrio fucatur lana veneno,
Nec casia liquidi conrumpitur usus olivi;
At secura quies, cæt.—Georg. 2, 461.

[2] In its disregard of time and distance this story resembles that of the expedition of Darius to the Wolga, Her. 4. (See Mr. Grote's remarks, Hist. of Greece, 4, 356.)

which we can rely is, that Cambyses sent an exploring party before he set out on his march against Ethiopia, a wise precaution, not indicative of that frenzy which the Egyptians imputed to all his actions.

When they returned, provoked, as Herodotus says, at the message of the king, he set out for Ethiopia. The Greeks were left behind at Memphis, and we are consequently deprived of the benefit of their evidence, as to the real events of the expedition. Taking with him the whole of his land forces, he proceeded from Memphis to Thebes. Hence it is said he detached 50,000 men[1] with orders to reduce the Ammonians, and burn the temple of Jupiter; with the remainder he pursued his march towards Ethiopia. He had made no provision of magazines of corn, and before he had accomplished a fifth part of the way, the victuals which the soldiers carried with them failed. They then devoured the beasts of burthen, but even this did not induce Cambyses to renounce his project; he still pressed on. The soldiers supported themselves on herbs, as long as the ground furnished them with any supply; but when they came into the sand, such was the extremity of their suffering, that they cast lots among ten, and he on whom the lot fell was devoured by the rest. Then Cambyses repented, and led back his army to Thebes, abandoning his enterprise against Ethiopia.

It would not be easy, from the brief description of Herodotus, to decide the direction of Cambyses'

---

[1] This number far exceeds what would be necessary for the purpose of occupying the oases nor is it credible that Cambyses should have withdrawn all his native troops at once from Egypt

march beyond the frontiers of Egypt. Nature, however, has marked out the lines of communication between it and the country which he was endeavouring to reach, and they remain the same in all ages. He might have followed the Nile upwards from Syene, through Nubia and Dongola, to Gebel-el-Birkel, and so further to Meroe; but this would have occupied many months, and would not have involved him in that Desert of sand which ultimately compelled him to return. He might have struck at once from Syene into the Desert, to proceed by the track which the caravans from Sennaar now often take, and which Bruce and Burckhardt followed; but this would be inconsistent with the account of Herodotus, who represents the soldiers as supporting themselves on the scanty vegetation which they found, before they entered the sand. The third track is that which is most commonly pursued by caravans and travellers at the present day. From Syene they ascend the river to Korosko (Derr), about half way between the First and Second Cataract. Here an *Akaba* or mountain pass opens into the valley of the Nile, leading through the Desert, by a route of about 250 miles, to Abou Hammed, near the island Mogreb, where it rejoins the river just at the beginning of its great bend to the south-west[1]. The first part of the march, for about sixty miles, lies through a valley bordered by sandstone hills not wholly destitute of vegetation, since Hoskins was informed that the Bishareen Arabs come hither in the season to pasture their flocks[2]. Beyond

[1] See vol. i p. 26.
[2] Russegger, Reisen, 2nd B. P. 1, p. 423. Hoskins, p. 23.

this valley lies a plain of desert sand, called *Atmoor-bela-ma*, the sea without water, extending to the south for fifty miles, on the west to the Second Cataract, and on the east nearly to the Red Sea[1]. The desert is seen here in all its horrors, which have been in some measure relieved by a variety in the scenery while passing through the rocky valley. The want of water is aggravated by the illusion which presents everywhere lakes and pools to the traveller suffering the extremity of thirst. The wind, sweeping over the unsheltered plain, raises pillars of sand, which choke the breathing-passages, while the heat of the blast relaxes his strength and augments his distress. Even the obstinacy of Cambyses was compelled to yield to the sufferings of his followers and their dreadful effects; could he have struggled through the sand, there was still considerably more than 100 miles to be accomplished through a region of barren rock, before he could have reached the Nile at Abou Hammed. This desert, however, is not impassable for an army[2], if proper precautions be taken. In the reign of Augustus[3] the Ethiopians under Candace had advanced as far as Elephantine, the Roman garrison being weakened by the withdrawal of part of the troops under Ælius Gallus to attack the Arabians. Petronius, with about 10,000 infantry and 800 horse, first of all drove them from Elephantine into the fortress of Pselcis (Dakke), between Syene and Korosko, and then, as the remains of the

---

[1] See Russegger's Karte von Nubien.
[2] That it was commonly traversed in ancient times is evident from what Mr. Hoskins says, that hieroglyphics are found near some of the wells (p. 24).
[3] Strabo, 17, p. 822.

army had fled into the Desert, "passing through the tract of sand[1] where the army of Cambyses was overwhelmed, a violent wind falling upon them[2], came to Premnis, a strong place which he took, and then advanced against Napata." The Premnis here spoken of must be the *Primis Magna* of Ptolemy[3]. He places it *beyond* Napata, and just above Meroe, in his enumeration of towns on the eastern or right bank of the Nile. It must therefore have been somewhere near the termination of the pass of Korosko at Abou Hammed. Petronius was deterred from proceeding further south by the heat and the sand[4], and could not remain where he was with his whole army. He refortified Premnis, garrisoned it with 400 men, victualled it for two years, and returned to Alexandria. In his absence Candace attacked Premnis, but Petronius was in time to relieve the garrison, and compelled the queen to send an embassy to Caesar. In this age the Desert had been long known and often travelled by those who passed between Egypt and Meroe, but to Cambyses and his army its difficulties were unknown, and it is not wonderful that he should have been baffled in his attempt to cross it. The name of Magazine of Cambyses[5], which Ptolemy places

---

[1]. Θίνες was the appropriate name for these sandy regions. Clearchus (Athen. 8, 345) wrote a treatise, Περὶ Θινῶν, De Locis Arenosis.

[2] Strabo has confounded the expedition against Ethiopia with that against Ammonium, but it is evident he believed the army of Cambyses to have been in the sandy desert.

[3] Ptol. Geogr. 4, 7, p. 302, ed. Wilberg. Πρίμις Μεγάλη ξβ (62°) ιϛ (17°) Ἐντεῦθεν δὲ νησοποιεῖται ἡ Μερόη χώρα.

[4] Dion Cass. lib. 54, p. 734, Reiz. He calls Napata, Τανάπη.

[5] Καμβύσου Ταμεῖα, Ptolemy, 4, 7. It was on the *left* bank of the river. Ταμιεῖον was not merely a treasury, but a storehouse or magazine. (Pollux, 9, 5.) According to the account of Pliny, Petronius returned to Napata, on his second expedition, by the valley of the

in lat. 18°, shows that while the main army attempted the passage of the Desert, another part advanced by the valley of the Nile into Upper Nubia; and this country remained tributary to Persia[1].

His expedition against Ammonium has been attributed to the same uncalculating frenzy as that against Ethiopia, inflamed by the fanatical wish to destroy the celebrated temple of Ammon. At this time, however, Cambyses had committed no outrages against the Egyptian religion, and had his object been only to occupy Ammonium and destroy its temple, it might have been reached with much greater ease from Lower Egypt. It was evidently his design to take possession of all these Oases, which might serve as retreats and mustering-places for the discontented Egyptians, and nests for robbers who might interrupt commerce. This was a wise policy for the new sovereign of Egypt, and the Great Oasis was accordingly occupied under Darius his successor. The fate of the 50,000 men said to have marched against it was never distinctly known. They reached in safety the Great Oasis, which is nearly in the same latitude as Thebes, and about 120 miles distant from it; it was inhabited by Samians of the Æschrionian phyle, who had probably found their way to it from the north, as Ammonium

Nile, through Nubia and Dongola, for he enumerates the places which he took, in this order: Pselcis, Primis (Ibrim), Aboccis (Aboosimbel), Pthuris (Farras), *Cambusis*, Atteva, Stadisis, "ubi Nilus præcipitans se, fragore auditum accolis aufert." (6, 29.) This must be the Third Cataract, to which Pliny has transferred the popular account of the First.

[1] Her. 3, 97; 7, 69. Josephus, Ant. 2, 10, represents Cambyses as conquering the capital of Ethiopia and changing its name from Saba to Meroe. Diodorus (1, 34) speaks of Cambyses as occupying Ethiopia, meaning probably only Nubia.

appears to have had also a Greek population[1]. Their route after leaving it would lie through the Oasis of El Farafreh in lat. 27°, nearly opposite Siout in Egypt, and thence through the Oasis of El Bacharieh, or the Little Oasis, in lat. 28° 20'. But it was only known that they never reached Ammonium, and never returned. The Ammonians said that they had arrived about half way[2] between the Great Oasis and their own, and while sitting down to take their meal were overwhelmed by a sudden and violent wind which buried them under heaps of sand. No well-attested instance is known of a traveller being deprived of life by the fall of the moving pillars of sand in the Desert, much less of whole armies and caravans being buried by them[3]. Nor is there any necessity to have recourse to this supposition to explain the loss of Cambyses' army. They may have been misled by their guides; they may have found the wells dry or choked with sand, at which they expected to renew their supply of water; the wind may have obliterated the track by which they had advanced, and baffled their attempt to return. In all these cases they must perish miserably, and the traveller who saw their shrivelled bodies or their skeletons, covered with the drifted sand, would naturally suppose that its fall had buried them alive[4]. The expedition of Cyrus against

---

[1] Her. 2, 32. Vol. i: p. 72.
[2] Μεταξύ κου μάλιστα αὐτῶν τε καὶ τῆς Ὀάσιος· (Her. 3, 26.)
[3] Compare the accounts of Bruce (6, 458) with those of Burckhardt. (Nubia, 1, 207.)
[4] Ἄνεμος νότος ἐπὰν πνεύσῃ ἐν ἐκείνῳ τῷ χώρῳ, τῆς ψάμμου ἐπιφορεῖ ἐπὶ μέγα, καὶ ἀφανίζεται τὰ σημεῖα, οὐδὲ ἔστιν εἰδέναι ἵνα χρὴ πορεύεσθαι, καθάπερ ἐν πελάγει, τῇ ψάμμῳ· ὅτι σημεῖα οὐκ ἔστι κατὰ τὴν ὁδὸν, οὔτέ που ὄρος, οὔτε δένδρον, οὔτε γήλοφοι βέβαιοι ἀνεστηκότες, οἷς τισιν οἱ ὁδῖται τεκμαίροιντο ἂν τὴν πορείαν, καθάπερ οἱ ναῦται τοῖς ἄστροις. (Arrian, 3, 3, of the march of Alexander to Ammonium.)

the Massagetæ was rash; so was that of Darius against the Scythians; but the Desert expeditions of Cambyses were far more rash, because, like Napoleon in Russia, he committed himself to a strife with the powers of nature.

We are not informed when it was that Psammenitus endeavoured to raise an insurrection in Egypt, but it was probably during the absence of Cambyses on his Ethiopian expedition, when the country seems to have been left with few troops, except the Grecian, Phœnician and Cyprian mercenaries. It is therefore not wonderful that he treated Egypt on his return with much greater severity than before. Psammenitus, who might have retained the viceroyalty of Egypt, as Herodotus assures us, had he known how to remain quiet[1], was compelled to put himself to death by drinking bull's blood. Thebes first felt his vengeance, and here he began those outrages upon the religion of Egypt which made his name odious to the priesthood. Probably they had sympathized with the attempt of Psammenitus, and had ill concealed their joy at the disasters of Cambyses. The temples were not only stripped of their wealth in gold, silver[2] and ivory, which was carried to Persia, but burnt; and no doubt ruins which were the work of time and earthquakes, and the neglect which is the lot of a deserted capital, were attributed to this arch-enemy of their country and religion. The rage of Cambyses against the priesthood was inflamed by hatred and contempt for their rites and dogmas. The Persians were not monotheists, in the sense in which the Hebrews

[1] Her. 3, 15, [2] Diod. 1, 46.

were so; they worshiped the elements, earth, air, water, and before all fire; the whole circle of heaven was their supreme god; but they viewed with abhorrence the confinement of the deity within the walls of a temple and his representation under a human form. They offered sacrifices, but without altar, or fire, or libation, or sprinkling of sacred meal, or music[1]. These differences were quite sufficient to awaken the spirit of intolerance, which is naturally the strongest, when the most opposite opinions come into collision; when the monotheist is opposed to the polytheist, the iconoclast to the idolater[2]. In such conflicts a fanatical persecution is the first result; interest subsequently dictates toleration, if the parties have need of each other's services.

A circumstance occurred which called forth in all its bitterness the contempt of the Persian for Egyptian superstition. When Cambyses arrived at Memphis he found the people feasting and in holiday attire, and suspecting that it was a rejoicing for his own defeat, he summoned the magistrates of Memphis to his presence and asked them why these festivities were going on now, though he had seen nothing of the kind when he was in Memphis before. They replied that a god had appeared among them as he was wont to do, but at considerable intervals of time. He regarded their answer as a falsehood, and commanded them to be put to death. Next he sent for the priests, and as they gave him the same account, he said he would know whether a

---

[1] Herod. 1, 131.
[2] Cic. de Legg. 2, 10. Magis auctoribus Xerxes inflammasse templa Graeciae dicitur quod parictibus includerent deos quibus omnia deberent esse patentia ac libera, quorumque hic mundus omnis templum esset et domus.

god had really made his appearance among the Egyptians in the shape of a domesticated beast[1], and ordered Apis to be brought in. When he saw a young steer fantastically marked, he drew his short sword and aimed a blow at the belly of Apis, but struck him on the thigh. "O stupid mortals," he exclaimed, "are these your gods? creatures of flesh and blood, and sensible to the touch of steel! But ye shall not with impunity make me your laughing-stock." He then commanded the priests to be scourged, and every Egyptian to be put to death who should be found engaged in festivity. Apis died of his wound, and was buried by the priests without the knowledge of Cambyses. He had not before been of sound mind, and, as the Egyptians said, became quite mad from the moment of this impious deed. Heliopolis, the seat of the worship of the bull Mnevis, suffered equally with Memphis from his fanaticism: both here and at Thebes the obelisks bore marks of the fires in which the temples had been consumed[2]. Various other acts are recorded of him, indicative not so much of intolerance or cruelty, as of that heedlessness or insolence which in the gratification of curiosity overlooks the wound inflicted on the feelings of others. He went into the temple of Ptah and made great sport of the deformed and pygmy image of the god; he also entered the temple of the Cabiri, the reputed sons of Ptah, and burnt their wooden images. He opened many of the ancient tombs and inspected the mummies. "I am quite convinced," says He-

---

[1] Εἰ θεός τις χειροήθης ἀπιγμένος εἴη Αἰγυπτίοισι. (Her. 2, 28.)

[2] Strabo, 17, p. 805.

rodotus after relating these things, "that Cambyses was very mad; he would not else have treated temples and established usages with ridicule. For if one were to propose to all men to select from all the usages in the world those which they deemed the best, they would each, after deliberate comparison, fix on their own. None therefore but a madman would treat these things with ridicule. And that this is the judgement of all men respecting their own usages I infer from many other proofs, and from this instance more especially. Darius once called the Greeks who were near him to his presence, and asked them for what consideration they would devour their dead parents; and they answered, for none that could be named. After this Darius called the Callatian Indians, who are accustomed to eat their dead parents, and asked them by an interpreter in the presence of the Greeks, for what consideration they would agree to burn their parents' corpses; and they with a loud outcry begged him not to shock their ears with such horrid words. Well has Pindar written, that Usage is lord of all." Had Herodotus, who here expresses the feeling of his own humane and reverent mind, been acquainted with the history of persecution, he would hardly have concluded Cambyses to be mad, because he treated with contempt the religious convictions and practices of others.

The acts of cruelty which Cambyses subsequently committed, his putting to death his brother Smerdis and his wife[1], who was also his sister,—his murder

---

[1] We may observe that the cruelty of his behaviour towards his wife is aggravated into brutality in the Egyptian version of the story. (Her. 3, 32.)

of the son of Prexaspes and execution of twelve Persians—belong rather to Persian than Egyptian history. We might conclude from them that he was really frantic, were there not so many parallel instances of cruelty in the acts of oriental sovereigns, and even of the successors of Cambyses himself. When Oiobazus supplicated that one of his three sons might remain with him, the wise and humane Darius promised that, as he was his friend and his request was moderate, they should all be left, and ordered them immediately to be put to death[1]. In answer to a similar request, Xerxes commanded the eldest son of his host, Pythius the Lydian, to be cut in half[2], that the army might march between the portions of his body. If the lust and cruelty of Henry VIII. appear less brutal than those of Cambyses, it is only because Christian civilization and the forms of a constitutional government imposed a certain restraint on the English sovereign. Cambyses, no doubt, was subject to epilepsy, which may have weakened his power of self-control; but to the last he showed no want of vigour or sagacity. Diodorus has rightly described him by saying, "that he had by nature a touch of insanity and mental aberration, but that the greatness of his power had much more to do in making him cruel and insolent[3]."

Cambyses had spent between three and four years

[1] Her. 4, 84.
[2] Her. 7, 37.
[3] Καμβύσης ἦν μὲν φύσει μανικὸς καὶ παρακεκινηκὼς τοῖς λογισμοῖς· πολὺ δὲ μᾶλλον αὐτὸν ὠμὸν καὶ ὑπερήφανον ἐποίει τὸ τῆς βασιλείας μέγεθος. (Diod. Excerpt. p. 248.) Herodotus seems to doubt whether the misdeeds of Cambyses were the consequence of his outrage on Apis or of natural influences—εἴτε διὰ τὸν Ἆπιν, εἴτε καὶ ἄλλως, οἷα πολλὰ ἔωθεε ἀνθρώπους κακὰ καταλαμβάνειν (3, 33).

in Egypt, when he was recalled to Persia by the usurpation of the two Magi, one of whom pretended to be Smerdis, the brother of Cambyses, whom he had murdered by the hands of Prexaspes. He had already reached a town in Syria, which Herodotus calls Ecbatana, when he met the messenger who was on his way to Egypt, to call on the army to renounce their allegiance to him. Leaping hastily on his horse to proceed to Persia, he shook off the knob which closed the lower end of the sheath in which he wore his short sword, and the point protruding wounded him dangerously in the thigh, precisely where he had wounded the god Apis. The bone became carious, and he died in Ecbatana, according to an Egyptian oracle, which he had interpreted to mean that he should end his days, an old man, in the ancient capital of Media, where all his treasures were laid up. Such is the account of Herodotus, which was no doubt derived from the Egyptian priests, and is suspicious from its exhibiting a striking proof of the vengeance of their god and the infallibility of their oracle. Ctesias says, he died at Babylon of a wound in the thigh which he gave himself while planing wood for his amusement[1]. He had reigned over Egypt six years; no memo-

---

[1] I have not hitherto noticed Ctesias' account of the conquest of Egypt by Cambyses. According to him, Amyrtæus was king of Egypt at the time of the invasion. Combaphes, his chief eunuch, was induced by the promise of the satrapy to betray his master, and Amyrtæus being taken prisoner, was transferred to Susa, with six thousand Egyptians selected by himself. This is inconsistent with the Egyptian monuments, with Manetho and Herodotus. The only circumstance in regard to which I think Ctesias' account the more authentic is the death of Cambyses, which the Egyptians had an obvious motive to misrepresent, and which would be better known at Babylon than in Egypt.

rial of him has been found on a temple or palace of Egypt, where he only destroyed; but his shield, bearing date in his sixth year, is seen with those of Darius and Xerxes, on the road to Cosseir near the Red Sea[1], mixed with some of the most ancient of the Pharaohs. It was natural that his memory should be the object of unmitigated hatred and abhorrence to the Egyptians; even the Persians, who had called Cyrus their father, gave Cambyses the title of Lord, in token of his severe and haughty temper[2], yet with an acknowledgement of the vigour with which he governed his dominions.

The conquests of Cyrus and Cambyses had been rapidly made, and not consolidated by any systematic administration. In the arts of government the Medes and Persians were as much inferior to the Egyptians, as they were superior to them in military force, and they had much to learn in civilization from their new subjects. The first care of DARIUS (520 B.C.) was to unite the heterogeneous members of the empire by a uniform system of government, which should secure the prompt and effectual execution of the commands of the central power, and at the same time to exchange the method of irregular and indefinite contribution (called *gifts*) which had prevailed under Cyrus and Cambyses[3] for a fixed system of imposts. The scale of taxation for each province was fixed by the satrap; Darius

---

[1] Burton, Excerpta Hierogl. pl. viii. The land of *Pars* is distinctly mentioned in the inscription. Rosellini (M. Stor. 2, 169) mentions a statue on which the name of Cambyses is found, but only as a date.

[2] Her. 3, 89. Δαρεῖος μὲν ἦν κάπηλος· Καμβύσης δὲ δεσπότης· Κῦρος δὲ πατήρ.

[3] Her. 3, 89. Ἐπὶ Κύρου ἄρχοντος, καὶ αὖτις Καμβύσεω, ἦν κατεστηκὸς οὐδὲν φόρου πέρι ἀλλὰ δῶρα ἀγίνεον.

gained popularity for himself by making a considerable reduction upon the amount[1]. He divided his dominions into twenty provinces, each ruled by a viceroy called a satrap, who commanded the military forces, administered the affairs of the province, and collected the tribute which was systematically levied throughout the empire. The satrapy of Egypt, besides the country usually so called, included the coast of Libya as far as the Euesperidæ, a little westward of Cyrene, and the oases of the Libyan Desert. The country between the Nile and the Red Sea must also have been included in it, as the names of Persian sovereigns are found on the road to Cosseir. Ethiopia above Egypt, which had been subdued by Cambyses, paid no regular tribute, and was not included in the satrapy; but once in three years it brought a voluntary offering, consisting of two *chœnixes* (three pints) of gold dust, two hundred blocks of ebony, twenty tusks of ivory, and five youths[2]. The tribute paid by the satrapy of Egypt was seven hundred talents in money, independently of the produce of the fisheries of the Lake Mœris, which amounted to a talent a day during the six months that the water flowed in from the Nile, and a third part of that sum during the efflux[3]. Egypt had also to furnish 120,000 medimni of corn as rations for the Persian troops and their auxiliaries,

---

[1] Polyæn. 7, 11, 3.
[2] Her. 3, 97.
[3] Her. 2, 149. According to Diodorus (1, 52) the revenue of the Lake, which he reckons at a talent a day, without distinction of seasons, was assigned by Mœris to his queen for the expenses of her toilette (πρὸς μύρα καὶ τὸν ἄλλον καλλωπισμόν). This custom appears to have been Persian (Her. 2, 98), not Egyptian, and Herodotus describes the revenue of the Lake, as paid into the royal treasury (τὸ βασιλήϊον).

who were stationed in the White Fort of Memphis[1]. Except in the payment of this tribute (about 170,000*l*. sterling), which cannot be considered as oppressive to a country so productive as Egypt, no change appears to have been made in the administration. The nomarchs levied the tribute and handed it over to the satrap[2]. But Egypt could not reap the full benefit of the wisdom and humanity of Darius under the government of a satrap, whose character was more important to the country which be ruled than that of the distant sovereign: we know by modern examples, that the tribute rendered to a sultan may be far less onerous than the exactions of a pasha.

When Cambyses was recalled to Persia by the usurpation of the false Smerdis, he left Aryandes in command of Egypt, and Darius continued him in his post. Little is related of his government except his expedition into Libya. The jealousy which the Greeks of Asia and Europe felt of the Persian power naturally extended to the people of Cyrene and Barca, and they suspected their own reigning family of a design to perpetuate their dominion by allying themselves with Persia. The changes introduced by Demonax[3] into the constitution had been borne with impatience by the kings, whose prerogatives were transferred to the people; Arcesilaus III. had attempted to repossess himself of

---

[1] Herodotus (7, 187) reckons a military ration at a chœnix a day. The medimnus contained forty-eight chœnixes (Böckh, Haushaltung der Athener, 1, 99), consequently each man consumed annually about seven and a half medimni, and the garrison consisted of about 17,000 men. The allowance of a chœnix, however, is mentioned by Herodotus as a *minimum*.
[2] Arrian, Hist. 3, 5, 6.
[3] Her. 4, 161. Τῷ βασιλεῖ Βάττῳ τεμένεα ἐξελὼν καὶ ἱρωσύνας, τὰ ἄλλα πάντα, τὰ πρότερον εἶχον οἱ βασιλέες, ἐς μέσον τῷ δήμῳ ἔθηκε.

the ancient prerogatives and domains, and being worsted in the struggle, had fled to Samos. Here he collected a force, by means of which he re-established himself at Cyrene, and having treated his enemies with great rigour, and burnt alive many of them who had taken refuge in a tower, he was induced by the fear of vengeance and the recollection of an oracle to withdraw to Barca, where his father-in-law governed. At Barca he was killed by the inhabitants and some of the exiles from Cyrene. His mother Pheretime, who had fled to Cyprus when her son fled to Samos, had returned, and administered the government of Cyrene till his assassination. On that event she betook herself to Egypt, and represented to Aryandes that her son had incurred the hostility of his subjects by his submitting to pay tribute to Cambyses, and had been put to death because he leaned to Persia[1]. Aryandes thought he saw a favourable opportunity for reducing all the Libyans into a real dependence on Persia[2]; but he first sent a herald to Barca, to demand the persons who had killed Arcesilaus. The Barcæans adopted it as the act of all, and justified it by the tyranny of which he had been guilty. On this Aryandes sent all the disposable troops of Egypt with a fleet[3], under the command of Amasis and Badres, against Barca. They besieged it in vain for nine months, and ultimately obtained pos-

[1] Her. 4, 165. Προϊσχομένη πρόφασιν ὡς διὰ τὸν Μηδισμὸν ὁ παῖς οἱ τέθνηκε.
[2] Her. 4, 167. Dahlmann (Herodot, aus seinem Buche sein Leben, 2, p. 164) doubts this project of Aryandes.
[3] To separate the civil administration from the military power in the satrapies appears to have been a subsequent refinement of Persian policy. See Heeren, Ideen, 1, 1, 524, Germ.

session of it by stratagem and perjury. The generals were divided in opinion whether they should also attack Cyrene, but Aryandes recalled them, and they returned to Egypt, the land forces having been much harassed by the Libyans on their march. We know not how long Aryandes continued in his office of satrap. Darius had introduced a gold coinage, the Daric, a thing unknown before in Asia, and Aryandes, in imitation of his master, a silver coinage in Egypt. Considering how much inconvenience Egypt must have suffered from the want of this instrument of exchange, there seems no sufficient reason for imputing to Aryandes a desire to usurp the functions of sovereignty. But the actions of a satrap are watched with morbid jealousy by his superior, and Aryandes had probably raised discontent among the Egyptians by some disrespect to the national religion, so that they were on the point of revolting[1]. Darius, passing through the Arabian Desert, came in person to Egypt, which he had not visited since he had attended Cambyses as one of his body-guards[2], put Aryandes to death, and conciliated the Egyptians by the offer of a reward for the discovery of an Apis, whose place was at that time vacant. We do not know the exact year of this visit, but that it was subsequent to the Scythian expedition of Darius, which took place 508 B.C., we learn from an anecdote preserved both by Herodotus and Diodorus[3]. He wished to erect a statue of himself at Memphis, in front of the temple of Ptah, and *before* that of Rameses-Sesos-

---

[1] Polyæn. 7, 11, 7.
[2] Her. 3, 139.
[3] Her. 2, 110. Diod. 1, 58.

tris. The high-priest remonstrated, and ventured to observe, that he had not equalled the exploits of Sesostris; for that he had not been able, like him, to subdue the Scythians. Darius was so far from resenting this allusion to his unsuccessful expedition, that he was pleased with the priest's freedom of speech, and in reference to the long reign of Sesostris replied, that if he lived as long he hoped to accomplish as much. The Egyptians reckoned him after Menes, Sasyches, Sesostris, Bocchoris and Amasis, the sixth of their great legislators. We may therefore conclude, notwithstanding the silence of history, that he made regulations for Egypt which secured its religion from the outrages to which it had been exposed from the fanaticism of Cambyses and Aryandes, and protected the people from oppression. "Hating," says Diodorus, "the lawless violence of Cambyses against the Egyptian temples, he pursued a humane and pious course of life. He associated familiarly with the Egyptian priests, who imparted to him a knowledge of their theology and the history contained in their sacred books. Learning from these the magnanimity of their ancient kings and their mildness towards their subjects, he imitated their course of life, and was so much honoured by them, that he alone of the kings[1] during his lifetime was called a god by the Egyptians, and after his death received the same honours as the ancient kings who had reigned most equitably." The monuments confirm these accounts. He is

[1] Diod. 1, 95. He means of course the Persian kings, who are here opposed to the τὸ παλαιὸν νομιμώτατα βασιλεύσασι κατ' Αἴγυπτον. Comp. 1, 90. Δοκοῦσιν Αἰγύπτιοι τοὺς ἑαυτῶν βασιλεῖς προσκυνεῖν τε καὶ τιμᾷν, ὡς πρὸς ἀλήθειαν ὄντας θεούς.

the only Persian king whose name is accompanied with a titular shield, and whose phonetic shield bears the crest of the vulpanser and disk, "son of the Sun." It is remarkable, however, that neither his name nor that of any of the Persian monarchs, is found on a public monument within the limits of Egypt. On an ornament of porcelain preserved in the museum of Florence, he is called "beneficent god[1]," and this adoption of his name on an article of familiar use is perhaps the strongest proof of the affection which the Egyptians bore to his person. He even appears to have carried his conformity so far as to offer worship to their gods. At least he is represented in a sculpture with a sacerdotal ornament on his head, with a lighted lamp in each hand (the emblem of fire, the great divinity of Persia) before a shrine, in which stand Athor, and Osiris in the form of a mummy[2].

It was probably on occasion of this visit of Darius that the Persians obtained possession of the Great Oasis and the Oasis of Siwah, the temples in both bearing his inscriptions. He resumed the excavation of the canal between the Nile and the Red Sea, which Sesostris attempted and Neco partially executed. Its length, from near Bubastis to the Gulf of Suez, was four days' navigation. It should seem, however, that even Darius did not actually open a communication between the end of

---

[1] Rosellini, Mon. Stor. 2, p. 170. Wilkinson, M. and C. 1, 199. The same title is given to Xerxes in an inscription on the Cosseir road. (Burton, Exc. Hierog. pl. 14.)

[2] Champollion Figeac, L'Univers, pl. 87. The evidence which such a monument supplies of an actual offering of worship by Darius, is weakened by our finding a similar representation of Tiberius. See the same work, pl. 91.

the canal and the Red Sea, though he left a very narrow space between them[1]. He is said to have been deterred from cutting through this space, by the discovery that the level of the Red Sea was higher than that of Egypt[2]. The Macedonian rulers of Egypt appear to have been the first who made the communication perfect, and placed a lock at the entrance from the sea. The through-navigation would be practicable only during a few weeks of the year, when the Nile is highest.

The road from Coptos to Cosseir, judging from the inscriptions bearing the names of Persian sovereigns, must have been much frequented in these times, and was probably the principal channel of the trade with Arabia and the shores of the Persian Gulf. The increase of commercial intercourse with strangers is indicated by the number of contracts in the demotic character which bear date in the reign of Darius[3]. This character appears to have been invented for such uses, and no specimens of it are found older than Psammitichus[4].

The relations of Egypt with Greece probably remained friendly during the early part of the reign of Darius; the resort of Greeks thither for commercial purposes and the pursuit of knowledge continued. A change would take place after the revolt, as it is called, of the Ionian cities from the

---

[1] A monument with cuneiform characters was found by the French near the Bitter Lakes. See Rozière, Descr. de l'Egypte Antiq. Mém. 1, p. 265. It contains part of the name of Darius. (Lepsius, Einl. 1, 354, note.)

[2] Strabo, 17, p. 804, says, δόξῃ ψευδεῖ πεισθείς. See p. 401 of this vol.

[3] Champollion Figeac, L'Univers, p. 379.

[4] Rosellini, M. S. 2, 172, 174. Lepsins, Lettre à M. Rosellini, p. 19.

THE TWENTY-SEVENTH DYNASTY. 481

Persian power, and the burning of Sardis in 499 B.C.[1] The Egyptians formed a part of the fleet which Persia employed for the reduction of Miletus[2]. From that time, Greeks, at least Ionian Greeks, the principal travellers whether for profit or improvement, would be excluded from the dependencies of Persia, and Egypt would not be open to them again, until she regained a temporary independence under Inaros and Amyrtæus.

When Darius quitted Egypt, which he had probably visited in the interval between his return to Susa after his Scythian expedition[3] and the commencement of his wars with the Ionians, he appointed Amasis satrap of Egypt. He may have been the same who had led the Persian fleet against Barca; the evidence of his having held the office is, that a shield with this name and the word *Melek* inscribed over it, has been found on the Cosseir road[4]. The title is neither Coptic nor Persian, but Semitic; that it was familiar, however, to the Egyptians is evident from its occurrence in the list of the nations conquered by Sheshonk[5]. Amasis, the father of Psammenitus, cannot be meant, as we have his shields with the full Pharaonic titles. Another shield, preceded by the word *Melek*, has been found at the same place, and the characters which it contains have been read, "Nephra son of Amasis." It bears date the 30th year of Darius (B.C. 489), and therefore Nephra seems to have succeeded Amasis in the satrapy. The defeat of

---

[1] Fnes Clinton, Fast Hellen. sub anno.
[2] Her. 6, 6.
[3] Her. 5, 11. 25.
[4] Rosellini's Exc. Hierog. pl. 3, 4.
[5] See p. 350 of this vol.

Darius' troops at Marathon in the year 490, offered to the Egyptians a prospect of recovering their liberty, and while all Asia resounded with the preparations which he made for three years to invade Greece, and efface the dishonour of his arms[1], Egypt revolted (B.C. 486). He died (B.C. 485) just when his preparations for attacking Egypt and Athens were complete, and left the execution of his enterprises to his son XERXES. The latest record of Darius' reign is a contract in the demotic character, dated in the month Phamenoth of his 35th year. An inscription in the Cosseir road mentions his 36th year, but this was engraved under the reign of Xerxes, who having recovered possession of Egypt, considered his predecessor's reign as uninterrupted, notwithstanding the revolt at its close[2]. Herodotus and the lists agree in assigning 36 years as the length of Darius' reign.

We know not by whom the revolt of the Egyptians was headed, or what form of government was established during the brief interval of its independence. The entire history of this event, which was almost lost to the Greek historians in the magnitude of the impending struggle between Persia and Greece, is contained in a few words of Herodotus. Xerxes was disinclined from a Grecian war, but Mardonius exhorted him first to tame the insolence of the revolted Egyptians, and then to lead his army against Athens. The advice was sound as regarded the order of his operations. To have attacked Greece, before Egypt was reduced, would have deprived him

[1] Herod. 7, 1. 4.
[2] Rosellini, M. Stor. 2, 174. Burton, Exc. Hierog. 14, 3.

of the most valuable part of his naval force except the Phœnicians: it might have added an Egyptian fleet to the navy of the Greeks. In the year after the death of Darius, therefore, he made an expedition against Egypt, and having subdued it apparently with little difficulty (B.C. 484), reduced it to a condition of much more severe dependence than it had experienced under Darius[1], and appointed his brother Achæmenes satrap, who governed it for twenty-four years, till he lost his life in the revolt of Inaros, B.C. 460.

In the invasion of Greece, on which Xerxes entered after four years of additional preparation, by marching from Sardis in the spring of the year 480 B.C., the Egyptians bore a very important part. They furnished 200 ships. The Calasirians and Hermotybians (for the old names were still kept up) served on board of them as *epibatæ* or marines, and were armed specially for this service with boarding-spears and large hatchets[2]. They assisted in the construction of the bridge of boats by which the Persian army crossed the Hellespont, furnishing the ropes of papyrus as the Phœnicians did those of flax, and conveyed corn to the places at which magazines were to be established for the supply of the army[3]. In the battle of Artemisium they distinguished themselves above the whole fleet, and captured five Greek vessels with their crews[4]. None of them were enrolled in the land-army of Xerxes, but when the fleet lay at Phalerum, Mardonius disembarked the fighting portion of the crews, and

[1] Her. 7, 7.
[2] Her. 7, 89.
[3] Her. 7, 34. 25.
[4] Her. 8, 17.

they served as swordsmen in the battle of Platea[1]. The internal history of Egypt is an entire blank from this time to the death of Xerxes, no doubt because all access to that country was forbidden to the Greeks. The name of Achæmenes is not found on any Egyptian monument, but that of Xerxes occurs on the Cosseir road with the date of his seventh year[2]. Early in the history of hieroglyphical discovery, Champollion read the name of Xerxes in Egyptian and cuneiform characters on an alabaster vase in the royal library at Paris, confirming his own discoveries and those of Grotefend.

Xerxes was assassinated by ARTABANUS in the year B.C. 465, and after an interval of a few months[3] was succeeded by ARTAXERXES LONGIMANUS, the second of his sons, in 464 B.C. The commencement of his reign appeared to offer a favourable opportunity of revolt to the Egyptians[4]. The Persian power had been greatly weakened by the result of Xerxes' invasion of Greece. Not only had his immense fleet and army been destroyed, but the Greeks, following up their victory, had driven the Persians from the Thracian Chersonesus, from Byzantium, from the coasts of Asia Minor, and from Cyprus; and Xerxes in the latter part of his reign had abandoned himself to luxury and the baneful intrigues and jealousies of his court and harem. The first care of Artaxerxes was to punish the murderers of his father and brother, and substitute satraps friendly to his interests in those governments from

[1] Her. 9, 32.
[2] Burton, Exc. Hierog. pl. 14.
[3] Eusebius, Chron. p. 31, ed. Scaliger, makes Artabanus to have reigned seven months after his assassination of Xerxes and his eldest son Darius.
[4] Diod. 11, 71.

which he apprehended hostility¹. Artapanus, satrap of Bactria, made an obstinate resistance, and was only subdued after two pitched battles². The Egyptians thus obtained time for maturing their revolt. Inaros, the son of Psammitichus, probably a descendant of the Saitic princes, had made himself king of the Libyans who bordered on Egypt, and advanced with an army from Marea, the frontier town near the later site of Alexandria³. He was joined by nearly the whole population of Egypt, and all the Persian revenue officers were driven out. Inaros raised a body of native troops and enlisted mercenaries, but as it was evident that he would have to contend with the whole force of Persia, as soon as order was established at home, he was naturally led to seek an alliance with Athens. At this time an Athenian fleet of 200 triremes was engaged in operations against Cyprus. To them Inaros would naturally make his first proposals, but it is not probable that they would act upon them without authority from Athens. According to Diodorus, he promised, besides many other advantages, to share with them the sovereignty of Egypt⁴. Such prospects were irresistible to the Athenian people, in whom success had already opened boundless hopes of dominion; they could hardly plead self-defence, for with the possession of Cyprus they were secure against any molestation by Persia. Forty triremes⁵ were accordingly detached from

---

¹ Diod. 11, 71.
² Ctes. Pers. c. 31, ed. Baehr.
³ Thuc. 1, 104.
⁴ Diod. 11, 71.
⁵ Ctes. Pers. c. 32. Diod. 11, 74, says 200. The construction of Thucydides, 1, 104, Οἱ δὲ ἔτυχον γὰρ ἐς Κύπρον στρατευόμενοι ναυσὶ διακοσίαις ἦλθον, is ambiguous.

the fleet off Cyprus. Artaxerxes in the meantime had been collecting a fleet and army from all the satrapies of his empire, and was about to take the command in person, but on the advice of his friends gave it up to Achæmenes, who appears to have fled from Egypt to Persia after the first victory of Inaros[1]. Achæmenes, after a short interval employed in recruiting his army, advanced against Inaros, who had retired to the western side of Egypt to collect his forces from Libya and avail himself of the aid of the Athenians; and here at Papremis[2] a great battle was fought, in which Inaros slew Achæmenes with his own hand, and the Persians were defeated chiefly by the valour of the Athenians. The Persians fled to Memphis; the Athenians sailed up the river in pursuit of them, and having possessed themselves of two out of the three regions of the city, besieged the Persians and the Egyptians who adhered to them in the citadel called the White Fortress. Artaxerxes first endeavoured to oblige the Athenians to recall their fleet from Egypt by sending Megabazus with gold to Sparta, to induce the Peloponnesians to make an irruption into Attica. His money was expended in vain; Athens had just placed herself in security by the completion of the Long Walls[3], and had shown how formidable was her naval power by sailing round the Peloponnesus and burning the naval arsenal of the Lacedæmonians. On the return of Megabazus, Artaxerxes

---

[1] Diodorus, 11, 74, says that the Achæmenes who commanded the expedition was the son of Darius. Ctesias calls him Achæmenides, brother of Artaxerxes.

[2] See Mannert, Geogr. x. 1, p. 591, for the position of Papremis in the western part of the Delta. (Diod. 11, 74.)

[3] Thuc. 1, 108, 109.

collected another armament[1], of which he gave the command to Megabyzus the son of Zopyrus. The fleet was equipped in Cilicia, and being joined by the army which had marched from Persia, proceeded by the coasts of Syria and Phœnicia to Egypt. The Athenians and Egyptians were still blockading the White Citadel, which during more than a year they had been unable to reduce[2]. The news of the arrival of the Persians caused them to raise the siege and retire into Lower Egypt[3]. They established themselves in the island Prosopitis, formed by a canal from the Canopic branch of the Nile, by commanding the navigation of which they kept open their communication with the sea[4]. After the experience which they had had of Grecian valour, the Persians abstained from battles in the field[5]; availing themselves of the dry season, they succeeded at the end of fifteen months in diverting the water from the channel in which the Athenian fleet lay, and the ships being thus useless, the Egyptians were alarmed and made conditions for themselves. The Athenians burnt their triremes, and were preparing for a desperate defence: as they were still 6000 in number, the Persian commanders did not desire to drive them to extremities, and agreed to allow them to retire from Egypt. Through Libya they reached Cyrene, but only a small remnant returned in safety to Athens[6]. Inaros, and some of

[1] Diodorus says, of 300,000 men. This is a standing number with him. (11, 74, 75.)
[2] Diod. 11, 75.
[3] Ctesias speaks of an engagement in which Inaros was wounded and some of the Greeks killed (c.33), and Thucydides agrees with him.
[4] Champollion, Égypte sous les Pharaons, 2, 162. Ctesias calls the place to which Inaros fled Byblos, a name otherwise unknown to Egyptian topography.
[5] Diod. 11, 77.
[6] Thuc. 1, 110.

the Greeks, were carried to Susa; their lives were at first spared, according to the capitulation; but Amytis, the mother of Achæmenes, who had been killed by Inaros, succeeded, after five years, in persuading the king to give up Inaros to her, and he was crucified. Thannyris, the son of Inaros, succeeded him in his government of Libya[1]; Sarsames was made satrap of Egypt. A further misfortune befell the Athenians; fifty triremes, destined to reinforce the armament, touched at the Mendesian mouth, in ignorance of what had happened. They were attacked by the Phœnician fleet and the Egyptian land-forces[2], and nearly all destroyed. These transactions occupied a space of six years, from 462 to 456 B.C., but the chronology of each is not easily fixed.

The Persians thus obtained possession of the greater part of Egypt; but the marsh-lands near the mouths of the Nile, being extensive, difficult of access, and inhabited by a warlike population, were not subdued[3]. There was in this district an island called Elbo, in which Anysis many years before had taken refuge during the invasion of the Ethiopians[4]. Here Amyrtæus, descended from the Saitic dynasty, established himself and maintained his independence. The Athenians, during a temporary remission of their war with the states of Peloponnesus, after the peace of Five Years (B.C. 450), turned their attention again to Cyprus and Egypt[5], and sent sixty ships to the latter country on the invitation of Amyrtæus. In Cyprus they were victorious[6], but

[1] Herod. 3, 15. Ctes. c. 35.
[2] Thucyd. 1, 110.
[3] Thucyd. 1, 110.
[4] Herod. 2, 140.
[5] Thucyd. 1, 112. Plut. Cim. 18.
[6] Plut. Cim. 18.

the death of Cimon (B.C. 449) put an end to the expedition, and the ships that had sailed to Egypt returned at the same time to Athens without having accomplished anything. Amyrtæus made submission to the Persians, and his son Pausiris was allowed to succeed to his father's power[1]. No monuments remain of any of these rulers.

Of the condition of Egypt under the re-established rule of Persia, we obtain some incidental account from Herodotus. The intercourse of the Greeks with the interior of that country had necessarily been suspended, during the insurrection of Inaros and Amyrtæus; it was renewed after the Athenian fleet had withdrawn, and peace virtually, if not formally, been established between Greece and Persia. Artaxerxes resumed the mild and tolerant policy of Darius. Herodotus describes the state of things which he saw in Egypt, subsequently to the battle of Papremis[2], and probably to the suppression of the revolt in 456 B.C. The country appears to have been in profound peace, for Herodotus proceeded from the sea to the limits of Ethiopia without molestation. A traveller might even pass these limits and ascend the Nile as far as Meroe. Democritus, who was a little younger than Herodotus, and spent five years in Egypt, wrote a treatise on the sacred characters of Meroe[3]. The frontier towns and Memphis[4] were occupied by

---

[1] Herod. 3, 15.
[2] 3, 12.
[3] Diog. Laert. 9, 49. Fynes Clinton, F.H. sub an. 460 B.C. Herod. 2, 29. Eusebius (Chron. p. 53, ed. Scalig.) has a singular statement respecting Democritus and a Jewess learned in mysteries named Maria, which Scaliger (p. 419) thinks an interpolation of the monk Panodorus. See p. 91 of this vol. Jablonsk., Panth. Æg. Prol. cxliv.
[4] Her. 2, 30. 99.

Persian troops; but the worship at the temples, the celebration of the panegyries, went on as usual; Greeks were found in all the principal towns, engaged in commerce and unmolested by the Egyptians, notwithstanding the strong repulsion which manners and religion placed between them[1].

Yet on the first opportunity which the state of Persia appeared to offer for throwing off the yoke, the Egyptians were eager to avail themselves of it. No other nation which formed a part of the Persian empire was so loosely connected with the general body as Egypt. It was in contact with it at a single point only, and even there difficult of access. No other nation could boast of so long an antecedent independence as Egypt; the power of the Assyrians and Babylonians was of recent origin, compared with the monarchy of the Pharaohs. Religion, however, was the strongest obstacle to union between the Egyptians and their masters. Though persecution had ceased, the priests of the national religion had lost the ascendency which they had once enjoyed. They might possess their revenues without disturbance or diminution, and worship their native gods without hindrance; but they no longer chose their sovereign, enrolled him in their order, regulated his public policy, and controlled his daily actions. The tolerance which the Persians practised left the priests in possession of all their ancient power over the minds of the common people, whom it would be easy for them to stir up to rebellion, when a favourable occasion offered itself. During the reign of Artaxerxes, who governed with

[1] Herod. 2, 41.

great vigour for forty years, they remained quiet. The domestic quarrels of the Greeks, who were engaged in the latter part of it in the Peloponnesian War, prevented their giving aid to Egypt, which without it could have no hope of success in a revolt from Persia.

On the death of Artaxerxes, B.C. 425, the usual disputes respecting the succession distracted the monarchy. His legitimate successor, XERXES II., was immediately murdered by his brother SOGDIANUS, and he in turn by Ochus, who possessed himself of the throne under the name of DARIUS, and is distinguished by the addition of Nothus (illegitimate), B.C. 424. He was not allowed to retain it without a struggle. His brother Arsites raised a revolt, and was only subdued by the help of Greek mercenaries in the service of Persia. The satrap of Egypt, Arxanes[1], had declared himself for Ochus, when he rebelled against Sogdianus; but this was merely a declaration of the Persian forces in favour of one sovereign and against another, in which the Egyptians had no interest. When, however, a truce for fifty years had been made between the Peloponnesians, Lacedæmonians and Athenians, B.C. 421, the hope of Athenian aid, which was now the hinge of Egyptian policy in its relations with Persia, would naturally revive, and a revolt speedily followed[2]. It began in the second year of Darius Nothus; but was either suppressed or was very limited in its extent, till the tenth year of the same sovereign's reign, B.C. 414. In the interval the short truce

---

[1] Ctes. Pers. c. 47, ed. Baehr. ἀπέστη Περσῶν δευτέρῳ ἔτει Νόθου
[2] Syncell. p. 256 D. Αἴγυπτος Δαρείου.

between the contending powers in Greece had been broken, and the Athenians had engaged in the expedition to Sicily which in the following year produced such disastrous results. Egypt therefore had to struggle unaided for her independence. Once more we chronicle the events of Egyptian history by the years of a native dynasty.

Twenty-eighth Dynasty.

	Years.
AMYRTÆUS the Saite, reigned	6

It has been supposed that this Amyrtæus is the same person who established himself in the marshy regions of the Delta[1], nearly forty years before, and had there maintained an independent sovereignty, till this new revolt called him forth to place himself at the head of his countrymen. Nothing favours this supposition, except the identity of the name, and it involves serious chronological difficulties. Probably the Amyrtæus who constitutes the twenty-eighth dynasty was the grandson of him who fled into the marshes, and the son of that Pausiris to whom, according to Herodotus, the Persians conceded the sovereignty which his father had exercised. The attachment of the Egyptians to the ancient line of the Saitic kings sufficiently explains their placing Amyrtæus at the head of their re-established monarchy. History is entirely silent respecting the events by which they regained their independence. Their success might be aided by the revolt of the Persian satraps of Lydia and

[1] See p. 488 of this vol.

Caria, Pisuthnes and his son Amorges, whom the Athenians assisted by a body of mercenary troops under Lycon[1]. That they maintained friendly relations with Athens, which was then engaged in hostility with Persia, is evident from the mention of corn-ships sailing from Egypt to Athens, which the Peloponnesians planned to intercept at the Triopian Promontory[2]. To protect themselves from invasion by land on the part of the Persians, the Egyptians entered into an alliance with the Arabians, without whose concurrence an army could not enter from Palestine. They also endeavoured, in conjunction with the Arabians, to obtain possession of Phœnicia, the great source of the naval power of Persia; but Pharnabazus suddenly appeared on the Phœnician coast with three hundred triremes and frustrated this design[3].

In this dearth of historical information the monuments give us valuable aid, by showing that Amyrtæus was sovereign of the whole kingdom of Egypt and its dependencies, and that Manetho was justified in assigning him that rank. In the temple of Chons at Karnak is an inscription, expressing that it had been repaired by him,—the first record of any such work, since Thebes was destroyed by Cambyses[4]. The temple of Eilithya, dedicated to Sevek, bears a record of a similar restoration by

---

[1] Ctes. Pers. 52. Thuc. 8, 5.
[2] Thuc. 8, 35, with Poppo's note.
[3] Diod. 13, 46. From Thuc. 8, 109 (τὰς διαβολὰς περὶ τῶν Φοινισσῶν νεῶν), it should seem as if Diodorus had confounded Pharnabazus with Tissaphernes. See Ley, Fata Egypti sub imperio Persarum, p. 55.
[4] Rosellini, Mon. Stor. 2, 201. There is some obscurity in the characters, but Egyptologists are generally agreed that the shield belongs to Amyrtæus. (Champollion-Figeac, L'Univers, p. 383.)

the same sovereign. The shield at Karnak appears also to express that he had been the conqueror of the "land of Heb," or the Great Oasis; and his name has been found on the temple in the Oasis of El Khargeh, in a position which shows that it was introduced subsequently to that of Darius[1]. At his death his body was placed in a magnificent sareophagus of green breccia. This was one of the trophies of the British expedition to Egypt, having been taken by the French from the mosch which had formerly been the basilica of St. Athanasius. Dr. E. D. Clarke supposed it to have been the sarcophagus of Alexander the Great; but it bears the shield of Amyrtæus[2], and by its size and beauty of execution, proves that art had declined but little since the days of Psammitichus. Amyrtæus reigned only six years, and the Saite dynasty expired with him (B.C. 408); an additional proof that he is not the Amyrtæus of Herodotus, who was succeeded by his son Pausiris.

Twenty-ninth Dynasty. Four Mendesian kings.

	Years.	
1. NEPHERITES, reigned	6	
2. ACHORIS	13	
3. PSAMMUTHIS	1	
4. NEPHERITES	0	4 months.
	20	4 months.

[Eusebius in Syncellus adds a fifth, Muthis, reigning one year. In the Armenian, Muthis is placed before Nepherites.]

It may appear singular that no attempt should

[1] Wilkinson, Mod. Egypt and Thebes, 2, 367.
[2] Rosellini, Mon. Stor. 2, 205; an engraving of it is given in the great French work on Egypt, Ant. vol. 5, pl. 40.

have been made by Persia to recover its dominion over Egypt, especially at the extinction of the Saitic dynasty, and that a new family should have been allowed quietly to possess itself of the throne. Just at this time, however, the Persian power was shaken by a revolt of the Medes[1], who had endeavoured in the time of Cambyses to regain their lost ascendency in what was called the conspiracy of the Magi, and had never been reconciled to the monopoly of the great offices of government which the Persians had assumed. How long the revolt lasted, and whether it was put down easily or not, we are not informed, our whole knowledge of the event being derived from a short passage in Xenophon; but while it lasted it must have precluded all thoughts of attempting the reduction of Egypt. Darius Nothus died soon after, B.C. 405, and was succeeded by Artaxerxes Mnemon. The ambition of his brother Cyrus led to the expedition of the Ten Thousand Greeks, which he was preparing from the time of their father's death[2], till the year B.C. 401. Cyrus having perished in the battle of Cunaxa, the first care of Artaxerxes was to recover his authority in Asia Minor, which had been the government of Cyrus and had joined in his revolt. He was thus brought into hostility with Sparta; Clearchus, the Lacedæmonian, had been the leader of the Greek mercenaries of Cyrus; the oppressed cities of Ionia called for protection on Sparta, which, by the issue of the Peloponnesian War, had been placed in the

---

[1] Xen. Hell. 1, 2, ad fin. Καὶ ὁ ἐνιαυτὸς ἔληγεν οὗτος, ἐν ᾧ καὶ Μῆδοι, ἀπὸ Δαρείου, τοῦ Περσῶν βασιλέως, ἀποστάντες πάλιν προσεχώρησαν αὐτῷ. This was B.C. 409.

[2] Xen. Anab. 1, 1.

hegemonia of Greece and was protectress of its liberties. When she prepared, in obedience to this call, to invade Asia, she made an alliance with Nephreus, king of Egypt, the Nofreopth of the monuments[1], and NEPHERITES of the lists, and he sent a hundred triremes and large supplies of corn[2]. The ships which conveyed it entering the port of Rhodes, which was in possession of Conon, who commanded the Persian fleet, were all taken. The success of Dercyllidas and Agesilaus (399–394 B.C.) fully occupied the Persian arms in Asia Minor for several years, and it was not till the power of Athens revived, and a league was formed in Greece against Sparta by the influence of Persian gold, that Artaxerxes could attend to the re-establishment of his authority in other parts of his dominions. The peace of Antalcidas, concluded B.C. 387, freed him from all further apprehension on the side of Greece, by sacrificing the liberty of the Asiatic cities, and leaving the principal states of the mother-country nearly balanced in power, and each prepared to resist the ascendency of another.

His first attack, for which he had been collecting forces during several years, was made on Cyprus. If held by a hostile naval power, it not only gave the command of the southern coast of Asia Minor, of Syria and Phœnicia, but even of Egypt. Evagoras of Salamis had availed himself of the weakness of Persia, to make himself master of

---

[1] Rosellini, Mon. Stor. 2, 209. His name is not found on any building in Egypt, but on a statue in the Museum of Bologna.

[2] Diod. 14, 79. Justin calls the king of Egypt *Hercynio* (6, 2). Achoris?

nearly the whole island¹. In the war which re-
sulted, Evagoras was powerfully aided by the Egyptians. Nepherites was dead. We know nothing
more of the events of his reign than his alliance
with Sparta, unless he is the Psammitichus of
whom Diodorus relates a disgraceful transaction².
After the death of Cyrus, the satraps of Asia Minor, who had favoured his cause, were alarmed
for their own safety, and Tamos, the satrap of Ionia,
had put his children and property on board ship,
and taken refuge in Egypt with Psammitichus, who
basely seized the fleet and the property, and put
Tamos and his children to death, notwithstanding
the ancient relations of friendship between them.
The chronology of this period is uncertain, and we
cannot tell whether the infamy of the act belongs
to Amyrtæus or Nepherites³.

When Evagoras sought the succour of the Egyptians, ACHORIS was on the throne. Artaxerxes had
been long preparing his attack, and had collected a
fleet of 300 triremes with a corresponding land-
force, while Evagoras had endeavoured to protect
himself by forming an alliance with Egypt, Arabia,
Tyre and Caria⁴. Achoris, besides furnishing him
with supplies of corn, sent him fifty triremes, which
were engaged in the unsuccessful naval battle fought
by Evagoras with the Persians off Citium, in the year

[1] Isocr. Evag. ed. Battie, 2, p. 101.
[2] Diod. 14, 35.
[3] Diodorus calls Psammitichus a descendant of the ancient king of that name, which suits best with Amyrtæus, who was a Saite. As the flight of Tamos took place soon after the death of Cyrus (B.C. 401), it is probable that it fell within the life of Amyrtæus, but that Diodorus has confounded him with Psammuthis.
[4] Diod. 15, 2. Βαρβάρων is an unquestionable corruption for Ἀρά-βων. Isocrates u. s. says he had taken Tyre by assault.

385 B.C. After this defeat he visited Egypt, to arrange with Achoris the means of carrying on the war. Achoris encouraged him to persevere, and entered into a league against Persia with the people of Barca[1]; but the pecuniary assistance which he gave him was less than Evagoras had expected, and he ultimately made peace with Artaxerxes on condition that he should pay an annual tribute to Persia, but retain the rank of a dependent king[2]; and thus the Cyprian war ended, after eight years spent in preparation and two in actual hostility[3]. Egypt, however, found an unexpected ally. Gaos, the son of Tamos, commanded the Persian fleet, and dreaded the displeasure of Artaxerxes, by whom his father-in-law Teribazus had been imprisoned. Availing himself of his popularity with the fleet, he induced the commanders of the triremes to revolt, and entered into a treaty with Achoris. Sparta joined the league. She had brought ignominy on herself by sacrificing the Asiatic Greeks to Persia in the peace of Antalcidas, and was desirous of recovering her ascendency and her reputation by a new war[4]. The death of Gaos by treachery, in the year 383[5], prevented any hostile operations against Persia. Tachos succeeded to him, and fortified himself on the coast of Asia Minor, between Smyrna and Phocæa, but dying soon after, the league fell to pieces. Sparta, by a change of policy, began

---

[1] Theopompus ap. Phot. clxxvi., who seems to make the Cyprian war end under Nectanebus.
[2] Diod. 15, 9. Ὑπακούειν ὡς βασιλεὺς βασιλεῖ προστάττοντι.
[3] Isocr. Evag. p. 102, ed. Battie.
Isocrates places this peace six years after the naval defeat. See the chronology discussed by Mr. Pynes Clinton, F. H. vol. 2, p. 278.
[4] Diod. 15, 9.
[5] Diod. 15, 18.

THE TWENTY-NINTH DYNASTY.

to court the aid of Persia, in order to make herself sovereign of Greece[1], and seized the citadel of Thebes 381 B.C. During these events, Egypt was unmolested by the Persians, but towards the close of the reign of Achoris, very formidable preparations were made by Pharnabazus for its invasion. To repel them Achoris collected a large body of Greek mercenaries, twelve or twenty thousand; and as he had no general capable of commanding them, he invited Chabrias the Athenian. Chabrias undertook the command, if Diodorus be correct, without the approbation of the people, and was recalled on the remonstrances of the satrap, who regarded it as a violation of the peace existing between Persia and Egypt[2]. He appears, however, to have remained long enough in Egypt to assist Nectanebus in establishing his power, on the extinction of the Saitic dynasty[3], and rapidly trained the Egyptians into accomplished seamen[4].

Memorials of Achoris are found in several places, as at Medinet-Aboo on a restoration of a building erected by Thothmes IV., and probably destroyed by Cambyses, and among the ruins of Karnak. The quarries of Mokattam also contain his shield; and there is a sphinx in the Museum of Paris, on the base of which his name is found hieroglyphically written, with the addition, " beloved of Kneph[5]."

[1] Diod. 15, 19.
[2] Diod. 15, 29. Corn. Nep. Chabrias, 3.
[3] Corn. Nep. Chabrias, 2. "Chabrias multa in Europa bella administravit quum dux Atheniensium esset; in Ægypto sua sponte gessit. Nam Nectanabin adjutum profectus regnum ei constituit."
[4] Polyænus, 3, 2, 7.
[5] Rosellini, Mon. Stor. 2, p. 213. Champollion-Figeac, L'Univers, p. 384.

Of the short reign of Psammuthis there is no record in history, but his shield has been found at Karnak[1]; NEPHERITES is equally unknown in history and in the monuments. The Muthis of Eusebius appears to have originated from a repetition of the last syllable of Psammuthis, whom he follows in the Armenian, reigning like Psammuthis one year.

Thirtieth Dynasty. Three Sebennytic kings.

	Years.	
1. NECTANEBES, reigned	18	10 (Euseb.)
2. TEOS	2	2
3. NECTANEBUS	18	8
	38	20

The accession of NECTANEBES, or Nectanebus, the first king of the Sebennytic dynasty, falls probably in the year B.C. 380. He was immediately called upon to defend his kingdom against the invasion which Pharnabazus was preparing when Achoris died. The Athenians had not only recalled Chabrias, in obedience to the demands of Persia, but had sent Iphicrates, to lead the Greek mercenaries in the Persian service[2]. The movements of the satrap were slow, for all his measures were subject to the control of the king, and awaited his sanction for their execution. At length, however, the fleet and army mustered at Acre, the nearest harbour on the Syrian coast where such a fleet could lie[3]. The land-forces consisted of 200,000 barbarians and 20,000

---

[1] Rosellini, Mon. Stor. 2, p. 214.
[2] Corn. Nep. Iphicrates, 2.
[3] Πτολεμαΐς, ἣν "Ακην ὠνόμαζον πρότερον· ᾗ ἐχρῶντο ὁρμητηρίῳ πρὸς τὴν Αἴγυπτον οἱ Πέρσαι. (Strabo, 16, 758.) It was while the armament was mustering here that the defection of Datames from the Persians took place. (Corn. Nep. Dat. 5.)

Greeks[1]; the fleet of 300 triremes, 200 triacontors (galleys of thirty oars each), and a great number of corn-ships. They began their march at the opening of summer, B.C. 373, the fleet accompanying the army. Nectanebes had improved the time which the long delay of Pharnabazus had given him. Every navigable branch of the Nile was fortified by two towers, joined by a boom which prevented the entrance of a fleet. Pelusium, the key of Egypt, had been strengthened with peculiar care; the roads had been laid under water, the navigable channels made dry by embankments, and every weak point protected by fortifications. Pharnabazus and Iphicrates found that they had no chance of capturing Pelusium, and sailed away to the Mendesian mouth. Landing here with 3000 men, they attacked the fort by which the entrance was protected; the garrison, of about equal numbers, marched out to give them battle, and being defeated, the Persians entered the fort along with the flying Egyptians. Dissensions arose between the generals, which prevented any results of this first success. Iphicrates, who had heard from the prisoners that the troops had all been withdrawn from Memphis, would have sailed thither before they could return. Pharnabazus thought this too hazardous, and wished to wait till the whole Persian army came up. Iphicrates then proposed to undertake the adventure with his own mercenary troops alone. This also Pharnabazus refused, fearing, it is said, that Iphicrates designed to conquer

[1] I give these numbers on the authority of Diodorus; they seem exaggerated.

Egypt for himself, but as is more likely, because he did not choose, on his own responsibility, to attempt a movement, which could be justified only by an improbable success. Meanwhile the Egyptians rallied their forces, garrisoned Memphis, and attacked the fortress at the mouth of the Mendesian branch, which the Persians had seized. They had the advantage in all the encounters which took place; as the summer advanced the waters of the Nile began to rise, and their efflux being retarded by the strength of the Etesian winds, the whole country was covered with the inundation. The Athenian and Persian generals had committed the same error, which led to the destruction of St. Louis and his army, in 1249, and which Bonaparte avoided in his campaign of 1798[1], and were compelled to return into Syria. Their discomfiture produced a quarrel between Pharnabazus and Iphicrates, who fearing the fate of Conon, soon after secretly embarked for Athens. Pharnabazus sent an embassy thither, and accused him to the people of being the cause of the ill-success of the Egyptian expedition; they replied, that if they found him guilty they would punish him; and soon after gave him the command of their whole fleet[2]. We find him in

[1] " Les Chrétiens étaient entrés dans Damietta, le 7 Juin ; c'est l'époque des plus basses eaux ; le Nil ne commence à croître que quinze jours plus tard, au solstice d'été ; et il s'élève lentement jusqu'à l'équinoxe, où l'on coupe ses digues. Un grand maître dans l'art de la guerre, comparant son expédition à celle de Saint Louis, nous fait sentir tout le prix du temps perdu par les croisés. ' Si le 8 Juin 1249,' dit Napoléon, ' Saint Louis eût manœuvré comme ont fait les Français en 1798, il serait arrivé le 26 Juin au Caire ; il aurait conquis la Basse-Égypte dans le mois de son arrivée. Il aurait attendu ensuite dans l'abondance d'une capitale, le débordement, puis la retraite, des eaux.' " (Sismondi, Hist. des Français, 5, 149, ed. de Bruxelles.)

[2] Diod. 15, 43.

the autumn of the same year, B.C. 373, commanding in the waters of Corcyra[1].

If even with the aid of Grecian mercenaries, Persia could not succeed in reducing Egypt, there was little likelihood that its own resources should avail for this purpose. The state of Greece precluded the hope of obtaining aid from thence. Sparta was engaged from 371 B.C. to the battle of Mantinea, 362 B.C., in a deadly warfare with Thebes, while Artaxerxes vainly endeavoured to reconcile them[2], that he might employ the Greek forces in his own service. Athens, though not directly embroiled in the conflict between Sparta and Thebes, sat by, watching its events, and flinging its weight alternately into the lighter scale. Egypt therefore enjoyed peace during the remainder of the life of Nectanebes. His name, spelt *Nacht ef neb*[3], occurs at Philæ on a temple dedicated to Athor, and on the rocks of the island of Beghe; at Coptos, in a church built out of the fragments of an old Egyptian edifice; and at Medinet Aboo in a small building of elegant workmanship, in which he is represented offering to Amun Re and the other gods of Thebes[4]. According to Pliny he cut out an obelisk from the quarry, which Ptolemy Philadelphus afterwards floated down the Nile, and erected in honour of his sister in the Arsinoite nome[5]. Its excavation

---

[1] Clinton, F. H. sub anno.
[2] Diod. 15, 70. Xen. Hist. 7, 1, 33, seq.
[3] Rosellini, Mon. Stor. 2, p. 220.
[4] Wilkinson, Manners and Customs, 1, 209, quotes a Greek papyrus in the possession of Signor Anastasy, which describes Nectanebns as restoring the temple of Mars at Sebennytus with great splendour, in obedience to a dream.
[5] He calls the king Necthhebix (36, 8), and according to the common reading (36, 13), makes him to have lived 500 years before Alexander the Great. The Bamberg

probably took place towards the end of the reign of Nectanebes, as it remained without an inscription. The celebrated Lions of the Fontana di Termini at Rome, now placed in the Museum of Egyptian antiquities in the Vatican, show that the art of sculpture, in the execution of animals, had declined but little; they are the last specimen of Egyptian sculpture executed under native princes[1].

Eusebius has shortened the duration of the Sebennytic dynasty from thirty-eight years to twenty, and the reign of Nectanebes from eighteen to ten. That the Greek text of Manetho is correct is in part proved by a stele preserved at Rome, on which his thirteenth year is mentioned[2].

TEOS (361 B.C.), the successor of Nectanebes according to Manetho, is evidently the Tachos of the Greek historians. In what relation he stood to his predecessor we are not informed, probably that of son. The empire of Artaxerxes was at this time surrounded with enemies[3]. The maritime provinces of Asia had before revolted, and the generals and satraps, Ariobarzanes of Phrygia, Mausolus of Caria, Orontes of Mysia, were preparing to march against the Great King. The Syrians and Phœnicians, and the adjacent litoral states of Cilicia, Pisidia and Lycia, had joined the league. The Spartans were hostile to him, because he had demanded that the

---

MS. reads—"Nechthebis regis D ante Alexandrum Magnum;" and Bunsen supposes that Pliny wrote "regis Δ," i. e. fourth king, copying some Greek author. (Urkundeubuch, p. 84, 89. Germ.)

[1] Rosellini, Mon. Stor. 2, 222.

[2] Champollion-Figeac, L'Univers, p. 385.

[3] Diod. 15, 90. Ὑπὸ τὸν αὐτὸν καιρὸν ἔδει πρός τε τὸν τῆς Αἰγύπτου βασιλέα πολεμεῖν καὶ πρὸς τὰς κατὰ τὴν Ἀσίαν Ἑλληνίδας πόλεις καὶ Λακεδαιμονίους καὶ τοὺς τούτων ξυμμάχους σατράπας καὶ στρατηγούς, τοὺς ἄρχοντας μὲν τῶν παραθαλασσίων τόπων, συντεθειμένους δὲ κοινοπραγίαν.

Messenians should be included in the terms of the peace made in 361 after the battle of Mantinea[1]. The finances of Persia were disordered by the loss of revenue arising from so many revolts, and the necessity of great armaments to suppress them. These circumstances appear to have emboldened Tachos no longer to act on the defensive, but to attack Persia. Rheomithres was sent to him on the part of Orontes and the other revolted satraps, and received from him 500 talents of silver and fifty ships of war. With these he sailed to Leuce on the coast of Asia Minor, but on his arrival seized the rebel chiefs and sent them bound to Artaxerxes, making his own peace by giving up to the king the money with which he had been furnished to carry on war against him[2]. Tachos raised a fleet of 200 sail, with an army of 80,000 Egyptians and 10,000 Greek mercenaries. The Greek troops he placed under the command of Agesilaus, who at the age of eighty, and with a body maimed and scarred by war, undertook this office, through restlessness and love of gain[3]. If we may believe Xenophon, Tachos had promised him the supreme command; on his arrival with a thousand Spartan hoplites, he found that only the subordinate command of the Greek mercenaries was destined for him, Chabrias the Athenian commanding the fleet, and the king himself being supreme[4]. This first

---

[1] Diod. 15,89. Xen. Ages. 2,28.
[2] Diod. 15, 92.
[3] Plut. Agesilaus, 36.
[4] Diodorus says, that Chabrias took the command of the fleet without authority from Athens. Τοῦ δὲ ναυτικοῦ τὴν στρατηγίαν ἐνεχείρισε Χαβρίᾳ τῷ Ἀθηναίῳ, δημοσίᾳ μὲν ὑπὸ τῆς πατρίδος οὐκ ἀπεσταλμένῳ, ἰδίᾳ δὲ ὑπὸ τοῦ β σιλέως συστρατεύειν πεπεισμένῳ (15, 92). This so closely resembles 15, 29, where, speaking of Achoris, Diodorus says, Οὐκ ἔχων στρατηγὸν

gave him offence, and a difference of opinion soon arose between him and Tachos respecting the conduct of the war. Agesilaus advised that Tachos should remain in Egypt, and commit active operations to his generals—advice that we cannot wonder Tachos should have declined, since two of these generals were foreigners, of a nation notoriously ready to embrace the side which policy or profit recommended. He placed Nectanebus, his brother or brother-in-law [1], at the head of the Egyptian land-forces, and advanced into Phœnicia. The measures which he had adopted to raise money for this expedition on the recommendation of Chabrias had been very unpopular. The Athenian general had represented to him how much money that might be usefully employed for the service of the state was expended on religious rites, and recommended the abolition of many of the priesthoods. The priests, unwilling to renounce their offices, gave up their private property to the king. But when they had made this sacrifice, he ordered them to expend in future only a tenth part of what they had been accustomed to lay out on religious rites, and to make a loan of the rest to him, till the expiration of the war with Persia. Besides this, Chabrias advised him to impose a house-tax and a poll-tax, a duty of an obolus on the sale of every artaba (nine gallons) of corn, and a tax of a tenth of the profits of navigation, manu-

ἀξιόχρεων μετεπέμψατο Χαβρίαν τὸν 'Αθηναῖον· οὗτος ἄνευ τῆς τοῦ δήμου γνώμης προσδεξάμενος τὴν στρατηγίαν ἀφηγεῖτο τῶν κατ' Αἴγυπτον δυνάμεων, that he has probably repeated himself. It is not likely that Chabrias should twice have gone to Egypt unauthorized. It is certain that he was here now, without a commission from the state. See Plut. Ages. 37.

[1] The Nectanebus who revolted was nephew to Tachos. (Plut. Ages. 37.)

factures, and every kind of occupation. All the gold and silver bullion was to be brought to the king, who gave an assignment on the nomarchs for its repayment from the taxes[1]. These devices of the Athenian financier must have been very distasteful to the Egyptians, who appear hitherto to have been lightly taxed[2]. A people enthusiastic in the defence of their religion and their liberties have submitted cheerfully to much greater sacrifices, but the Egyptians were not threatened by any imminent danger, and might reasonably regard Tachos as engaged in a war of ambition rather than of self-defence. The general who had been left in command of Egypt during his absence, though so nearly related to him[3], perceiving the discontent of the people, sent a message to his son Nectanebus, exhorting him to claim the crown. Nectanebus had been detached with some Egyptian troops to besiege the strong places of Syria, and adopting the suggestion of his father[4], induced the generals by gifts and the soldiers by promises to espouse his cause. He endeavoured to persuade Agesilaus and Chabrias to employ their forces also for the establishment of his power. Chabrias was desirous of supporting Tachos; Agesilaus had been mortified and offended by him, and as the Egyptians generally had declared for Nectanebus, refused to fight against those whom he had been sent to aid[5]. He dispatched messengers to Sparta, instructed to make

---

[1] Aristotelis (sive Anonymi) Οἰκονομικά, c. 23, ed. Goettling, where many singular expedients, on the part of states and financiers for raising money, are collected.

[2] See p. 36 of this vol.
[3] See note 1, p. 506.
[4] Diod. 15, 92.
[5] Plut. Agesil. 37.

representations favourable to Nectanebus; the rivals also sent each his ambassador. The Spartans, after deliberation, left it to Agesilaus to act as he thought most advantageous for his country. He carried over not only the Spartans, but all the mercenaries to the side of Nectanebus, and the Athenians, at the instigation of Persia, recalled Chabrias[1]. Tachos, thus abandoned by his troops, native and foreign, first retired to Sidon[2], and then crossing the Desert, which extends on both sides of the Euphrates[3], came to the king at Babylon or Susa, by whom he was favourably received, and according to Diodorus, entrusted with the command of an expedition against Egypt.

This expedition Artaxerxes Mnemon did not live to carry into execution. He died in the year B.C. 359, and was succeeded by his son Darius Ochus, sometimes also known by the name of Artaxerxes. He was at once cruel and unwarlike[4]; he had secured his own succession by murders surpassing the ordinary measure of oriental barbarity; the kingdom was distracted by the revolt of the satraps which we have already mentioned. He suspended therefore all operations against Egypt; Tachos was retained at the Persian court, and soon ended his days there, a victim to indulgence in its luxuries, so different from the simple habits of the Egyptians[5].

---

[1] I refer to this period what Diodorus (15, 29) relates of the reign of Achoris. See notes, p. 499 and 505.
[2] Xenoph. Ages. 2, 30.
[3] Diod. 15, 92. Ὁ Ταχὼς καταπλαγεὶς ἐτόλμησε διὰ τῆς Ἀραβίας ἀναβῆναι πρὸς τὸν βασιλέα. This is the Arabia of Xenophon's Anabasis (1, 5), lying south of the Araxes.
[4] Diod. 16, 40.
[5] Ælian, V. Hist. 5, 1. Diodorus makes him return to Egypt and recover his throne by the aid of Agesilaus (15, 93), but the best authorities are against him. See Wesseling ad loc.

But though delivered for the present from a foreign invasion, Egypt was divided by a civil war. A native of Mendes, whose name has not been preserved, had risen up in opposition to Nectanebus, had been proclaimed king, and raised a large army, composed, like that which Sethos led against Sennacherib, not of the hereditary soldiery, but of the unwarlike population[1]. The inhabitants of a country like Egypt, however, covered with trenches and embankments, soon grow dexterous in the use of the spade for fortification. Agesilaus, who was now in the service of Nectanebus, became suspected by him, in consequence of a message from the Mendesian, tempting his fidelity, and though urged by Agesilaus to attack the enemy forthwith, Nectanebus left the open country and took possession of a large town, where, as Agesilaus foresaw, the numbers of the enemy and their familiarity with the art of entrenchment would enable them to hem him in[2]. This they had nearly accomplished, and supplies began to fail. Nectanebus was now eager to march out and give battle, and the Greeks joined with him in demanding it. But Agesilaus saw that the trench which the besiegers had drawn around the town, with the exception of a single point, would prevent their own forces from being concentrated. At nightfall therefore he persuaded Nectanebus to join him in an united and rapid attack on the part which remained open, and they

---

[1] Μιγάδες καὶ βάναυσοι καὶ δι' ἀπειρίαν εὐκαταφρόνητοι. (Plut. Ages. 38.) These were the class especially aggrieved by the new system of taxation.

[2] Κελεύοντος αὐτοῦ διαμάχεσθαι τὴν ταχίστην, καὶ μὴ χρόνῳ πολεμεῖν πρὸς ἀνθρώπους ἀπείρους ἀγῶνος, πολυχειρίᾳ δὲ περιελθεῖν καὶ περιταφρεῦσαι δυναμένους, ἀπεχώρησεν εἰς πόλιν εὐερκῆ καὶ μέγαν ἔχουσαν περίβολον. (Plut. Ages. 38.)

forced their way through, routing the troops opposed to them, before the others could assemble to support them. Soon after he gained a decisive victory by superiority of tactics. Being greatly outnumbered by the Egyptians, he took post where both his flanks were covered by a canal, and thus avoiding the danger of being surrounded, he easily defeated those who attacked him in front, and routed them with great slaughter. NECTANEBUS II. was thus secured on the throne.

Agesilaus immediately set sail on his return to Sparta. As it was already mid-winter, he coasted along Libya, not venturing to stand straight across the Carpathian sea, and had reached the port of Menelaus, opposite to Crete, on his way to Cyrene, where he died in his 84th year[1]. With the departure of the Greeks, in the end[2] of the year 359 B.C., our knowledge of the internal state of Egypt, during the reign of Nectanebus, ceases, till 350 B.C., when Persia resumed and carried into effect the project of reconquest. It is probable that hostilities never entirely ceased between the kingdoms. Ochus made more than one unsuccessful attempt to enter Egypt[3], and was defeated by the skill of Lamins of Sparta and Diophantus of Athens, whom Nectanebus placed at the head of his forces[4].

Ochus was an indolent and unwarlike prince, but the ridicule with which he had been covered by the

---

[1] Plut. Ages. 40.
[2] Μέσου χειμῶνος ὄντος ἀποπλεῖ οἴκαδε. (Xenoph. Ages. 2, 31.)
[3] Ἀποστέλλων δυνάμεις καὶ στρατηγοὺς, πολλάκις ἀπετύγχανε.
(Diod. 16, 40.) The language of Isocrates, 1, p. 280, ed. Battie, may seem to imply that Ochus had commanded in person.
[4] Diod. 16, 48.

defeat of his attacks on Egypt, roused him at last to make a great effort. Not only had his name become a by-word among the Egyptians for heaviness and sloth[1], but the dependent rulers of Cyprus and Phœnice were encouraged to follow the example of Egypt[2]. The Persian empire was evidently in danger of dissolution, but the vigorous exertions to which Ochus was stimulated preserved it for a quarter of a century. He began by reducing Cyprus and Phœnicia. Sidon, the most flourishing of the Phœnician cities, had made great preparations for defence, but it was surrendered by the treachery of its king Tennes, and the inhabitants, having first destroyed their fleet, burnt themselves, their wives and children and slaves[3]. Cyprus also was subdued[4]. The states of Greece were invited to furnish mercenaries; Athens and Sparta promised neutrality, but declined co-operation; the Thebans, Argives and Asiatic Greeks sent together 10,000 men, and Ochus, after the destruction of Sidon, advanced by the same route as Cambyses to the desert which separates Egypt from Palestine[5]. In passing the Serbonian Lake, part of his army were lost in the quicksands called Barathra which border the coast[6]. Had Tennes, the king of Sidon, been alive, he might have saved the Persians from this disaster, for he was well acquainted with the approaches to Egypt

---

[1] Ὦχον οἱ Αἰγύπτιοι τῇ ἐπιχωρίῳ φωνῇ Ὄνον ἐκάλουν, τὸ νωθὲς αὐτοῦ τῆς γνώμης διαβάλλοντες. (Ælian, V. H. 4, 8.) The Coptic for ass is Eio.
[2] Diod. 16, 40.
[3] Diod. 16, 45.
[4] Diod. 16, 46.
[5] It appears to me that the account quoted by Longinus from Theopompus (p. 450 of this vol.), describes the expedition of Ochus.
[6] This is probably the event, which Diodorus (1, 30) has exaggerated into the swallowing up of whole armies. Comp. Par. Lost, 2, 593, ... "the Serbonian bog, Where armies whole have sunk.

and the proper points for making a descent[1]. Nectanebus had not neglected the means of defence. He had under arms 60,000 of the Hermotybians and Calasirians, 20,000 Libyans, and an equal number of Greek mercenaries. In sea-going ships he was far inferior to the Persians, who had the command of the Cyprian and Phœnician navies, but he had a large fleet of boats adapted for fighting on the branches of the Nile; and he had rendered the frontier towards Arabia nearly impregnable, by a continuous chain of entrenchments and fortifications. Pelusium was garrisoned by 5000 Greeks, under the command of Philophron. The Thebans in the Persian army, eager to maintain the glory which they had acquired at Leuctra and Mantinea, advanced alone and rashly, across a deep canal to attack Pelusium. The garrison sallied out and a fierce conflict ensued, which lasted till night. Next day the whole body of Greek mercenaries were brought up in three divisions, each under the joint command of a Greek and a Persian. Lacrates, who commanded the Thebans, cut the banks of the canal, letting off the water, and having filled it up with earth, planted his military engines on the embankment. These soon made breaches in the walls; but the besieged rapidly raised new walls behind, and erected wooden towers upon them. Ochus might have returned again discomfited, but in the meantime a great calamity had befallen Nectanebus. It was evidently his policy to avoid a pitched battle and let the enemy exhaust their strength, in

[1] Diod. 16, 43.

endeavouring to reduce the number of strong positions which he occupied; but the eagerness of his Greek auxiliaries to fight prevented his carrying this plan into execution, and he was outmanœuvred by the enemy. With 30,000 Egyptians, 5000 Greeks, and half the Libyan auxiliaries, he was guarding an important passage. Nicostratus, the commander of the Argives who were before Pelusium, was guided by some Egyptians whose wives and children were in the power of the Persians as hostages, to an obscure branch of the river, by which he brought up his fleet and secretly fortified himself on the Egyptian side. When he was discovered, the garrison of a neighbouring fortress, Greek mercenaries to the number of 5000, under the command of Cleinias of Cos, marched out against them, and a pitched battle ensued, in which the troops of Nectanebus were nearly all cut to pieces. He was alarmed, and apprehending that the rest of the Persian forces might cross the river and cut off his retreat on Memphis, marched thither with all his army. Diodorus severely censures him, and alleges that he was ruined by the over-confidence arising from previous success—success of which the merit belonged not to him, but to Diophantus and Lamins. His own narrative, however, justifies no other censure on Nectanebus, than perhaps a want of vigilance in allowing Nicostratus to fortify a position in his rear. When that position was made good by a victory, nothing appears to have been left for Nectanebus but to retire on Memphis, before he was intercepted. The garrison of Pelusium perceived that any further resistance was vain, and surrendered to Lacrates on condition that they should be transported to Greece with their property untouched. This condition was violated by the Persian troops, who endeavoured to plunder the Greeks as they marched out. Lacrates, indignant at this breach of his pledged word, attacked the Persians and killed some of them. Bagoas, their commander, complained to Ochus, but he justified the Greeks, and ordered the Persians who had broken the truce to be put to death. Mentor, the commander of another division of the Persian army, soon reduced Bubastis and the other cities of Lower Egypt. They were all occupied by mixed garrisons of Greeks and Egyptians, and as he caused the rumour to be spread that those who surrendered should be treated with kindness, while a more terrible fate than that of Sidon awaited all who made resistance, they were eager to anticipate each other in submission. Nectanebus found that he could not maintain himself at Memphis, and fled into Ethiopia, having reigned between eight and nine years. His flight closed the Thirty Dynasties of the Pharaohs—a succession unexampled in ancient or modern times [1].

Ochus took possession of all Egypt, razed the walls of the principal towns, and plundered the temples. It is said that he imitated the outrages

[1] Lynceus (who lived 280 B.C. See Clinton, F. H. 3, 498) says that Nectanebus was taken prisoner and invited to supper by Ochus. The feast appeared mean to Nectanebus, who requested to be allowed to order his former cooks to prepare an Egyptian supper. When Ochus had partaken of it he exclaimed, "O Egyptian, what folly to leave such feasts as these, and set your heart on a more spare diet!" (Athen. 4, p. 150.) Persian diet, however, was more luxurious than Egyptian.

of Cambyses, killed Apis and gave his flesh to the cooks, and commanded an ass to receive the honours due to the god. When he subsequently fell a victim to assassination by Bagoas, who made dagger-handles of his thigh-bones, and gave his flesh to cats, superstition saw in this a retribution corresponding to that which fell on Cambyses[1]. The temples were not only stripped of the gold and silver which they contained, but rifled of their ancient records, which Bagoas subsequently restored for a large sum to the priests[2]. The Greek mercenaries were dismissed with munificent rewards; Pherendates was made satrap of Egypt, and Ochus, in 350 B.C., led back his army in triumph to Babylon.

Of the administration of the Persians in Egypt during the remainder of the reign of Ochus and that of Darius Codomannus, nothing is known. The long struggles of Sparta, Athens and Thebes, for supremacy in Greece, had ended in their subjugation by Macedonia, and one of the first uses which Philip made of the command which he acquired by the battle of Chæronea, was to prepare an expedition against Persia. His own assassination by Perdiccas prevented his execution of this plan, but it was resumed by Alexander, who crossed the Hellespont in 334 B.C. The battle of the Granicus gave him possession of Asia Minor; that of Issus, of Syria; the sieges of Tyre and Gaza, of the coast of Phœnicia, Palestine, and the Idumean Arabia[3]. Seven days' march brought him from Gaza

---

[1] Ælian, V. Hist. 6, 8. Suid. s.v. Λαβαίς. Ὦχος. Ælian. Hist. Anim. 10, 28.
[2] Diod. Sic. 16, 15.
[3] Arrian, Hist. 3, 1.

to Pelusium, the fleet accompanying him. Mazaces, whom Darius had appointed satrap of Egypt, did not attempt resistance. The Persian armies had been driven across the Euphrates, and the Egyptians were prepared to welcome the conquerors of their own masters. Having placed a garrison in Pelusium, he marched through the desert country along the eastern bank of the Nile to Heliopolis, and crossing the river there came to Memphis, where his fleet, which had sailed up the Nile, was awaiting him. Greek philosophy had banished fanaticism from his mind, and policy clearly dictated that he should conciliate the Egyptians, whose religious feelings had been deeply wounded by the Persians. Having sacrificed to the other gods and Apis, he descended the Nile by the Canopic branch, and fixed the site of the new city, which still preserves his name and attests his sagacity. Hence, after founding a temple to Isis, he set out for the oracle of the Libyan Ammon, a divinity whom Greeks and Egyptians agreed to honour. His expedition was performed along the coast of Libya as far as Parætonium, thence through the Desert to the Oasis of Siwah. On his return he avoided the dangers to which he had exposed himself, and took the shorter route by the Natron Lakes to Memphis[1]. Here, while recruits were raising in Greece,

---

[1] On the point whether Alexander returned by Parætonium or the Natron Lakes, two generals of Alexander, Aristobulus and Ptolemy Lagi, were at variance in their memoirs. Aristobulus did not write his history, however, till he was 84 (see St. Croix, Examen Critique, p. 43), and may have forgotten minute circumstances. I have followed Ptolemy, whose account is the more probable. Curtius agrees with Aristobulus, and makes Alexander found Alexandria on his way home (4, 33).

to repair the losses which his army had sustained in the battles of the Granicus and Issus, and the sieges of Tyre and Gaza, he employed himself in arranging the future administration of Egypt. Two Egyptians, Doloaspis and Petisis, were appointed nomarchs of Upper and Lower Egypt; but Petisis declining the office, the whole kingdom was placed under Doloaspis. Cleomenes, a native of Naucratis, had the chief administration of the finances, and was instructed to allow the kingdom to be governed entirely according to its ancient laws and customs; the inferior nomarchs collected the tribute and paid it to Cleomenes, by whom it was transferred to the Macedonians. Thus foreigners were prevented from coming into collision with the Egyptians, in the odious character of tax-gatherers, but all real power was placed in the hands of the Macedonians. A fleet of thirty triremes and four thousand men[1] sufficed to maintain his conquest. The command of the garrisons of Pelusium and Memphis was given to *companions* of the king; other Greeks held the offices of præfect of Libya and Arabia, the command of the army, the mercenaries, and the fleet. Alexander introduced the principle, which the Romans afterwards carried out in the administration of Egypt, not to allow any one man to have sole authority in a kingdom so fertile and so strong by natural position, and from various causes so prone to revolt[2]. Cleomenes, however, the præfect of Arabia, after Alexander's departure,

[1] Q. Curt. 4, 33.
[2] Tac. Hist. 1, 11; Ann. 2, 59. Ita visum expedire provinciam aditu difficilem, annonæ fœcundam, superstitione ac lascivia discordem ac mobilem, insciam legum, domi retinere. (Arrian, 3, 5, 10.)

appears to have availed himself of the power which his office as chief financier gave him, to usurp a kind of supremacy[1], and various acts of extortion are recorded of him, in the interval between the conquest of Egypt and the establishment of the Ptolemaic monarchy[2]. He repeated the threat of Nectanebus, to suppress some of the priesthoods on account of their number, and the largeness of the sums expended on religious ceremonies, and thus obtained from the priests considerable sums, not only from their private property, but from the treasures of the temples.

Alexander left Memphis early in the spring of 331 B.C., and having crossed the Nile and its various canals on bridges, passed the Desert, and at Tyre joined his fleet, which had preceded him. He never again visited Egypt; but his corpse was brought hither from Babylon and deposited at Alexandria in a sarcophagus[3], within a funeral hypogæum[4]. In the division of his empire Egypt was chosen for his portion by Ptolemy, the son of Lagus, with whom begins a new period of its history.

[1] Κλεομένης Αἰγύπτου σατραπεύων. (Arist. Œconom. c. 32.)
[2] Arist. u. s.
[3] Juvenal, Sat. 10, 172.
[4] Lucan, Pharsal. 10, 19, speaking of Julius Cæsar,—

Effossum tumulis cupide descendit in antrum.
Illic Pellæi proles vesana Philippi
Felix prædo jacet.

INDEX.

A.

ABABDEH, the, i. 65.
Abaris (Auaris), ii. 181, 193, 320.
Aboosimbel (Aboccis), i. 24; ii. 465 note.
——, Greek inscription there, ii. 413.
——, temple of, ii. 276.
Abydos, i. 46.
——, Tablet of, ii. 108, 160, 200.
Acacia, i. 145.
Achoris, ii. 497.
Actisanes, ii. 368 note.
Adonis, mourning for, i. 415.
Ægyptus, ii. 311.
Æra, not used by the Egyptians, ii. 95.
Æsculapius, i. 396.
——, worship paid to his serpent, ii. 2.
Africa, whether circumnavigated by the Phœnicians, ii. 401.
Africanus, Julius, ii. 89.
Agesilaus, his campaign in Egypt, ii. 505.
Alabaster, quarries of, i. 49.
Alabastron, i. 49, 233.
Alexander, his supposed sarcophagus, ii. 494.
Alexandria, its population, i. 179.
——, foundation of, ii. 516.
Alluvium, deposit of, i. 78, 150.
Alphabetical characters, when arranged, ii. 323.
Alum, i. 75; ii. 433.
Amasis, ii. 425.
——, his laws, ii. 48.
—— (satrap), ii. 481.
Amenmeses, ii. 338 note.
Amenophis I., ii. 206.
—— II., ii. 232.
—— III., ii. 234.
Amenthe, i. 394, 484.
Ammonium, i. 71.
——, expedition of Cambyses against, ii. 465.
Amosis, ii. 204.
Amun, i. 369.
Amun Khem, i. 375; ii. 328.
Amunt, i. 383.
Amuntuanch, ii. 250.
Amyrtæus, ii. 488, 492.
Anaglyphs, i. 321.
Anatomy, whether known in Egypt, i. 271; ii. 123.
Anaxagoras, his doctrine concerning God, i. 438.
Androsphinx, i. 137, 172.
Animals, sanctity of, in India, ii. 11.
——, Egyptian worship of, ii. 1-27.
——, as military ensigns, ii. 7.
Anouke, i. 385.
Anubis, i. 424.
—— with head of jackal, i. 425.
Anysis, ii. 362.
Aphrodite, Celestial, i. 386.
Apion, ii. 180.
Apis, his worship when introduced, ii. 6.
——, honours paid to him, ii. 23.
——, his marks, ii. 22.
——, *Epiphaneia* of, ii. 389, 468.
——, mummies of, ii. 24.
Apollodorus, his list of kings, ii. 97, 194 note.
Arabic numerals, i. 344.
Arch, its antiquity, i. 259.
Ark of the Covenant, i. 460.
Armais, ii. 312.
Aroeris, *see* Haroeris.
Art, Egyptian, i. 202; ii. 352, 389.
——, ——, influenced by religion, i. 265, 268.
——, ——, its progress the same as that of civilization, i. 273.
——, decline of, ii. 340, 504.
Artaxerxes Mnemon, ii. 504.
Arutu, nation, ii. 223.
Ases (Asseth), i. 330; ii. 189 note.
Ashes, criminals plunged in, ii. 150.
Asp, emblem of the Sun, ii. 21.
Asphaltum, its use in embalmment, i. 498.
Assyrian empire, ii. 339.
Assyrians, their power, ii. 186, 212.
Atet, fortress, ii. 259.

Atinre, ii. 251.
Athens, whether a colony from Sais, ii. 395.
——, its alliances with Egypt, ii. 486, 493.
Athom, i. 393.
Athor, i. 386.
Atlantis, island, its submersion, ii. 404, 439.
Atmoo, i. 393.
Atmosphere of Egypt, its effect on colours, i. 262.
Auaris (Abaris), ii. 181.
Automoli, ii. 393, 395.
Azotus, siege of, ii. 391.

B.

B, pronounced as *ou*, i. 393.
Bab, its signification, i. 166.
Babylon, ii. 227.
——, Egyptian, ii. 287.
Babylonians, their inventions, i. 340.
Bagoas, ii. 514.
Bahr-be-la-Ma, i. 70, 79.
Bahr-Jusuf, i. 50, 113, 147.
Barabras, i. 103.
Barathra, ii. 511.
Barbarians, all other nations so called by the Egyptians, ii. 248.
Bari, i. 210, 459, 501, 508.
Basalt, i. 263.
Basis, ii. 126.
Bas-relief, Egyptian, its peculiarity, i. 272.
Beans, an impure vegetable, i. 447.
Beard, absence of, in African nations, ii. 167.
Beitoualli, temple of, ii. 268.
Belzoni, i. 24, 128.
——, tomb discovered by, i. 167.
Berbers, ii. 248.
Besa, i. 454.
Birket-el-Kerun, i. 51; ii. 156.
Blemmyes, i. 28.
Bocchoris, ii. 359, 361.
——, his legislation, ii. 58.
Boeckh, his view of Manetho's chronology, ii. 94 note.
Bonaparte, his campaign in Egypt, ii. 502.
Book of the Dead, i. 485.
Books not in common use in Egypt, i. 284.
Bow, mode of drawing, i. 223.
Breccia, quarries of, i. 63.
Bridge in Egyptian monuments, ii. 258 note.
—— of boats over the Hellespont, ii. 483.

Bridges, none on the Nile, i. 211.
Bubastis, ii. 345.
Bull, of what a type, ii. 19.
Bunsen, his mode of reconciling Eratosthenes and Manetho, ii. 99, 131.
Busiris, king, ii. 81.
——, city, i. 56.
Buto, goddess, i. 382.
Byblos, i. 410, 414.

C.

Cabiri, i. 381, 397.
Cadmus, the historian, ii. 68.
Calasirians, i. 221; ii. 42, 390, 483.
Camels in Egypt, i. 76; ii. 450.
Canal, between the Nile and the Red Sea, ii. 291, 399, 479.
Cancer, Tropic of, i. 28.
Candace, her war with the Romans, ii. 463.
Canopi, i. 405.
Canopic mouth, first frequented by the Greeks, ii. 64.
Captives represented on furniture, i. 235.
Caravan routes from Egypt to Meroe, i. 26; ii. 462.
Carchemish, battle of, ii. 408.
Carians in Egypt, i. 465.
——, their settlement in Egypt, ii. 383.
Caricature, i. 269.
Carthaginians, their naval power, ii. 455.
Casluhim, ii. 190.
Caste, law of, ii. 30, 44, 46.
Cat, sanctity of, ii. 4.
——, consecrated to the Moon, ii. 21.
Cataracts, i. 14, 19, 22, 31.
Cavalry, not used in Egypt, i. 226.
Cedar, oil of, i. 493, 497.
Ceilings, astronomical, i. 168, 169.
Cemeteries, Egyptian, on the western side of the Nile, i. 501, 502.
Cerberus, i. 407.
Chabrias, his campaigns in Egypt, ii. 499, 505.
Chæremon, his work on Hieroglyphics, ii. 365 note.
Charon, i. 509.
Chebros, ii. 209.
Cherubim, i. 460.
Chemi, name of Egypt, ii. 115.
Chemistry, origin of the name, i. 215.
Chesebt, metal, ii. 227, 259.
Chinese writing, i. 308.
Chiun, worship of, ii. 325.
Choachutæ (not Cholchytæ), i. 505.
Chons, i. 384.
Chronicle, the Old Egyptian, ii. 95.

INDEX. 521

Chronology, Egyptian, ii. 91, 93, 197.
Circesium, battle of, ii. 408.
Circumcision, i. 448-450.
Clemens Alexandrinus, his enumeration of Egyptian priests, ii. 103.
Coinage not known in Egypt, i. 345.
—— by the Persians, ii. 477 introduced
Colchians, their similarity to the Egyptians, ii. 283.
Colossal in art, its effect, i. 266.
Colour, conventional, of the male and female in Egyptian painting, i. 98.
—— applied to sculpture, i. 262.
Comasiæ, i. 458.
Comastes, i. 458; ii. 31.
Concharis, ii. 189.
Concubines, their children legitimate, ii. 58.
Constellations, influence of, i. 456.
Copper mines, i. 61; ii. 140.
Coronation, ceremonies of, ii. 326.
Corslet, linen, of Amasis, i. 215; ii. 432.
Cosseir road, inscriptions in, ii. 148, 480, 482, 484.
Cotton, whether used in bandages, i. 493.
——, whether grown in Egypt, i. 188; ii. 432.
Cranium, the Egyptian, distinguishable by its hardness, i. 248 note.
Criosphinx, i. 137 note, 172.
Crocodile, not now found in Lower Egypt, i. 94.
——, mode of its capture, i. 203.
——, its import in mythology, i. 393.
——, worship of, i. 35; ii. 20.
——, symbol of Typhon, ii. 19.
——, —— of darkness, i. 457.
——, ornaments bestowed upon, ii. 16.
Crown of Upper and Lower Egypt, i. 247 note.
Cubit, Egyptian, i. 345.
Cycle, Sothiac, i. 333.
——, its commencement, ii. 294.
Cynocephalus, i. 428.
——, emblem of Thoth, ii. 19.
Cyprus, conquest of, ii. 329.
——, its relations to Persia, ii. 485, 496.
Cyrene, foundation of, ii. 420.
——, war of Apries against, ii. 424.
——, of Aryandes against, ii. 476.

D.

Dahæ, ii. 223.
Danaus, story of his migration, ii. 64, 310.

Danaides bring the mysteries of Demeter to the Peloponnesus, i. 468.
Darius Hystaspis, ii. 473.
—— Ochus, ii. 508.
—— Codomannus, ii. 515.
Dead, state of, according to the Hebrews, i. 473, 476 note.
——, according to the early Greeks, i. 474.
Debtor and creditor, law of, ii. 58.
Decans, i. 342.
Delta, apex of, i. 54.
——, its formation, i. 78; ii. 125, 127.
Demigods, their reigns, ii. 111.
Democritus, ii. 77.
——, his visit to Egypt, ii. 489.
Demotic character, when first introduced, ii. 480.
Desert, the, between Palestine and Egypt, ii. 449.
——, between Egypt and Ethiopia, ii. 462.
Dialect, sacred, i. 316, 320.
Dicæarchus, ii. 78, 165.
Diodorus, ii. 79-87.
——, variations between him and Herodotus, ii. 86.
Divination, i. 452.
Doric order, its origin, i. 255.
Draughts, game of, i. 242; ii. 333.
Dromos, i. 260.
Dynasty, its meaning, ii. 112.
Dynasties of Manetho, whether contemporaneous, ii. 96, 185.

E.

Egypt, extent of its coast, i. 58.
——, want of harbours, i. 59.
——, fertility of its soil, i. 86.
——, temperature, i. 92, 94.
——, healthiness, i. 92.
——, cheapness of living, i. 181.
——, native name of, i. 215.
——, fecundity of women in, i. 182 note.
——, its monarchy one, ii. 97.
——, taxation under the Persians, ii. 473.
——, amount of population, i. 179.
——, state under the Persians, ii. 490.
Eimopht, i. 397.
Elbo, island of, ii. 363, 379.
Election of kings, ii. 31.
Elephant, found in Egyptian pictures, ii. 221.
Elephantiasis, i. 93.
Eleusinian Mysteries, i. 470.
Elians, their visit to Egypt, ii. 411.
Embalmment, its antiquity, ii. 123.

Embalmment, its purpose, i. 476.
——, different mode of, i. 491.
Emeph, i. 373.
Emeralds, mines of, i. 64.
Epagomenæ, i. 330.
Epiphaneia of Apis, ii. 22.
Eratosthenes, ii. 78, 97.
Ergamenes, i. 27.
Etesian winds, i. 81, 347.
Ethiopia, conception of, in the age of Herodotus, ii. 456.
Ethiopian monarchy, extent of, ii. 363.
Ethiopians, visit of gods to, i. 458.
Ethiopic language, ii. 365 note.
Eunuchs, whether known in ancient Egypt, ii. 164.
Evagoras, his alliance with Egypt, ii. 497.
Eusebius, his chronology, ii. 90.
——, arbitrary changes in, ii. 179 note.
Exodus of the Israelites, ii. 313-325.
Eye of Osiris, i. 403.
Eyes, artificial, i. 497.
"Eyes of the King," ii. 290 note.
Ezekiel, his prophecy against Egypt, ii. 419.

F.

Factories of the Greeks in Egypt, ii. 431.
Famine in Egypt, i. 85.
Fanbearers, ii. 36.
Feast of the gods with the Ethiopians, i. 458.
Fekkaroo, ii. 331, 333.
Fish forbidden to priests, i. 447.
Fish of the Nile, their species, i. 205.
Flint knives, i. 492.
Flowers in Egypt not fragrant, i. 89.
——, their symbolical import, ii. 15.
Forest, petrified, near Cairo, i. 78.
Fortification, art of, i. 230 note.
Fowl, domestic, whether known in Egypt, i. 207.
Frog, emblem of Life, i. 416.
Fruits of Egypt, i. 198.
Furniture, buried with deceased persons, i. 504.
Fyoum, i. 50.

G.

Gardening, art of, i. 199.
Gardens of Solomon, i. 200.
Germanicus, his visit to Thebes, ii. 228.
Giligammæ, ii. 305.
Gloves, worn by northern captives, ii. 221.
Gods, division of, i. 366, 367.
——, reign of, ii. 113.
Gold mines, i. 64.

Goshen, its position, ii. 231.
Grain, what species cultivated in Egypt, i. 187.
Granite, quarries of, i. 32.
Greeks, their contempt for barbarians, ii. 77.
——, their neglect of foreign languages, ii. 387.
Grottos of Benihassan, i. 47.
—— of Koum-el-Ahmar, i. 49.
Gymnastic exercises, i. 222, 237, 240, 272.

H.

Ham, name of, i. 96.
Hapimoou, i. 396.
Harka, i. 385.
Haroeris, i. 392, 421.
Harper's Tomb, ii. 334.
Harpocrates, i. 411, 422.
Hatching by artificial heat, i. 207.
Hawk, emblem of Horus, ii. 19.
Head-stool, used by the Egyptians, i. 236.
Heavens, emblematic figure of, i. 169, 395.
Hecatæus of Miletus, i. 101; ii. 68.
Hellanicus, ii. 68.
Hellenion, factory of the Greeks in Egypt, ii. 431.
Henneh, use of, i. 251.
Heracleopolis, ii. 154.
Hermapion, his interpretation of an obelisk, i. 291.
Hermes, books of, ii. 103.
Hermes Trismegistus, i. 427.
Hermotybians, i. 221; ii. 42.
Herodotus, ii. 70-76.
——, his deficiency in calculation, ii. 395.
Heroes, worship of, i. 431.
——, reign of, ii. 113.
Hestia, i. 385.
Hieroglyphics, i. 283-324.
——, knowledge of them how far diffused, i. 285; ii. 76.
——, order of reading them, i. 310.
Hierogrammateus, i. 451; ii. 104.
Hincks, Dr. E., ii. 159.
——, his modifications of Champollion's system, i. 324.
Hipparchus, discoverer of the precession of the equinoxes, i. 338.
Hippopotamus, i. 203.
——, symbol of crime, ii. 119.
——, symbol of darkness, i. 407.
Hippys of Rhegium, ii. 68.
Homer, his account of Thebes, i. 178; ii. 66.
——, his account of Pharos, ii. 65.

Horapollo, i. 288.
Hor-hat, his emblem, i. 261, 392.
Horologium, i. 328 ; ii. 103.
Horoscopus, i. 451, 456 ; ii. 103.
Horse, its use, i. 195-197.
Horus, god, i. 420.
——, king, ii. 247.
——, " the golden," ii. 149.
Hyksos, their invasion, ii. 181.

I.

Iamblichus, i. 360.
Iatromathematic, i. 348.
Ibis, emblem of Thoth, ii. 20.
Ichneumon, ii. 157.
Ichthyophagi, act as interpreters, ii. 457.
Idumæans, ii. 449.
Illumination in honour of Neith, i. 466.
Inaros, ii. 485.
India, supposed early connexion with Egypt, i. 105-110.
——, tenure of land in, ii. 29.
——, sanctity of plants and animals in, ii. 11.
Interest, rate of, ii. 59.
Interpreters, caste of, ii. 45, 387.
Io, legend of, ii. 1, 63.
Ionic order, its origin, i. 255.
Iphicrates, his campaigns in Egypt, ii. 500.
Is, bituminous springs of, ii. 228.
Isaiah, his prophecies against Egypt, ii. 376.
Isiac rites, i. 469.
Isis, i. 405.
Islands of the Blessed, i. 68, 481, 486.

J.

Jablonsky, Pantheon Ægyptiorum, i. 355, 371.
Jebusites, ii. 188.
Jehovah, his name unknown to the Jews in the time of Moses, ii. 324.
Jeremiah, his prophecy against Apries, ii. 417.
Jerusalem, capture of, by Sheshonk, ii. 349.
——, ——, by Neco, ii. 406.
——, ——, by Nebuchadnezzar, ii. 416.
Jews, not the same as the Hyksos, ii. 187.
——, their departure from Egypt, ii. 313.
——, Manetho's account of, ii. 319.
——, employed in brickmaking, ii. 230.

Jewish laws, resemblance to the Egyptian, ii. 53.
Josephus, his unfairness, ii. 187, 188, 196.
Judgement of kings, posthumous, ii. 34.
Judgement-scene, i. 406, 429.
Jukasa, land of, ii. 228.

K.

Kanana, land of, ii. 256.
Karnak, royal tablet of, ii. 108, 229.
——, statistical tablet of, ii. 222.
Khamsin, i. 68 note.
Kings of Egypt, their mode of life, ii. 32.
——, number of, ii. 190 note.
Kneph, i. 373.
Korosko, Akaba of, ii. 462.
Kufa, nation, ii. 220.
Kuphi, i. 446.

L.

Labyrinth, i. 53 ; ii. 172-176, 384.
Lacrates, commands the Theban troops in Egypt, ii. 512.
Lakes, the Bitter, ii. 400.
Land, threefold division of, ii. 28, 37.
——, tenure of, in Egypt, ii. 28.
Lark, crested, venerated by the Lemnians, ii. 17.
Laterculus of Syncellus, ii. 95, 194 note.
Latus, the fish, i. 41.
Law, administration of, ii. 41, 51.
——, Egyptian, its humanity, ii. 53.
Layard's Nineveh, ii. 225, 339.
Legislators, Egyptian, ii. 33.
Lemanen, nation, ii. 226.
Leopard's skin, worn by priests, i. 503.
Lepidotus, the fish, i. 411.
Leprosy among the Jews, ii. 322.
Lepsius, his discovery of marks of rise of the Nile in Nubia, i. 22.
——, reading of the name Osortasen, ii. 160.
——, —— of the name of the builder of the Labyrinth, ii. 173.
——, —— of the name Set, ii. 254.
Leto, i. 386.
Lex talionis, ii. 55.
Library of the Rameseion, i. 155.
Libyans, ii. 118.
Linant, his discoveries in the Fyoum, i. 51 ; ii. 156.
Lion-hunt, ii. 331.
Lion, tamed, accompanying the king, i. 229.
Lions, of the Fontana di Termini, ii. 504.

524 INDEX.

Lotus, the sacred, i. 90.
———, its use for food, i. 190.
Ludim, nation, ii. 263.
Ludun, nation, ii. 221, 257.
Lydia, had a partly Semitic population, ii. 264.

M.

Magicians of Egypt, i. 456.
Mandoulis, i. 394.
Mandoo, i. 394.
Maneros, song of, i. 238.
Manes, reign of, ii. 92.
Manetho, ii. 88, 92.
———, whether his dynasties were consecutive, ii. 96–100.
———, duration of his dynasties, ii. 110, 177.
Manmisi, i. 38, 255 ; ii. 237.
Manoskh, i. 75.
Marriage of sisters and brothers, ii. 57.
Mars, i. 434, 465.
———, worship of, at Papremis, i. 465.
Marshes of Egypt, character of the population of, ii. 64, 488.
Mashiosha, ii. 329.
Mauthemva, ii. 234, 237, 246.
Medicine, i. 345.
Megabazus, his mission to Sparta, ii. 486.
Melampus, i. 399, 401, 467 ; ii. 311.
Melek, on Egyptian monuments, ii. 442, 481.
Memnon, ii. 241–246.
Memnonia, unhealthy employments carried on there, i. 491.
Memphis, etymology of, ii. 114.
Mendes, worship of the goat there, ii. 6, 126.
Mennahom, nation, ii. 329.
Menzaleh, lake of, i. 55.
Meroe, i. 10, 104 ; ii. 364.
———, whether the civilization of Egypt was derived thence, ii. 50 note, 171.
Metempsychosis, i. 108, 477–484 ; ii. 10.
Mexican writing, i. 308.
Milesians, their settlement in Egypt, ii. 359, 384.
Military age, i. 181.
Mines, the working of, ii. 55.
———, emerald, i. 64.
Minotaur, legend of, ii. 1.
Mizraim, ii. 115.
Mnevis, worship of, ii. 6.
Mœris, lake, i. 51 ; ii. 155, 229.
———, its fisheries, i. 204.
———, etymology of, ii. 155.
Mokattam, quarries of, i. 139.

Moloch, his worship, ii. 325.
Momemphis, ii. 384.
Mons Casius, ii. 192 note.
Months, Egyptian, their names, i. 330.
Monuments, public, their superiority to all other evidence, ii. 200.
Mora, game of, i. 243.
Mountains of the Moon, i. 7.
Mourning, i. 490.
Mouse, an emblem of destruction, ii. 373.
Mummies of animals, i. 142, 144, 165 ; ii. 5.
Mummies, pledged for debt, ii. 59.
———, kept in houses, i. 500.
———, Greek, i. 494.
Mummy, derivation of, i. 498.
———, introduced at banquets, i. 238.
Mysteries, i. 467.
———, Eleusinian, i. 471.

N.

Nænia, metrical, i. 490 note.
Naharaina, ii. 211, 217, 227.
Nahsi, ii. 264, 305.
Namhu, ii. 264.
Nantef, ii. 170.
Napata, i. 18 ; ii. 464.
Nasamones, ii. 305.
Natron Lakes, i. 70.
Natron, its use in embalmment, i. 493.
Naucratis, ii. 67.
Navigation, disesteemed in Egypt, ii. 45.
Nebuchadnezzar, his invasion of Egypt, ii. 419.
Nectanebus I., ii. 500.
Nectanebus II., ii. 510.
Nefruatep, ii. 170, 190.
Negro in Egyptian monuments, ii. 219.
——— physiognomy different from the Egyptian, i. 97.
Neith, i. 388.
Nemroud, Egyptian tablets found at, ii. 225, 339 note.
Nemt-amen, peculiarity of, ii. 212.
Nenii, supposed Nineveh, ii. 225.
Neocoros, ii. 31.
Neo-Platonists, i. 354.
Nepenthe, ii. 66.
Nephra, son of Amasis, ii. 481.
Nephthys, i. 423.
Netpe, i. 398, 496.
Nevopth, tomb of, i. 48 ; ii. 168.
Niger, the, confounded with the Nile, i. 6.
Nile, its changes of colour, i. 87.
———, figure of, i. 396 ; ii. 238.
Nile-water, i. 87, 237.

Nile, omens derived from, ii. 128.
Niloa, i. 395, 463.
Nilometer, i. 33.
Nilos, town, i. 396.
"Nine Bows," nation of, ii. 210, 252, 306 note.
Nineveh, capture of, ii. 408.
Nitocris, her history, ii. 150.
———, queen of Babylon, ii. 442.
No-Ammon, i. 151.
Nofre, i. 394.
Nomes, their division, ii. 49.
———, twelve predominant, ii. 51.
Noph, ii. 341.
North, symbol of, ii. 349.
Nubia, its climate and soil, i. 29.

O.

Oaths by vegetables, ii. 15.
Obelisk of St. John Lateran, i. 274; ii. 218.
—— of Nectanebus, ii. 503.
—— of Luxor, i. 171.
—— of Heliopolis, i. 55.
—— of the Fyoum, i. 52; ii. 158.
—— of Karnak, i. 173.
—— of Monte Citorio, i. 274; ii. 389.
—— of Apries, i. 275.
—— of the Piazza del Popolo, i. 277.
—— of Philæ, i. 31, 298.
Obelisks, placed in pairs, i. 171.
—— in the quarries of Syene, i. 218.
—— of the Roman times, i. 277.
———, mode of raising, i. 343.
Obliteration of names, i. 417.
Ocean, whether an Egyptian name for the Nile, i. 508.
Officers of state, ii. 36.
Onions, whether worshiped in Egypt, ii. 14.
Orphic doctrines, i. 372, 379, 382, 388, 402, 477.
Osarsiph, ii. 320.
"Osirian," appellation of deceased persons, i. 487; ii. 297.
Osiride columns, i. 258.
Osiris, i. 398–407.
———, forty-two assessors of, i. 169,407.
———, mythe of, i. 408.
———, porcelain figures of, i. 495.
—— eye of, i. 503.
Osymandyas, tomb of, i. 153, 155; ii. 280.
———, circle of, i. 341.
Otsch, fortress, ii. 259.
Oxyrrynchus, town, i. 49.
Oxyrrynchus, fish, ii. 19.

P.

Paamyles, i. 408.
Paamylia, i. 467.
Painting, art of, i. 164, 271.
—— of tombs, i. 164.
Pallaces, of Jupiter, i. 170.
Palm, emblematic, i. 428.
Palm-tree, its uses, i. 88.
———, Theban (Doum), i. 94, 198.
Panegyries, hall of, i. 175.
———, where held, i. 463.
Papremis, i. 434, 465.
Papyri, age of the earliest, ii. 102.
———, funeral, i. 487.
Papyrus, its manufacture, i. 90.
———, use for food, i. 190.
—— of Sallier, ii. 288.
Paraschistes, i. 492.
Pastophori, i. 451; ii. 105.
Pathros, i. 387 note.
Patnouphis, title of Hermes, i. 427.
Pepi, ii. 146.
Persea, i. 198; ii. 13.
Perseus, i. 46.
———, tower of, i. 58.
Persian conquest of Egypt, its effect, ii. 68.
Perspective, its neglect in Egyptian art, i. 269.
Petesuchis, ii. 174.
Pethempamenthes, title of Osiris, i. 405, 415.
Petronius, his expedition against Napata, ii. 464.
Phagrus, the fish, i. 411.
Phanes, his treachery, ii. 449.
Pharos, Homeric description of, ii. 65.
Pheron, ii. 293, 302, 336.
Philistus, ii. 77.
Philitis, ii. 192.
Phœnicians, said to have circumnavigated Africa, ii. 401.
———, their connexion with Egypt, ii. 192.
Phœnix, i. 333.
Phre, i. 390 note.
Phrygians, claim superior antiquity to the Egyptians, ii. 396.
Physicians, i. 345; ii. 39.
Pilgrimages, i. 464.
Pindar, his doctrine of transmigration, i. 481.
Pithom, ii. 231.
Plague, the, i. 93.
Plants, sanctity of, ii. 12.
Plato, his testimony to the antiquity of Egypt, i. 3.
———, of the forms of Egyptian art, i. 264.

Plato, his visit to Egypt, i. 55.
——, his doctrine of transmigration, i. 483.
Plutarch, de Iside et Osiride, i. 353.
Plutus and Pluto the same, i. 401.
Poetry, historical, in Egypt, ii. 107.
Polycrates of Samos, his history, ii. 434.
Polygamy, i. 450; ii. 58.
Potipherah, i. 390 note.
Pount, land, ii. 219.
Precession of the equinoxes, i. 337.
Premnis (Primis Magna), ii. 464.
Priesthood, effects of their power, ii. 35.
——, their condition and influence, ii. 37.
Priests, whether judges, ii. 41.
Primis (Ibrim), ii. 465 note.
Processions, i. 457.
Prophetes, i. 451, 454; ii. 31, 104.
Proscynema, i. 504.
Prussian Expedition their discoveries, i. 133, 155.
Psammitichus I., ii. 382.
—— II., ii. 410.
—— III., assassinates Tamos, ii. 497.
Pschent, i. 247 note, 392; ii. 327.
Pthuris (Farras), ii. 465 note.
Pulley, whether known to the Egyptians, i. 343 note.
Pylon, meaning of, i. 37.
Pyramids, proportions of, i. 118.
——, mode of erecting, i. 125.
——, their number, i. 133.
——, in Upper Egypt, i. 148.
——, builders of, ii. 132–138.
——, Ethiopian, i. 12.
Pyramidion of obelisk gilded, ii. 218.
Pythagoras, his visit to Egypt, ii. 388 note.
——, his residence in Egypt and doctrine, i. 279, 326, 327, 340, 350, 438, 477; ii. 67.

Q.

Qoorneh, sepulchres of, i. 163.
Quails in Egypt and the Desert of Sinai, i. 206.
Queens, their prerogatives, ii. 127.

R.

Ra, i. 390.
Raameses, city, ii. 231.
Rain in Egypt, i. 94.
Rameses I., ii. 249.
—— II., ii. 268.
—— III., ii. 271.
Rameses IV., ii. 325.
—— V.–XIV., ii. 336–338.
Rampsinitus, ii. 336.
Ranpo, i. 435.
Re, i. 390.
Rebo, nation, ii. 333.
Records, antiquity of, in Egypt, ii. 100.
Red Sea, routes from Egypt to, i. 43, 62.
Rehearsing, sign of, in Egyptian pictures, ii. 327 note.
Rekamai, i. 46.
Remai, ii. 146.
Remanen, nation, ii. 226, 257.
Rent, its proportion to produce, ii. 29.
——, its amount in Egypt, ii. 29.
Resurrection, doctrine of, i. 473, 489.
Rhadamanthys, etymology of, i. 486.
Rhodopis, ii. 152.
Rot, ii. 264.
Rotno, nation, ii. 221, 257.

S

Sabaco, ii. 368.
Sacrifices, human, i. 440–443; ii. 64.
Sacrilege, law of, ii. 56.
Saf, "Lady of Letters," i. 155; ii. 239.
Sagdas, i. 446.
Sais, ii. 379, 380.
Samaritan Pentateuch, ii. 315.
Sandstone rock, its extent in Egypt, i. 35.
Sasychis, ii. 346.
Sataspes, voyage of, ii. 403.
Scape-goat, i. 444.
Scarabæus, sanctity of, ii. 12, 21.
Scythians, their invasion of Egypt, ii. 397.
Seb, i. 397.
Sebek, i. 392.
Sebekatep, sovereigns of this name, when they lived, ii. 190.
Semueh, ii. 216.
Sennacherib, ii. 371.
Septuagint, its variation from the Hebrew, ii. 315.
Serapis, i. 431.
Serbonian bog, ii. 511.
Serpent, emblem of Agathodæmon, i. 375.
—— of Æsculapius, ii. 2.
Serpents, winged, ii. 20.
Sesonchis, ii. 346.
Sesonchosis, ii. 165.
Sesostris, ii. 164.
——, his emblems, ii. 166.
Set, name of Typhon, i. 418; ii. 254.
Sethos, ii. 371.

INDEX.   527

Sethroite nome, ii. 181, 187.
Shairetaan, ii. 331.
Sharu or Kharu, nation, ii. 270.
Sharpe, Samuel, i. 257 note; ii. 209 note.
Sheol of the Hebrews, i. 401.
Shepherd kings, ii. 180.
Shepherds, disesteemed in Egypt, ii. 318.
Sheshonk, his invasion of Judæa, ii. 109.
Sheto, nation, ii. 260, 278, 288.
Shields, royal, titular and phonetic, ii. 147.
Shishak, ii. 347.
Shos, ii. 256, 270.
Sidon, capture of, by Ochus, ii. 511.
Sidonians, ii. 221.
Silco, king of the Blemmyes, i. 28.
Silphium, ii. 305, 423.
Simoum, i. 68 note.
Sinai, peninsula of, i. 61.
Singara, ii. 227, 263.
Skhai, ii. 251.
Slaves, protected by law, ii. 54.
—— did not attend on the king, ii. 33.
Socari, i. 381.
Soldiery, Egyptian, their migration to Ethiopia, ii. 393.
Solomon, his connexion with Egypt, ii. 344.
Sothiac period, ii. 94 note, 294.
Sothis (Isis and Dog-star), i. 334.
——, spurious work of Manetho, ii. 88 note.
Soul, wicked, its punishment, i. 480.
South, symbol of, ii. 349.
Sphinx, meaning of, i. 137.
——, female, i. 137.
Sphragistes, i. 442.
Stability, emblem of, i. 380, 415.
Standard of kings, ii. 149.
Stele, its meaning, ii. 225 note.
Stibium, use of, i. 251.
Stolistes, ii. 104.
Stork, veneration of, ii. 17.
Suchus, i. 392.
Sukiim, ii. 348 note.
Sun, a divinity, i. 395.
——, Fountain of the, i. 72.
—— worshipers, ii. 109, 251.
—— in a state of weakness during winter, i. 420.
Swine, use of, in agriculture, i. 184.
——, herds of, i. 463 note.
——, sacrifice of, i. 400, 466.
——, emblem of gluttony, i. 480.
Swineherds, excluded from temples, ii. 44.
Syncellus, George the, ii. 91.

"Syrians of Palestine," the Jews, ii. 448.

T.

Tablet of Abydos, i. 45; ii. 108.
—— of Karnak, ii. 108.
——, statistical, of Karnak, ii. 222.
Tachos, ii. 504, 508.
Tahai, nation, ii. 222.
Taia, ii. 234, 246.
Tamhu, nation, ii. 264.
Tamos, his assassination by Psammitichus III., ii. 497.
Tanis, ii. 341.
Taochi, ii. 223.
Taricheutæ, i. 491.
Tau, or *crux ansata*, its signification, i. 294 note, 303.
Tau, placed on the tongue, ii. 32.
Taxation in Egypt, ii. 36.
Thammuz, mourning for, i. 415.
Thebes, origin of the name, i. 149 note.
——, once co-extensive with Egypt, ii. 98.
Theology, Egyptian, its threefold source, i. 368.
Theosophy, Egyptian, i. 363.
Thermuthis, i. 384, 435.
Thesmophoria, i. 468.
Thieves, how organized in Egypt, ii. 56.
This, its site, ii. 113.
Thoth, i. 426.
——, worshiped in Nubia, i. 23, 27.
Thotbmes I., ii. 209.
—— II., ii. 213.
—— III., ii. 215.
—— IV., ii. 233.
Thunder, rare in Egypt, i. 455.
Thuoris, ii. 302.
Tides at Suez, ii. 401 note.
Timæus, king of Egypt, ii. 189.
Tirhakah, i. 16, 56, 161; ii. 234, 370.
Tithrambo, i. 435.
Titular name, whether incorporated, ii. 161 note.
Tohen, nation, ii. 259, 329.
Tokari, nation, ii. 331.
Tombs, royal, i. 167.
Tools, buried with artificers, i. 504.
Toparchies, ii. 51.
Tourah, quarries of, i. 140.
Tpe, i. 496.
Transmigration of souls, i. 479.
Trees, sanctity of, ii. 13.
Triaconterides, i. 472.
Troglodytes, i. 65.
Tropic of Cancer, i. 28, 33.
Trumpet, of late introduction in Greece, i. 281.

Truth, goddess of, i. 407, 429, 445, 509; ii. 53.
Turin, papyrus of, ii. 104.
Turks, their similarity to the Hyksos, ii. 195.
Typhon, his emblem, i. 417.
——, mythe of, i. 408–419.
Typhonia, i. 255, 261.
Tyre, siege of, by Shalmaneser, ii. 417.
——, ——, by Nebuchadnezzar, ii. 418.
Tyrians, camp of, ii. 386.

U.

Uchoreus, ii. 102.
Unity of God, i. 437.
Urim and Thummim, ii. 53 note.

V.

Vava, nation, ii. 223.
Venus, Egyptian, i. 386.
Viscera, the, considered as the cause of sin, i. 488.
——, their embalmment, i. 492.

W.

Wadi Magara, i. 64; ii. 140.
Water, mode of raising, i. 189.
Weeks, reckoning by, i. 336.
Wells, Artesian, i. 73.
Winckelmann, his opinions of Egyptian art, i. 265 note.
Wine, its growth in Egypt, i. 190.
Women, their condition in Egypt, ii. 57.

Women, whether admitted to the priesthood, i. 452; ii. 38.
——, never appear reading or writing, i. 284.
Wood, semicircle of, used to support the head, i. 236.
Woods used in carpentry, i. 220.
Wool, its use for garments, i. 194.
Woollen wrappers of mummies, i. 131, 140, 492.
Worship of animals among the African nations, ii. 12.
Wounding the forehead in mourning, i. 465.
Writing, art of, its antiquity in Egypt, ii. 102, 142.

X.

Xois, ii. 179, 185.

Y.

Young, Dr., his discoveries in hieroglyphics, i. 296.

Z.

Zagreus, i. 402.
Zerach, ii. 354.
Zet, ii. 358.
Zoan, ii. 340.
Zodiac, signs of, i. 341.
——, not known to ancient Egyptians, ii. 8.
Zoega, i. 355.
Zuchis, ii. 421 note.

THE END.

www.ingramcontent.com/pod-product-compliance
Lightning Source LLC
Chambersburg PA
CBHW062029290426
44108CB00032B/2721